EDENS ZERO

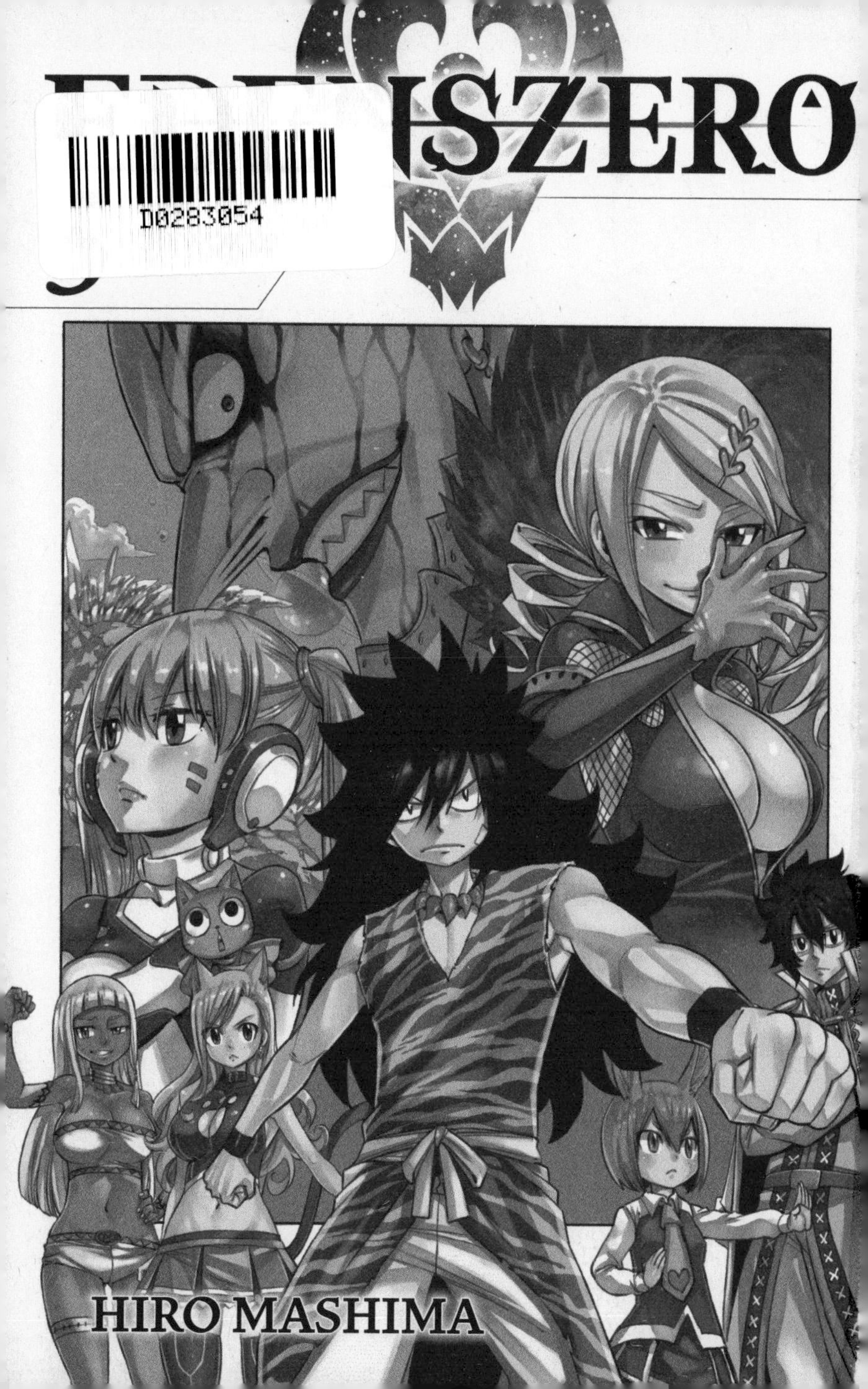

HIRO MASHIMA

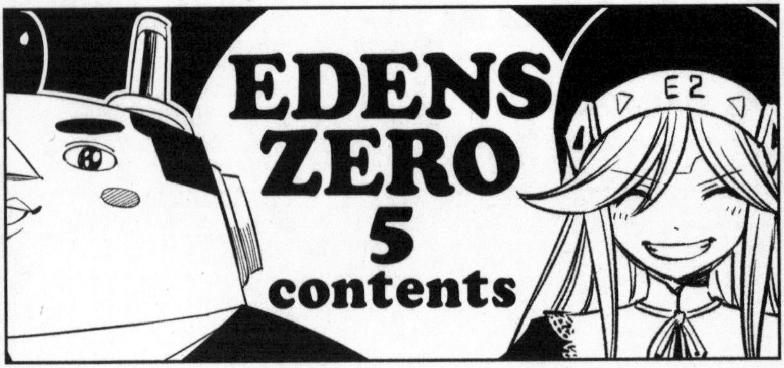
EDENS ZERO
5
contents
E2

EDENSZERO

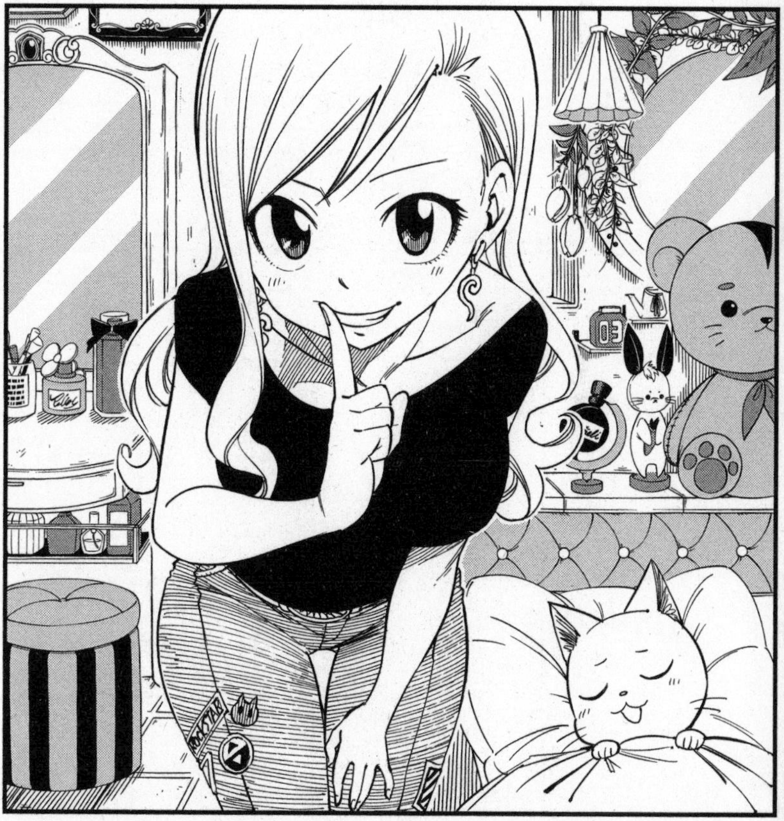

CHAPTER 33: THE GIRL ON THE HILL

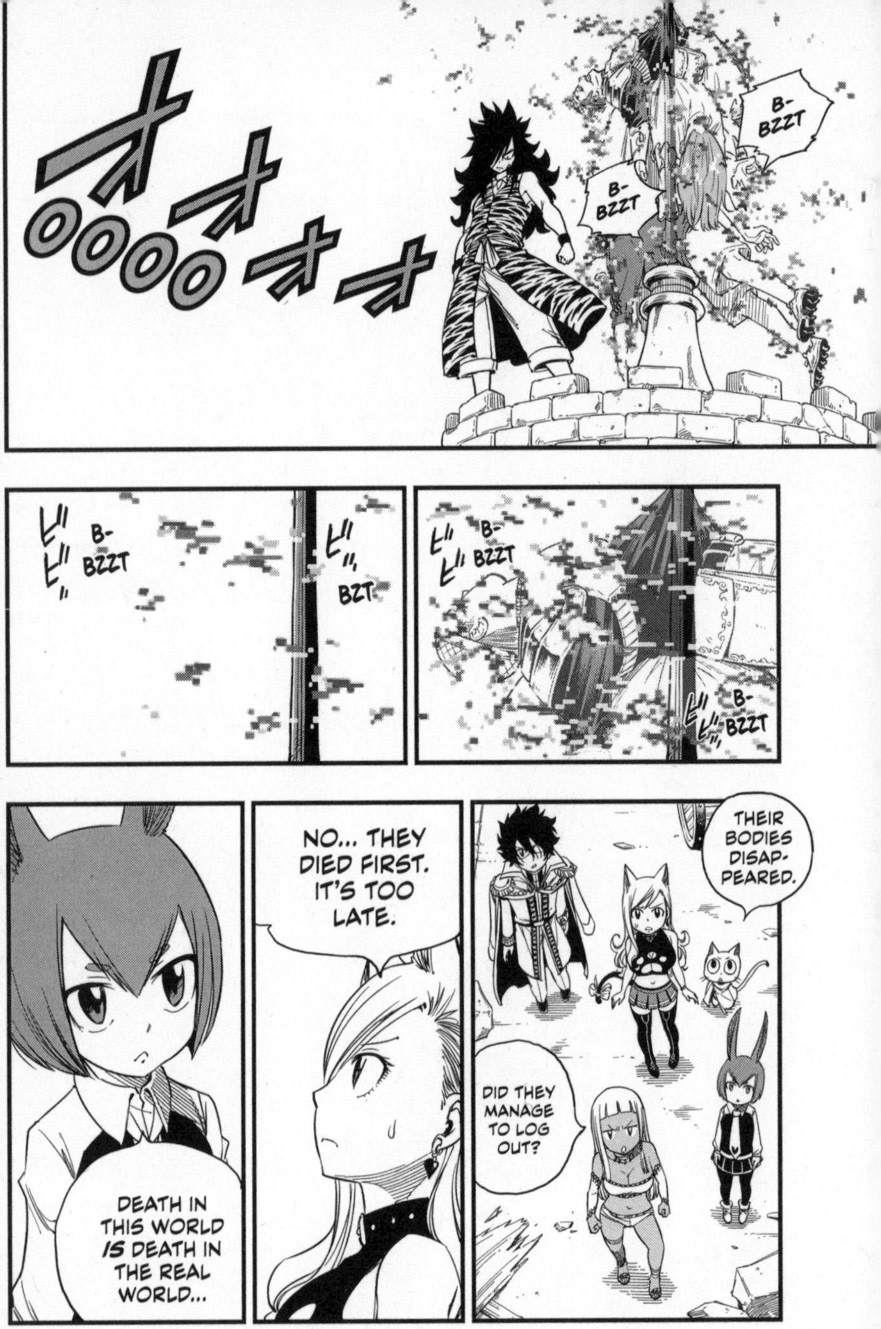
オオオオ
OOOO
B-BZZT
B-BZZT
ビビ
B-BZZT
ビビ
B-BZZT
ビビ
B-BZZT
ビ"
BZT
THEIR BODIES DISAP-PEARED.
DID THEY MANAGE TO LOG OUT?
NO... THEY DIED FIRST. IT'S TOO LATE.
DEATH IN THIS WORLD *IS* DEATH IN THE REAL WORLD...

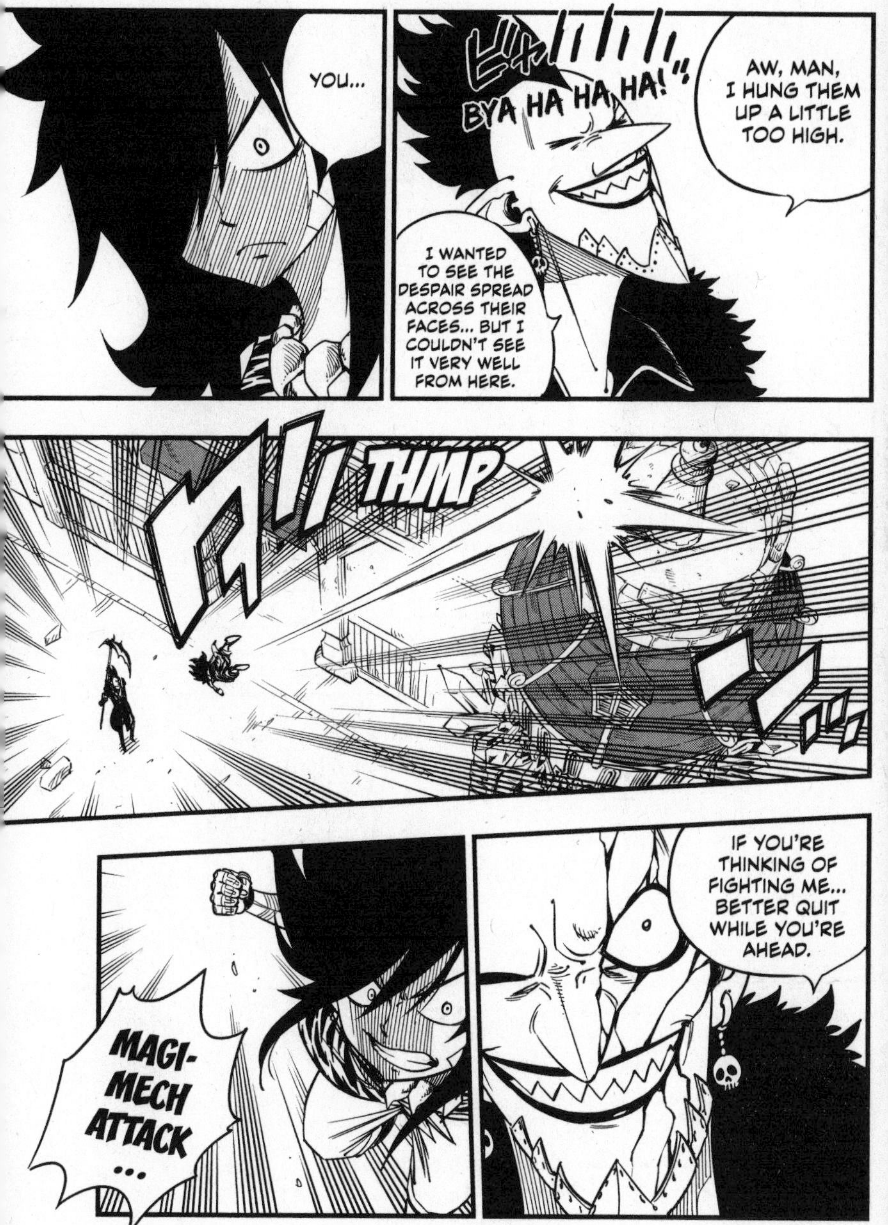
BYA HA HA HA!!
AW, MAN, I HUNG THEM UP A LITTLE TOO HIGH.
I WANTED TO SEE THE DESPAIR SPREAD ACROSS THEIR FACES... BUT I COULDN'T SEE IT VERY WELL FROM HERE.
YOU...
THMP
IF YOU'RE THINKING OF FIGHTING ME... BETTER QUIT WHILE YOU'RE AHEAD.
MAGI-MECH ATTACK ...

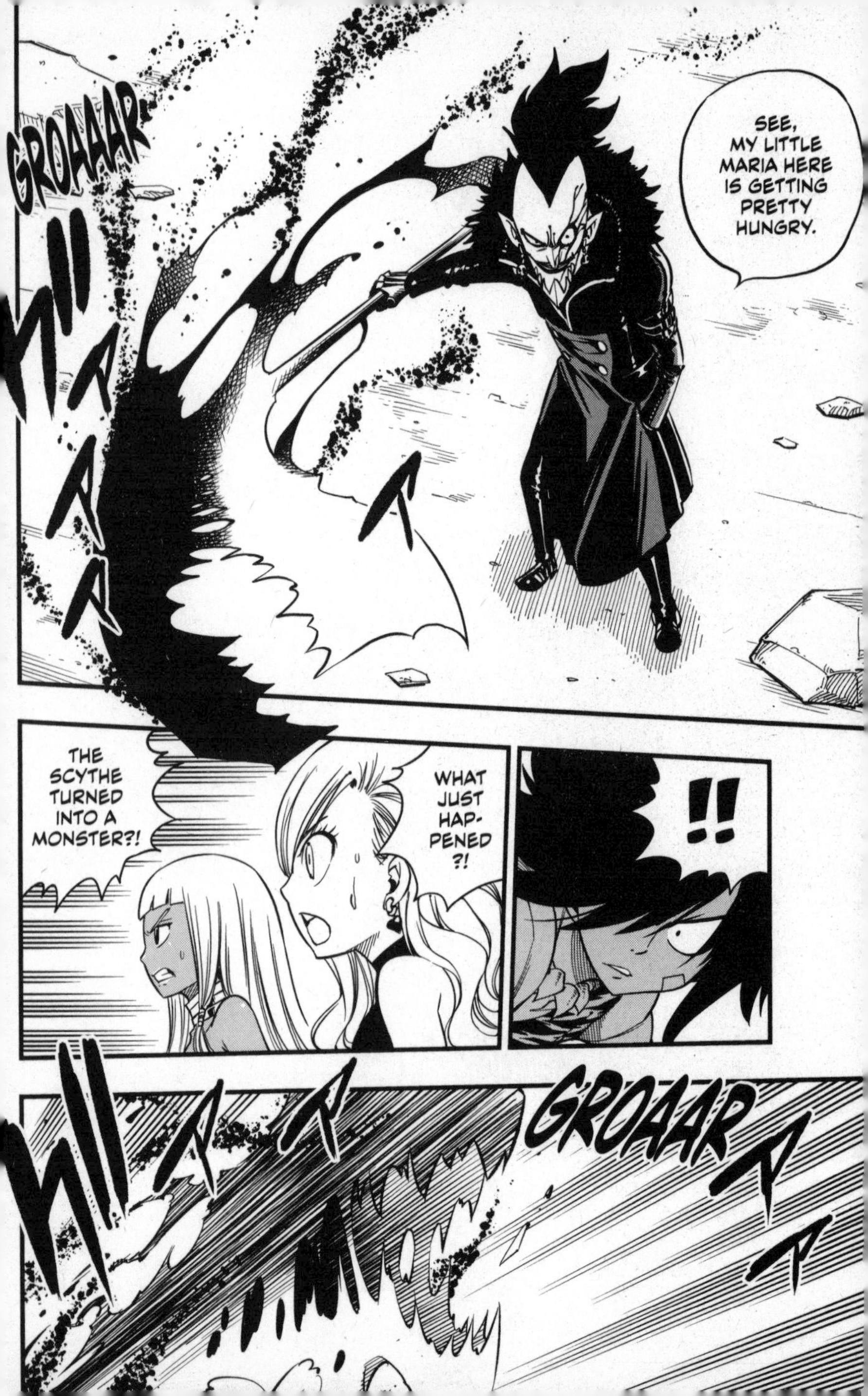
SEE, MY LITTLE MARIA HERE IS GETTING PRETTY HUNGRY.
GROAAAR
!!
WHAT JUST HAP-PENED?!
THE SCYTHE TURNED INTO A MONSTER?!
GROAAR

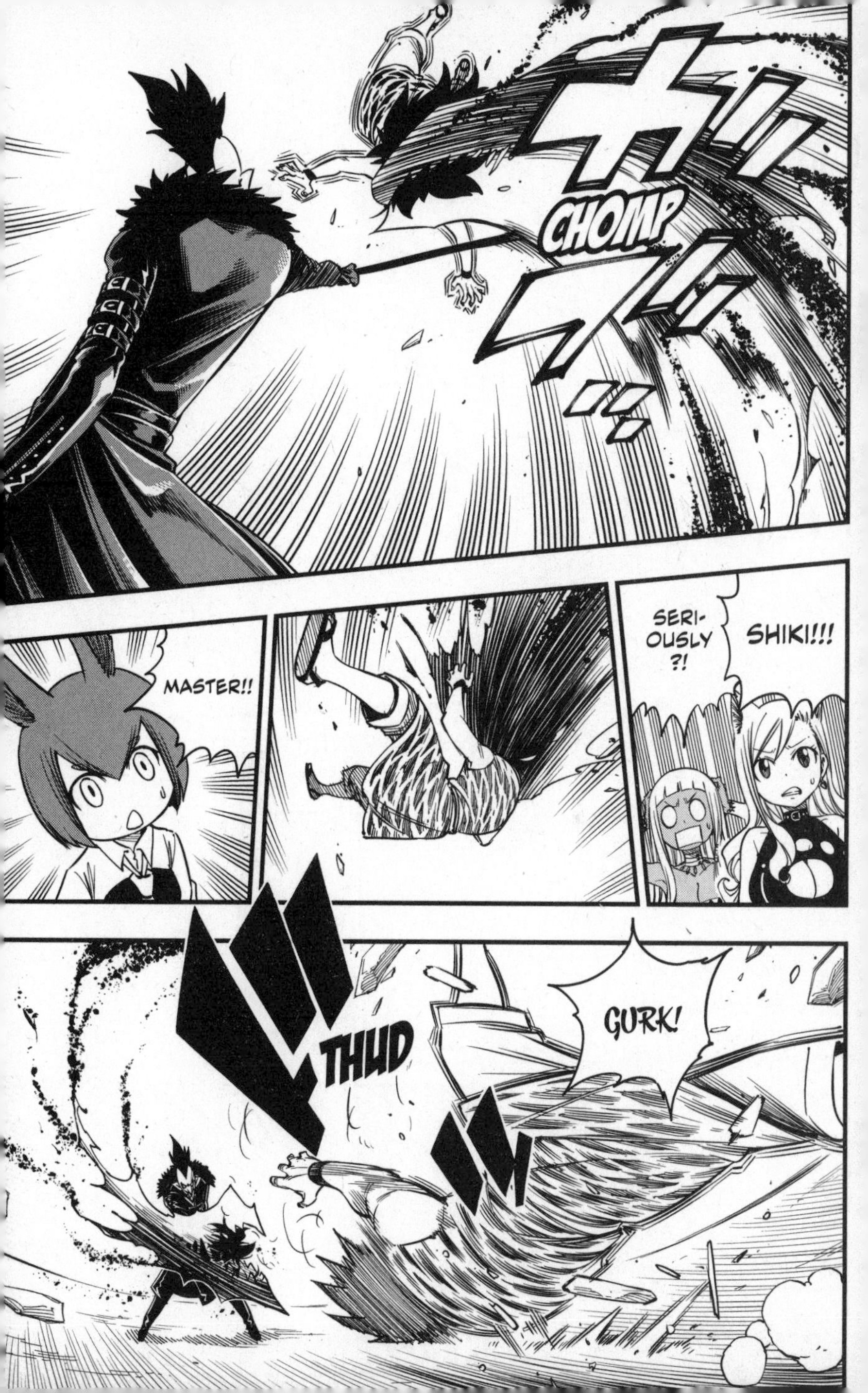
CHOMP
SHIKI!!!
SERI-OUSLY?!
MASTER!!
GURK!
THUD

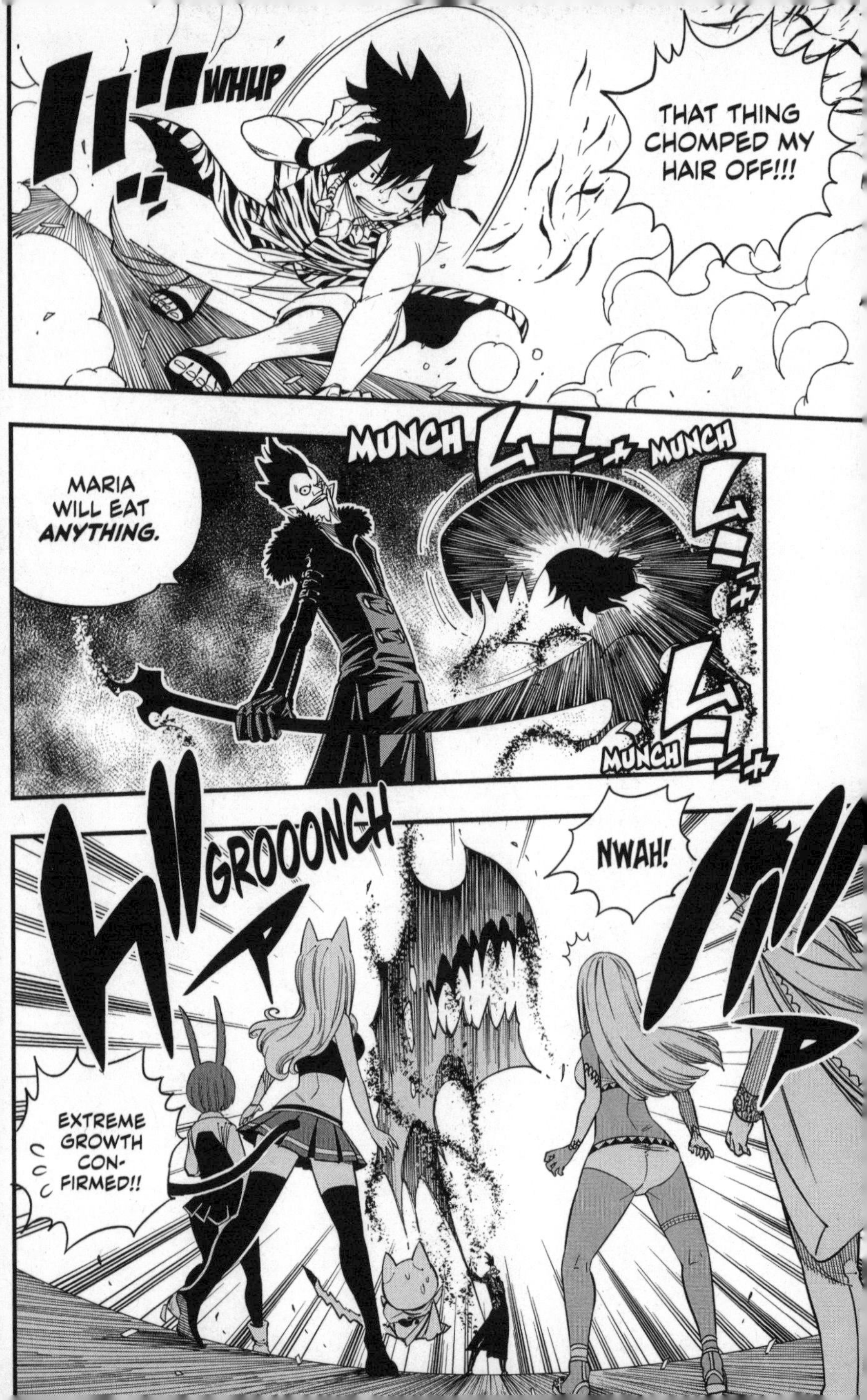

THAT THING CHOMPED MY HAIR OFF!!!
WHUP
MUNCH
MUNCH
MARIA WILL EAT ANYTHING.
MUNCH
NWAH!
GROOONCH
EXTREME GROWTH CON-FIRMED!!

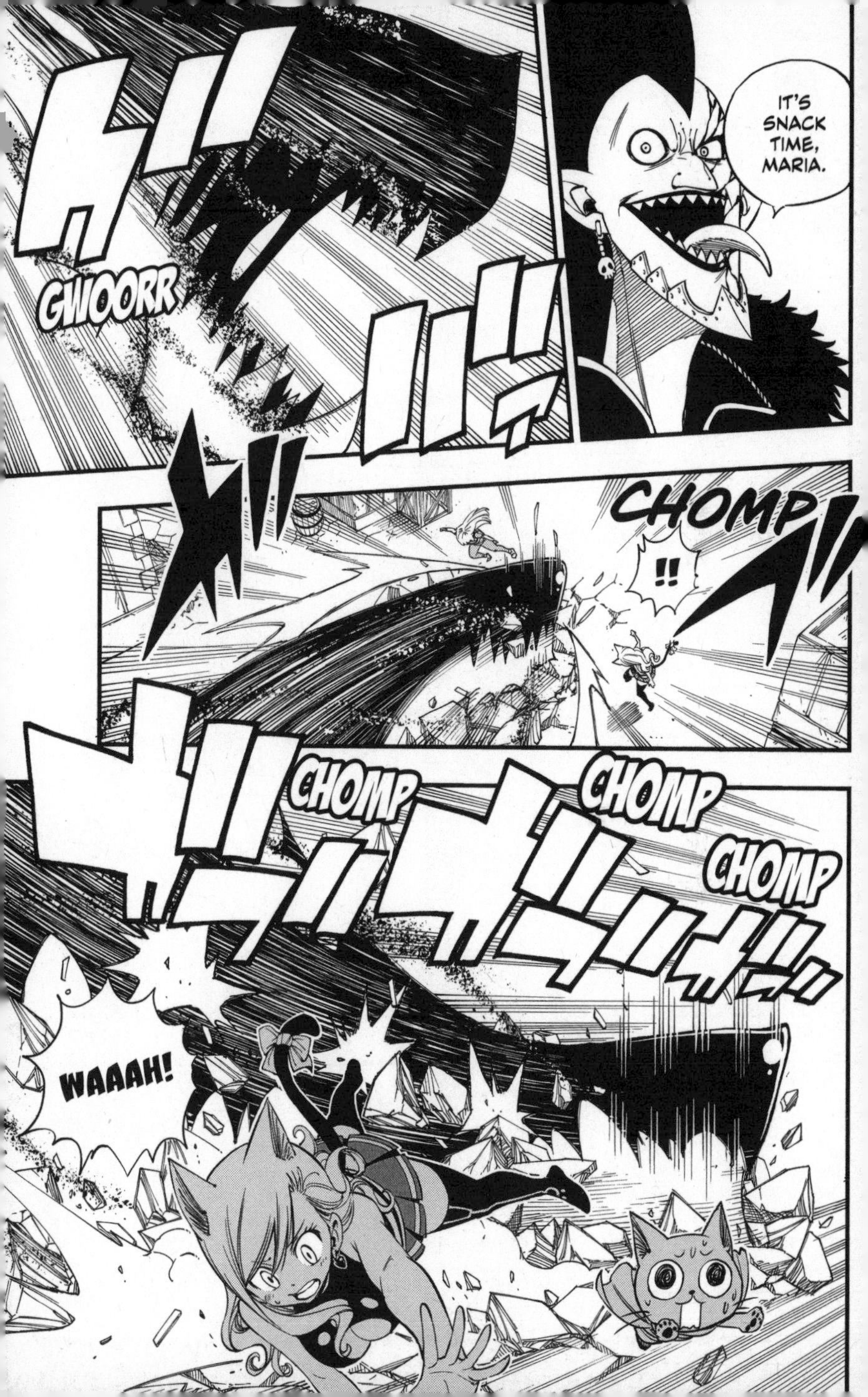
IT'S SNACK TIME, MARIA.
GWOORR
CHOMP
!!
CHOMP
CHOMP
CHOMP
WAAAH!

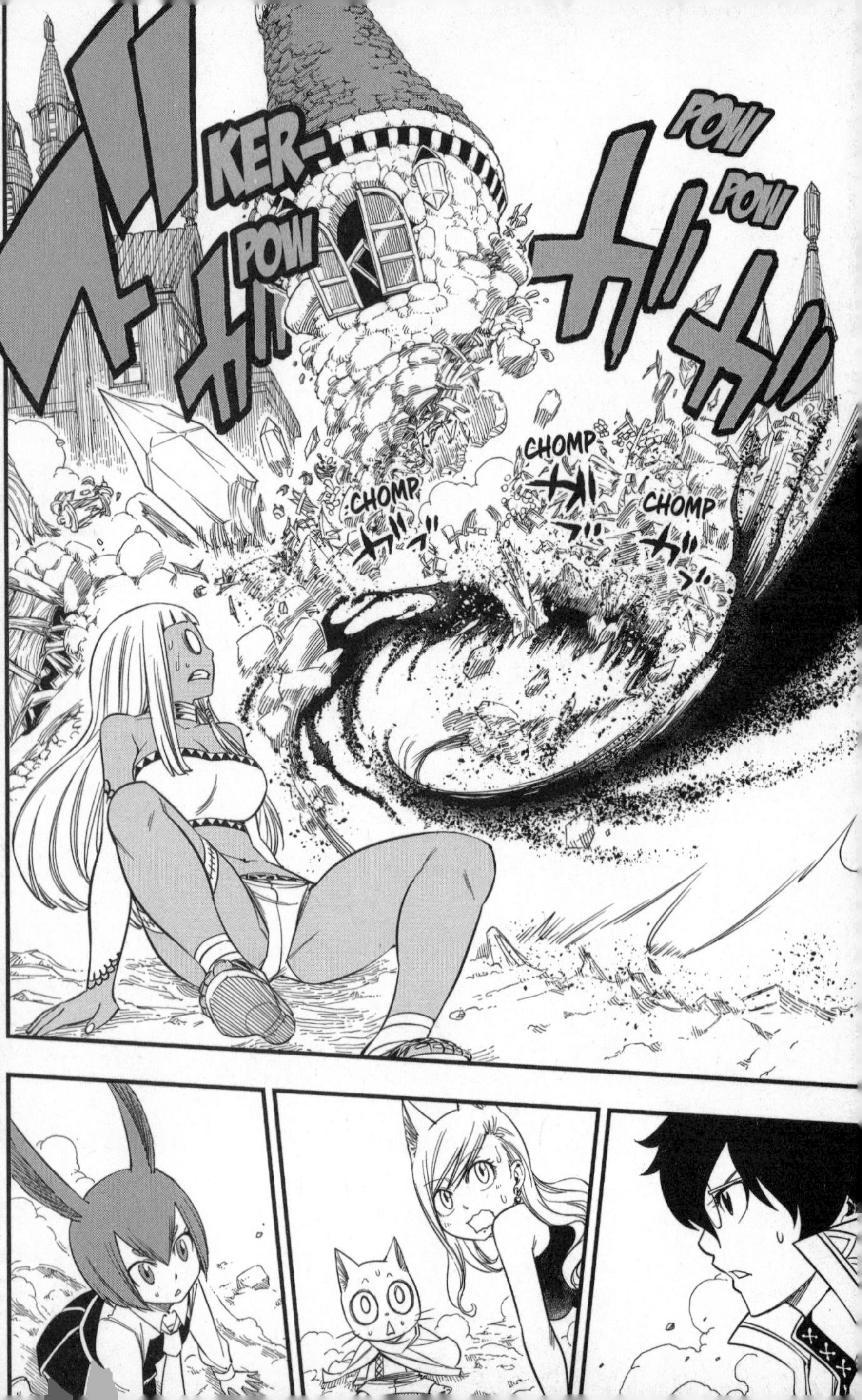
POW
POW
KER-
POW
CHOMP
CHOMP
CHOMP

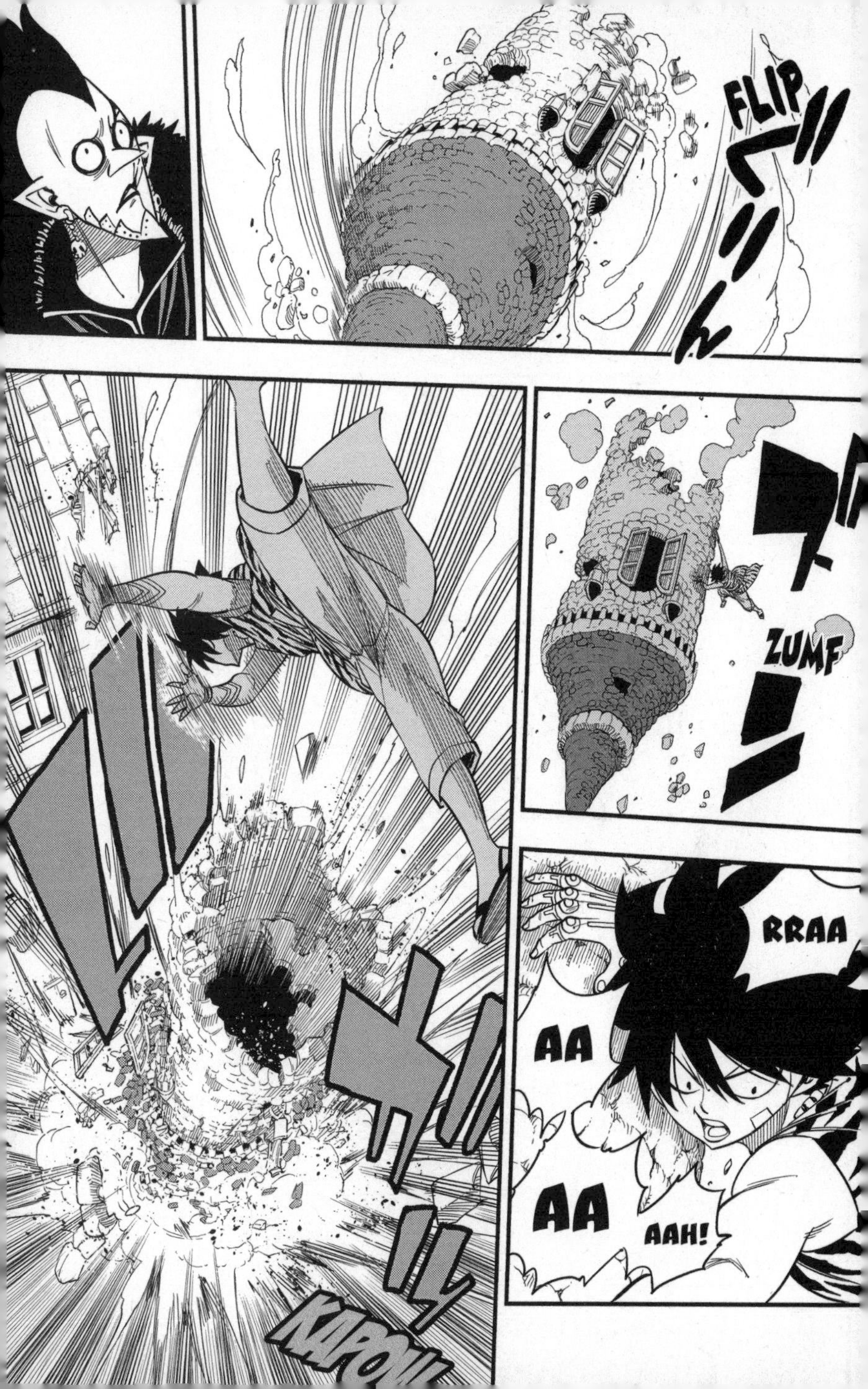
FLIP
ZUMF
RRAA
AA
AA
AAH!
KAPOW

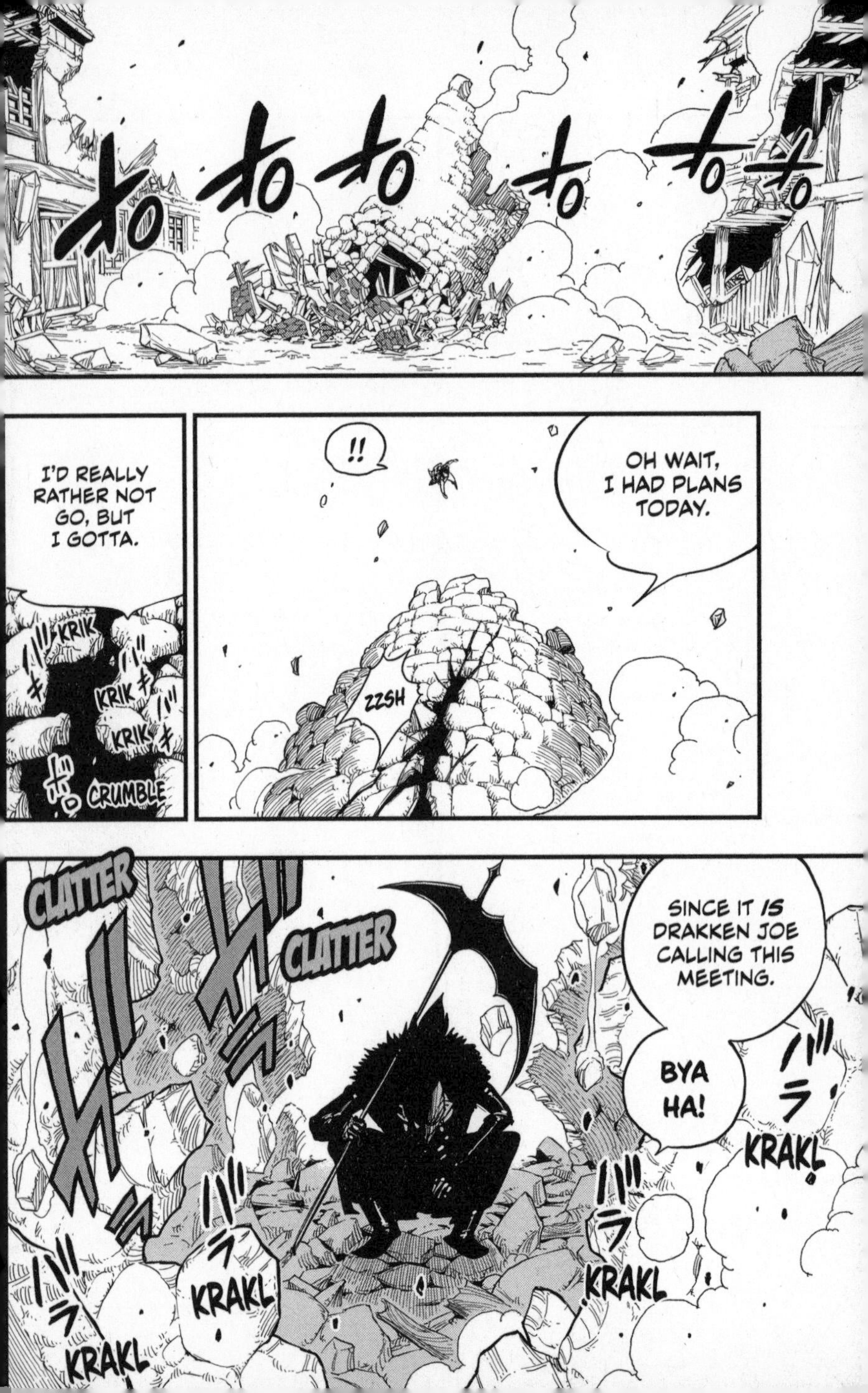
!!
OH WAIT, I HAD PLANS TODAY.
ZZSH
I'D REALLY RATHER NOT GO, BUT I GOTTA.
KRIK
KRIK
KRIK
CRUMBLE
SINCE IT *IS* DRAKKEN JOE CALLING THIS MEETING.
BYA HA!
KRAKL
KRAKL
CLATTER
CLATTER
KRAKL
KRAKL

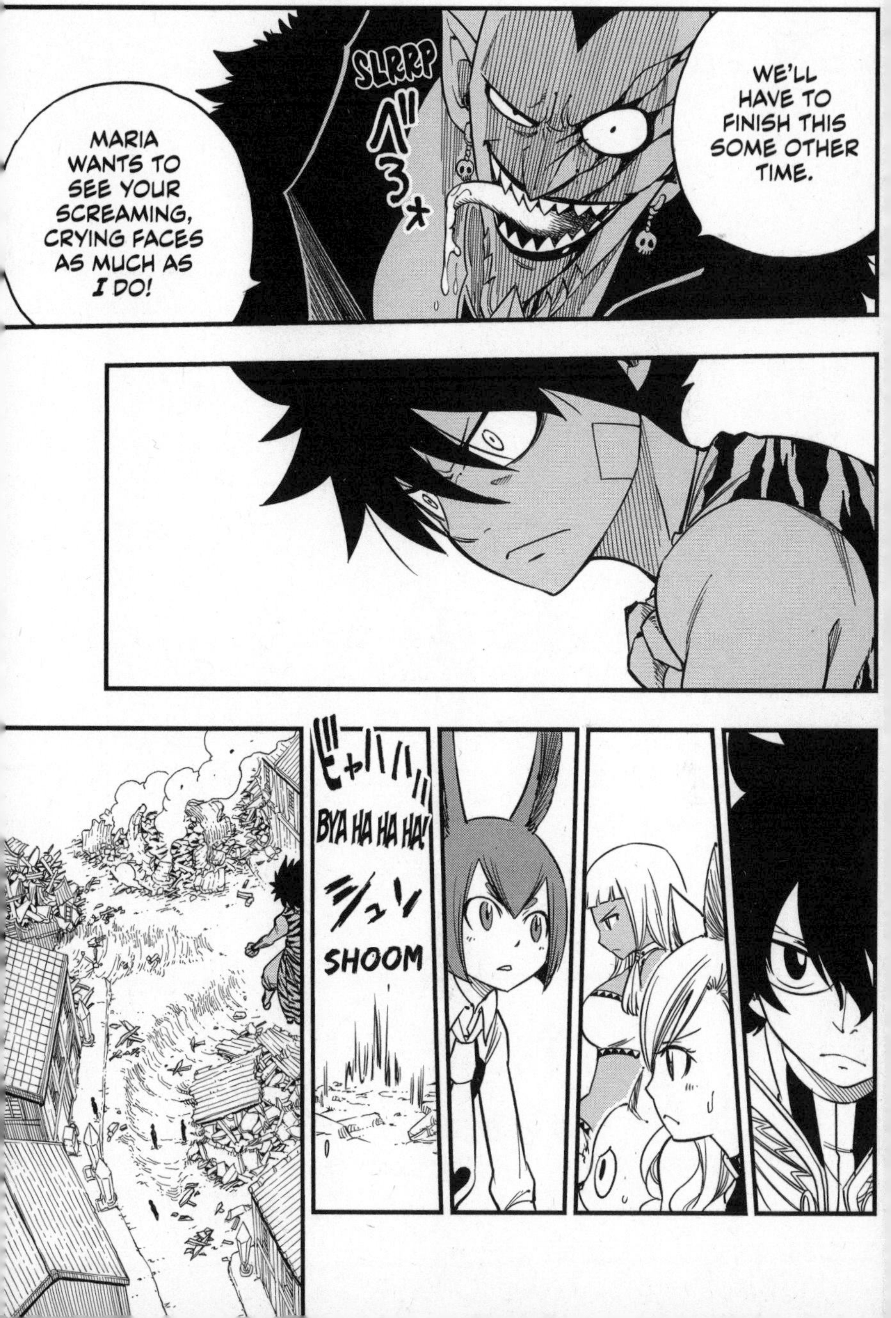
WE'LL HAVE TO FINISH THIS SOME OTHER TIME.
SLRRP
MARIA WANTS TO SEE YOUR SCREAMING, CRYING FACES AS MUCH AS I DO!
BYA HA HA HA!
SHOOM

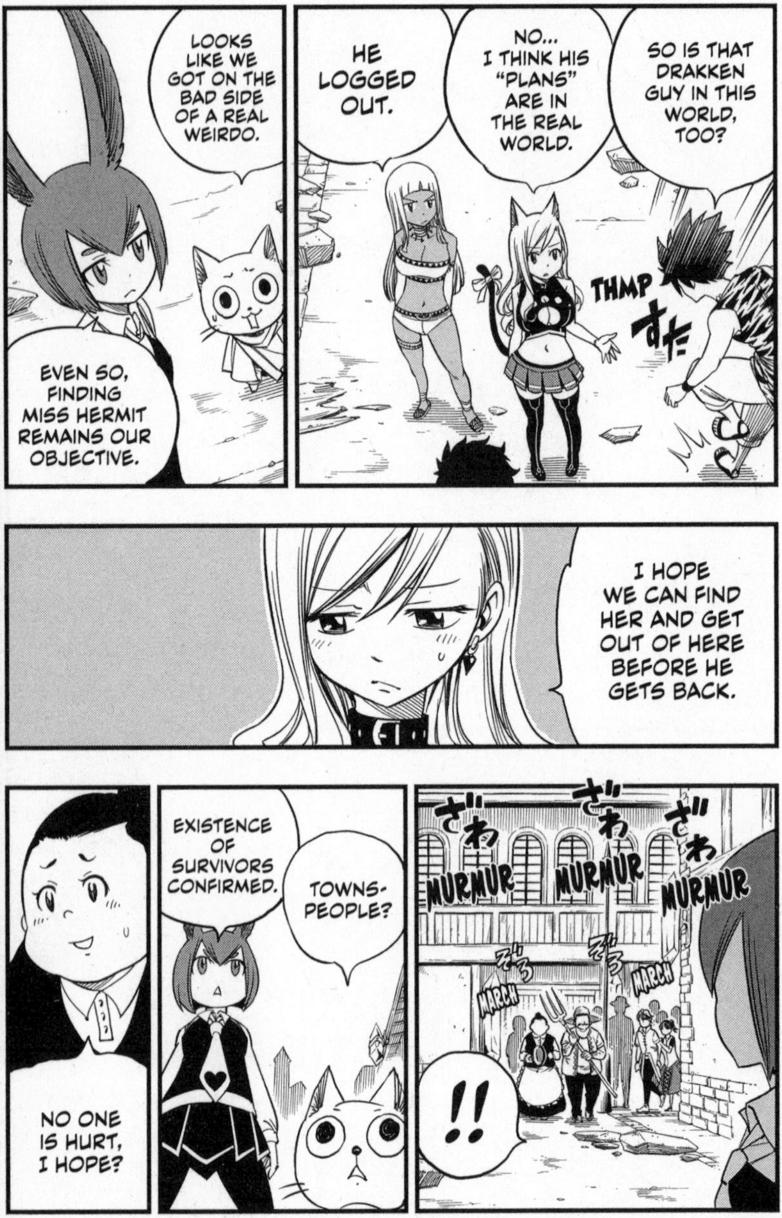
SO IS THAT DRAKKEN GUY IN THIS WORLD, TOO?
NO... I THINK HIS "PLANS" ARE IN THE REAL WORLD.
HE LOGGED OUT.
THMP
すた
LOOKS LIKE WE GOT ON THE BAD SIDE OF A REAL WEIRDO.
EVEN SO, FINDING MISS HERMIT REMAINS OUR OBJECTIVE.
I HOPE WE CAN FIND HER AND GET OUT OF HERE BEFORE HE GETS BACK.
ざわ
MURMUR
ざわ
MURMUR
ざわ
MURMUR
ぞろ
MARCH
ぞろ
MARCH
!!
TOWNS-PEOPLE?
EXISTENCE OF SURVIVORS CONFIRMED.
NO ONE IS HURT, I HOPE?

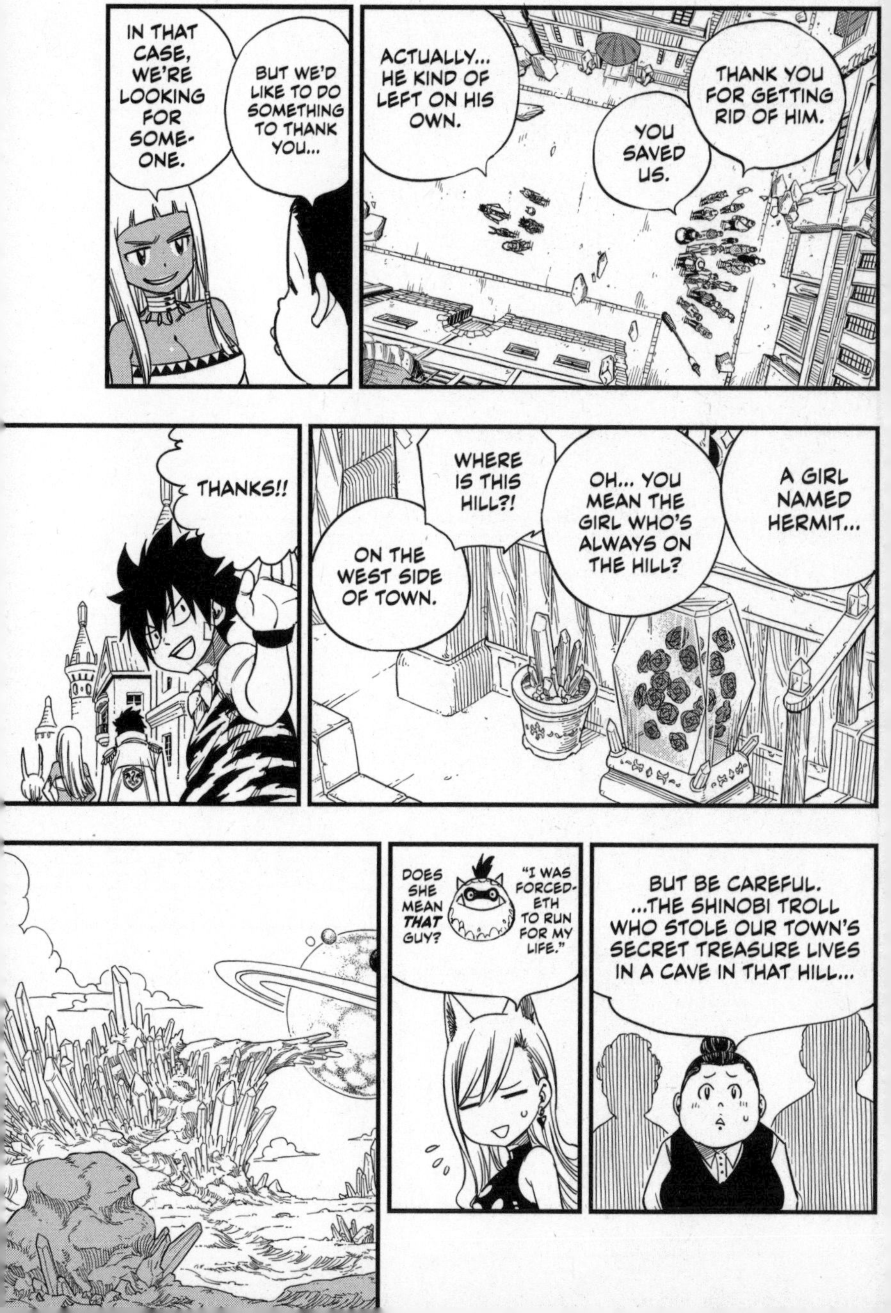
THANK YOU FOR GETTING RID OF HIM.
YOU SAVED US.
ACTUALLY... HE KIND OF LEFT ON HIS OWN.
BUT WE'D LIKE TO DO SOMETHING TO THANK YOU...
IN THAT CASE, WE'RE LOOKING FOR SOME-ONE.
A GIRL NAMED HERMIT...
OH... YOU MEAN THE GIRL WHO'S ALWAYS ON THE HILL?
WHERE IS THIS HILL?!
ON THE WEST SIDE OF TOWN.
THANKS!!
BUT BE CAREFUL. ...THE SHINOBI TROLL WHO STOLE OUR TOWN'S SECRET TREASURE LIVES IN A CAVE IN THAT HILL...
"I WAS FORCED-ETH TO RUN FOR MY LIFE."
DOES SHE MEAN *THAT* GUY?

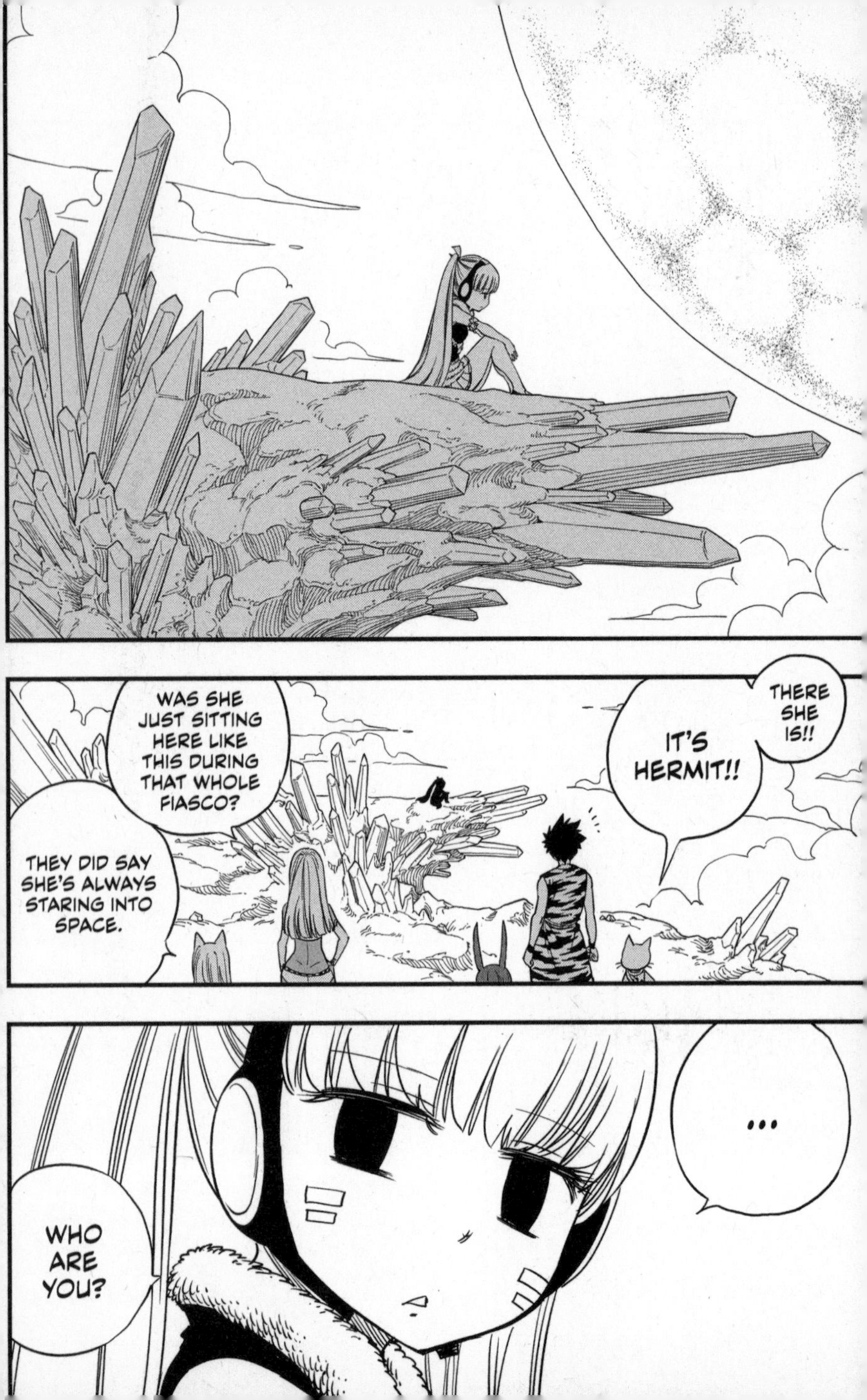
THERE SHE IS!!
IT'S HERMIT!!
WAS SHE JUST SITTING HERE LIKE THIS DURING THAT WHOLE FIASCO?
THEY DID SAY SHE'S ALWAYS STARING INTO SPACE.
...
WHO ARE YOU?

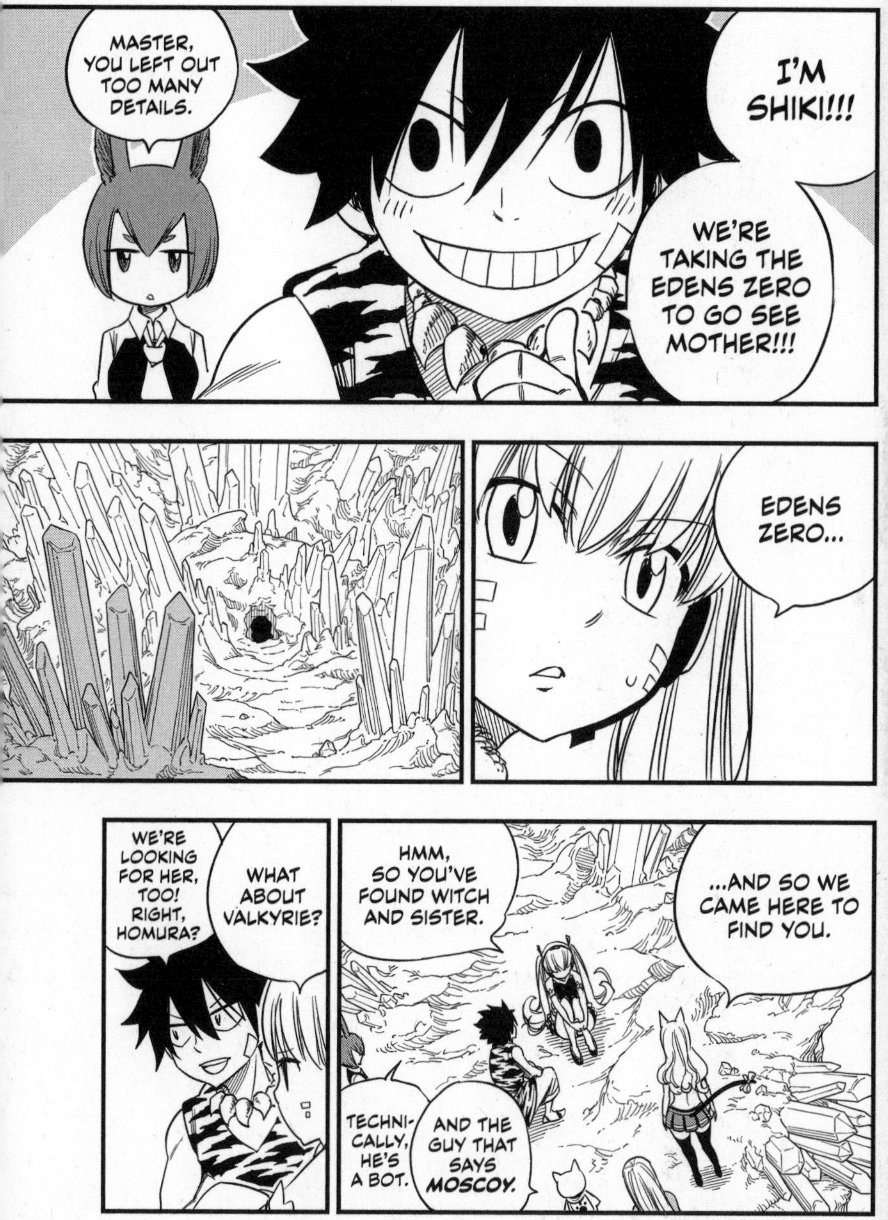
I'M SHIKI!!!
WE'RE TAKING THE EDENS ZERO TO GO SEE MOTHER!!!
MASTER, YOU LEFT OUT TOO MANY DETAILS.
EDENS ZERO...
...AND SO WE CAME HERE TO FIND YOU.
HMM, SO YOU'VE FOUND WITCH AND SISTER.
AND THE GUY THAT SAYS *MOSCOY*.
TECHNICALLY, HE'S A BOT.
WHAT ABOUT VALKYRIE?
WE'RE LOOKING FOR HER, TOO! RIGHT, HOMURA?

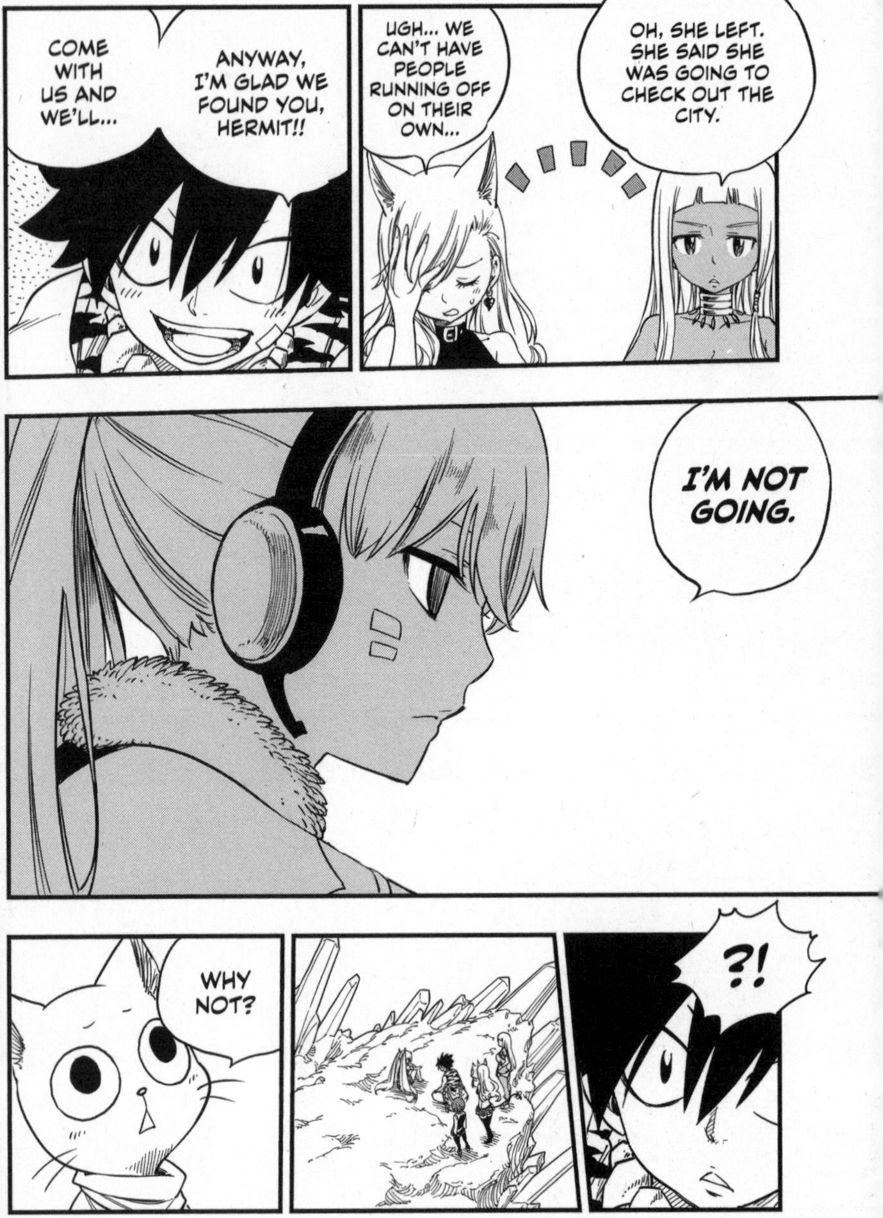
OH, SHE LEFT. SHE SAID SHE WAS GOING TO CHECK OUT THE CITY.
UGH... WE CAN'T HAVE PEOPLE RUNNING OFF ON THEIR OWN...
ANYWAY, I'M GLAD WE FOUND YOU, HERMIT!!
COME WITH US AND WE'LL...
I'M NOT GOING.
?!
WHY NOT?

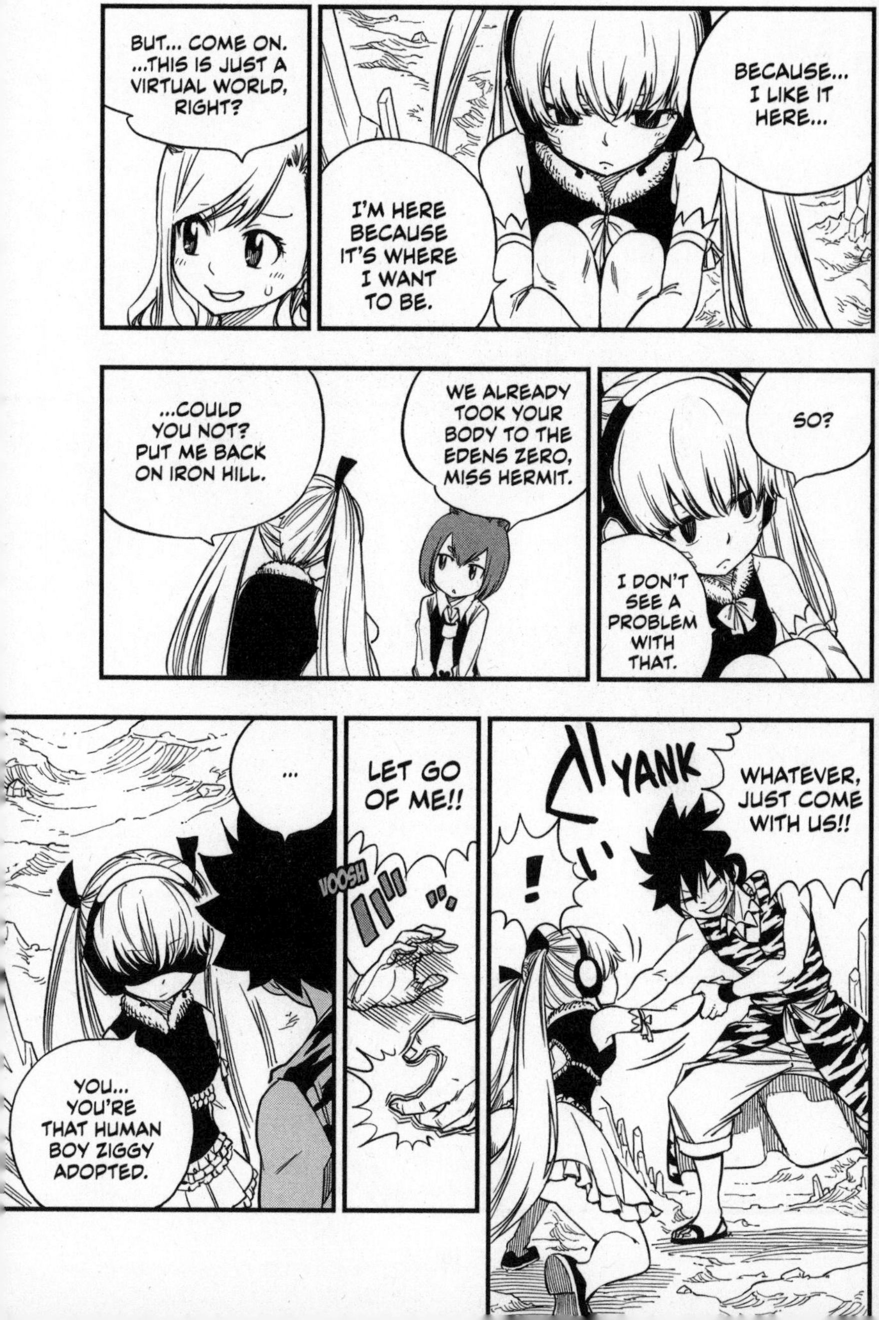
BECAUSE... I LIKE IT HERE...
I'M HERE BECAUSE IT'S WHERE I WANT TO BE.
BUT... COME ON. ...THIS IS JUST A VIRTUAL WORLD, RIGHT?
SO?
I DON'T SEE A PROBLEM WITH THAT.
WE ALREADY TOOK YOUR BODY TO THE EDENS ZERO, MISS HERMIT.
...COULD YOU NOT? PUT ME BACK ON IRON HILL.
YANK
WHATEVER, JUST COME WITH US!!
!
LET GO OF ME!!
VOOSH
...
YOU... YOU'RE THAT HUMAN BOY ZIGGY ADOPTED.

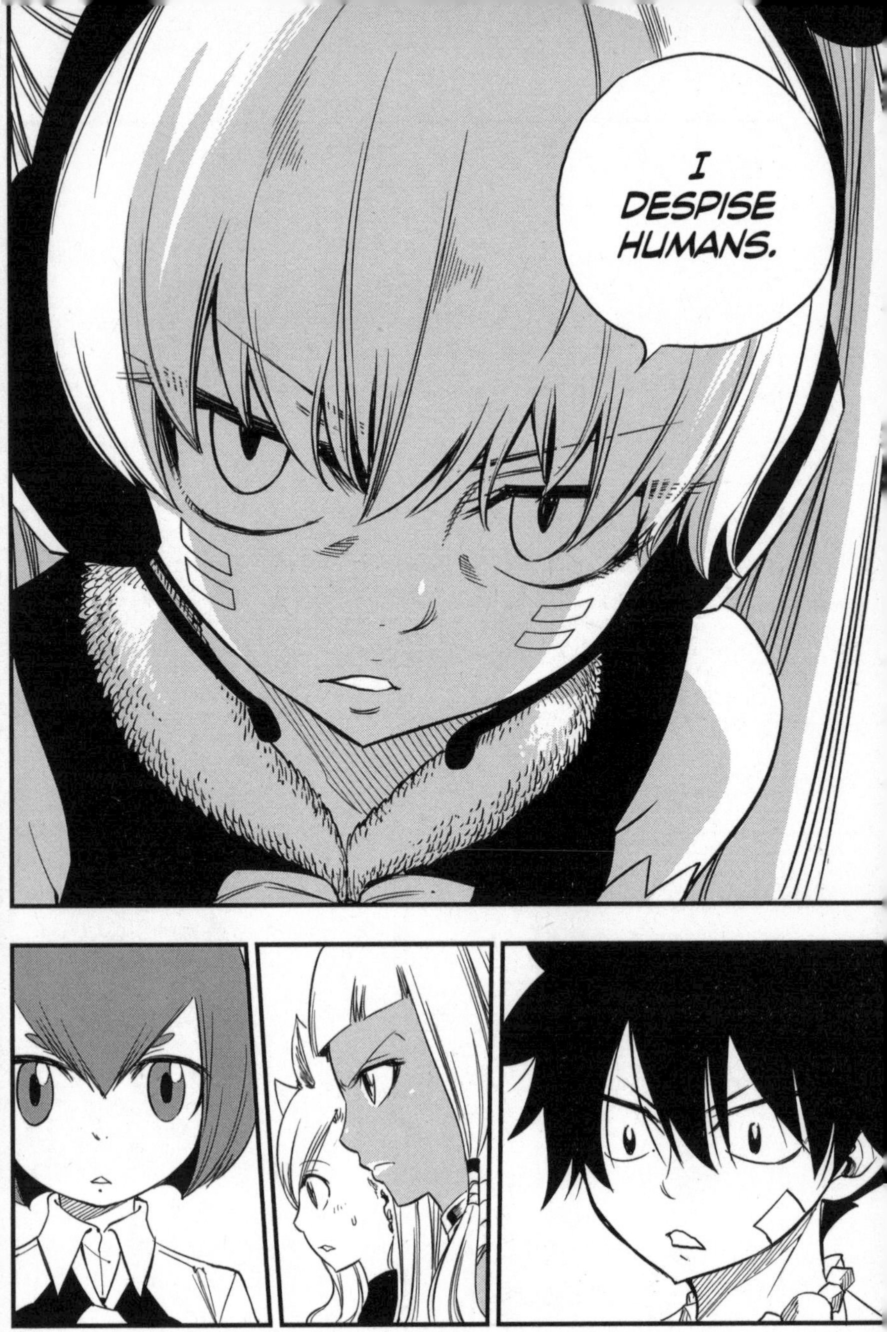
I DESPISE HUMANS.

THE CITY OF CRYSTA

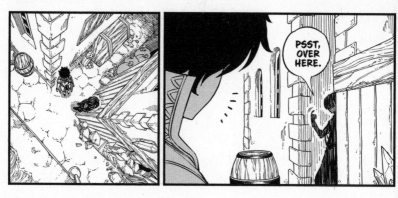

PSST, OVER HERE.

21

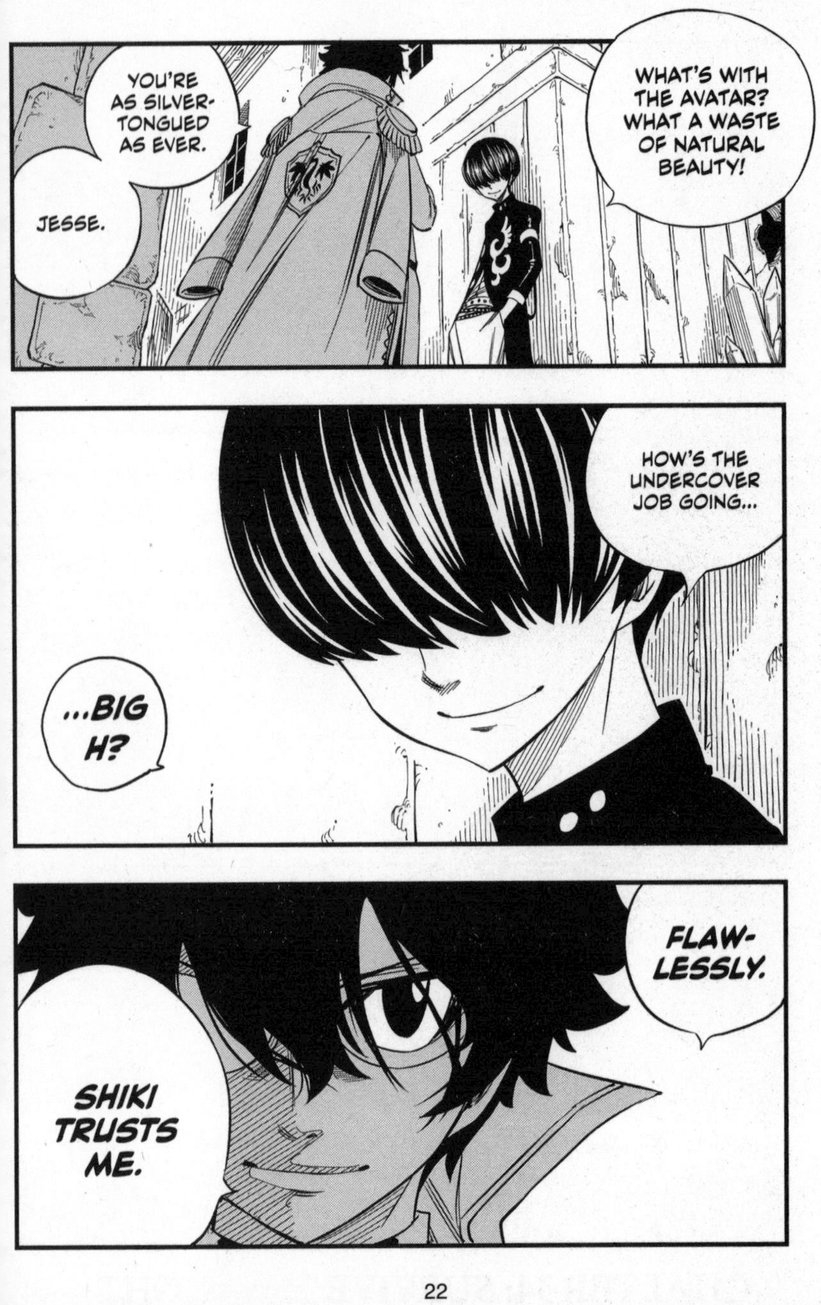
WHAT'S WITH THE AVATAR? WHAT A WASTE OF NATURAL BEAUTY!
YOU'RE AS SILVER-TONGUED AS EVER.
JESSE.
HOW'S THE UNDERCOVER JOB GOING...
...BIG H?
FLAW-LESSLY.
SHIKI TRUSTS ME.

EDENS ZERO

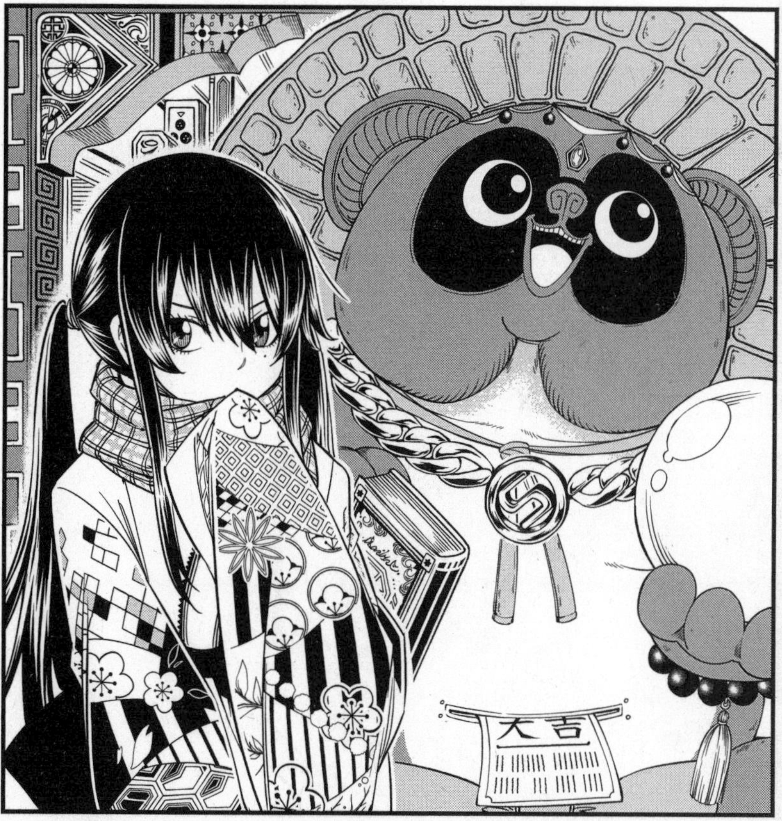
大吉

CHAPTER 34: SURVIVE THE NIGHT

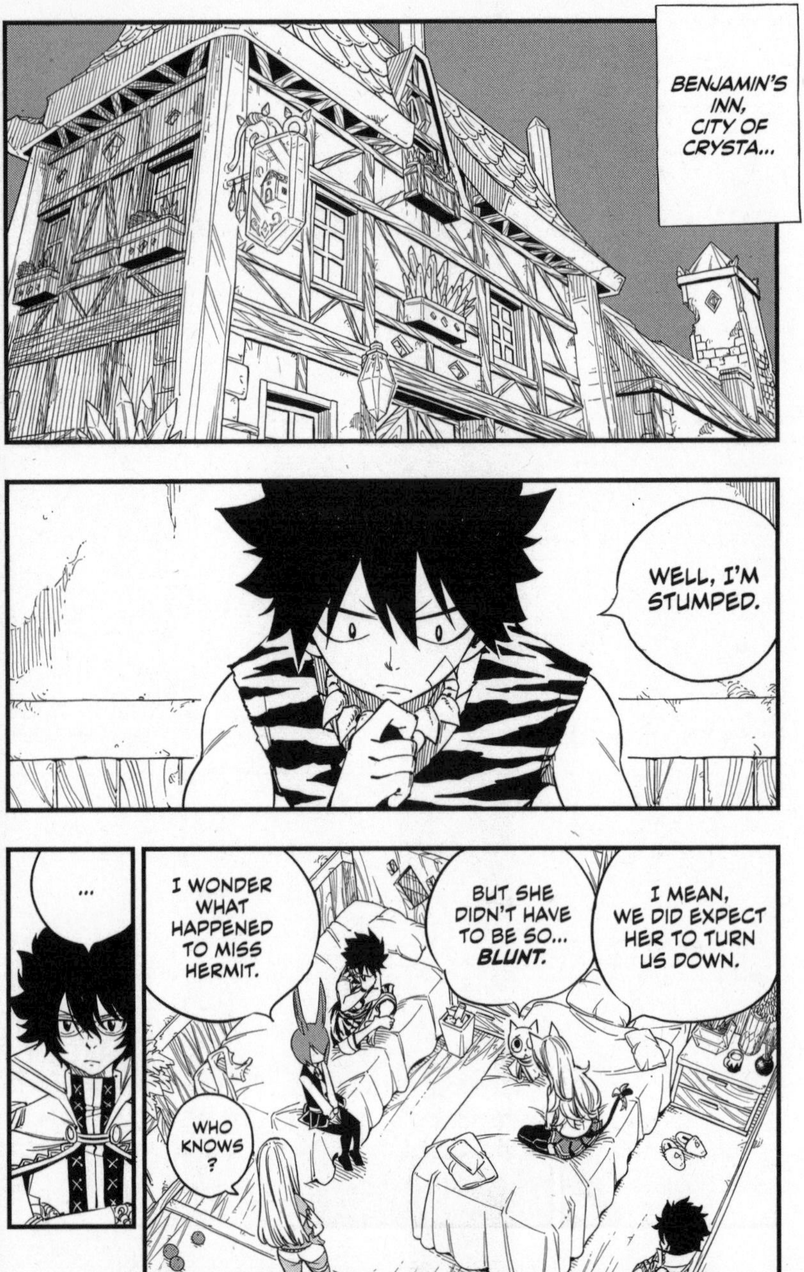
BENJAMIN'S INN, CITY OF CRYSTA...
WELL, I'M STUMPED.
I MEAN, WE DID EXPECT HER TO TURN US DOWN.
BUT SHE DIDN'T HAVE TO BE SO... *BLUNT.*
I WONDER WHAT HAPPENED TO MISS HERMIT.
WHO KNOWS?
...

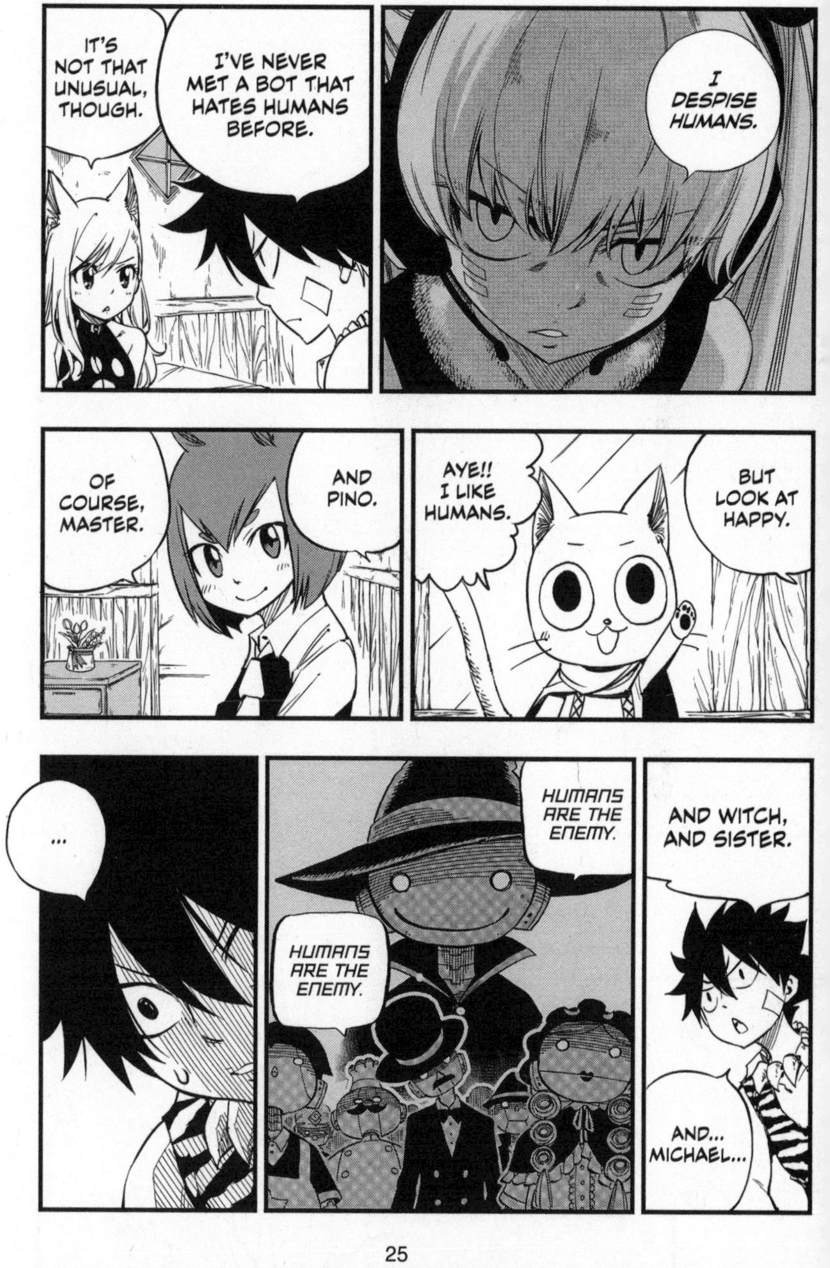
I DESPISE HUMANS.
I'VE NEVER MET A BOT THAT HATES HUMANS BEFORE.
IT'S NOT THAT UNUSUAL, THOUGH.
BUT LOOK AT HAPPY.
AYE!! I LIKE HUMANS.
AND PINO.
OF COURSE, MASTER.
AND WITCH, AND SISTER.
AND... MICHAEL...
HUMANS ARE THE ENEMY.
HUMANS ARE THE ENEMY.
...

HRRRNNG
DON'T CRY OVER STUFF THAT'S ONLY HAPPENING IN YOUR HEAD! IT'S SO OBNOXIOUS!
WELL... SHIKI WENT THROUGH A LOT BACK ON HIS HOME PLANET.
HOLD ON A MOMENT... I NEED TO GET SOMETHING OFF MY CHEST.
WHY SO FORMAL ALL OF A SUDDEN?
I DIDN'T REALIZE BOOBS WERE SO HEAVY.
My shoulders are stiff.
BOING
BOING
WOW, NOBODY CARES.
GONG
!!

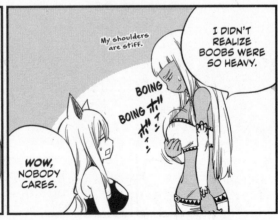

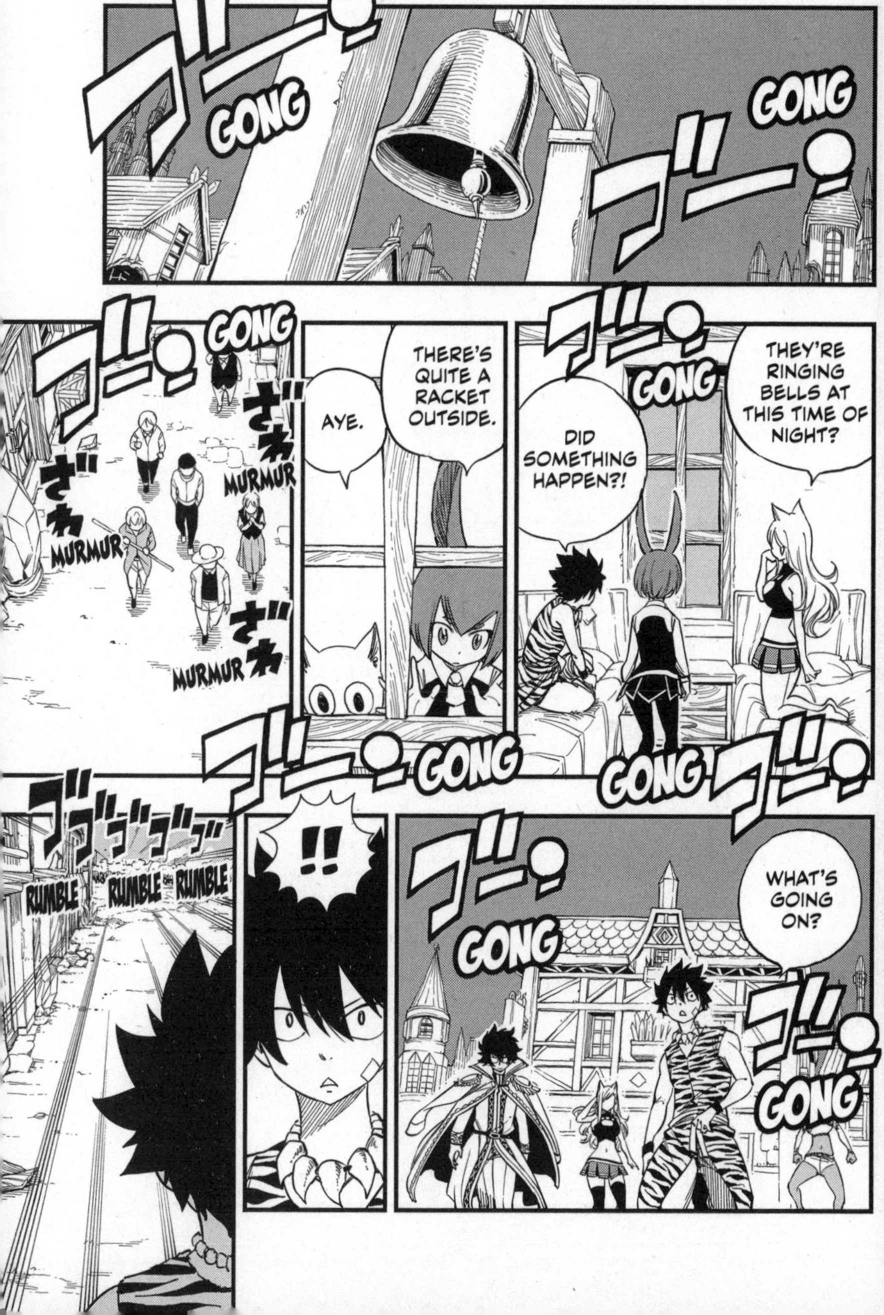
ゴーン
GONG
ゴーン
GONG
ゴーン
GONG
THEY'RE RINGING BELLS AT THIS TIME OF NIGHT?
DID SOMETHING HAPPEN?!
THERE'S QUITE A RACKET OUTSIDE.
AYE.
ゴーン
GONG
ざわ
MURMUR
ざわ
MURMUR
ざわ
MURMUR
ゴーン
GONG
GONG
ゴーン
ゴーン
WHAT'S GOING ON?
GONG
ゴーン
GONG
!!
ゴゴゴゴゴ
RUMBLE
RUMBLE
RUMBLE

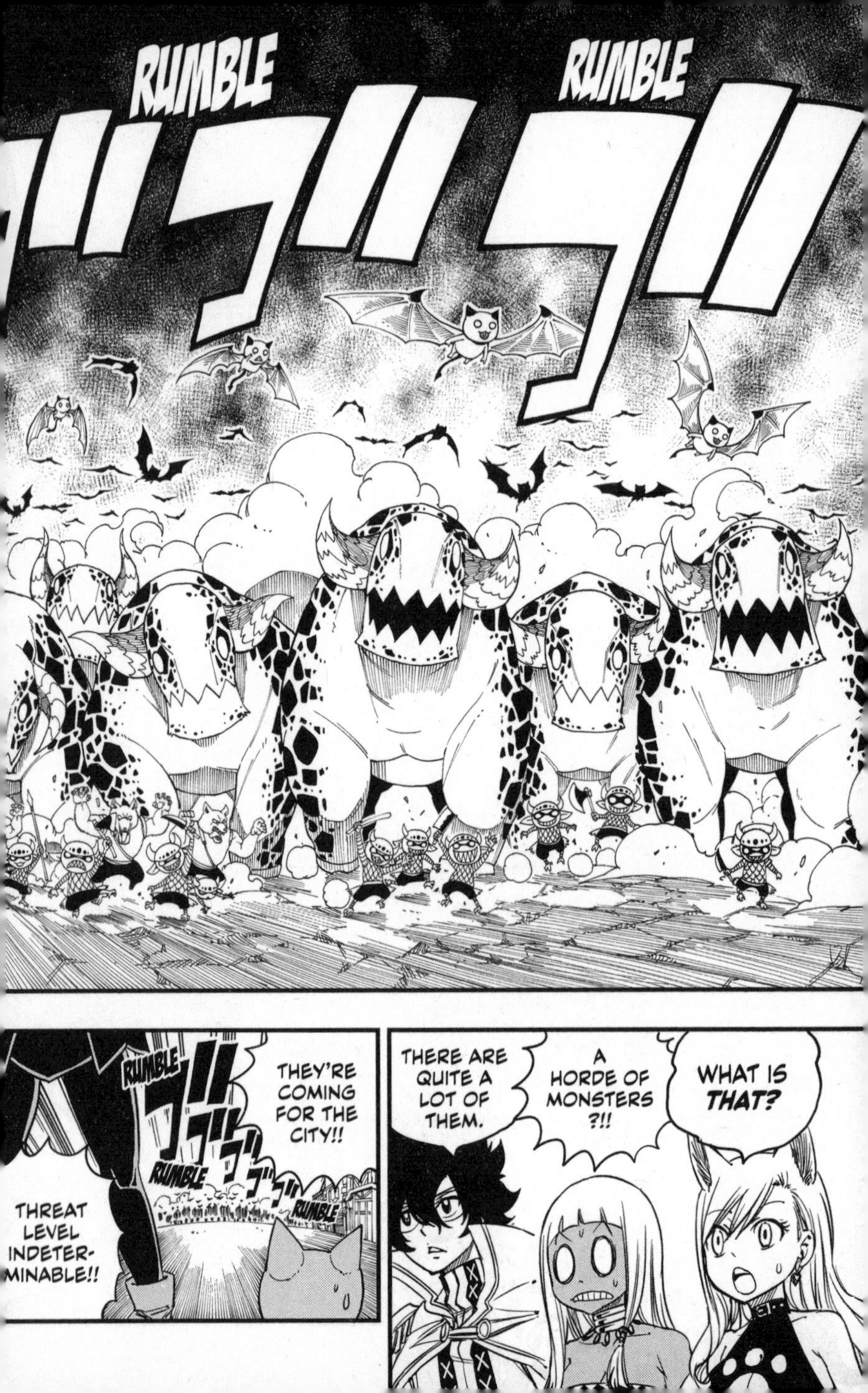
RUMBLE
RUMBLE
WHAT IS *THAT?*
A HORDE OF MONSTERS ?!!
THERE ARE QUITE A LOT OF THEM.
THEY'RE COMING FOR THE CITY!!
RUMBLE
RUMBLE
RUMBLE
THREAT LEVEL INDETER-MINABLE!!

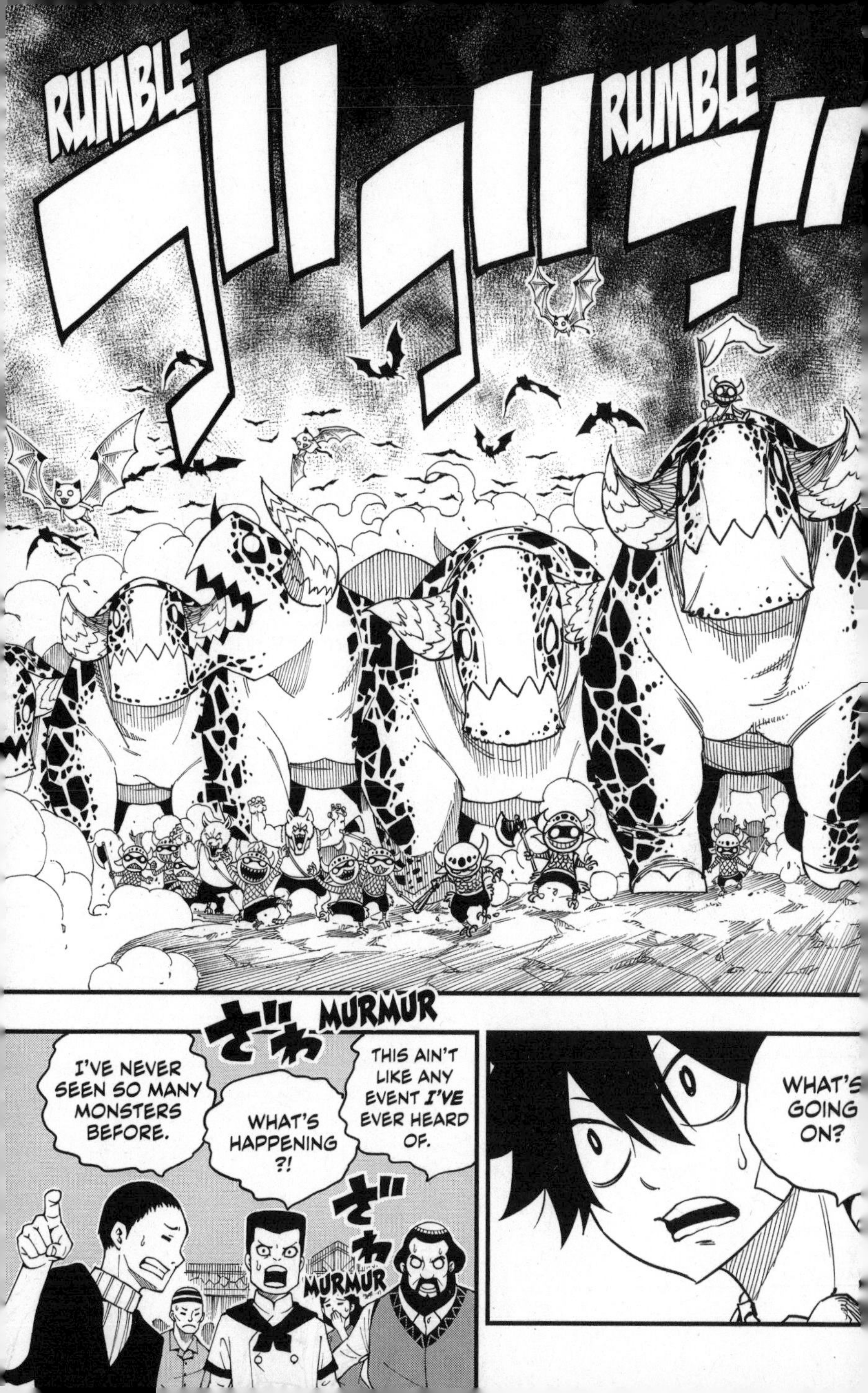
RUMBLE
RUMBLE
WHAT'S GOING ON?
THIS AIN'T LIKE ANY EVENT *I'VE* EVER HEARD OF.
ざわ MURMUR
WHAT'S HAPPENING ?!
I'VE NEVER SEEN SO MANY MONSTERS BEFORE.
ざわ MURMUR

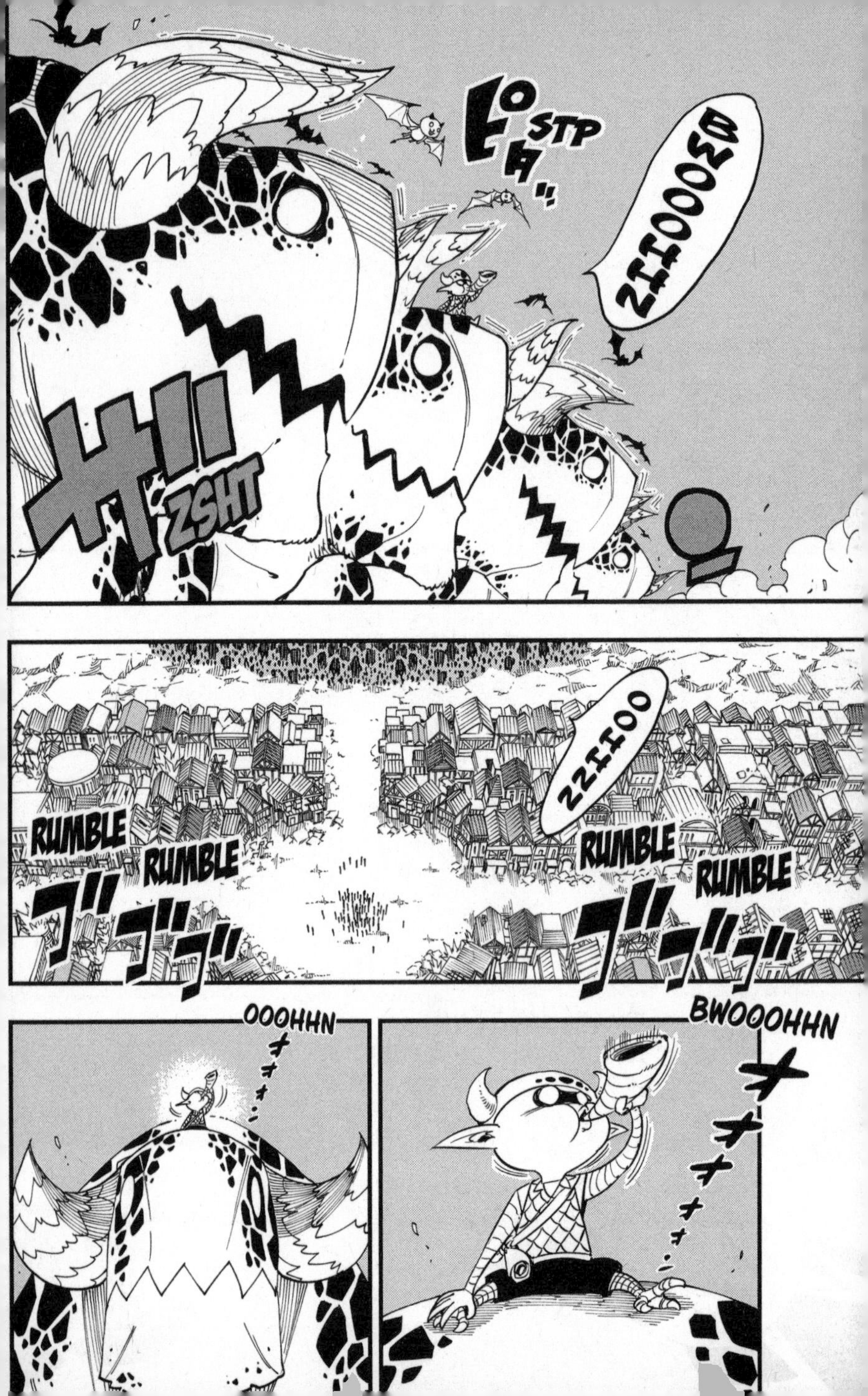
BWOOOHHN
STP
ZSHT
OOHHNN
RUMBLE
RUMBLE
RUMBLE
RUMBLE
BWOOOHHN
OOOHHN

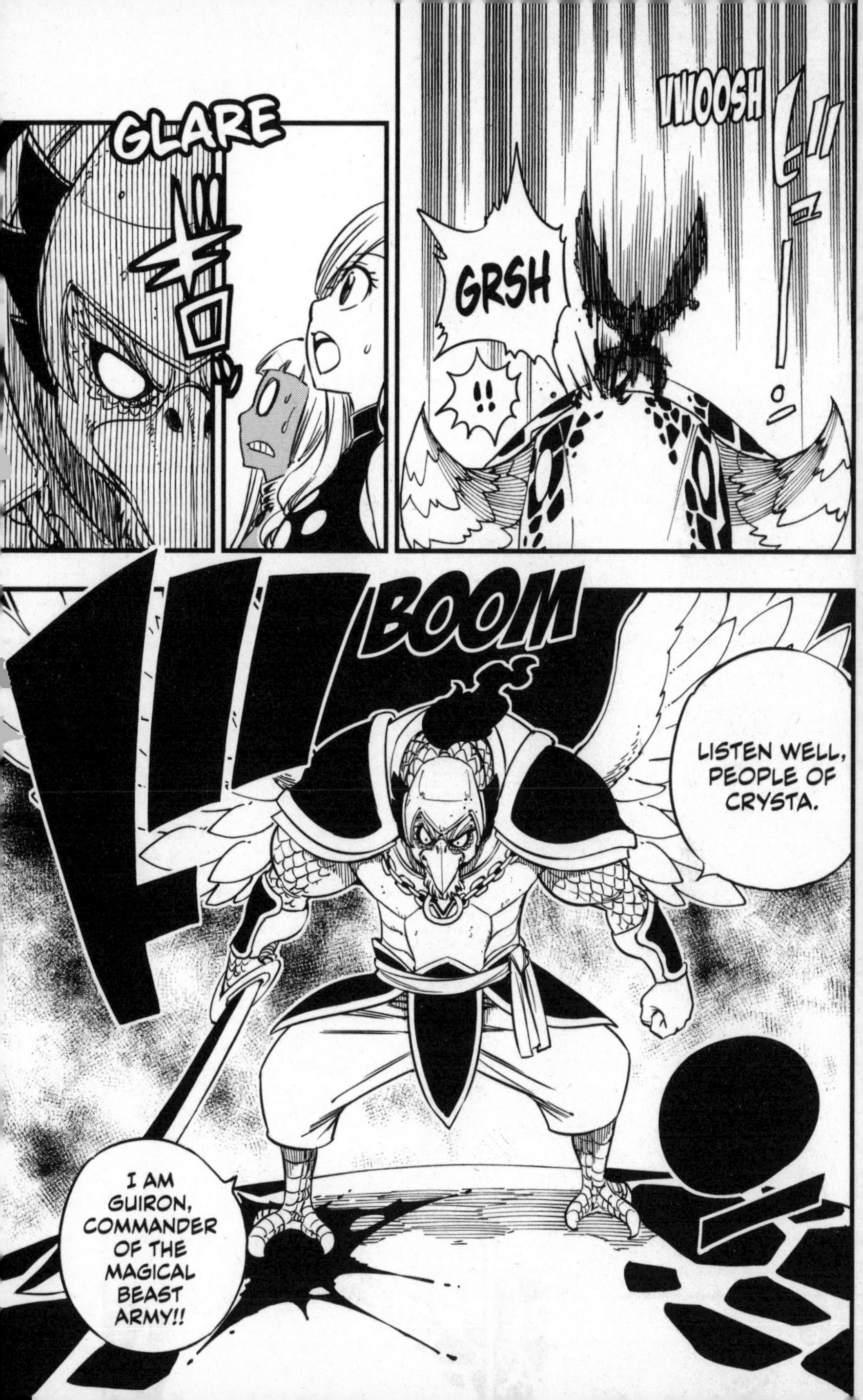
VWOOSH
GRSH
!!
GLARE
BOOM
LISTEN WELL, PEOPLE OF CRYSTA.
I AM GUIRON, COMMANDER OF THE MAGICAL BEAST ARMY!!

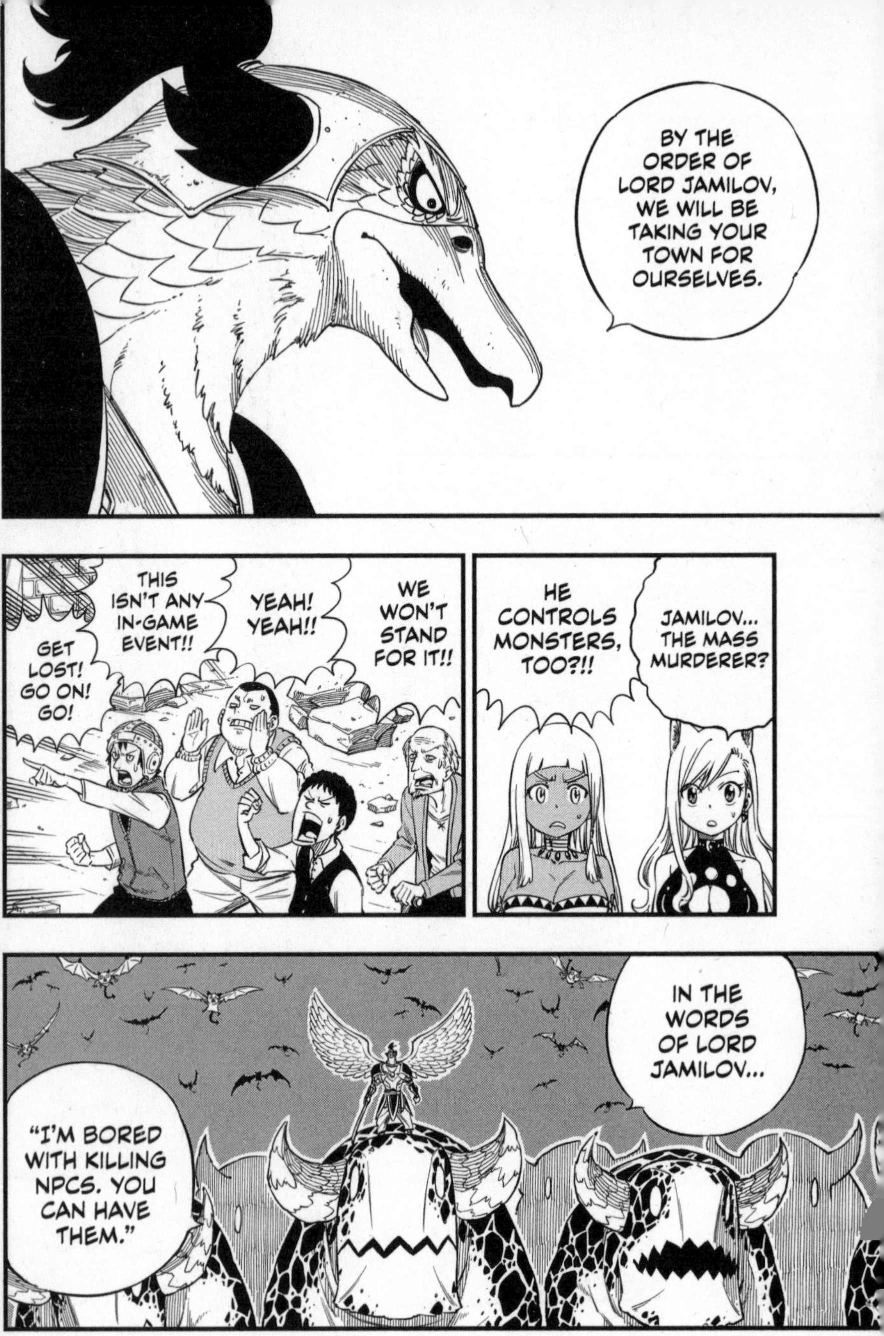
BY THE ORDER OF LORD JAMILOV, WE WILL BE TAKING YOUR TOWN FOR OURSELVES.
JAMILOV... THE MASS MURDERER?
HE CONTROLS MONSTERS, TOO?!!
WE WON'T STAND FOR IT!!
YEAH! YEAH!!
THIS ISN'T ANY IN-GAME EVENT!!
GET LOST! GO ON! GO!
IN THE WORDS OF LORD JAMILOV...
"I'M BORED WITH KILLING NPCS. YOU CAN HAVE THEM."

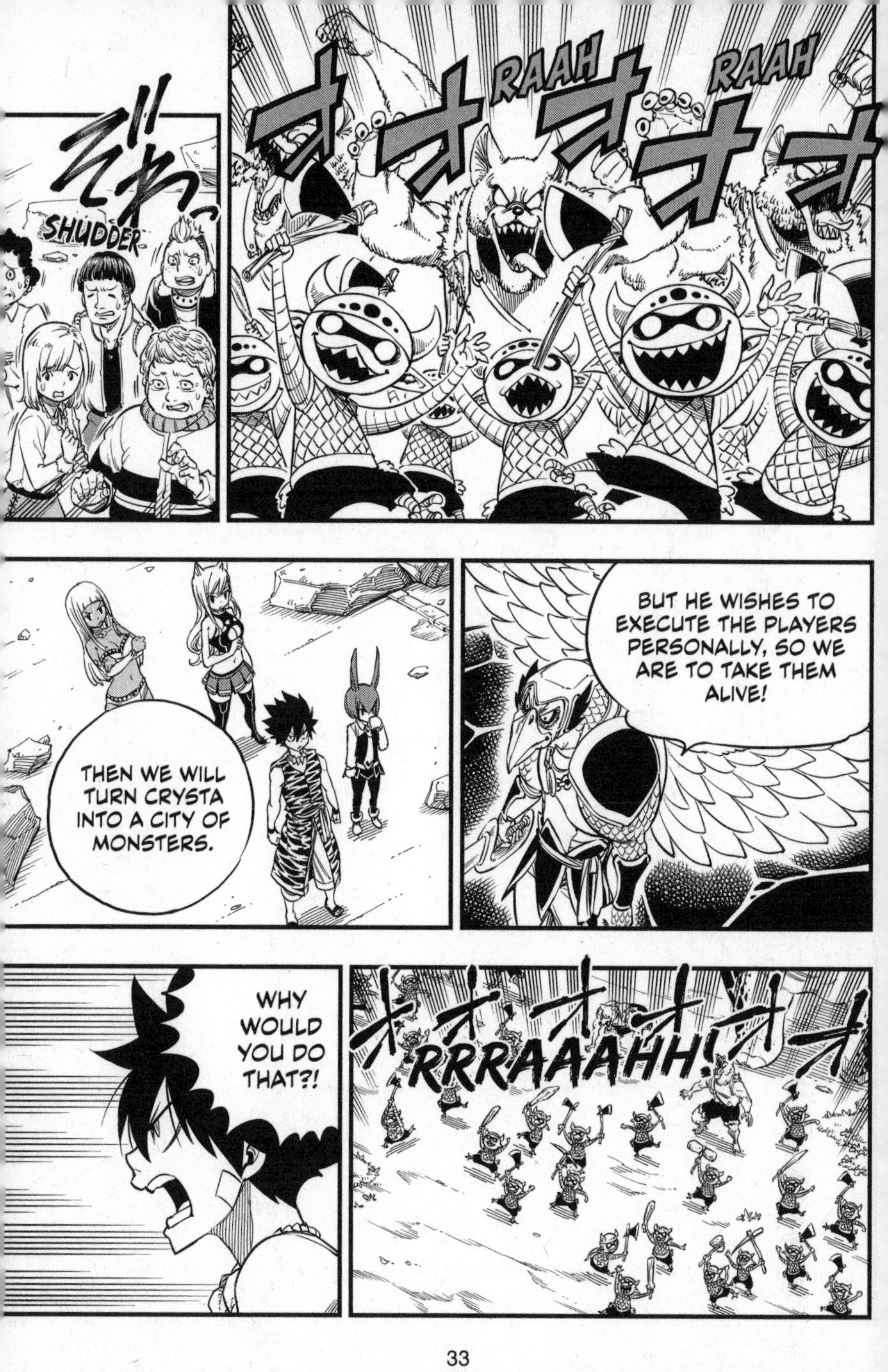
RAAH
RAAH
オオオオオ
ぞわっ
SHUDDER
BUT HE WISHES TO EXECUTE THE PLAYERS PERSONALLY, SO WE ARE TO TAKE THEM ALIVE!
THEN WE WILL TURN CRYSTA INTO A CITY OF MONSTERS.
オオオオオオ
RRRAAAHH!
WHY WOULD YOU DO THAT?!

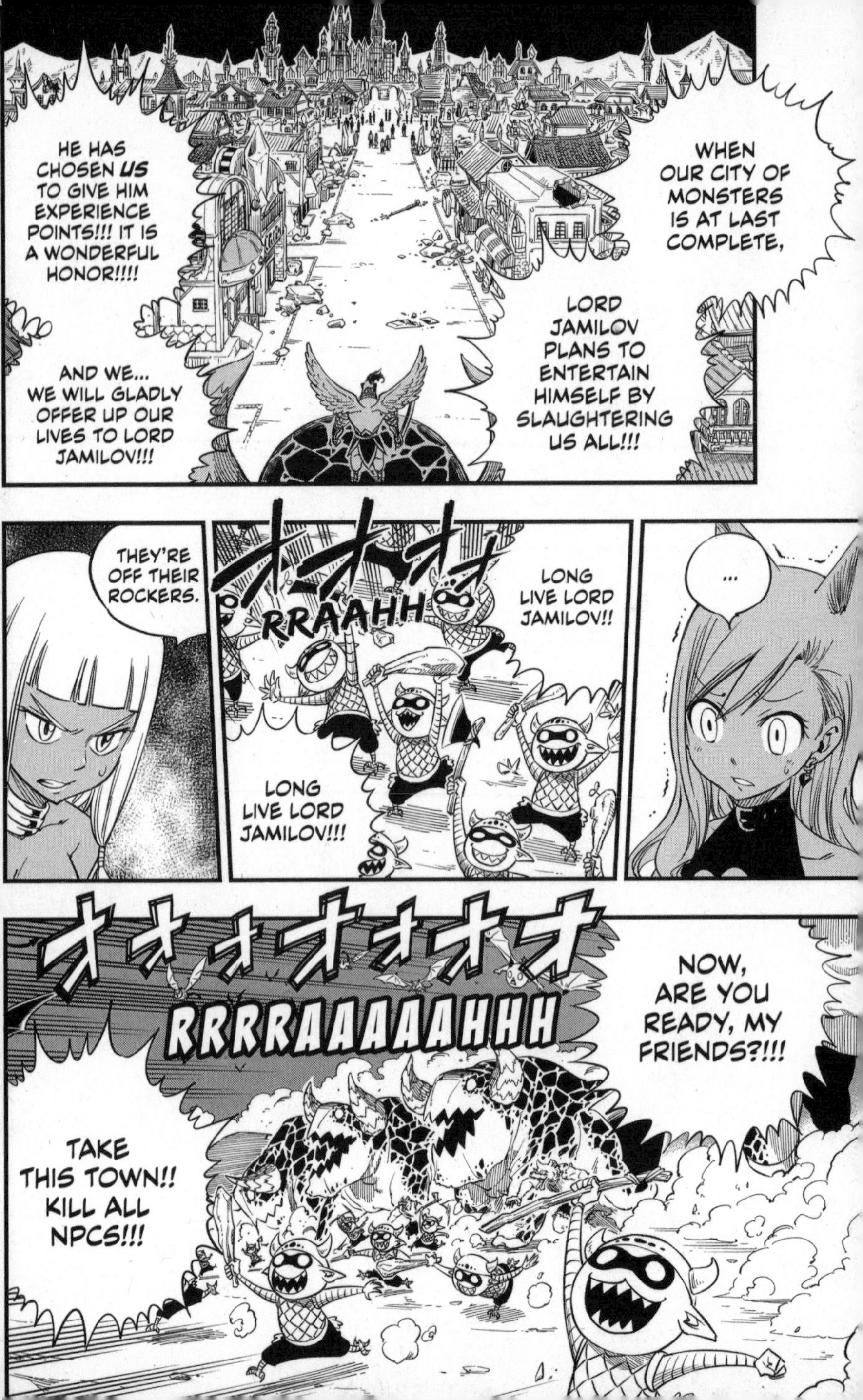

WHEN OUR CITY OF MONSTERS IS AT LAST COMPLETE,
LORD JAMILOV PLANS TO ENTERTAIN HIMSELF BY SLAUGHTERING US ALL!!!
HE HAS CHOSEN *US* TO GIVE HIM EXPERIENCE POINTS!!! IT IS A WONDERFUL HONOR!!!!
AND WE... WE WILL GLADLY OFFER UP OUR LIVES TO LORD JAMILOV!!!
...
RRAAHH
LONG LIVE LORD JAMILOV!!
LONG LIVE LORD JAMILOV!!!
THEY'RE OFF THEIR ROCKERS.
オオォオォオオ
RRRRAAAAAAHHH
NOW, ARE YOU READY, MY FRIENDS?!!!
TAKE THIS TOWN!! KILL ALL NPCS!!!

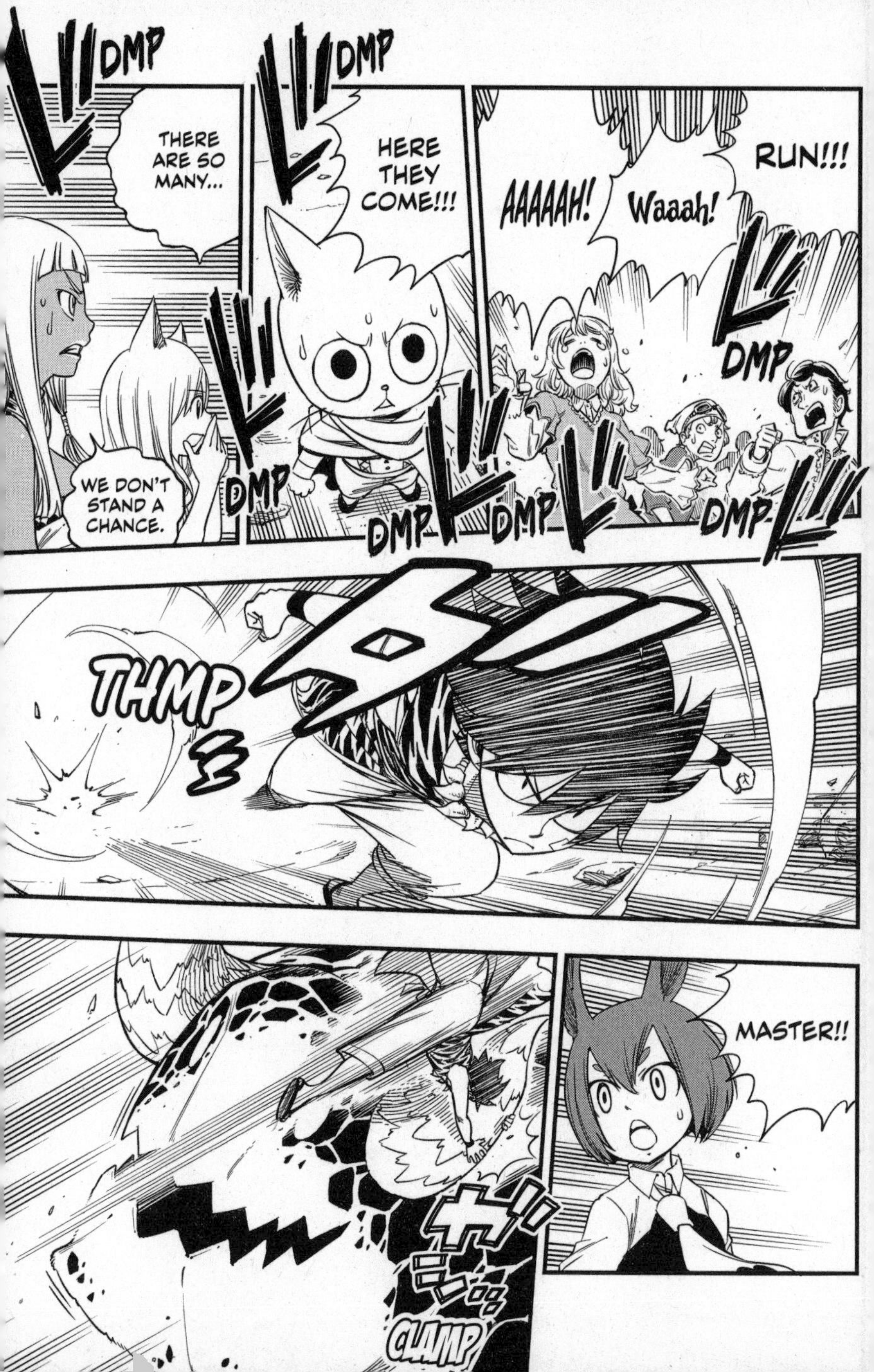
RUN!!!
Waaah!
AAAAAH!
DMP
DMP
DMP
DMP
HERE THEY COME!!!
DMP
DMP
DMP
THERE ARE SO MANY...
WE DON'T STAND A CHANCE.
THMP
MASTER!!
CLAMP

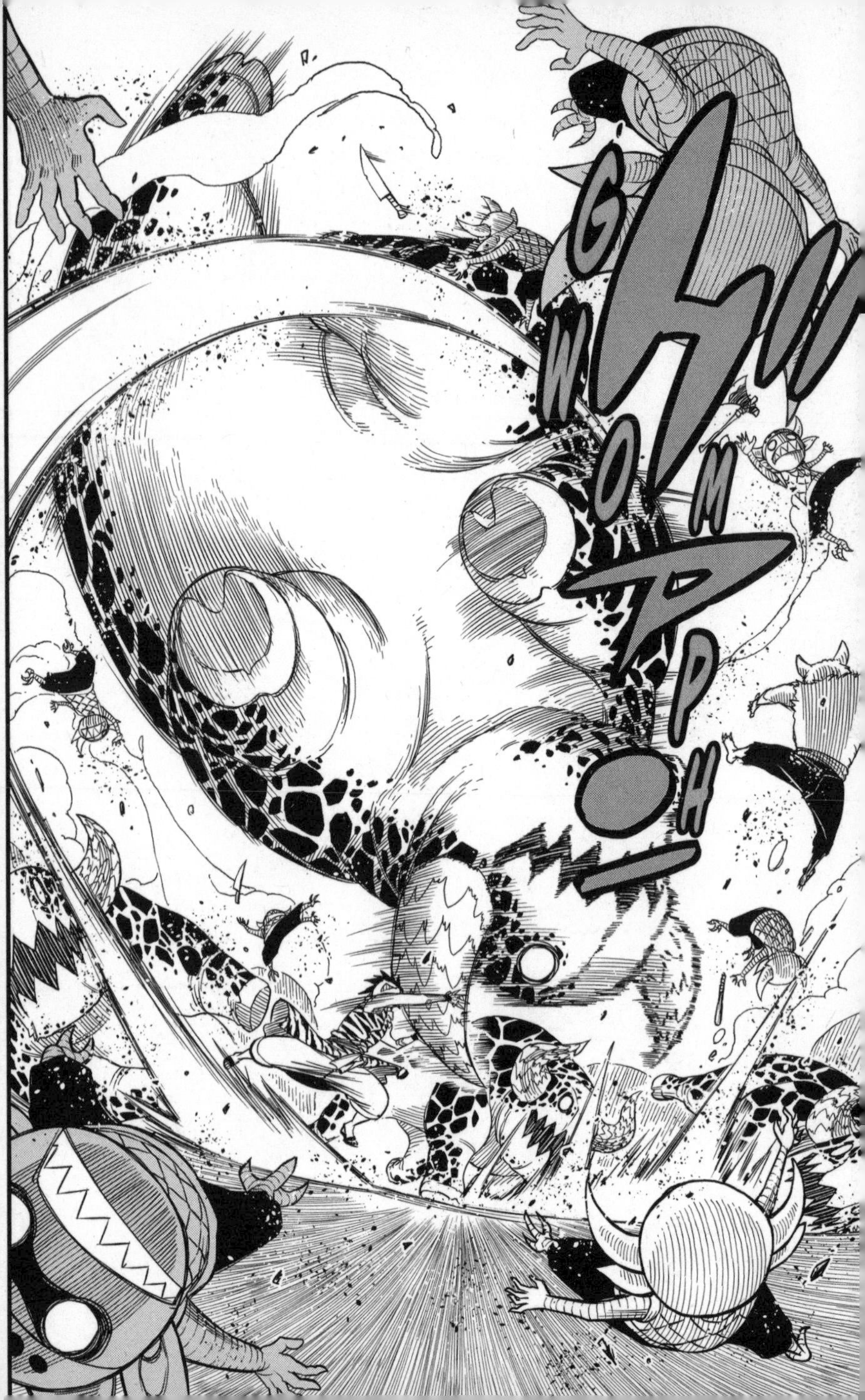
GWOMPH

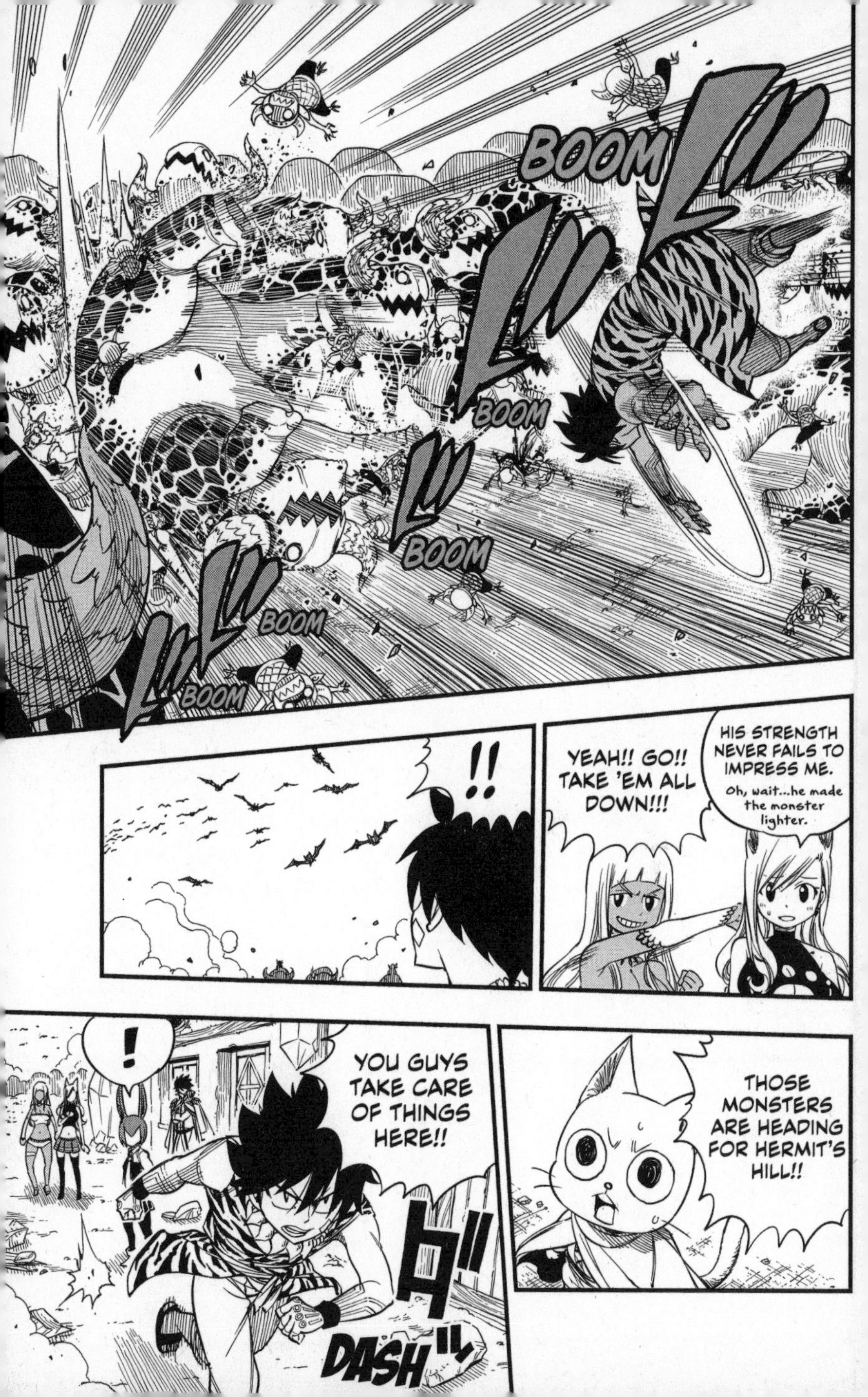
BOOM
BOOM
BOOM
BOOM
BOOM
HIS STRENGTH NEVER FAILS TO IMPRESS ME.
Oh, wait...he made the monster lighter.
YEAH!! GO!! TAKE 'EM ALL DOWN!!!
!!
THOSE MONSTERS ARE HEADING FOR HERMIT'S HILL!!
!
YOU GUYS TAKE CARE OF THINGS HERE!!
DASH

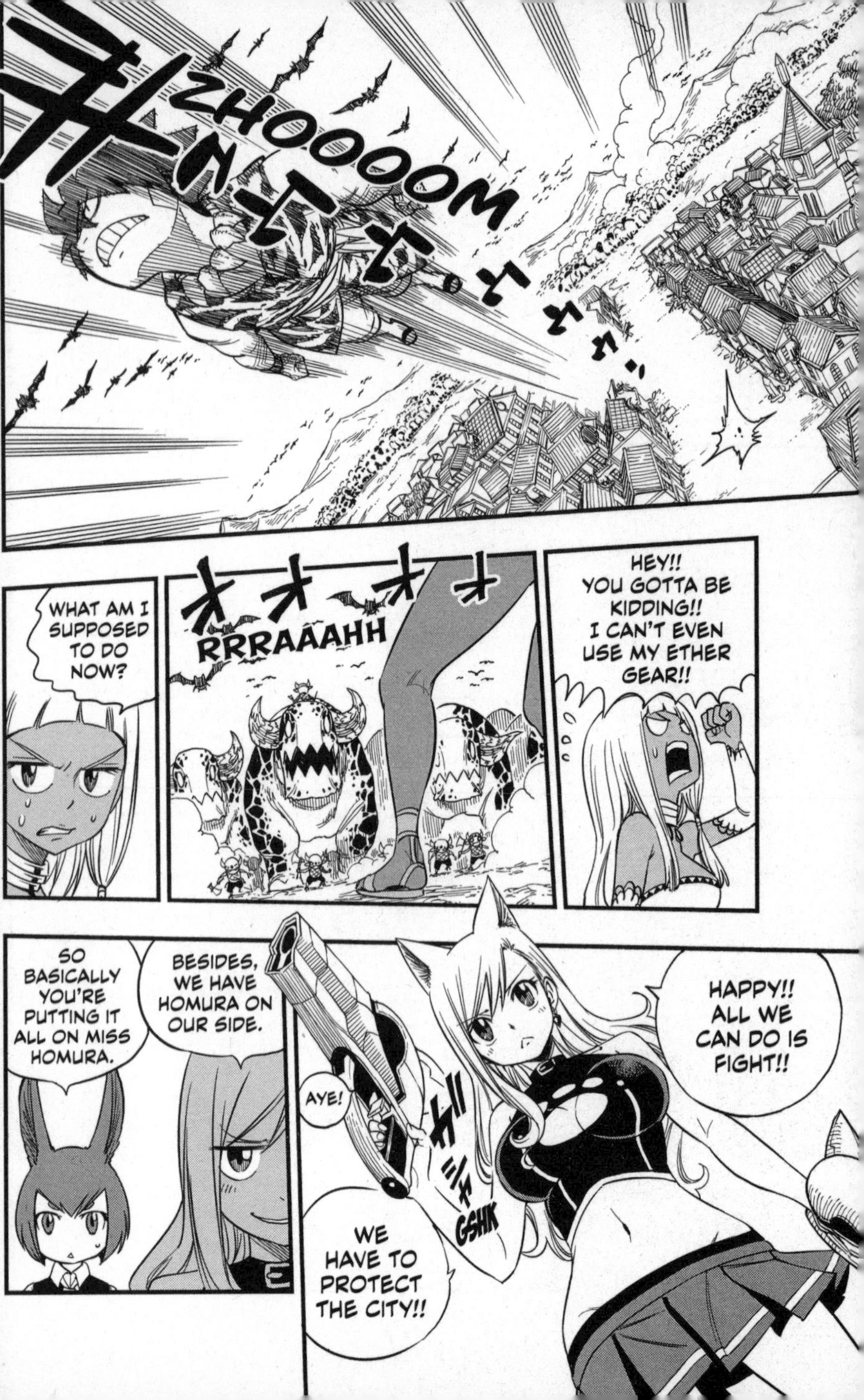
ZHOOOOM
HEY!! YOU GOTTA BE KIDDING!! I CAN'T EVEN USE MY ETHER GEAR!!
RRRAAAHH
WHAT AM I SUPPOSED TO DO NOW?
HAPPY!! ALL WE CAN DO IS FIGHT!!
AYE!
GSHK
WE HAVE TO PROTECT THE CITY!!
BESIDES, WE HAVE HOMURA ON OUR SIDE.
SO BASICALLY YOU'RE PUTTING IT ALL ON MISS HOMURA.

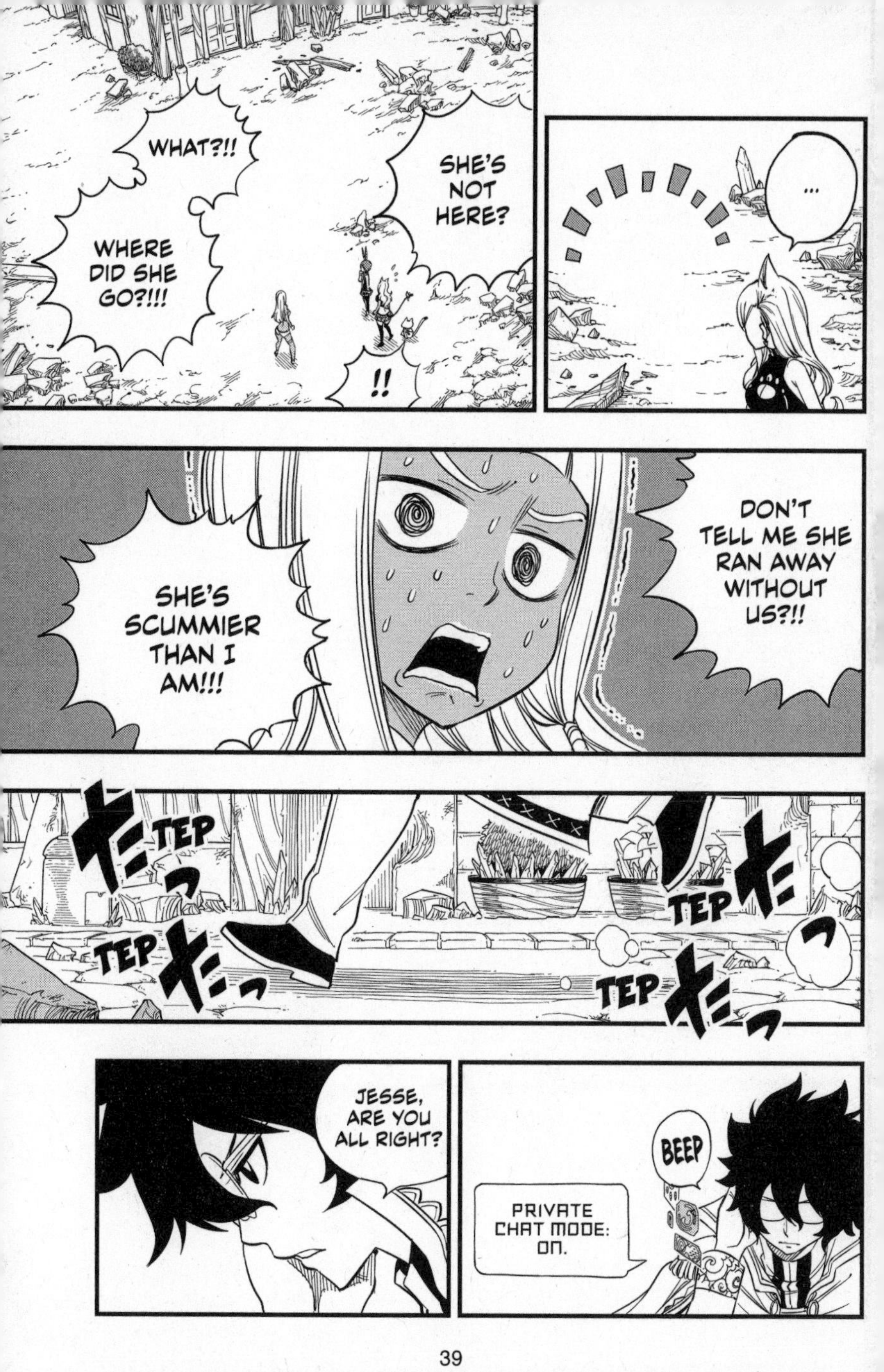
...
SHE'S NOT HERE?
WHAT?!!
WHERE DID SHE GO?!!!
!!
DON'T TELL ME SHE RAN AWAY WITHOUT US?!!
SHE'S SCUMMIER THAN I AM!!!
TEP
TEP
TEP
TEP
BEEP
PRIVATE CHAT MODE: ON.
JESSE, ARE YOU ALL RIGHT?

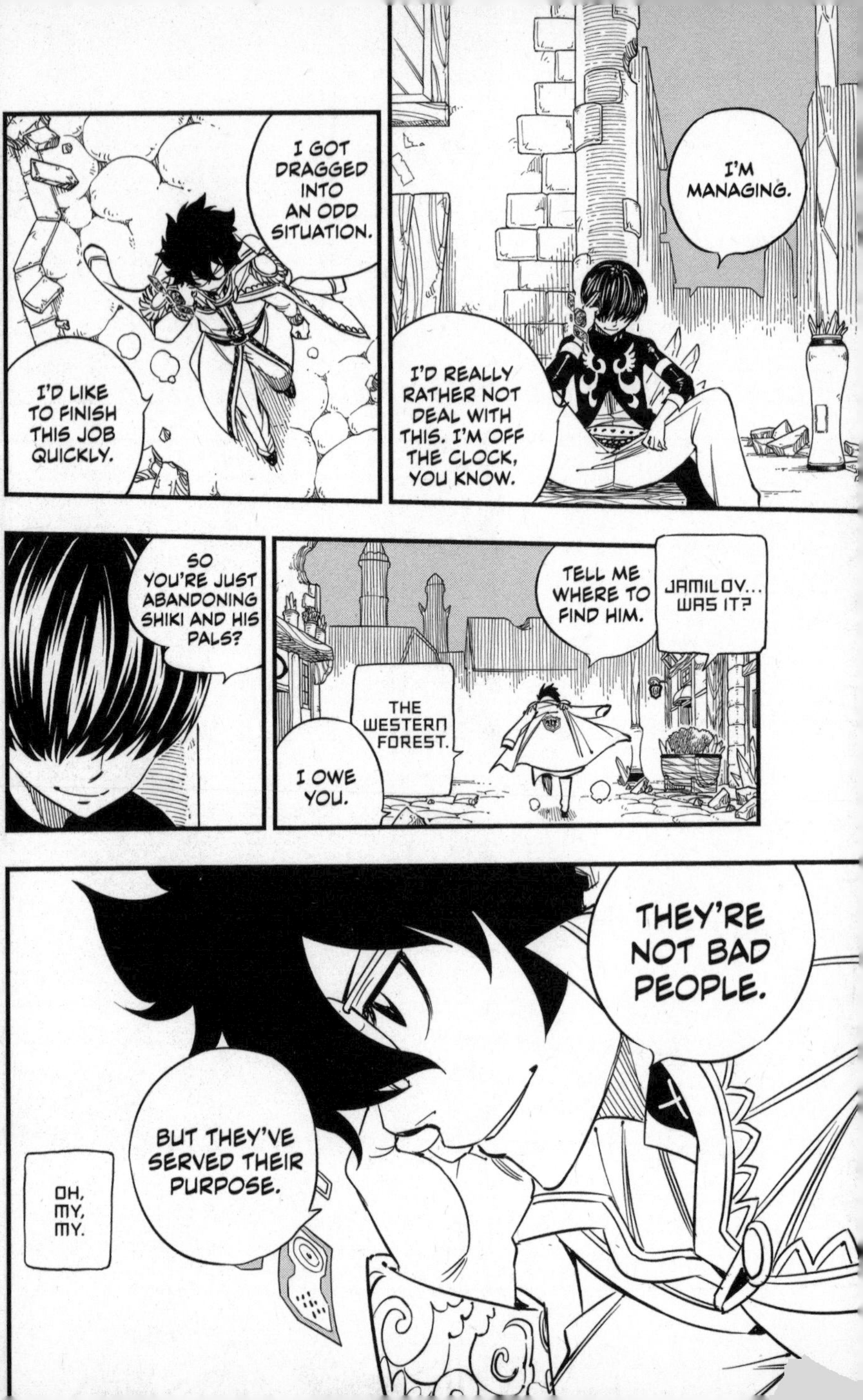
I'M MANAGING.
I'D REALLY RATHER NOT DEAL WITH THIS. I'M OFF THE CLOCK, YOU KNOW.
I GOT DRAGGED INTO AN ODD SITUATION.
I'D LIKE TO FINISH THIS JOB QUICKLY.
JAMILOV... WAS IT?
TELL ME WHERE TO FIND HIM.
THE WESTERN FOREST.
I OWE YOU.
SO YOU'RE JUST ABANDONING SHIKI AND HIS PALS?
THEY'RE NOT BAD PEOPLE.
BUT THEY'VE SERVED THEIR PURPOSE.
OH, MY, MY.

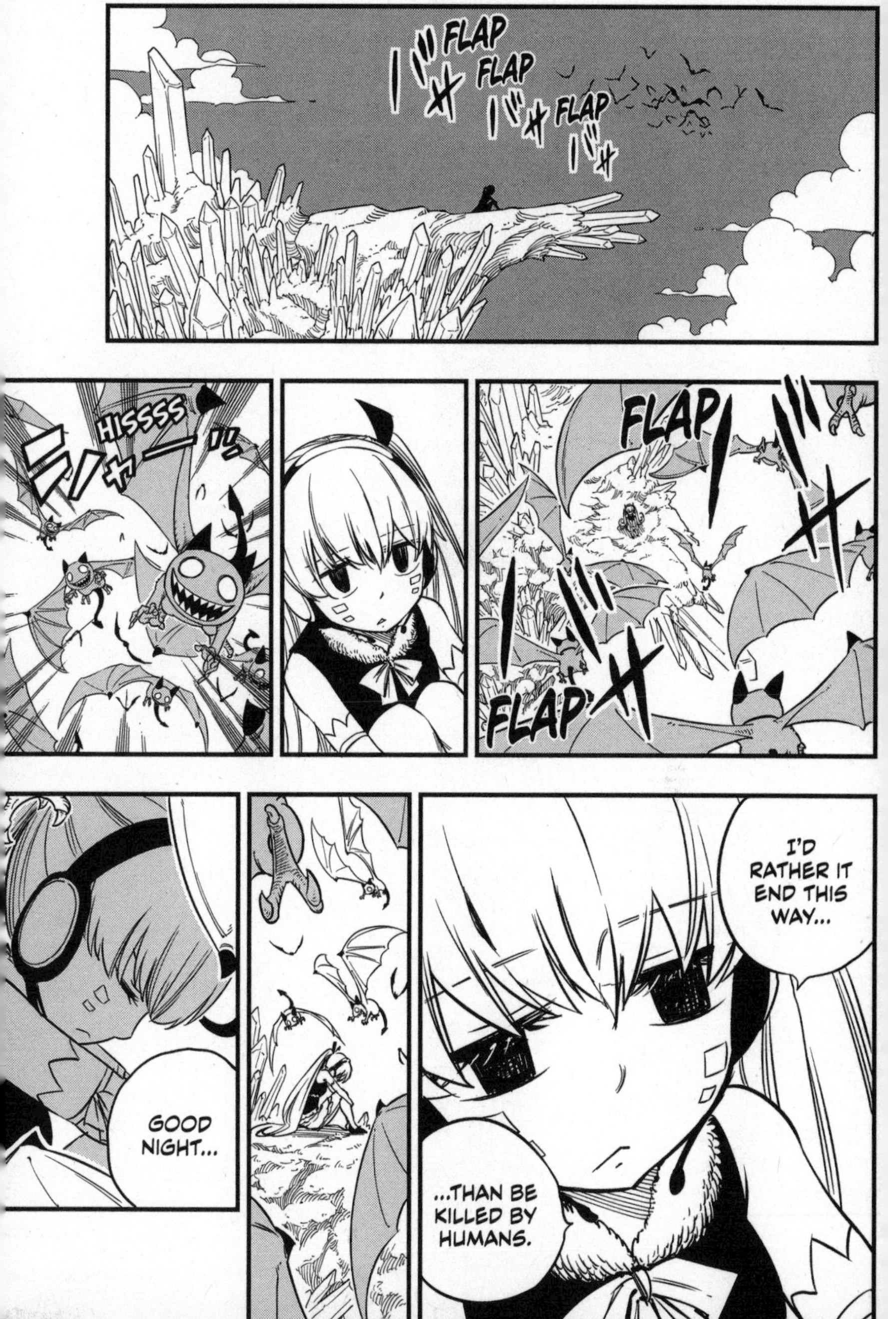
FLAP
FLAP
FLAP
FLAP
FLAP
HISSSS
I'D RATHER IT END THIS WAY...
...THAN BE KILLED BY HUMANS.
GOOD NIGHT...

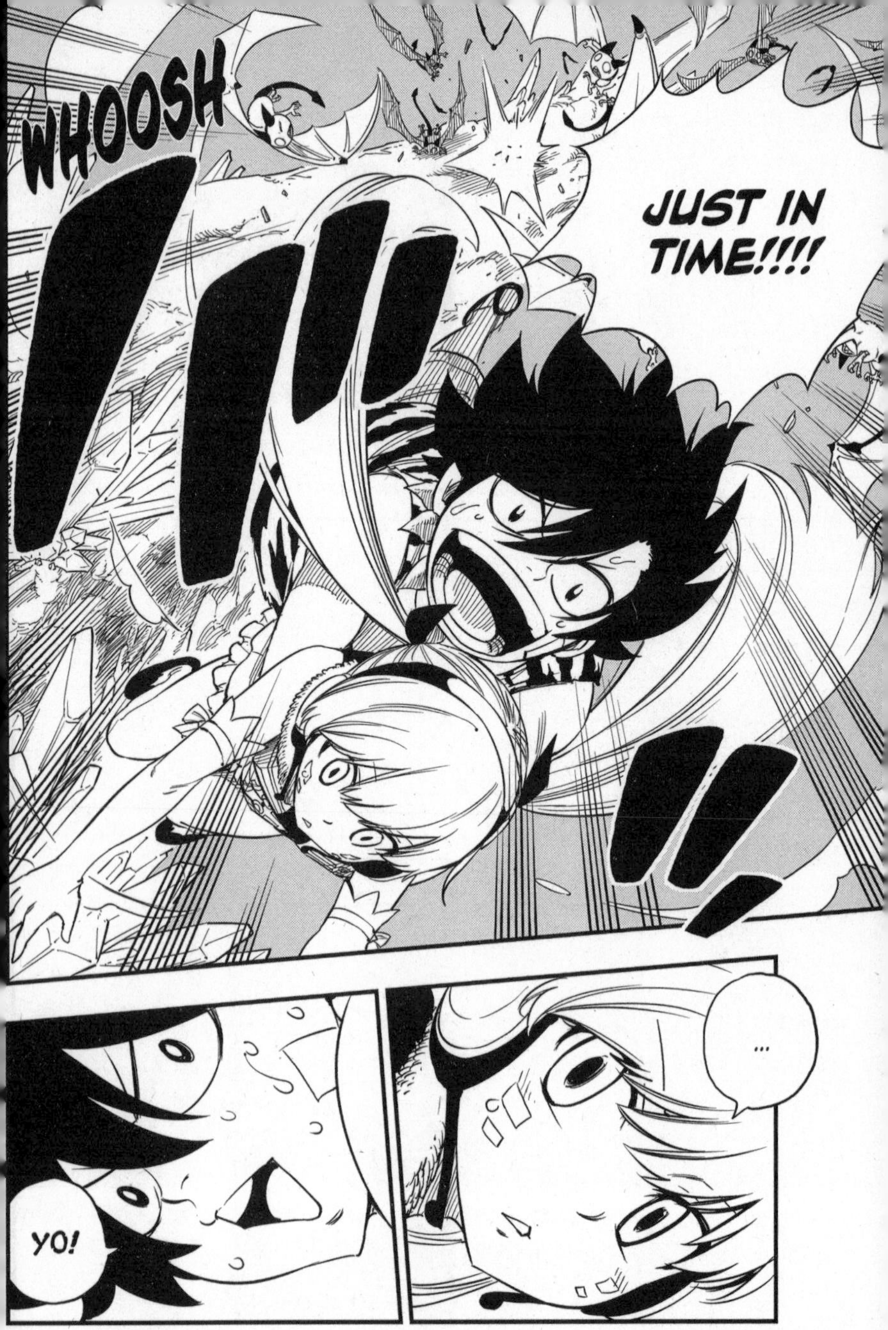
WHOOSH
JUST IN TIME!!!!
...
YO!

EDENS ZERO

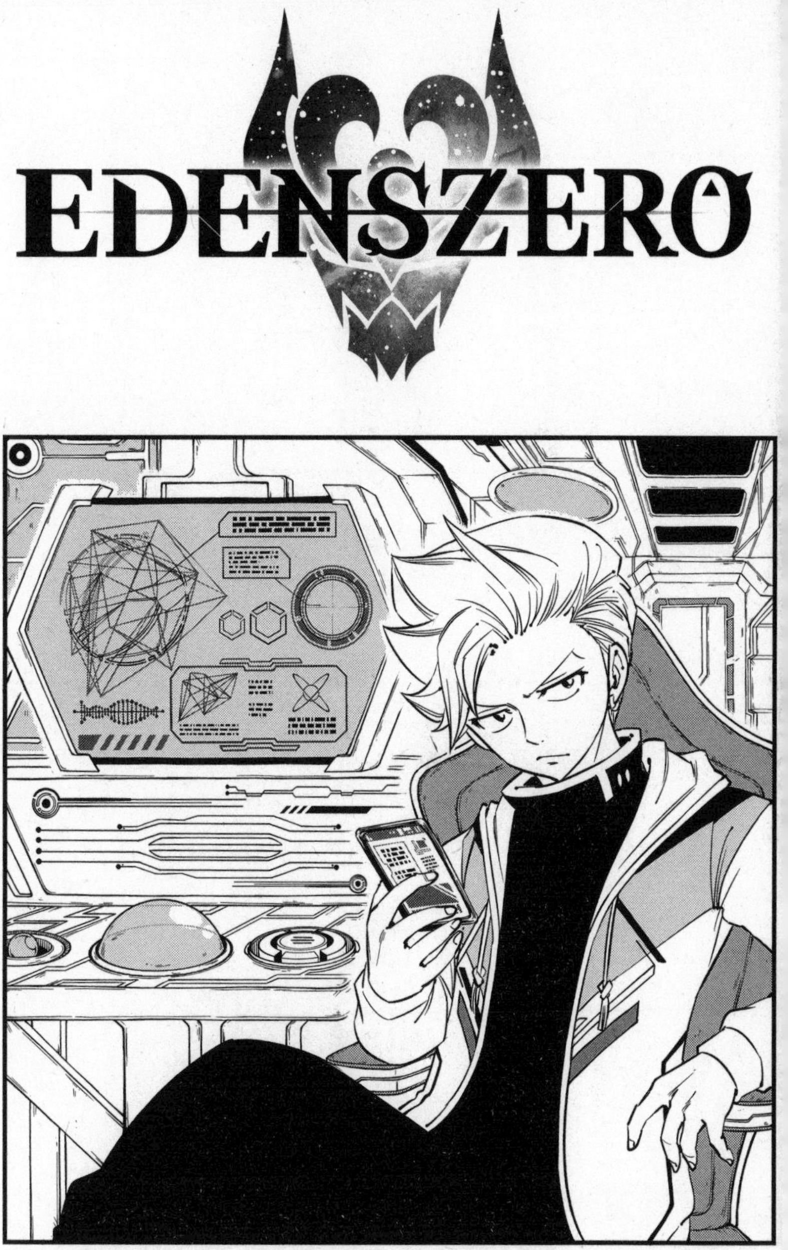

CHAPTER 35: THE GIRL AND THE MONSTER

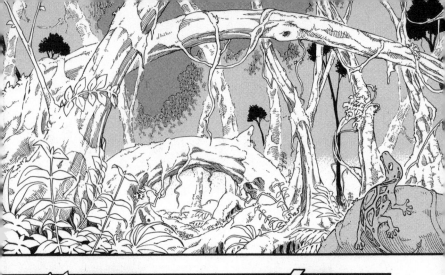

MONCH

MONCH

MONCH

もっ

もっ

ZMF

!

ZSH

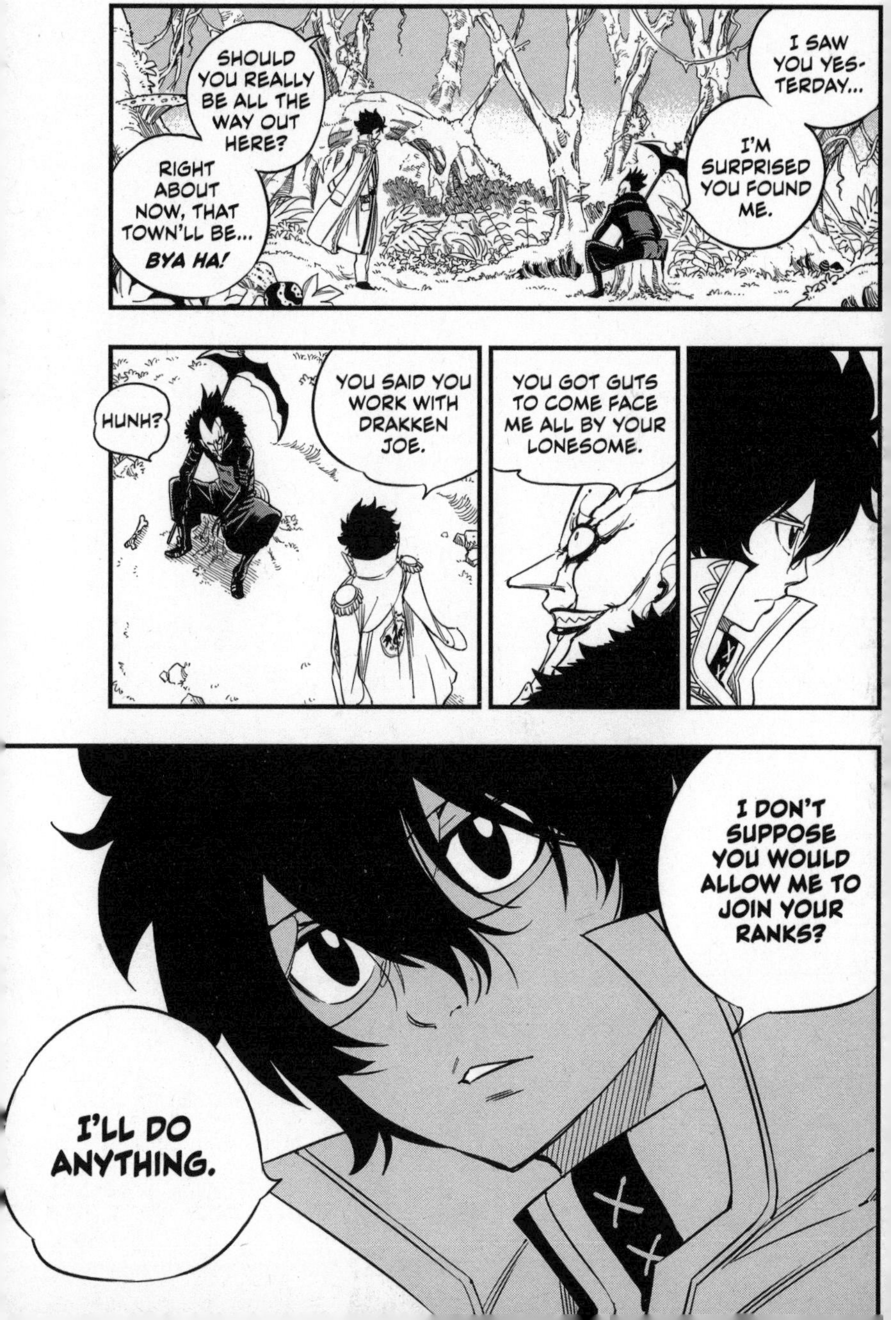
I SAW YOU YESTERDAY...
I'M SURPRISED YOU FOUND ME.
SHOULD YOU REALLY BE ALL THE WAY OUT HERE?
RIGHT ABOUT NOW, THAT TOWN'LL BE... *BYA HA!*
YOU GOT GUTS TO COME FACE ME ALL BY YOUR LONESOME.
YOU SAID YOU WORK WITH DRAKKEN JOE.
HUNH?
I DON'T SUPPOSE YOU WOULD ALLOW ME TO JOIN YOUR RANKS?
I'LL DO ANYTHING.

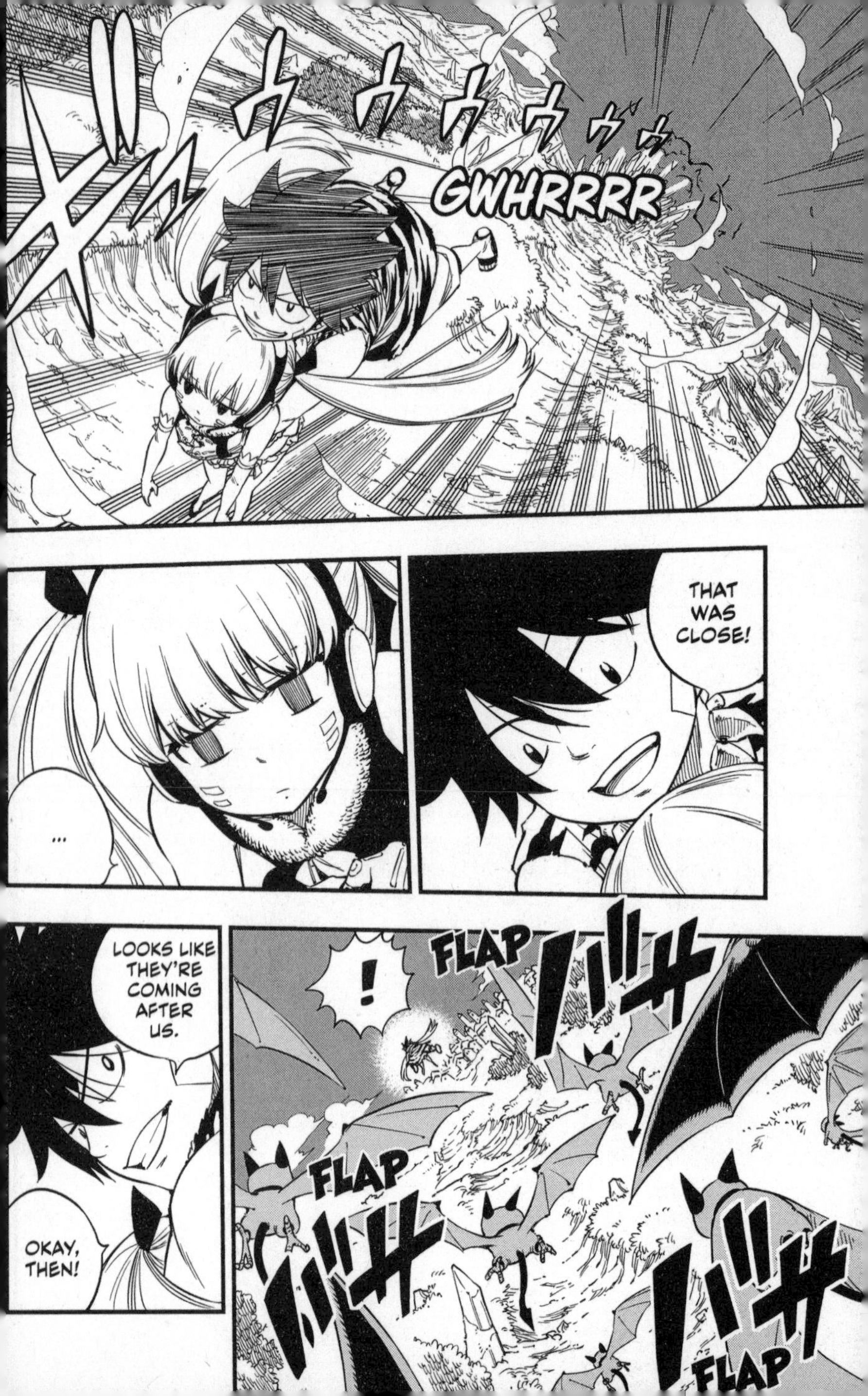
GWHRRRR
THAT WAS CLOSE!
...
FLAP
!
FLAP
FLAP
LOOKS LIKE THEY'RE COMING AFTER US.
OKAY, THEN!

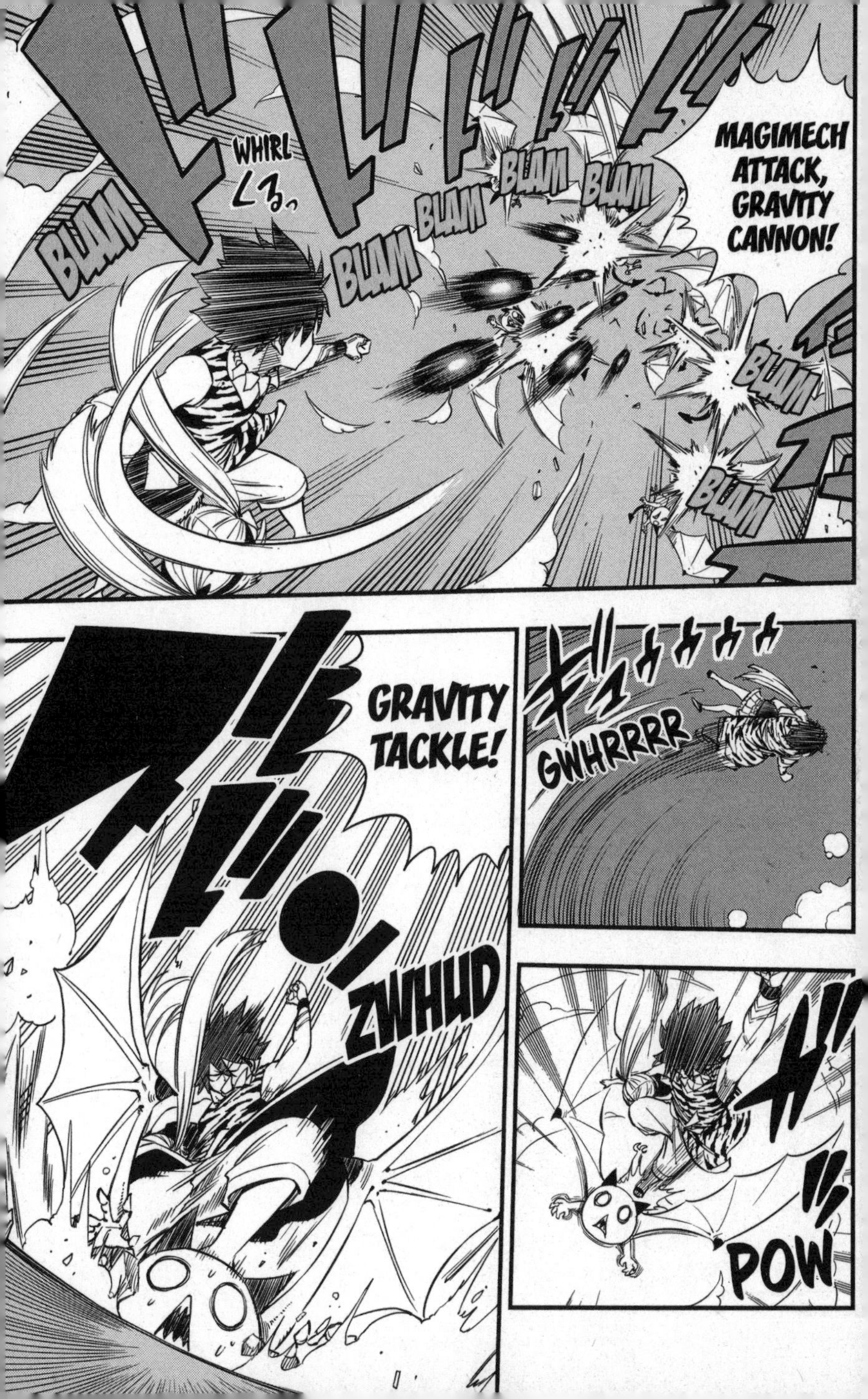
MAGIMECH ATTACK, GRAVITY CANNON!
BLAM
BLAM
BLAM
BLAM
BLAM
BLAM
WHIRL
くるっ
BLAM
GWHRRRR
POW
GRAVITY TACKLE!
ZWHUD

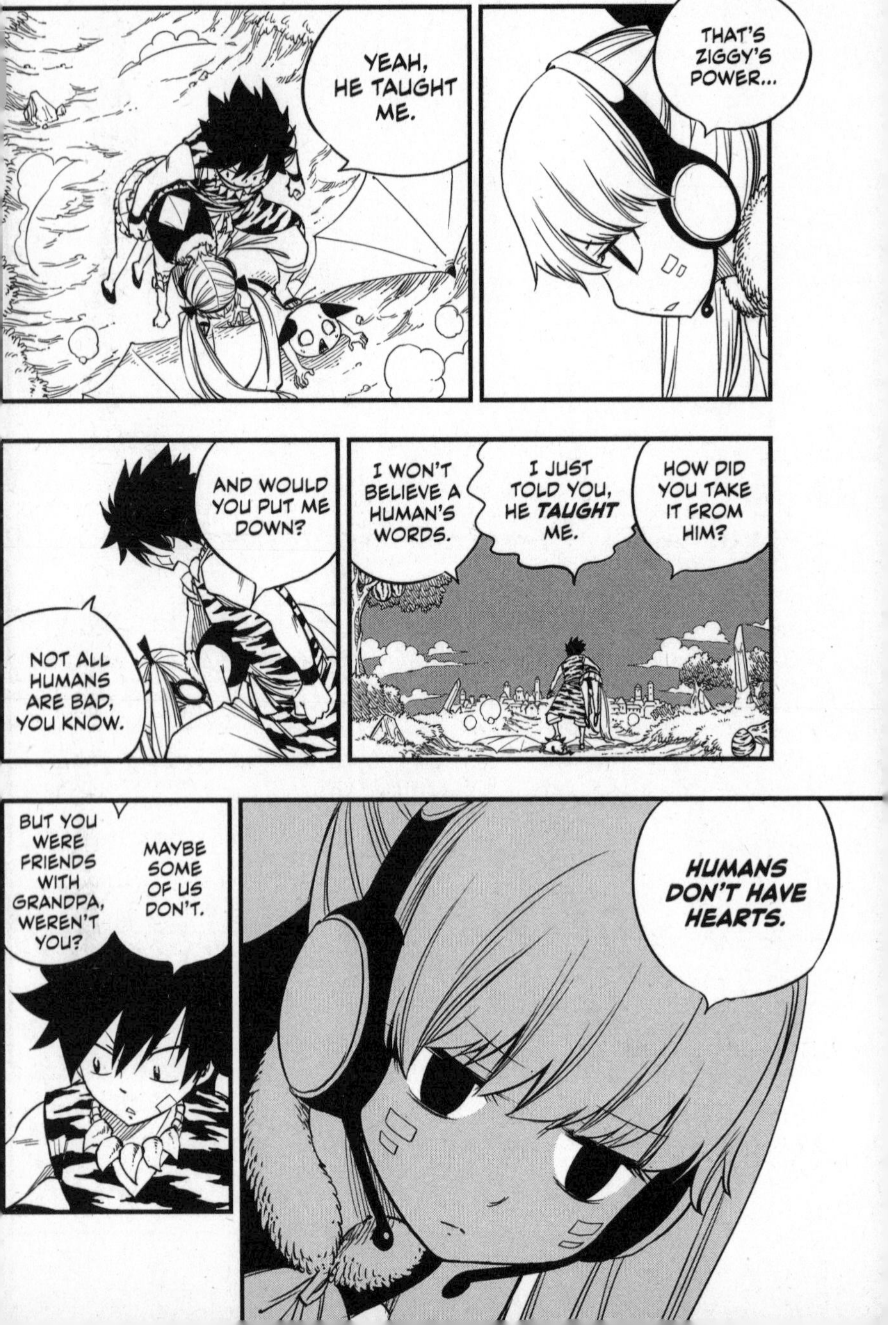
THAT'S ZIGGY'S POWER...
YEAH, HE TAUGHT ME.
HOW DID YOU TAKE IT FROM HIM?
I JUST TOLD YOU, HE *TAUGHT* ME.
I WON'T BELIEVE A HUMAN'S WORDS.
AND WOULD YOU PUT ME DOWN?
NOT ALL HUMANS ARE BAD, YOU KNOW.
HUMANS DON'T HAVE HEARTS.
MAYBE SOME OF US DON'T.
BUT YOU WERE FRIENDS WITH GRANDPA, WEREN'T YOU?

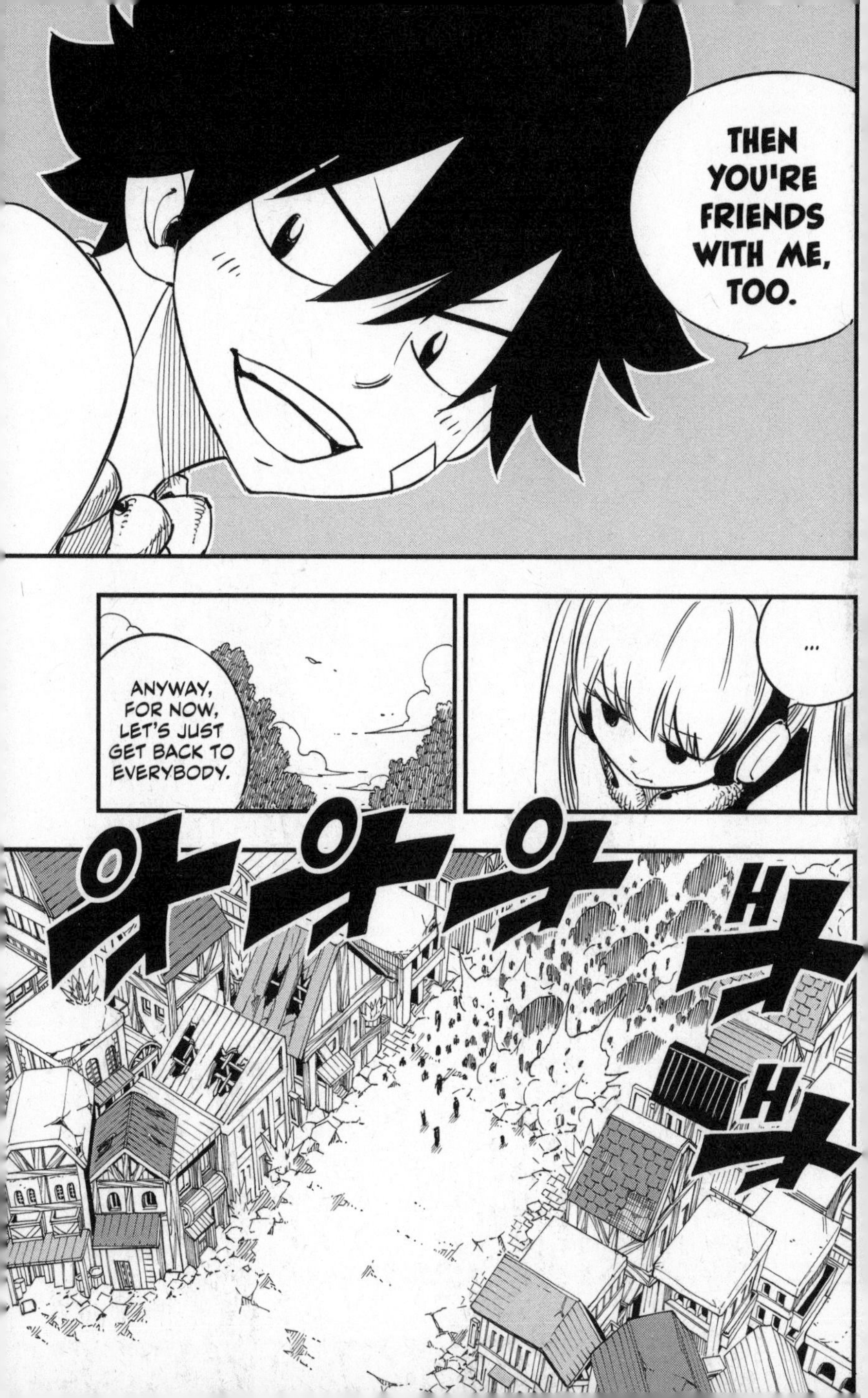
THEN YOU'RE FRIENDS WITH ME, TOO.
...
ANYWAY, FOR NOW, LET'S JUST GET BACK TO EVERYBODY.
H
H

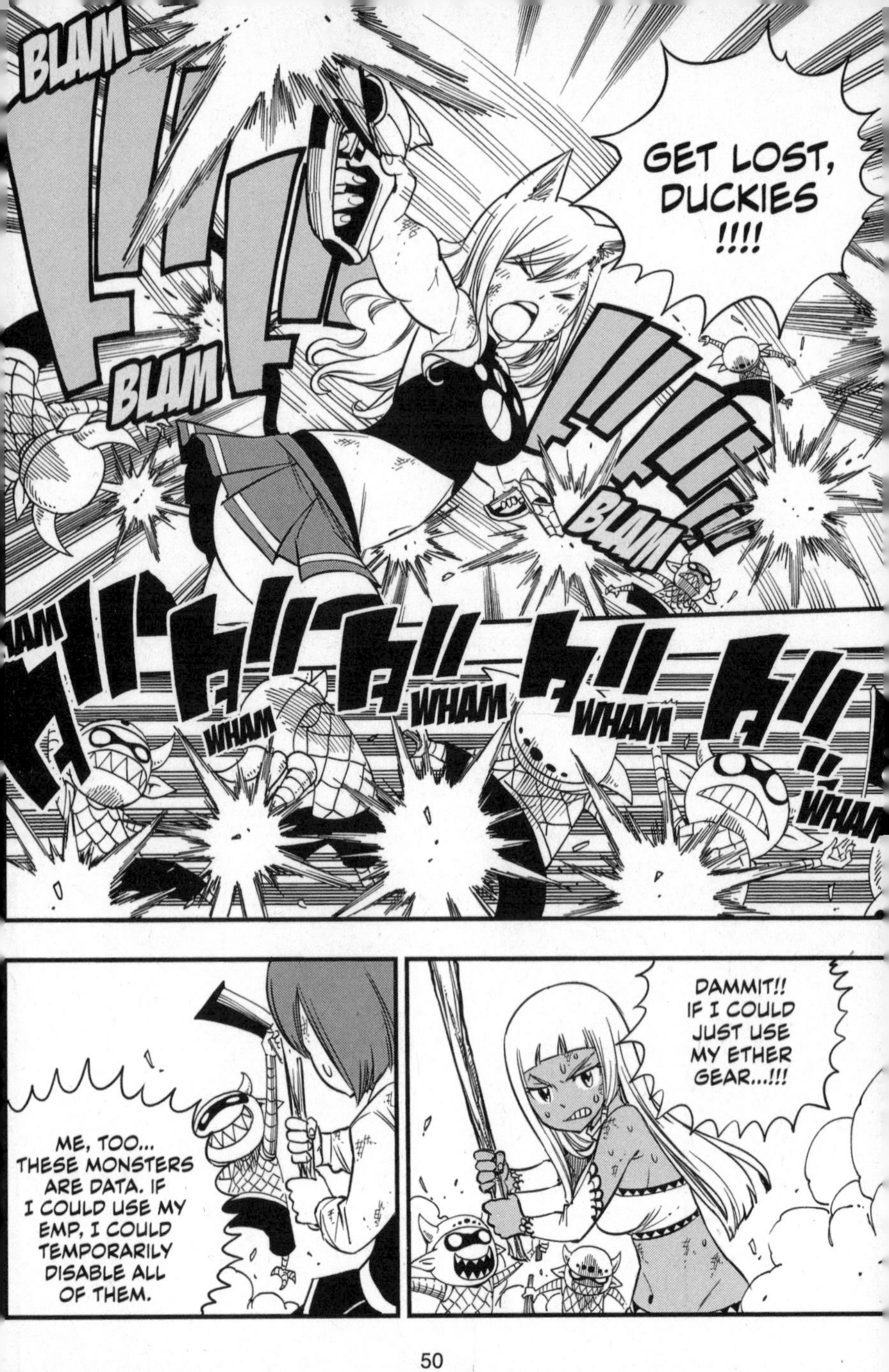
GET LOST, DUCKIES !!!!
BLAM
BLAM
BLAM
WHAM
WHAM
WHAM
WHAM
WHAM
DAMMIT!! IF I COULD JUST USE MY ETHER GEAR...!!!
ME, TOO... THESE MONSTERS ARE DATA. IF I COULD USE MY EMP, I COULD TEMPORARILY DISABLE ALL OF THEM.

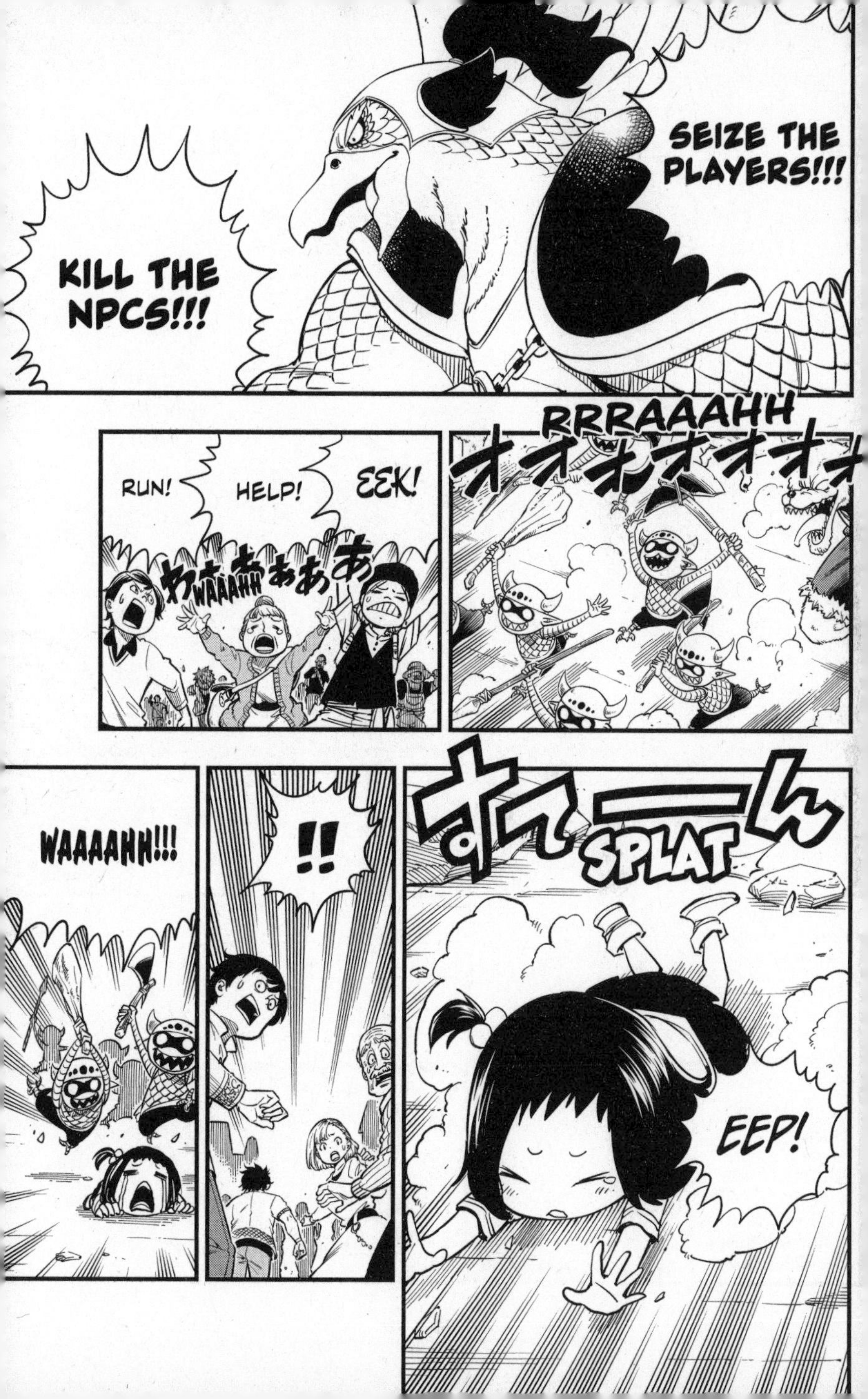
SEIZE THE PLAYERS!!!
KILL THE NPCS!!!
RRRAAAHH
オオオオオオオ
EEK!
HELP!
RUN!
わああああ
WAAAHH
すてーん
SPLAT
EEP!
!!
WAAAAHH!!!

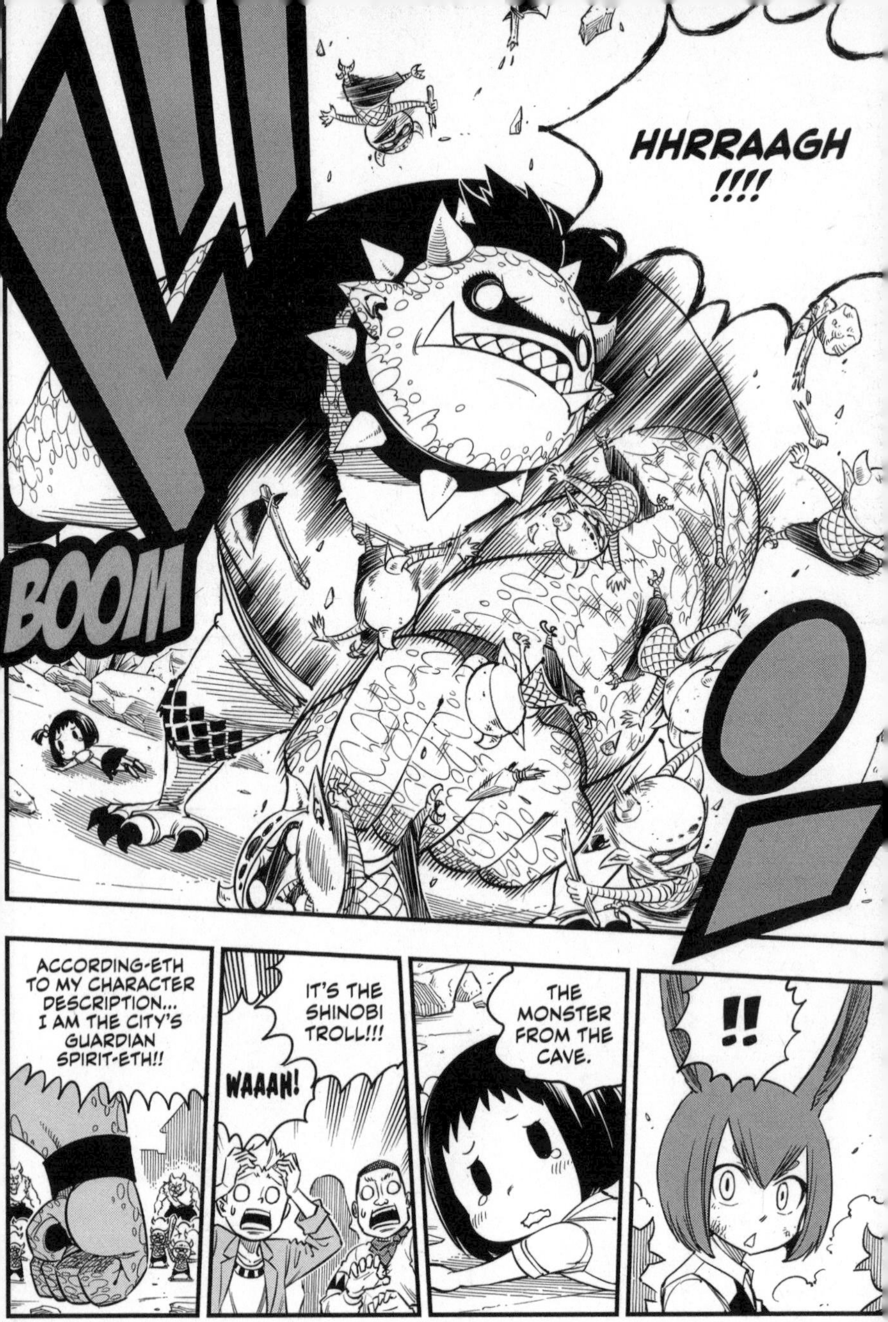
HHRRAAGH !!!!
BOOM
!!
THE MONSTER FROM THE CAVE.
IT'S THE SHINOBI TROLL!!!
WAAAH!
ACCORDING-ETH TO MY CHARACTER DESCRIPTION... I AM THE CITY'S GUARDIAN SPIRIT-ETH!!

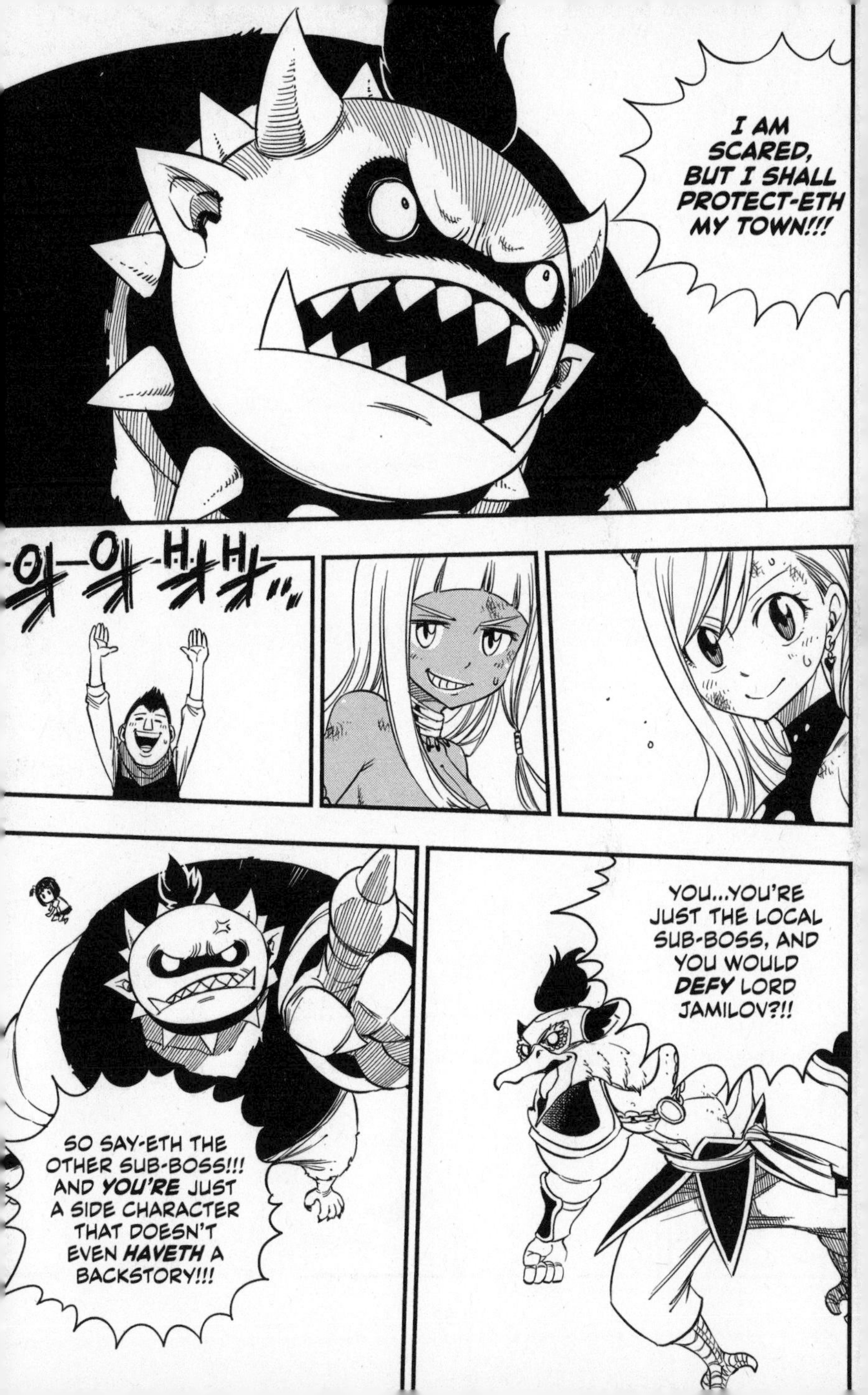
I AM SCARED, BUT I SHALL PROTECT-ETH MY TOWN!!!
YOU...YOU'RE JUST THE LOCAL SUB-BOSS, AND YOU WOULD DEFY LORD JAMILOV?!!
SO SAY-ETH THE OTHER SUB-BOSS!!! AND YOU'RE JUST A SIDE CHARACTER THAT DOESN'T EVEN HAVETH A BACKSTORY!!!

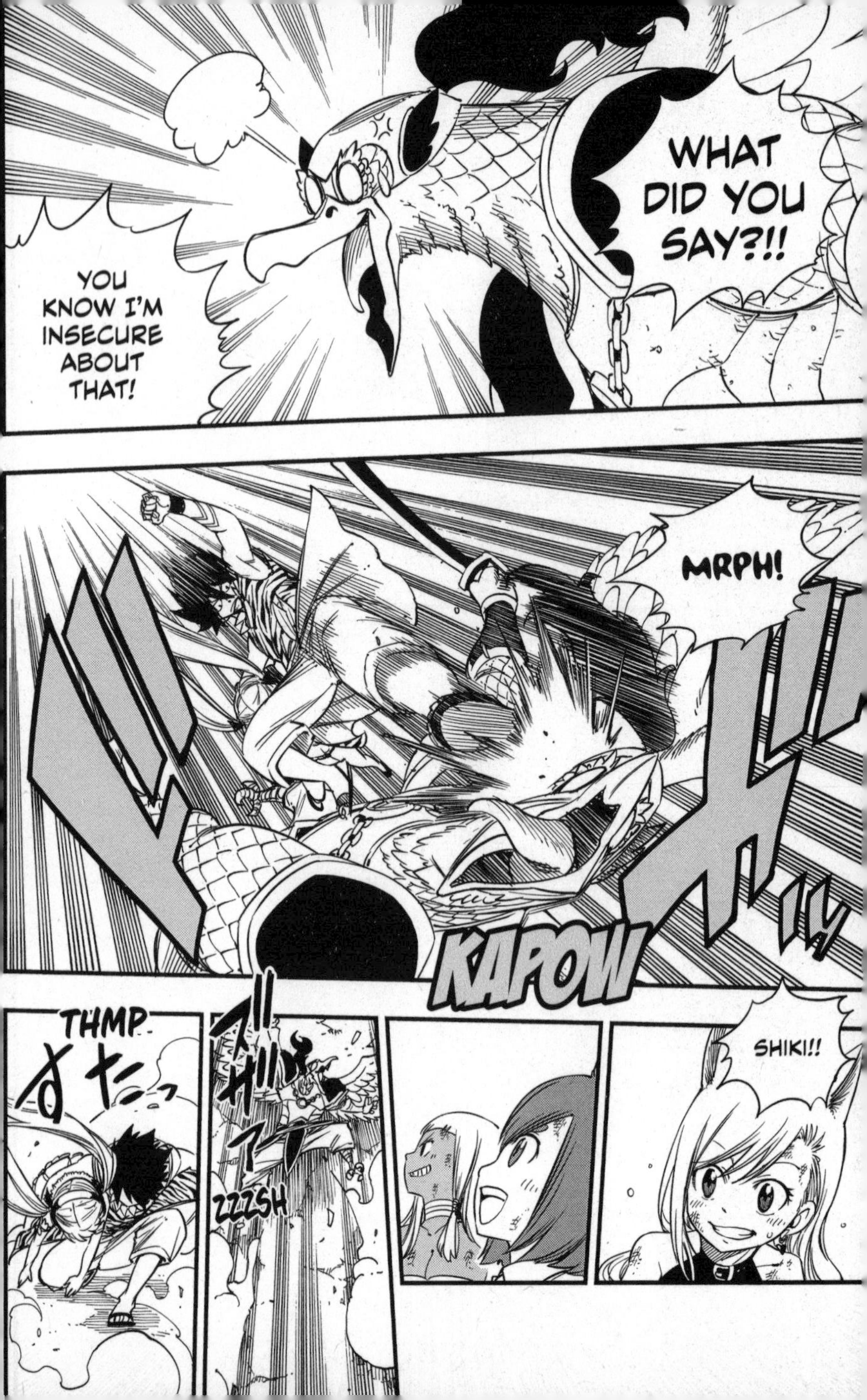
WHAT DID YOU SAY?!!
YOU KNOW I'M INSECURE ABOUT THAT!
MRPH!
KAPOW
SHIKI!!
ZZZSH
THMP

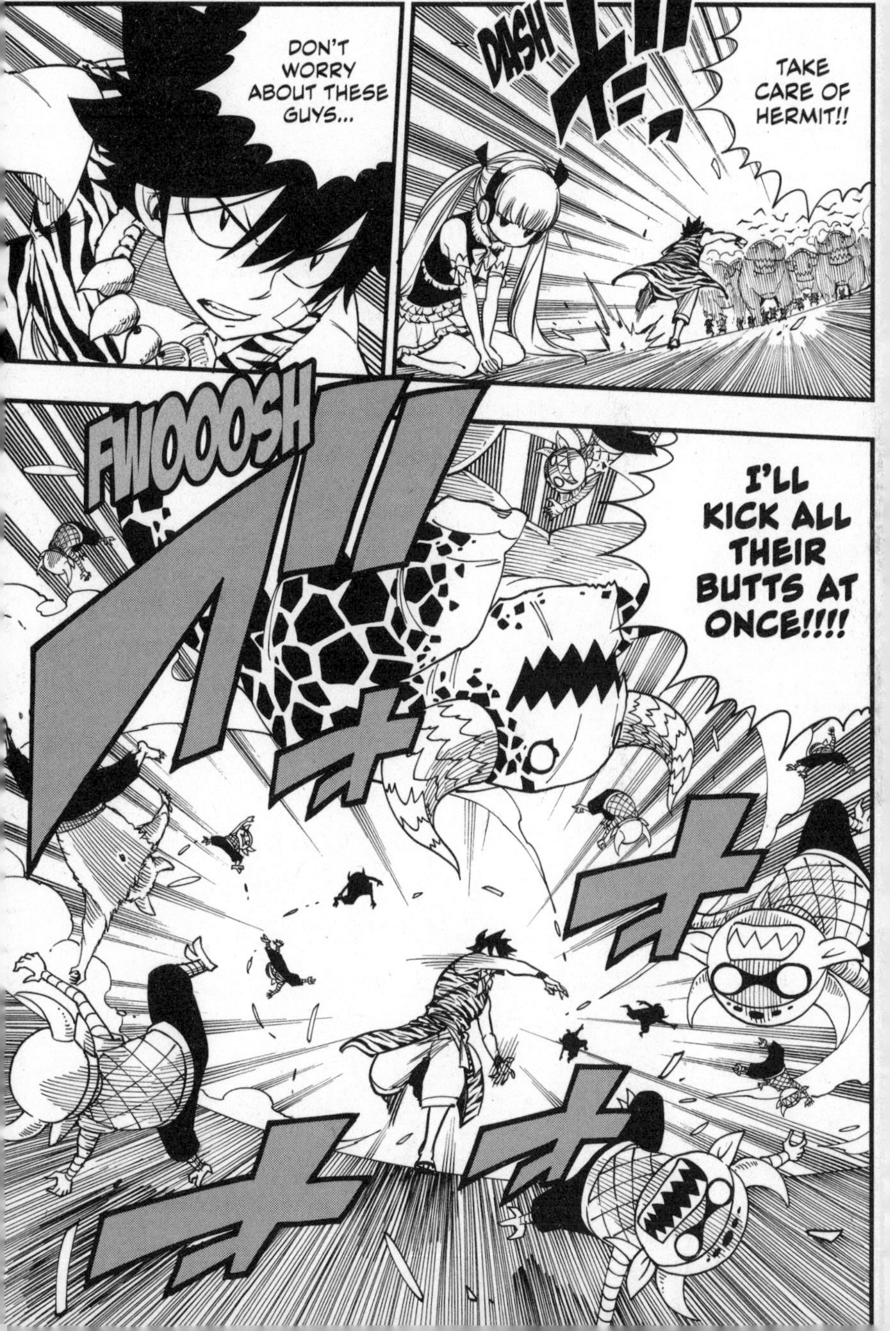
TAKE CARE OF HERMIT!!
DASH
DON'T WORRY ABOUT THESE GUYS...
I'LL KICK ALL THEIR BUTTS AT ONCE!!!!
FWOOOSH

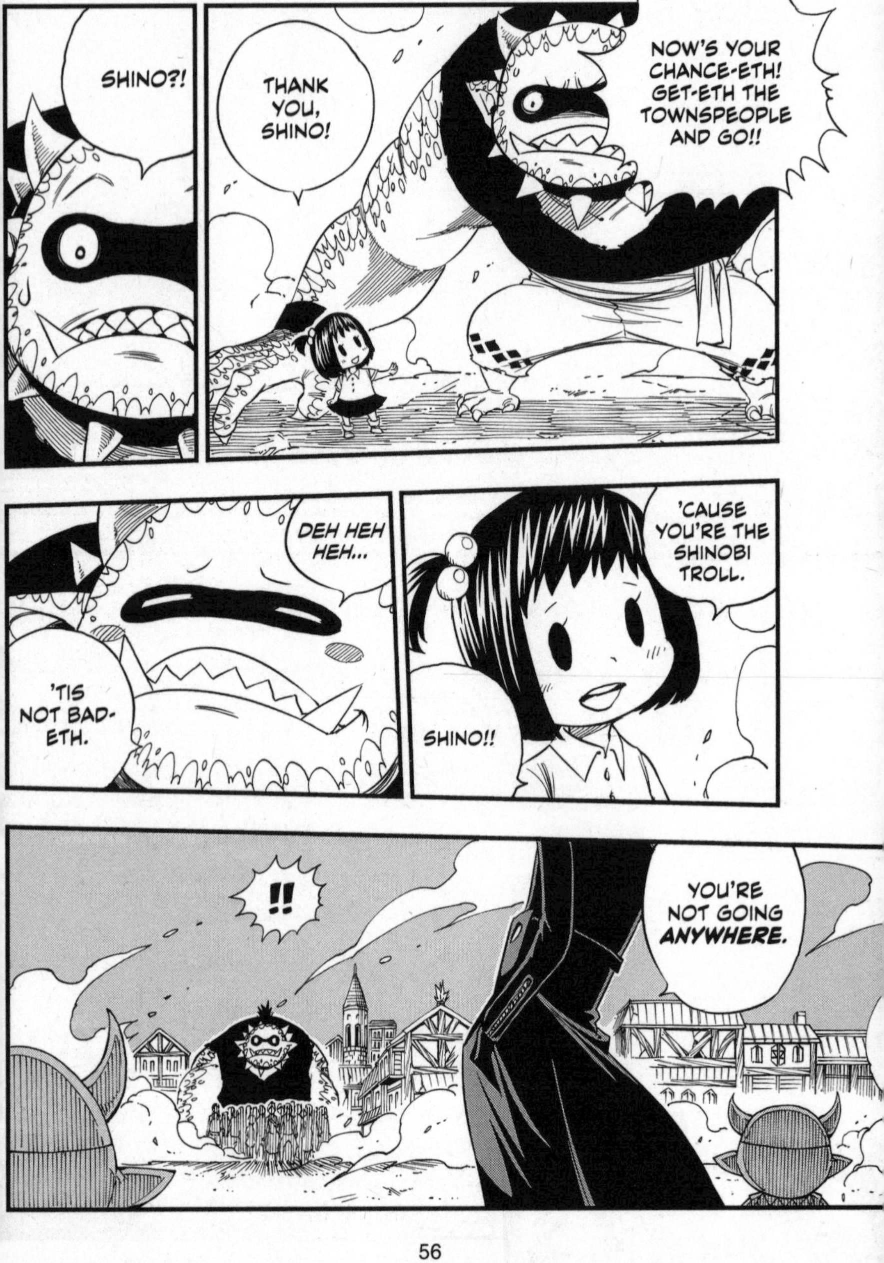
NOW'S YOUR CHANCE-ETH! GET-ETH THE TOWNSPEOPLE AND GO!!
THANK YOU, SHINO!
SHINO?!
'CAUSE YOU'RE THE SHINOBI TROLL.
SHINO!!
DEH HEH HEH...
'TIS NOT BAD-ETH.
YOU'RE NOT GOING *ANYWHERE.*
!!

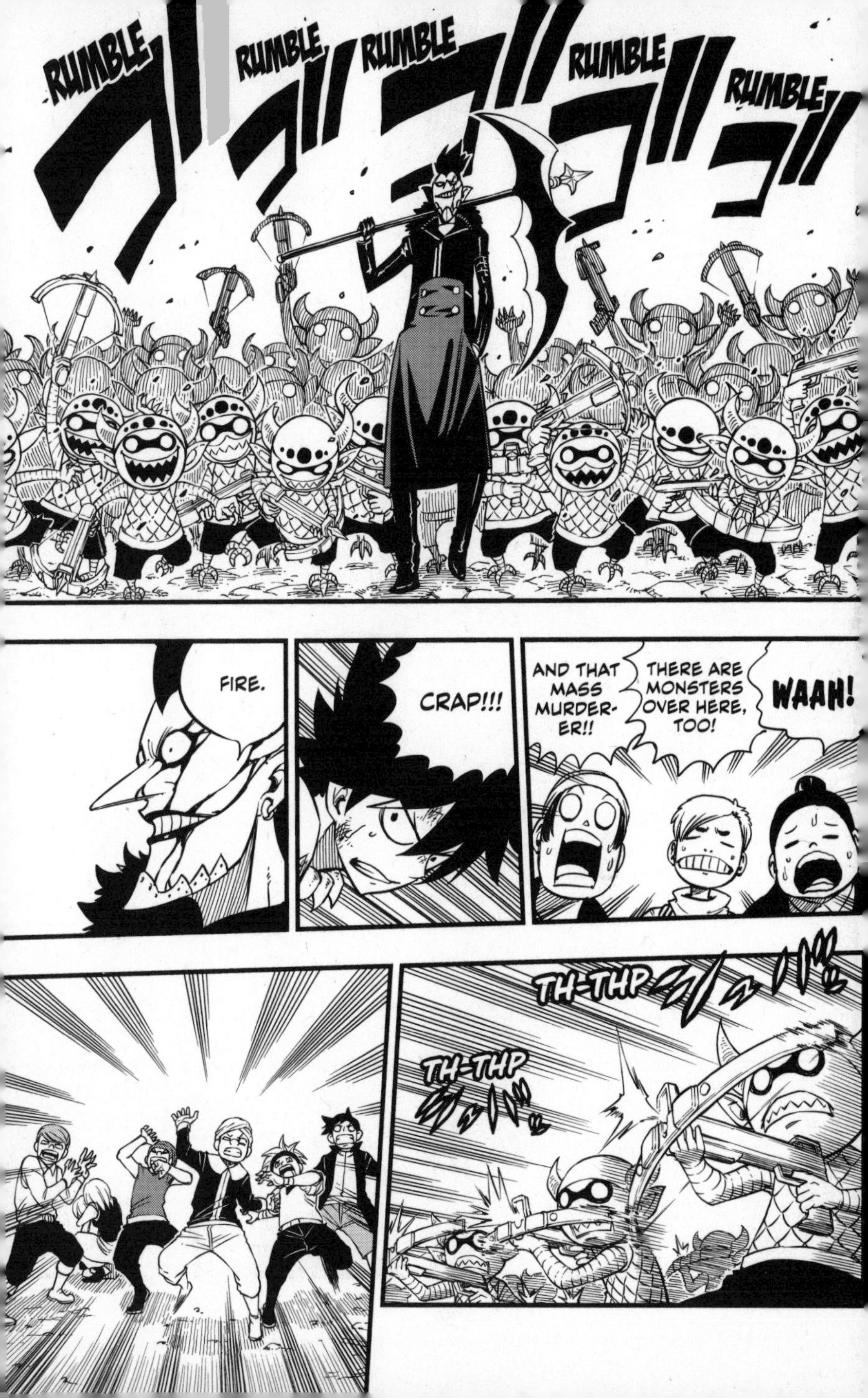
RUMBLE
RUMBLE
RUMBLE
RUMBLE
RUMBLE
WAAH!
THERE ARE MONSTERS OVER HERE, TOO!
AND THAT MASS MURDERER!!
CRAP!!!
FIRE.
TH-THP
TH-THP

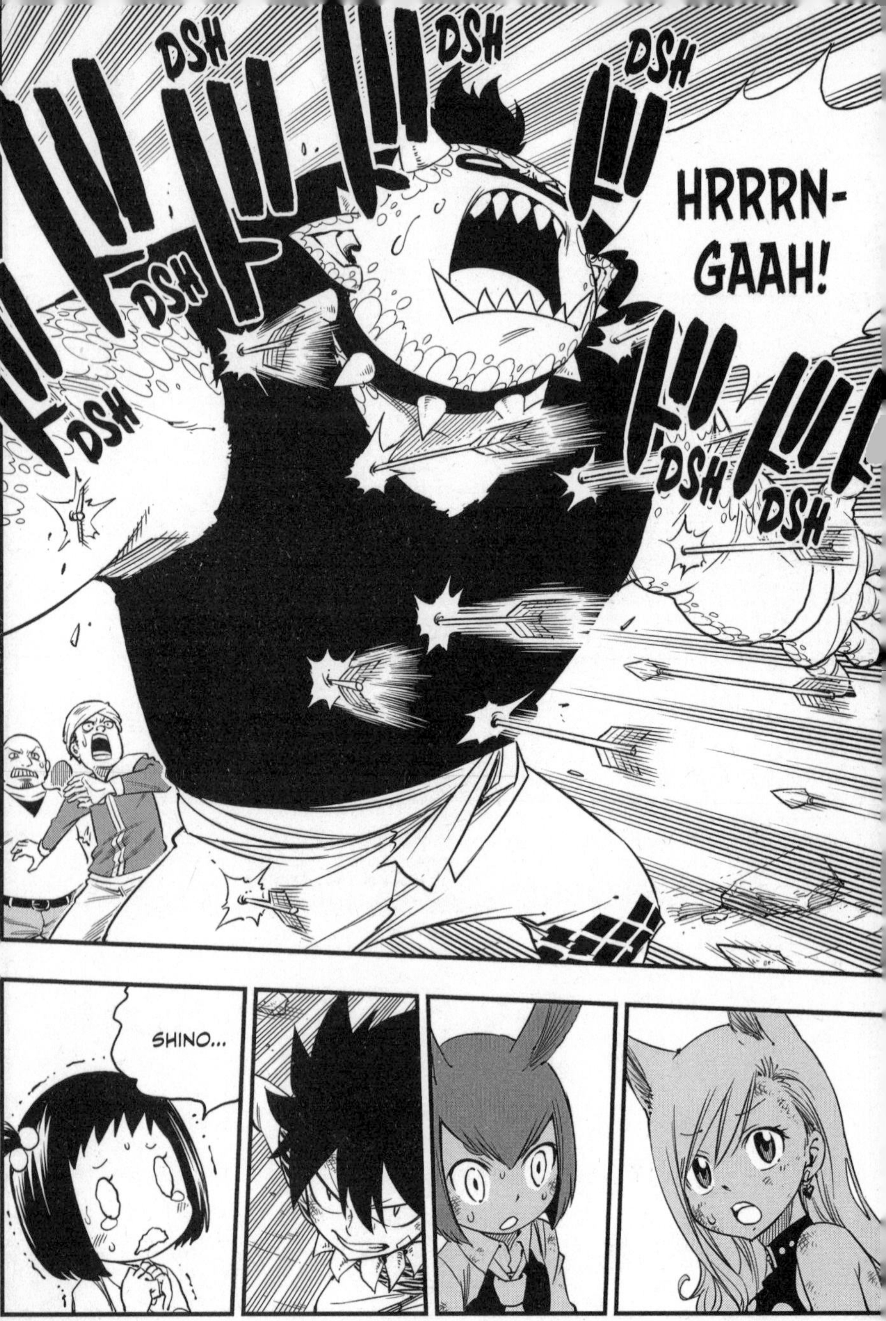
DSH
HRRRN-
GAAH!
DSH
DSH
DSH
DSH
DSH
DSH
DSH
SHINO...

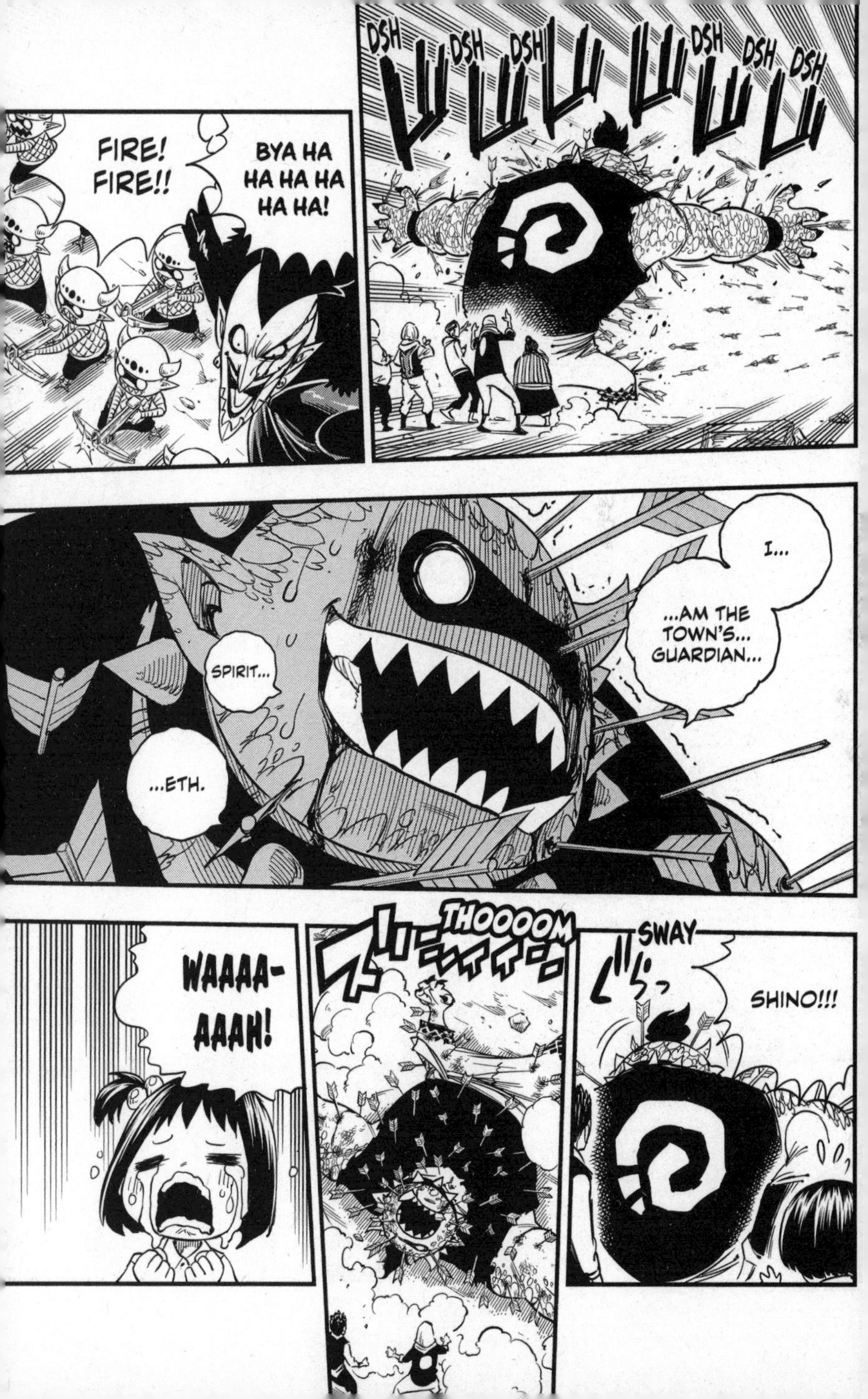
DSH DSH DSH DSH DSH DSH
BYA HA HA HA HA HA HA HA!
FIRE! FIRE!!
I...
...AM THE TOWN'S... GUARDIAN...
SPIRIT...
...ETH.
SWAY
SHINO!!!
THOOOOM
WAAAA-AAAH!

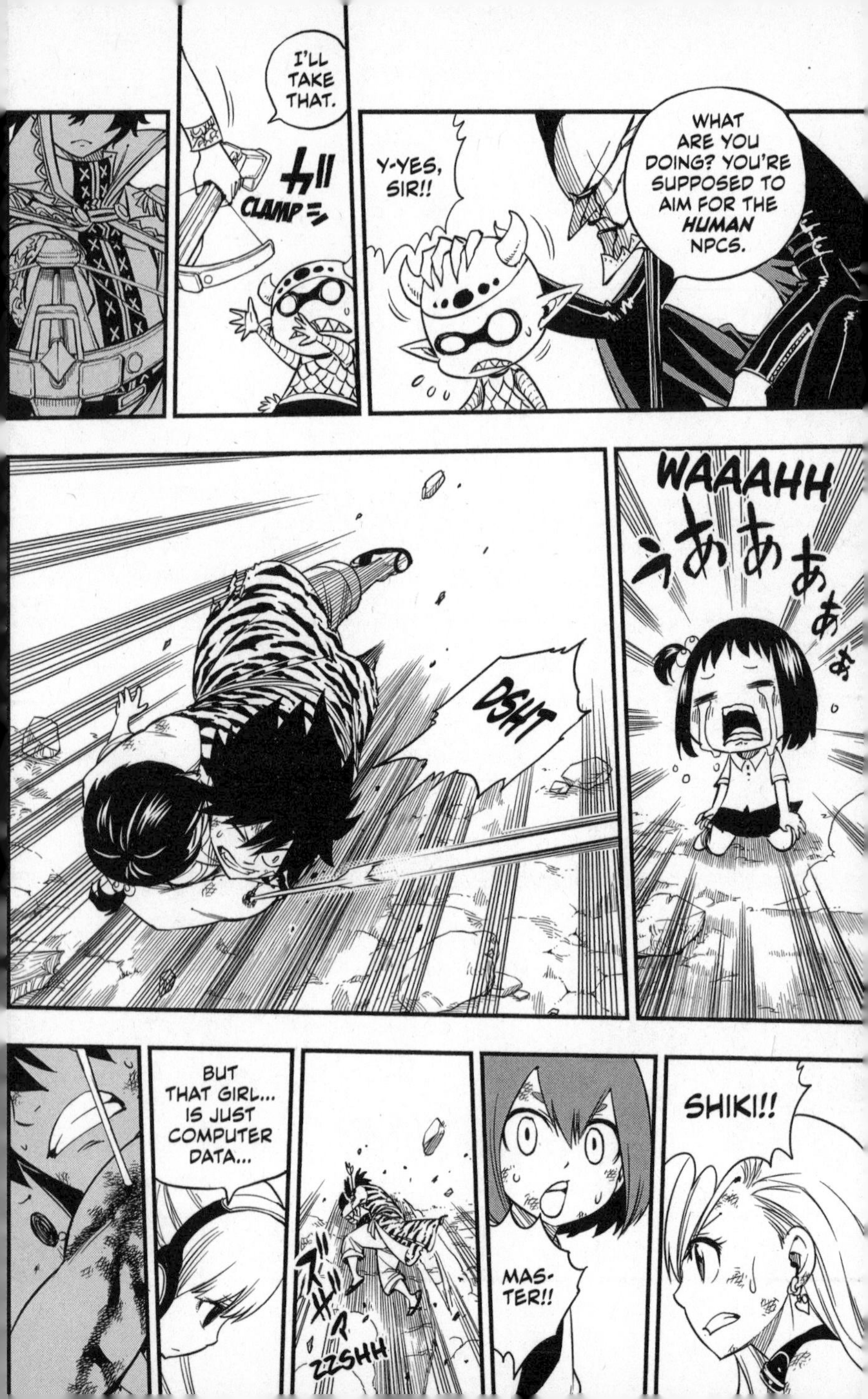
WHAT ARE YOU DOING? YOU'RE SUPPOSED TO AIM FOR THE HUMAN NPCS.
Y-YES, SIR!!
I'LL TAKE THAT.
CLAMP
WAAAHH
うあああぁぁ
DSHT
SHIKI!!
MAS-TER!!
ZZSHH
BUT THAT GIRL... IS JUST COMPUTER DATA...

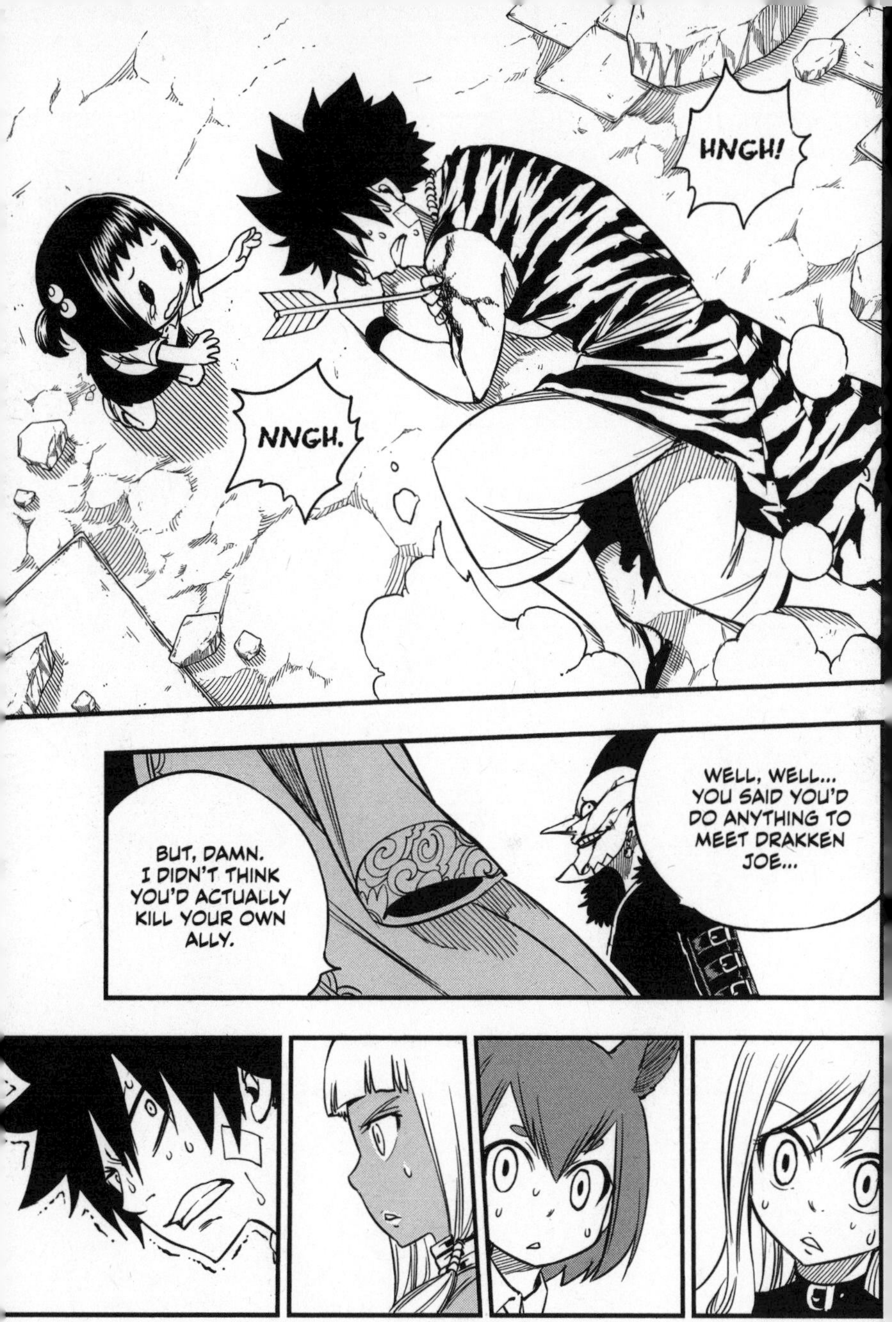
HNGH!
NNGH.
WELL, WELL... YOU SAID YOU'D DO ANYTHING TO MEET DRAKKEN JOE...
BUT, DAMN. I DIDN'T THINK YOU'D ACTUALLY KILL YOUR OWN ALLY.

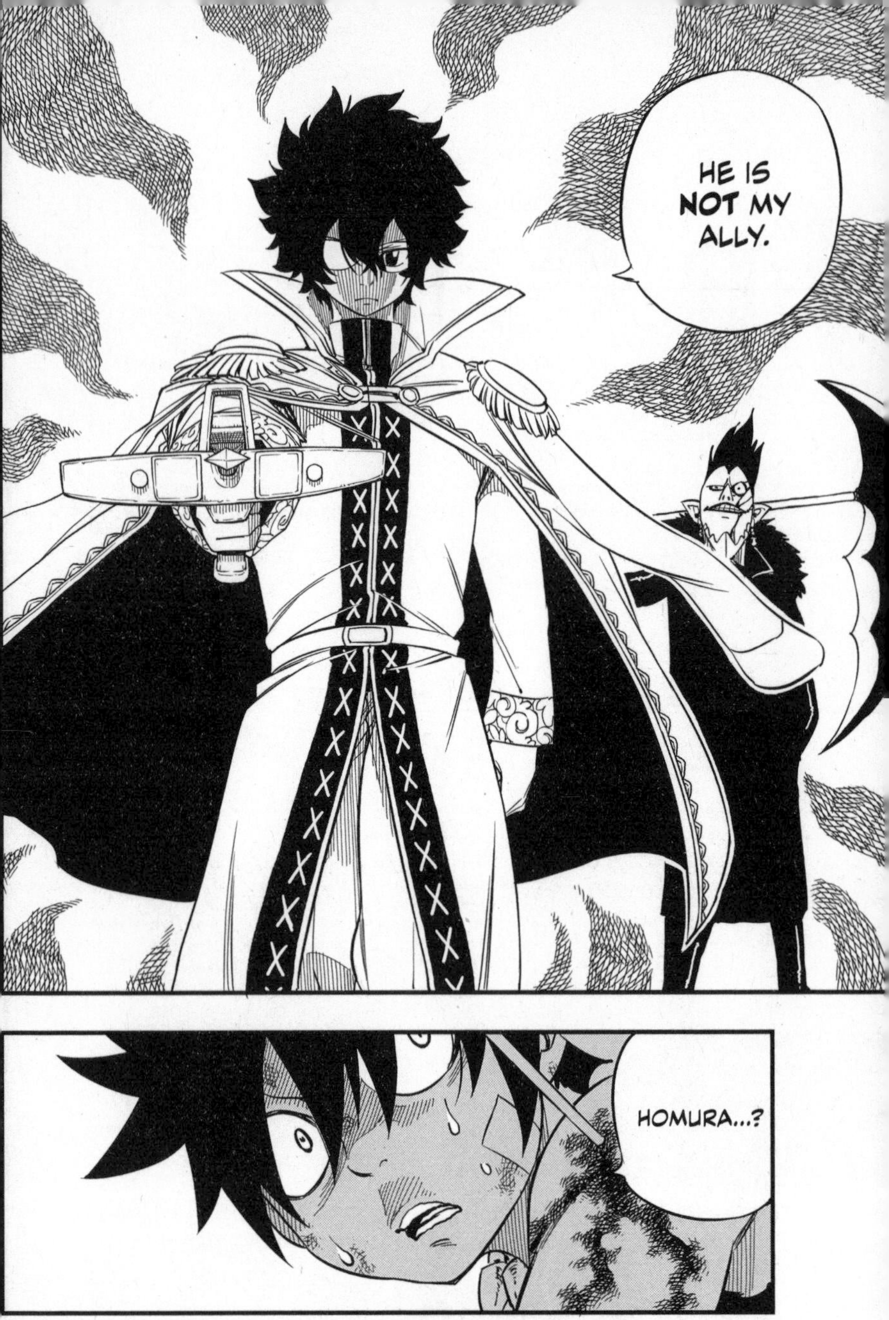
HE IS **NOT** MY ALLY.
HOMURA...?

EDENS ZERO

E4

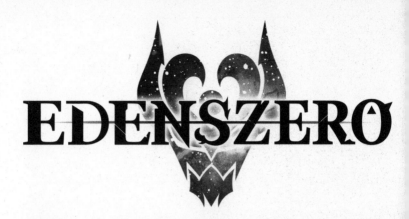

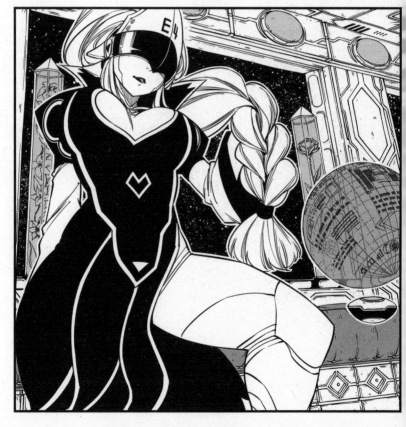

CHAPTER 36: THE G.I.A.

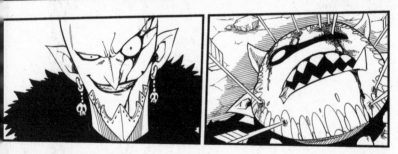

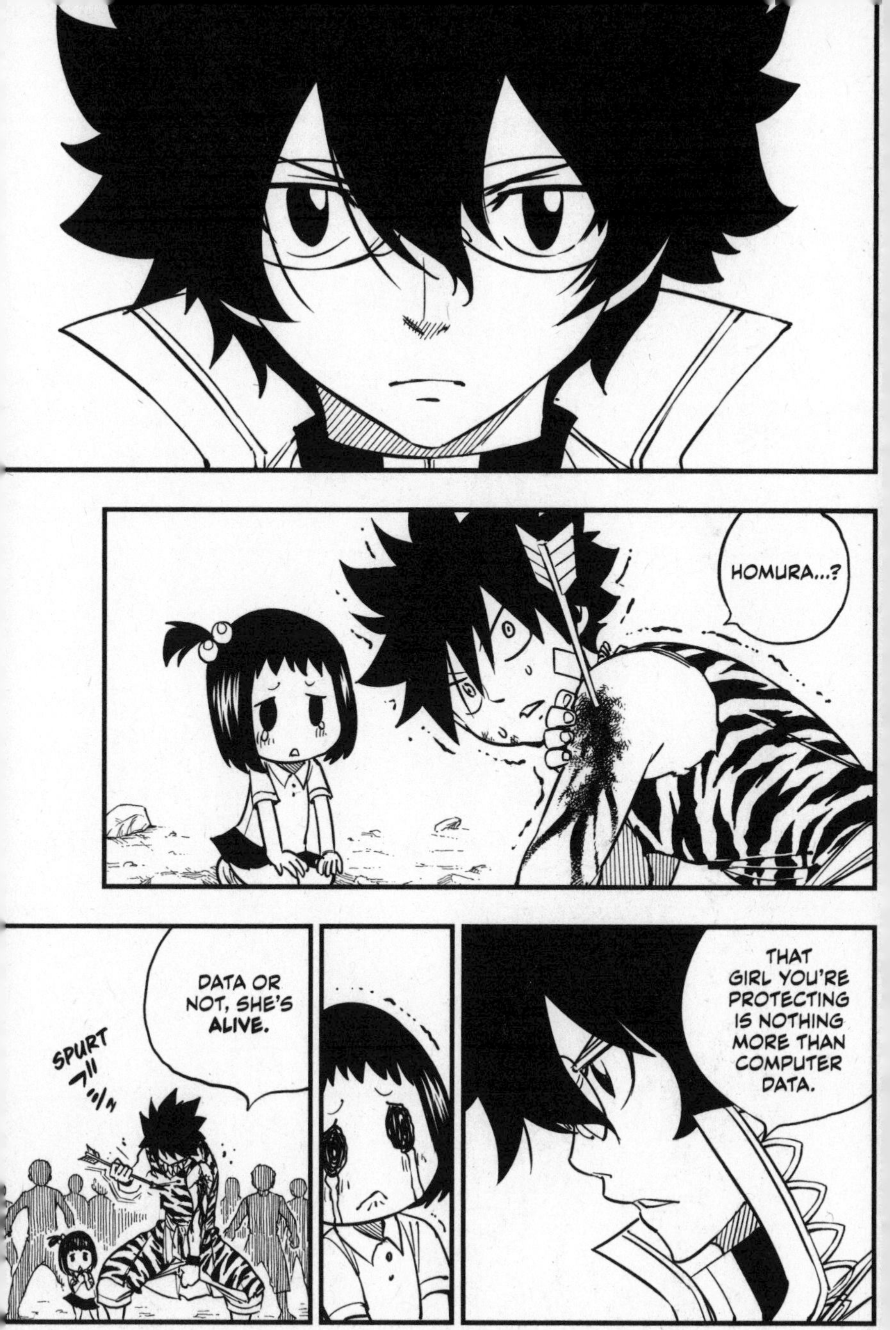
HOMURA...?
THAT GIRL YOU'RE PROTECTING IS NOTHING MORE THAN COMPUTER DATA.
DATA OR NOT, SHE'S ALIVE.
SPURT

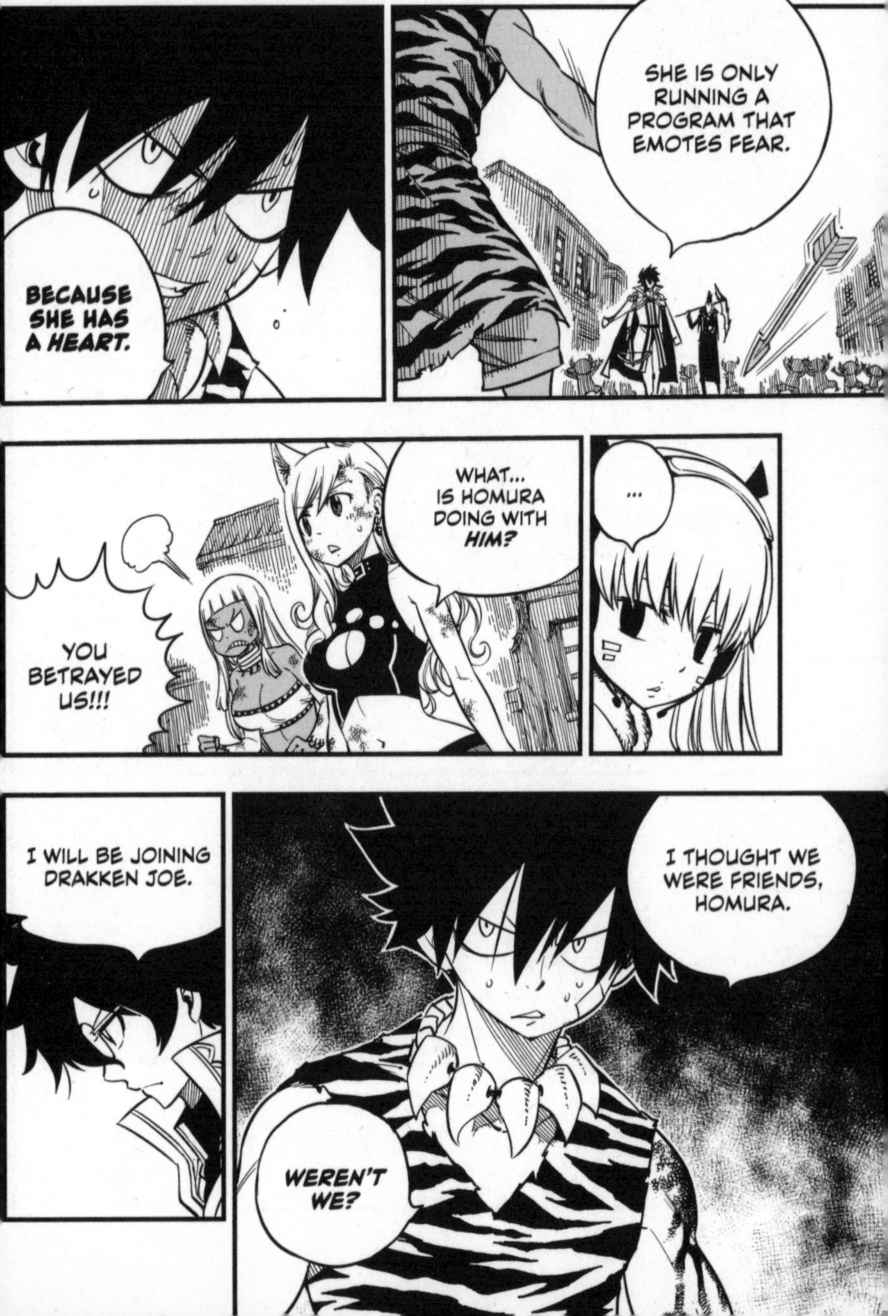
SHE IS ONLY RUNNING A PROGRAM THAT EMOTES FEAR.
BECAUSE SHE HAS A *HEART.*
...
WHAT... IS HOMURA DOING WITH *HIM?*
YOU BETRAYED US!!!
I THOUGHT WE WERE FRIENDS, HOMURA.
WEREN'T WE?
I WILL BE JOINING DRAKKEN JOE.

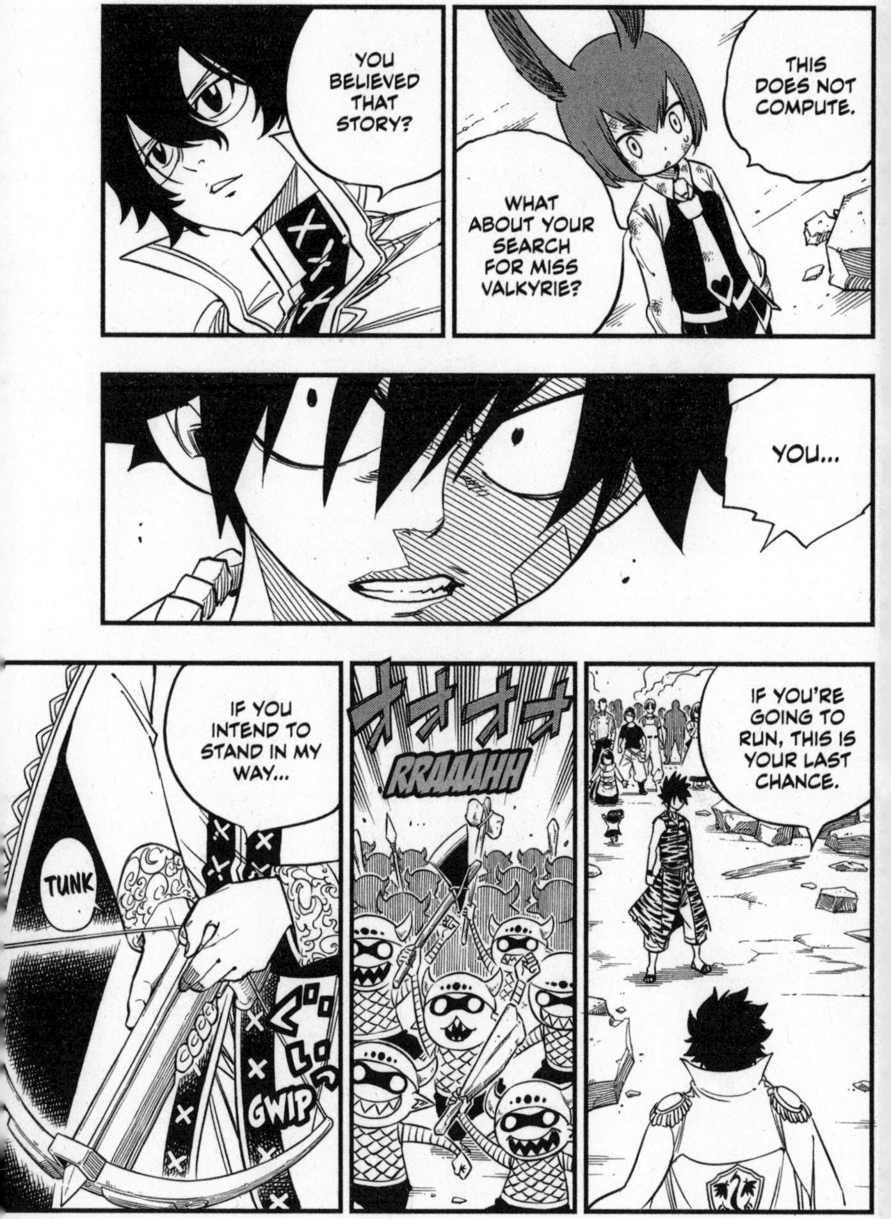

THIS DOES NOT COMPUTE.
WHAT ABOUT YOUR SEARCH FOR MISS VALKYRIE?
YOU BELIEVED THAT STORY?
YOU...
IF YOU'RE GOING TO RUN, THIS IS YOUR LAST CHANCE.
オオオオ
RRAAAHH
IF YOU INTEND TO STAND IN MY WAY...
TUNK
GWIP

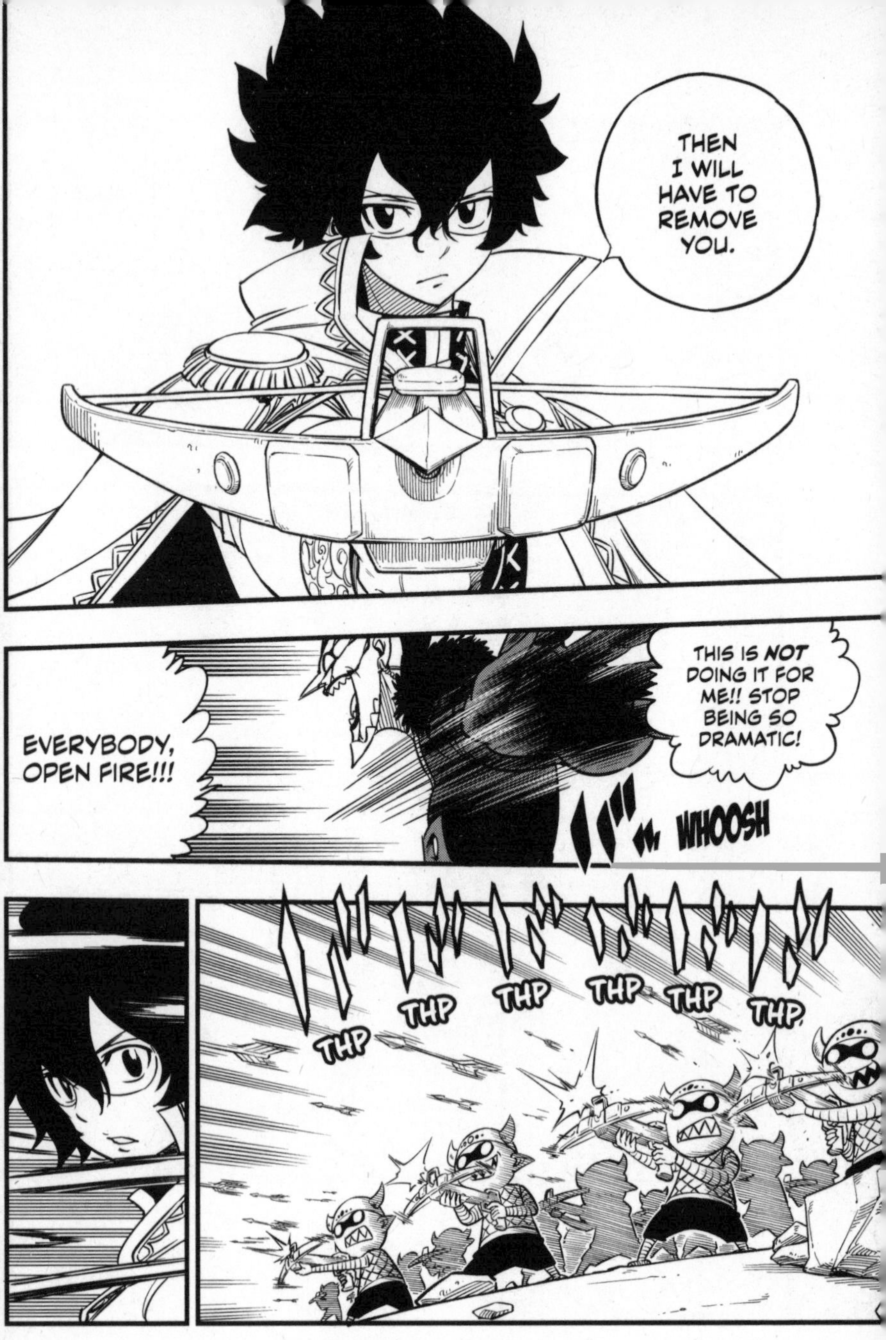
THEN I WILL HAVE TO REMOVE YOU.
THIS IS **NOT** DOING IT FOR ME!! STOP BEING SO DRAMATIC!
WHOOSH
EVERYBODY, OPEN FIRE!!!
THP
THP
THP
THP
THP
THP
THP

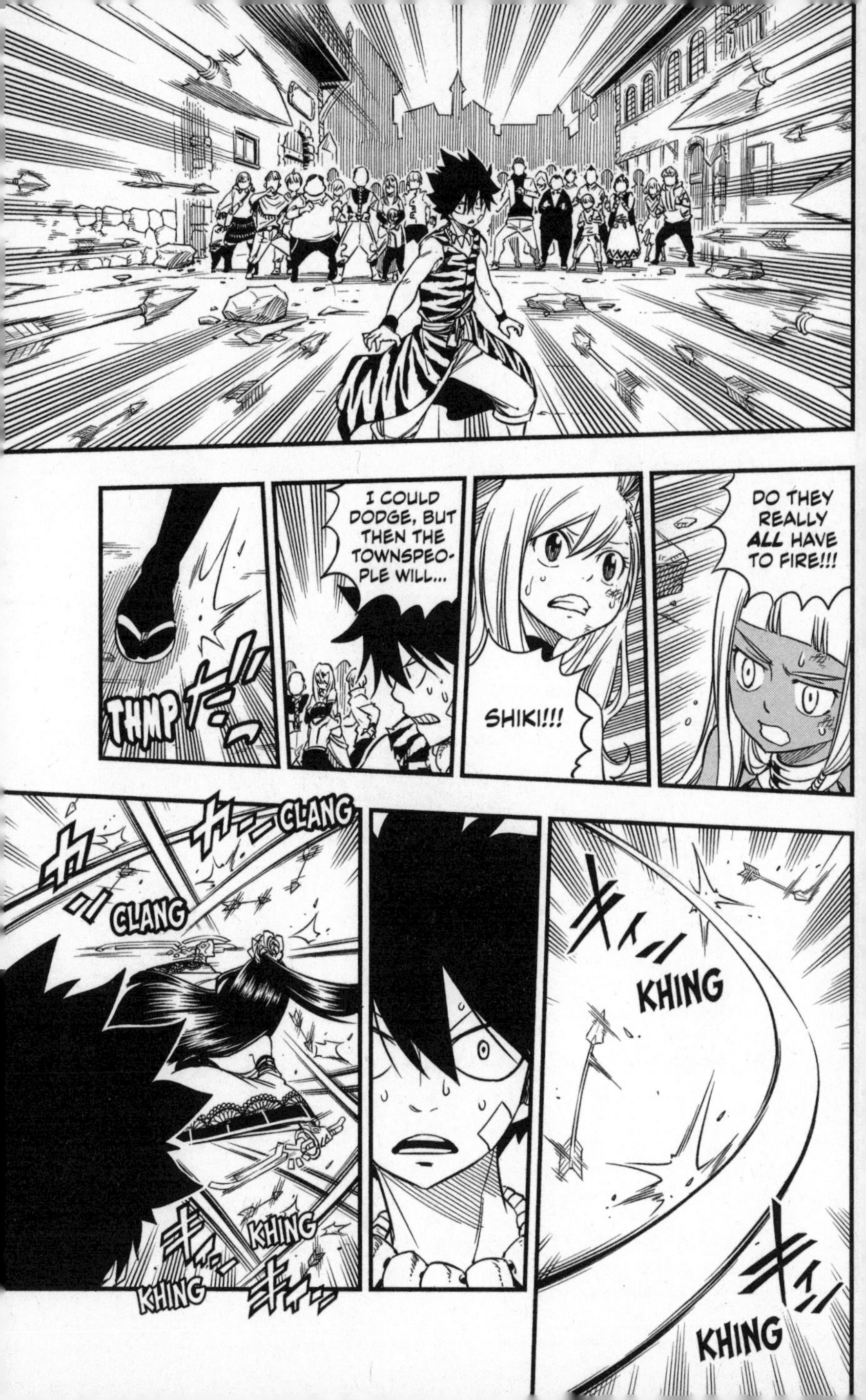
DO THEY REALLY ALL HAVE TO FIRE!!!
SHIKI!!!
I COULD DODGE, BUT THEN THE TOWNSPEO-PLE WILL...
THMP
KHING
KHING
CLANG
CLANG
KHING
KHING

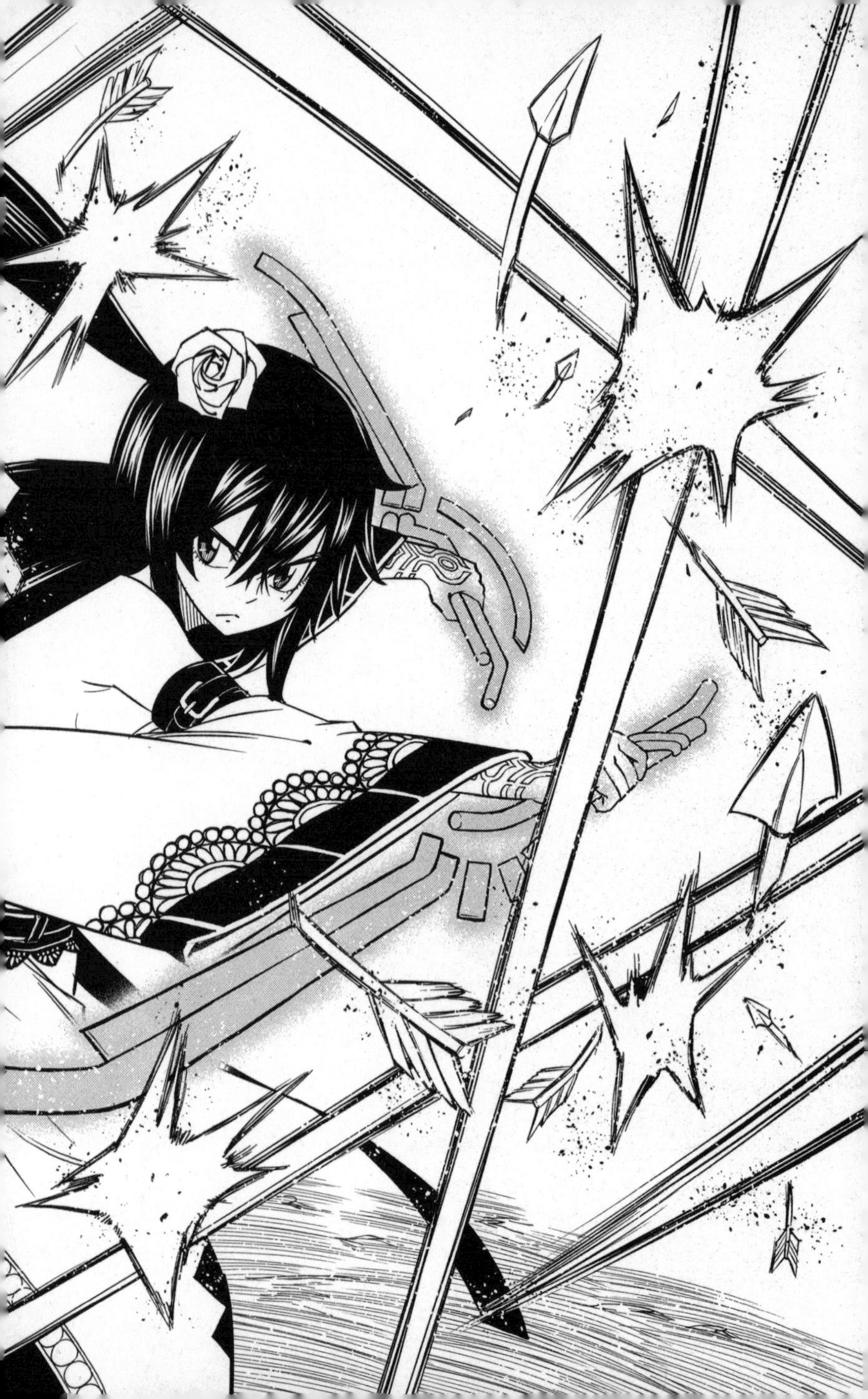

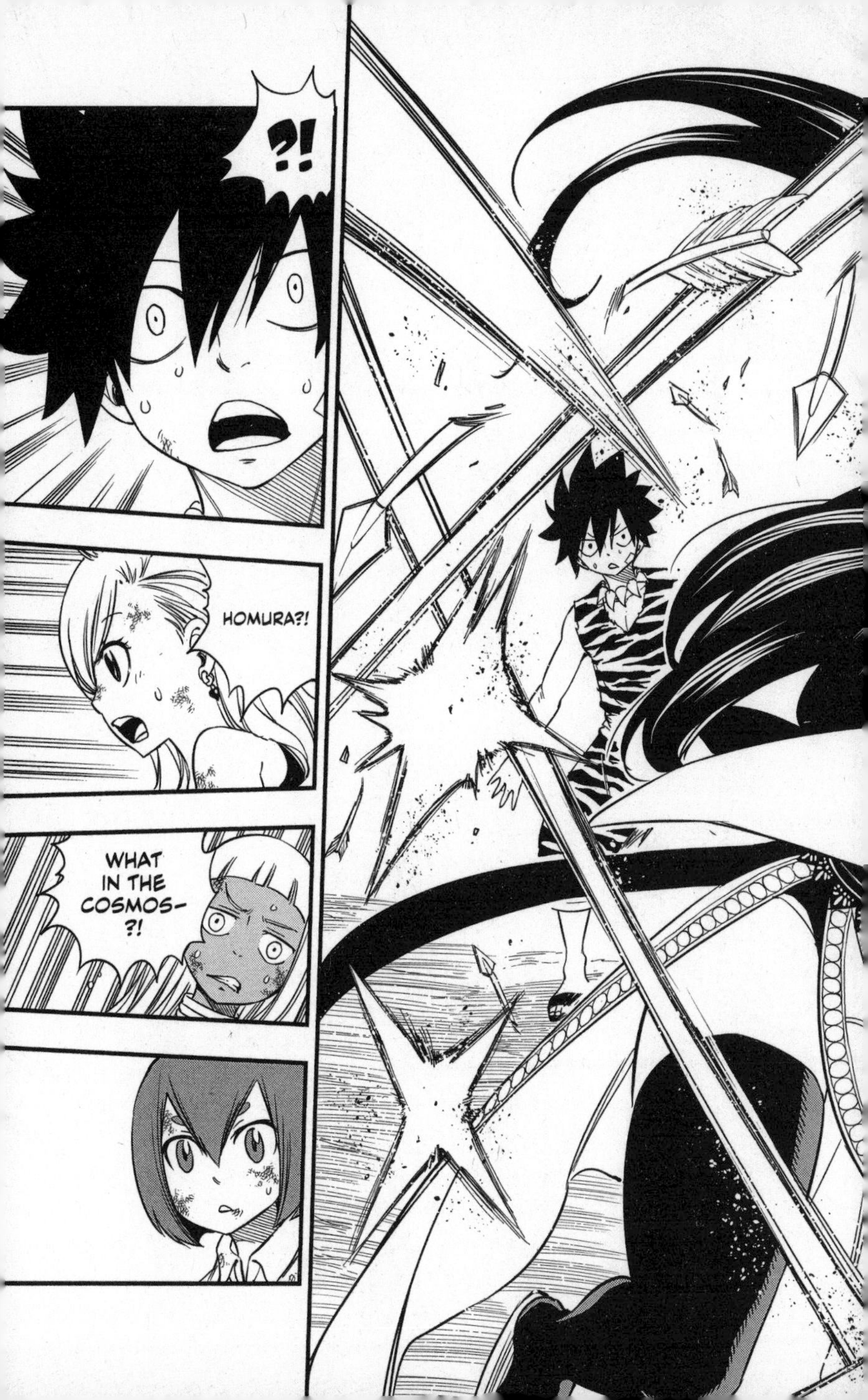
?!
HOMURA?!
WHAT IN THE COSMOS-?!

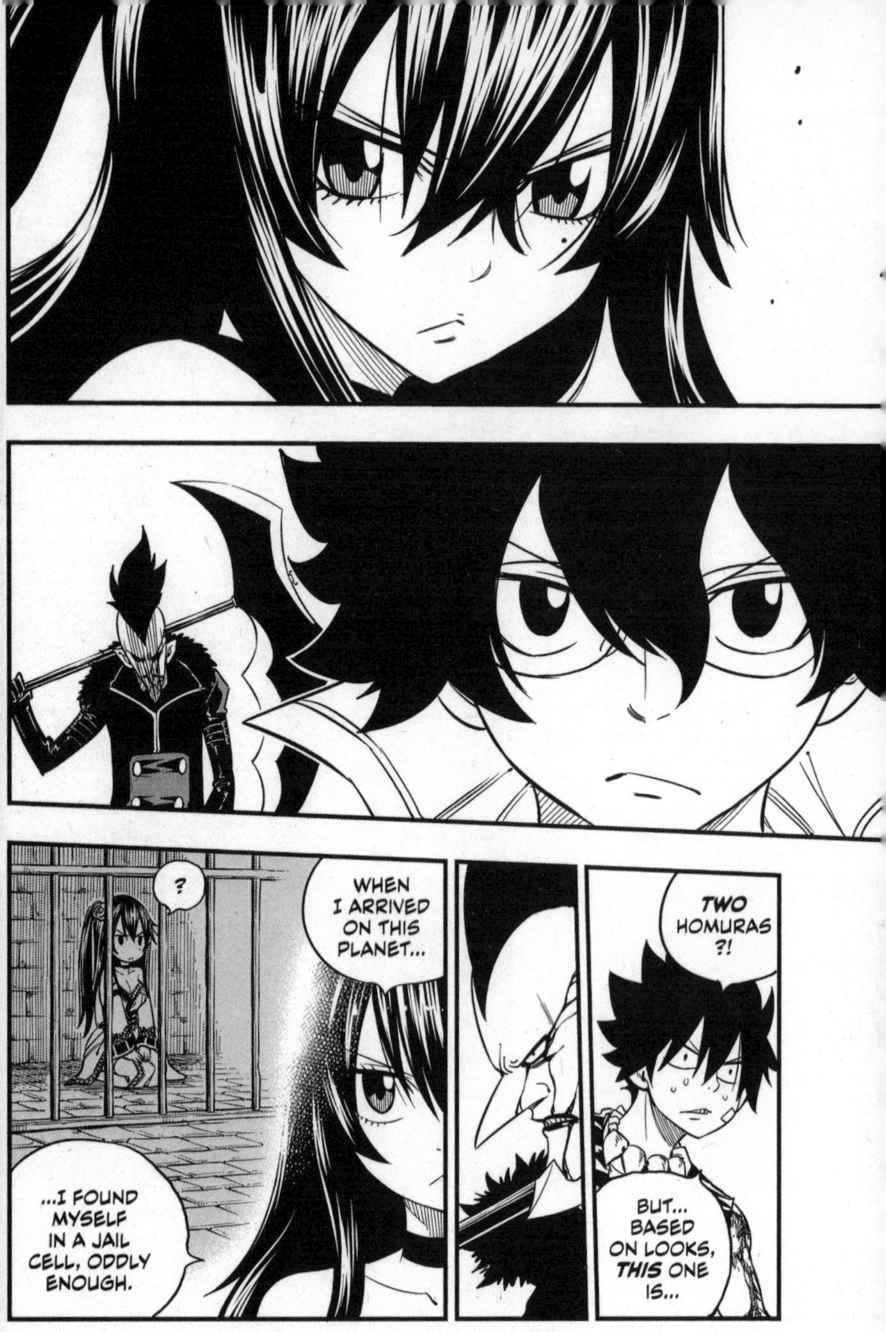
TWO HOMURAS ?!
BUT... BASED ON LOOKS, THIS ONE IS...
WHEN I ARRIVED ON THIS PLANET...
?
...I FOUND MYSELF IN A JAIL CELL, ODDLY ENOUGH.

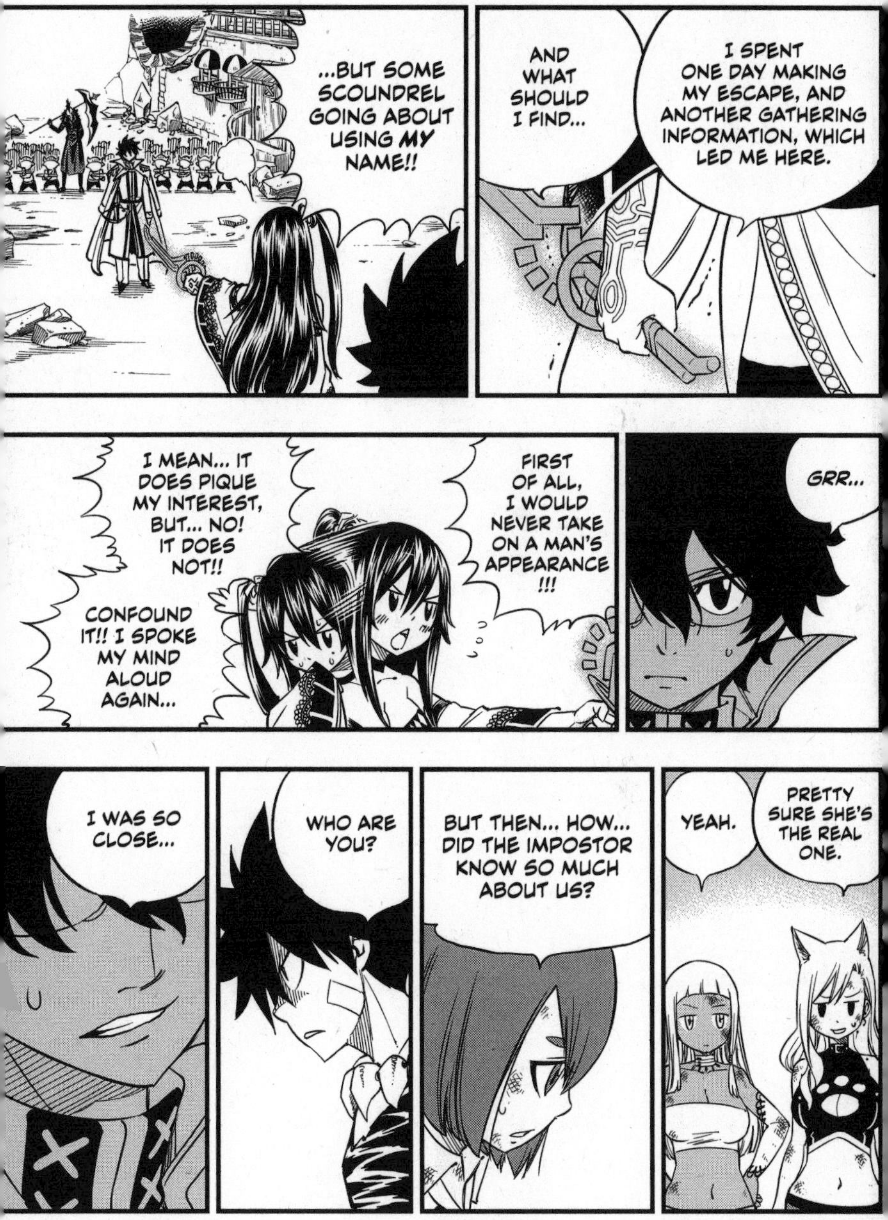
I SPENT ONE DAY MAKING MY ESCAPE, AND ANOTHER GATHERING INFORMATION, WHICH LED ME HERE.
AND WHAT SHOULD I FIND...
...BUT SOME SCOUNDREL GOING ABOUT USING *MY* NAME!!
GRR...
FIRST OF ALL, I WOULD NEVER TAKE ON A MAN'S APPEARANCE !!!
I MEAN... IT DOES PIQUE MY INTEREST, BUT... NO! IT DOES NOT!!
CONFOUND IT!! I SPOKE MY MIND ALOUD AGAIN...
PRETTY SURE SHE'S THE REAL ONE.
YEAH.
BUT THEN... HOW... DID THE IMPOSTOR KNOW SO MUCH ABOUT US?
WHO ARE YOU?
I WAS SO CLOSE...

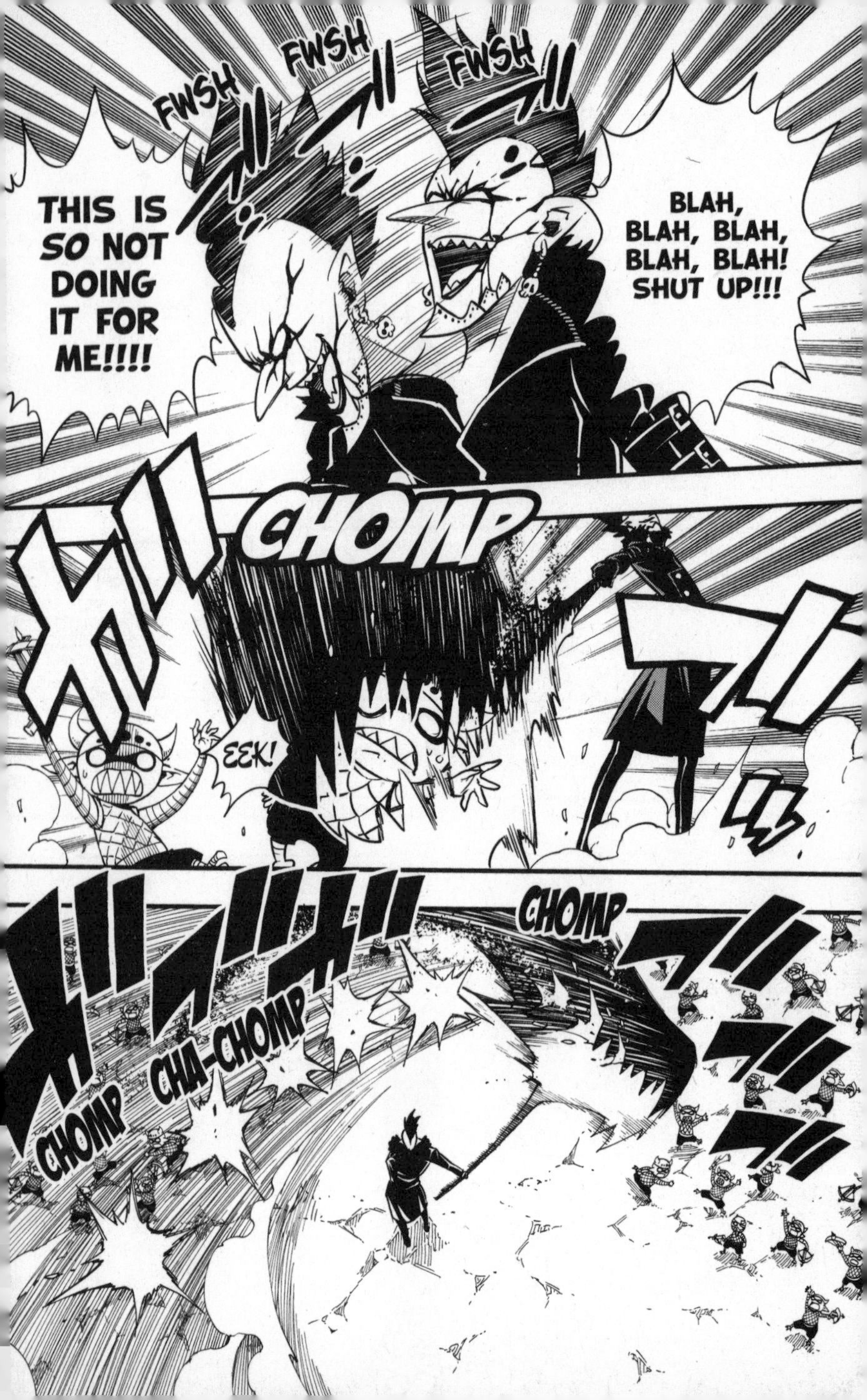
FWSH
FWSH
FWSH
BLAH, BLAH, BLAH, BLAH, BLAH! SHUT UP!!!
THIS IS SO NOT DOING IT FOR ME!!!!
CHOMP
EEK!
CHOMP
CHA-CHOMP
CHOMP

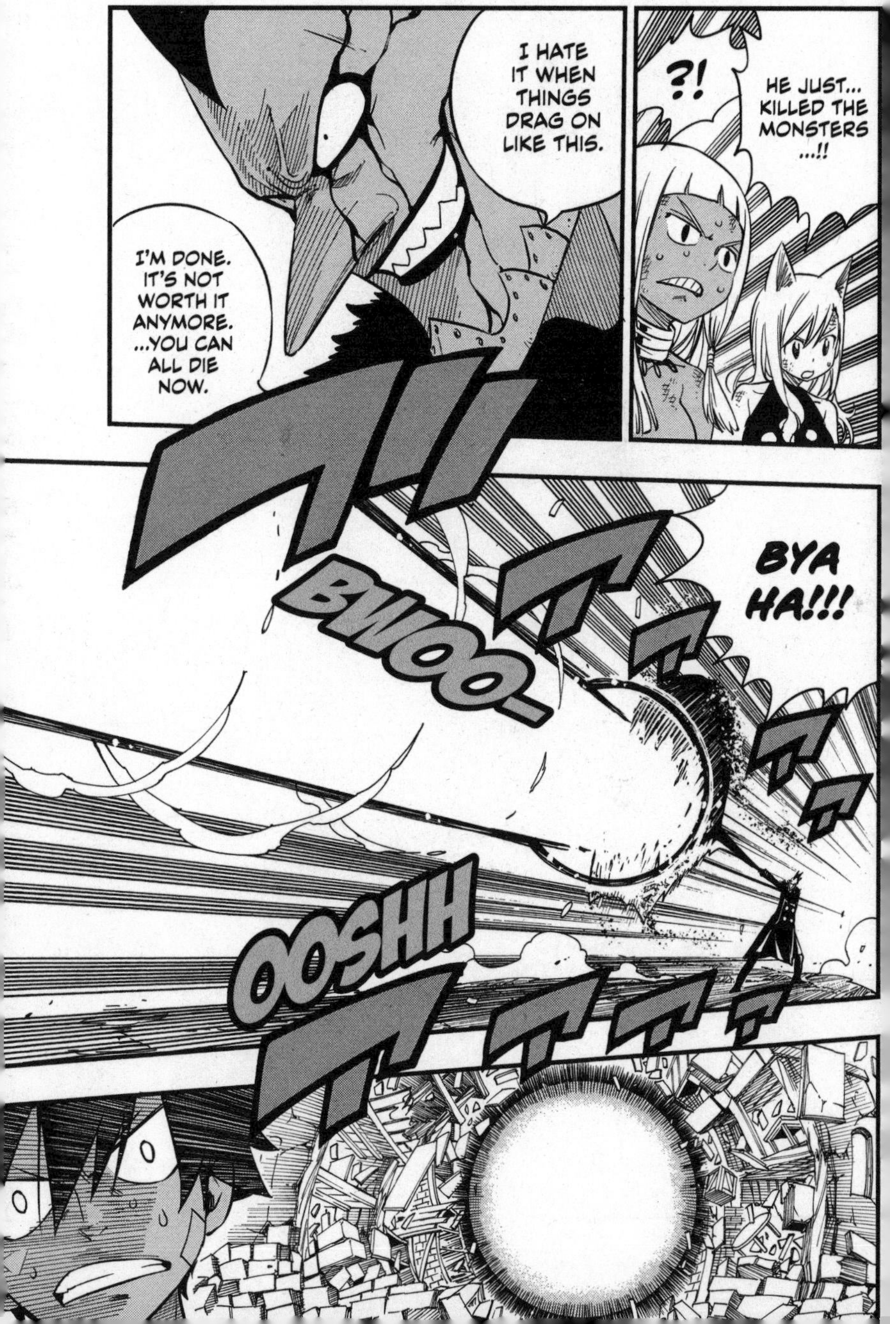
?!
HE JUST... KILLED THE MONSTERS ...!!
I HATE IT WHEN THINGS DRAG ON LIKE THIS.
I'M DONE. IT'S NOT WORTH IT ANYMORE. ...YOU CAN ALL DIE NOW.
BYA HA!!!
BWOO-
OOSHH

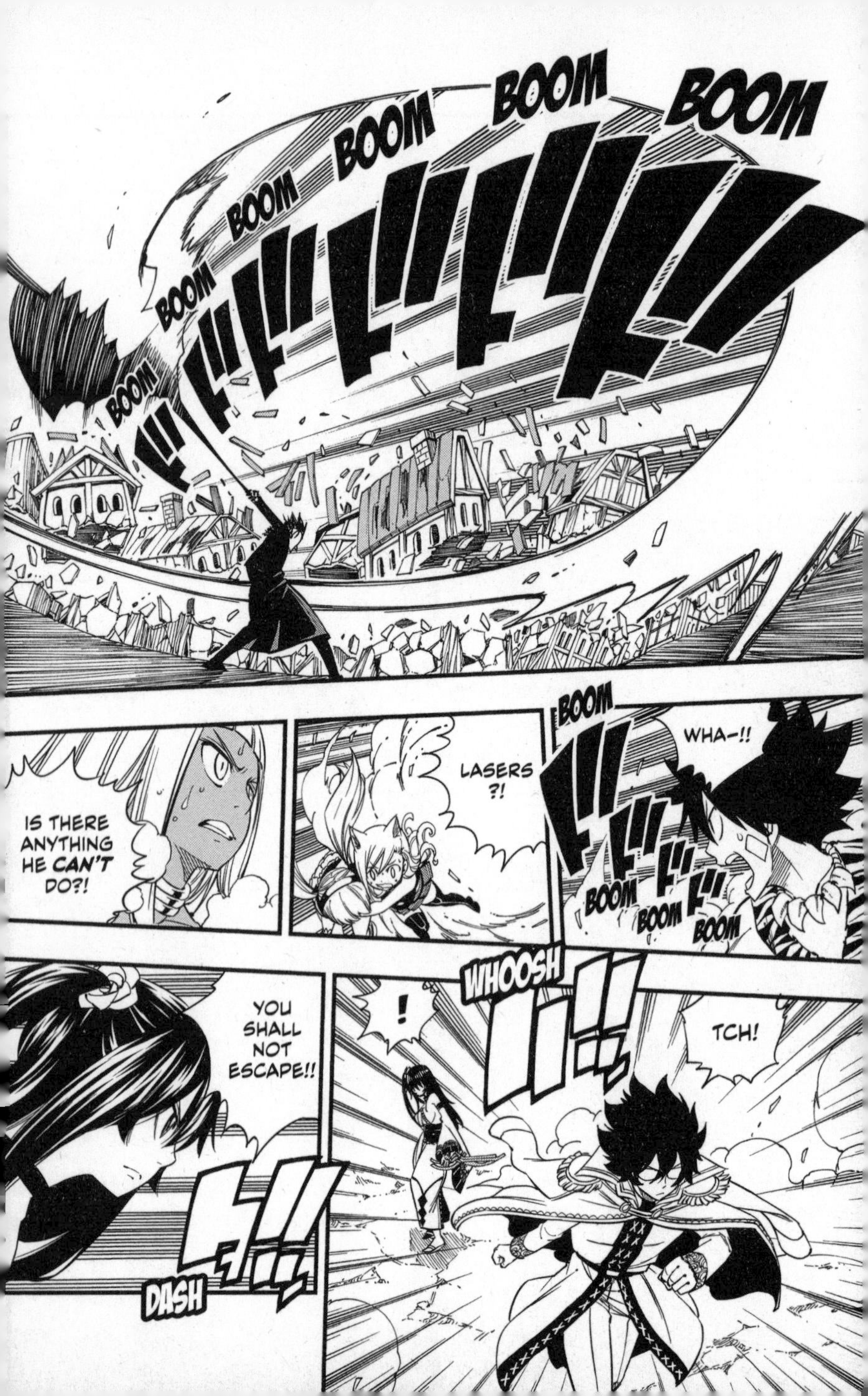
BOOM
BOOM
BOOM
BOOM
BOOM
BOOM
BOOM
BOOM
WHA-!!
BOOM
BOOM
BOOM
LASERS ?!
IS THERE ANYTHING HE **CAN'T** DO?!
WHOOSH
TCH!
!
YOU SHALL NOT ESCAPE!!
DASH

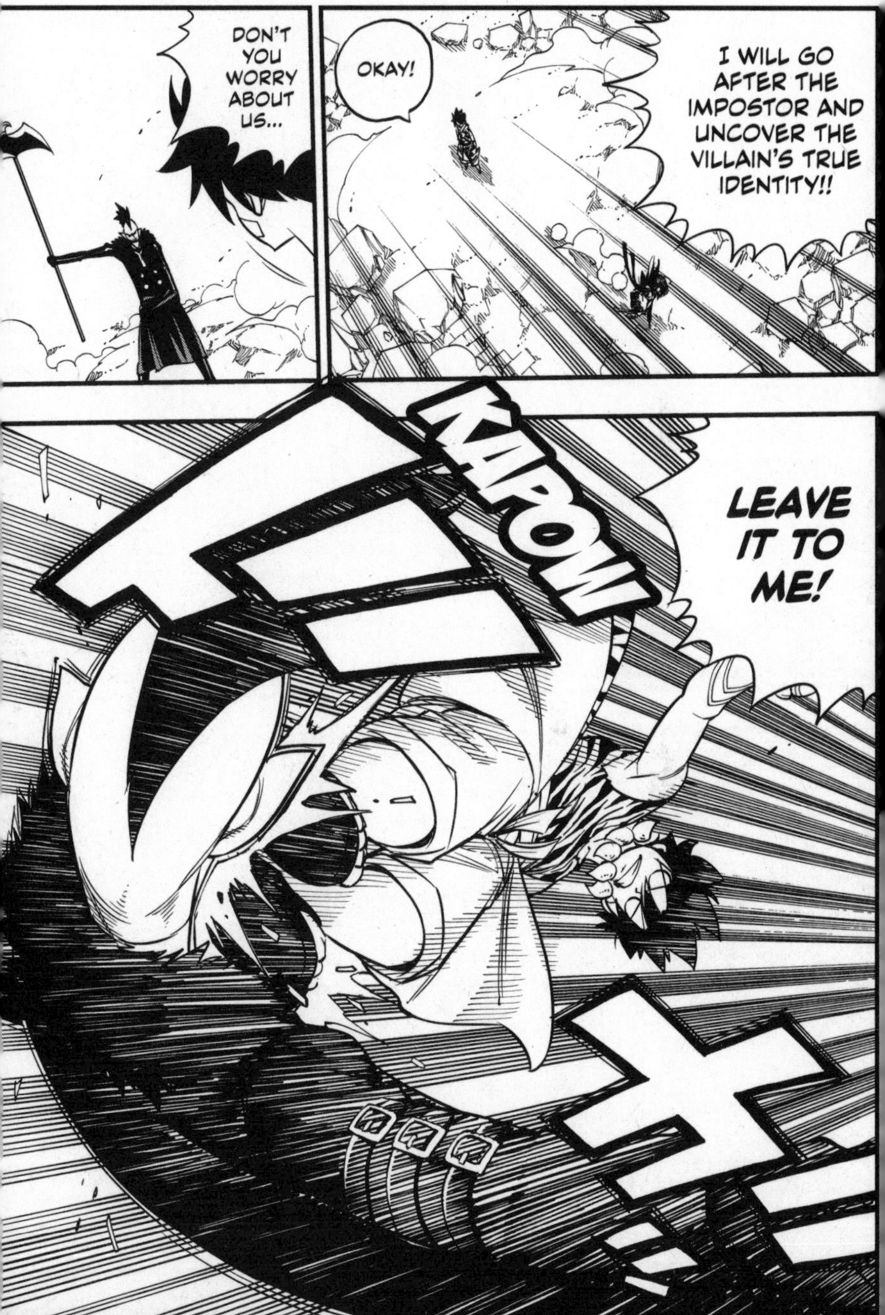
I WILL GO AFTER THE IMPOSTOR AND UNCOVER THE VILLAIN'S TRUE IDENTITY!!
OKAY!
DON'T YOU WORRY ABOUT US...
KAPOW
LEAVE IT TO ME!

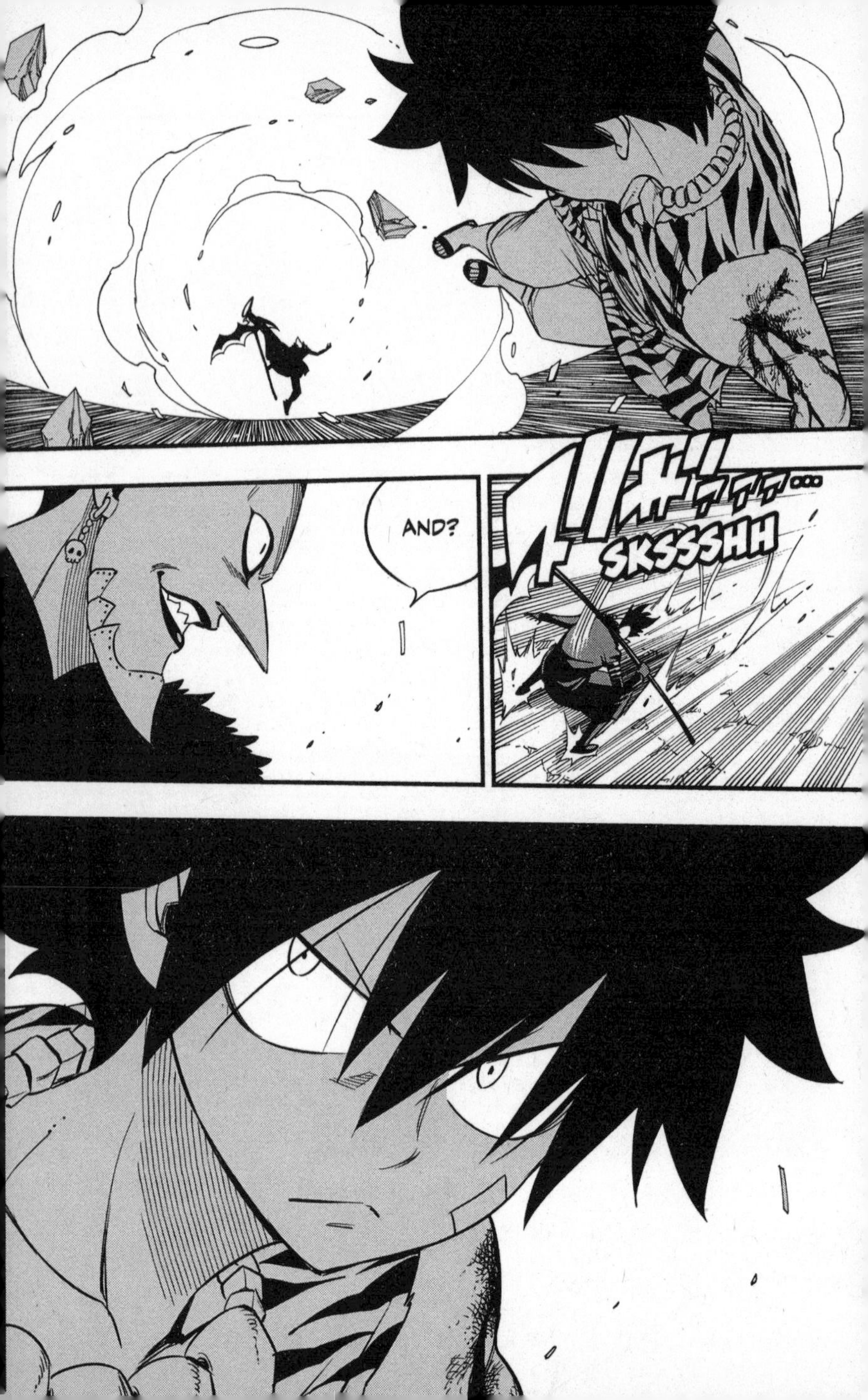

ズザザザ…
SKSSSHH
AND?

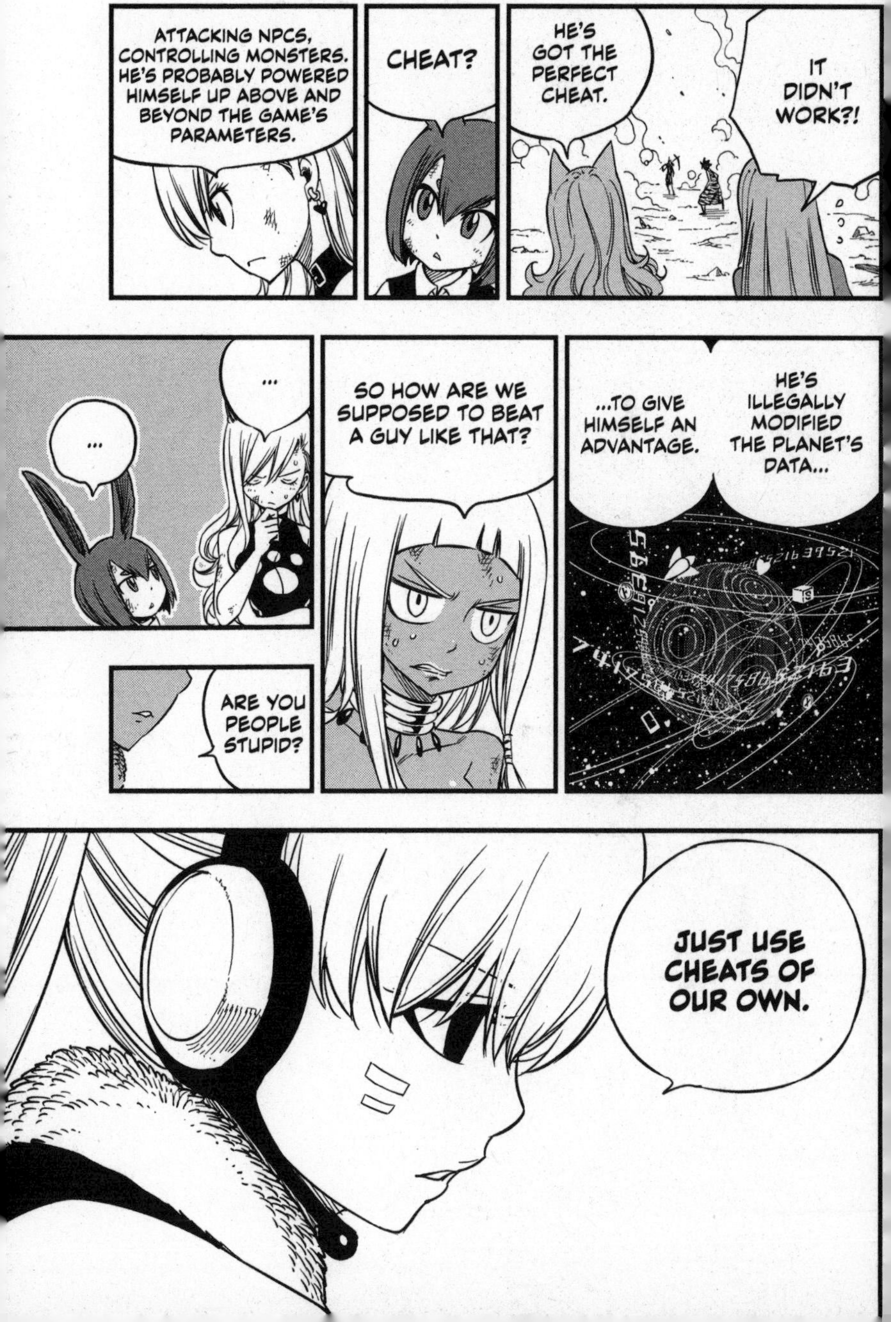
IT DIDN'T WORK?!
HE'S GOT THE PERFECT CHEAT.
CHEAT?
ATTACKING NPCS, CONTROLLING MONSTERS. HE'S PROBABLY POWERED HIMSELF UP ABOVE AND BEYOND THE GAME'S PARAMETERS.
HE'S ILLEGALLY MODIFIED THE PLANET'S DATA...
...TO GIVE HIMSELF AN ADVANTAGE.
SO HOW ARE WE SUPPOSED TO BEAT A GUY LIKE THAT?
...
...
ARE YOU PEOPLE STUPID?
JUST USE CHEATS OF OUR OWN.

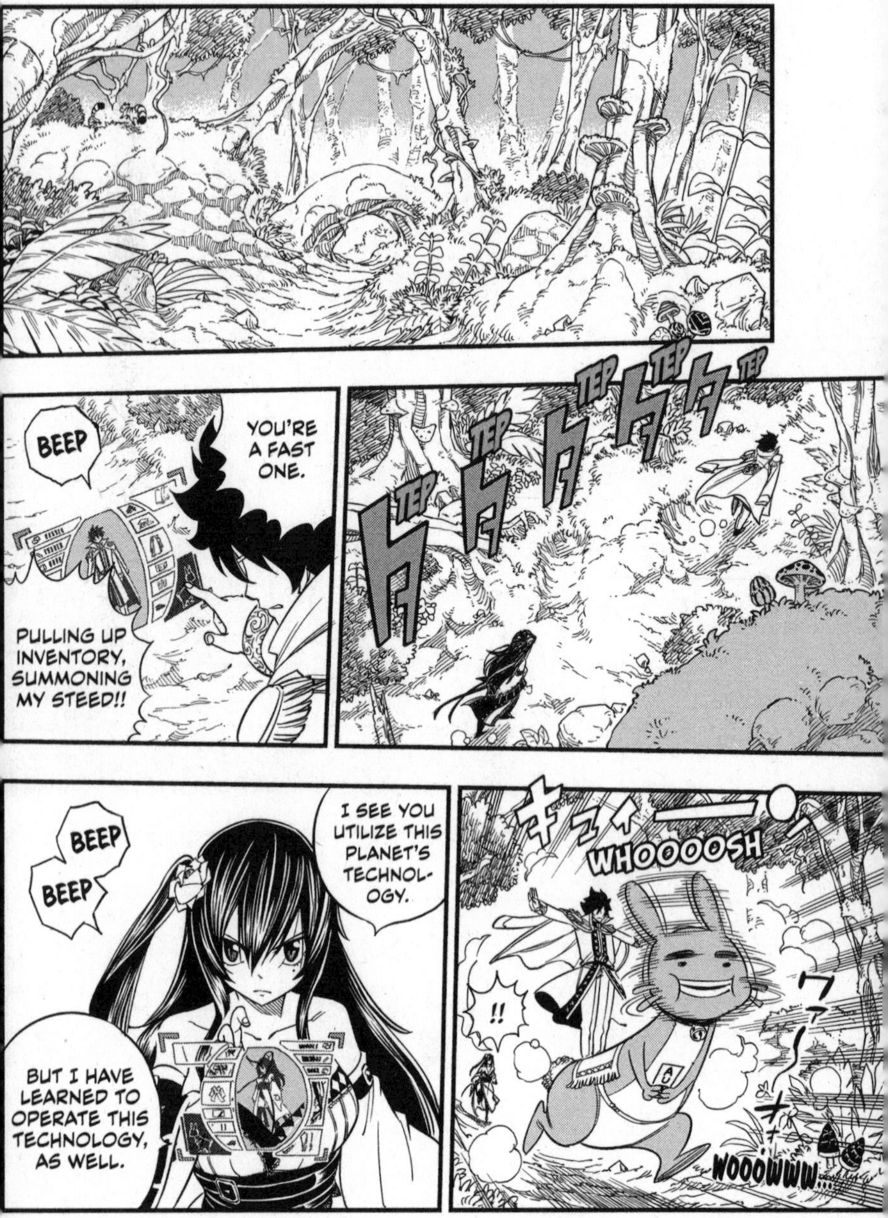
TEP TEP TEP TEP TEP
YOU'RE A FAST ONE.
BEEP
PULLING UP INVENTORY, SUMMONING MY STEED!!
WHOOOOSH
!!
WOOOWWW...
I SEE YOU UTILIZE THIS PLANET'S TECHNOLOGY.
BEEP
BEEP
BUT I HAVE LEARNED TO OPERATE THIS TECHNOLOGY, AS WELL.

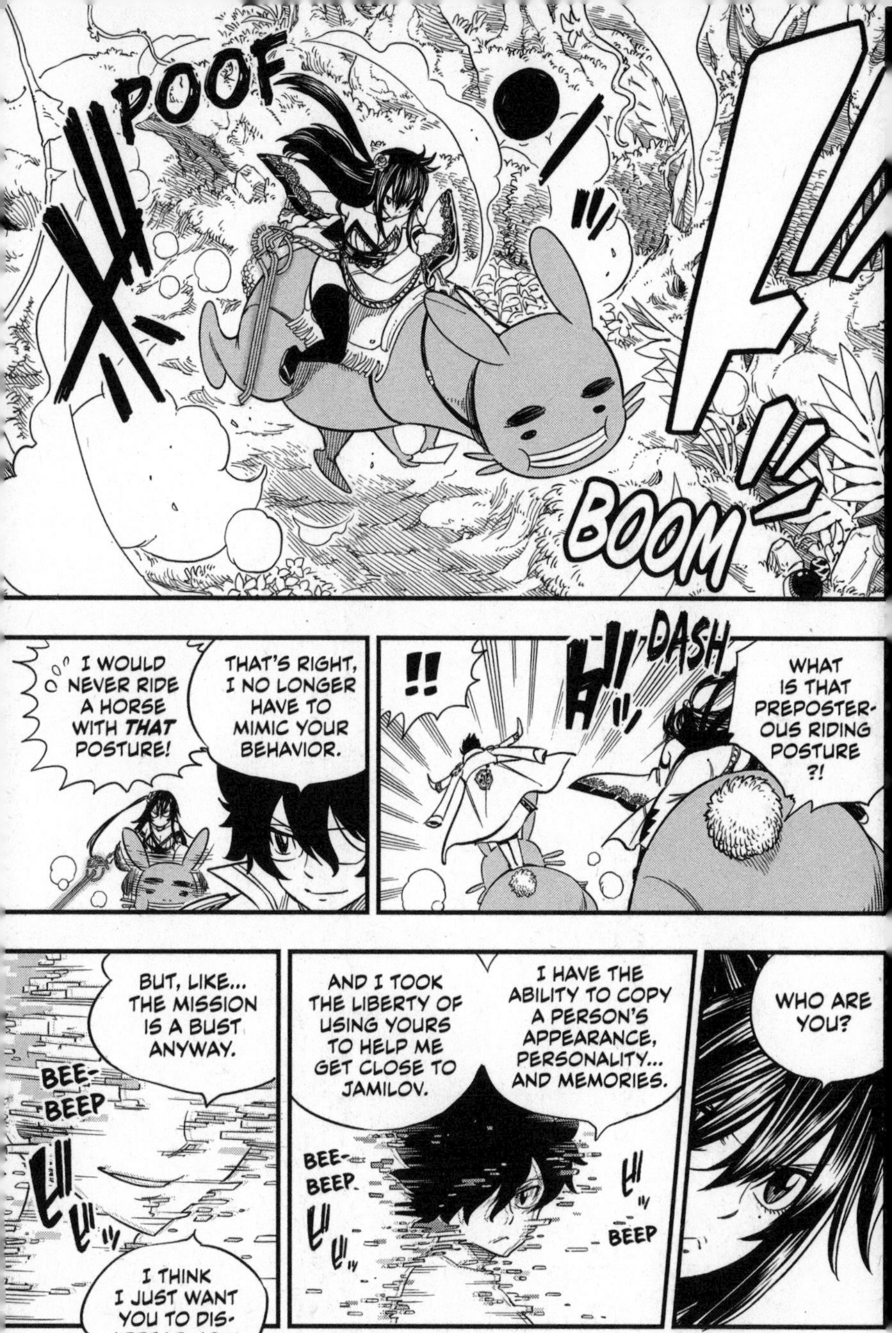
BOOM
POOF
DASH
WHAT IS THAT PREPOSTER-OUS RIDING POSTURE ?!
!!
THAT'S RIGHT, I NO LONGER HAVE TO MIMIC YOUR BEHAVIOR.
I WOULD NEVER RIDE A HORSE WITH *THAT* POSTURE!
WHO ARE YOU?
I HAVE THE ABILITY TO COPY A PERSON'S APPEARANCE, PERSONALITY... AND MEMORIES.
AND I TOOK THE LIBERTY OF USING YOURS TO HELP ME GET CLOSE TO JAMILOV.
BEEP
BEE-BEEP
BUT, LIKE... THE MISSION IS A BUST ANYWAY.
BEE-BEEP
I THINK I JUST WANT YOU TO DIS-APPEAR NOW.

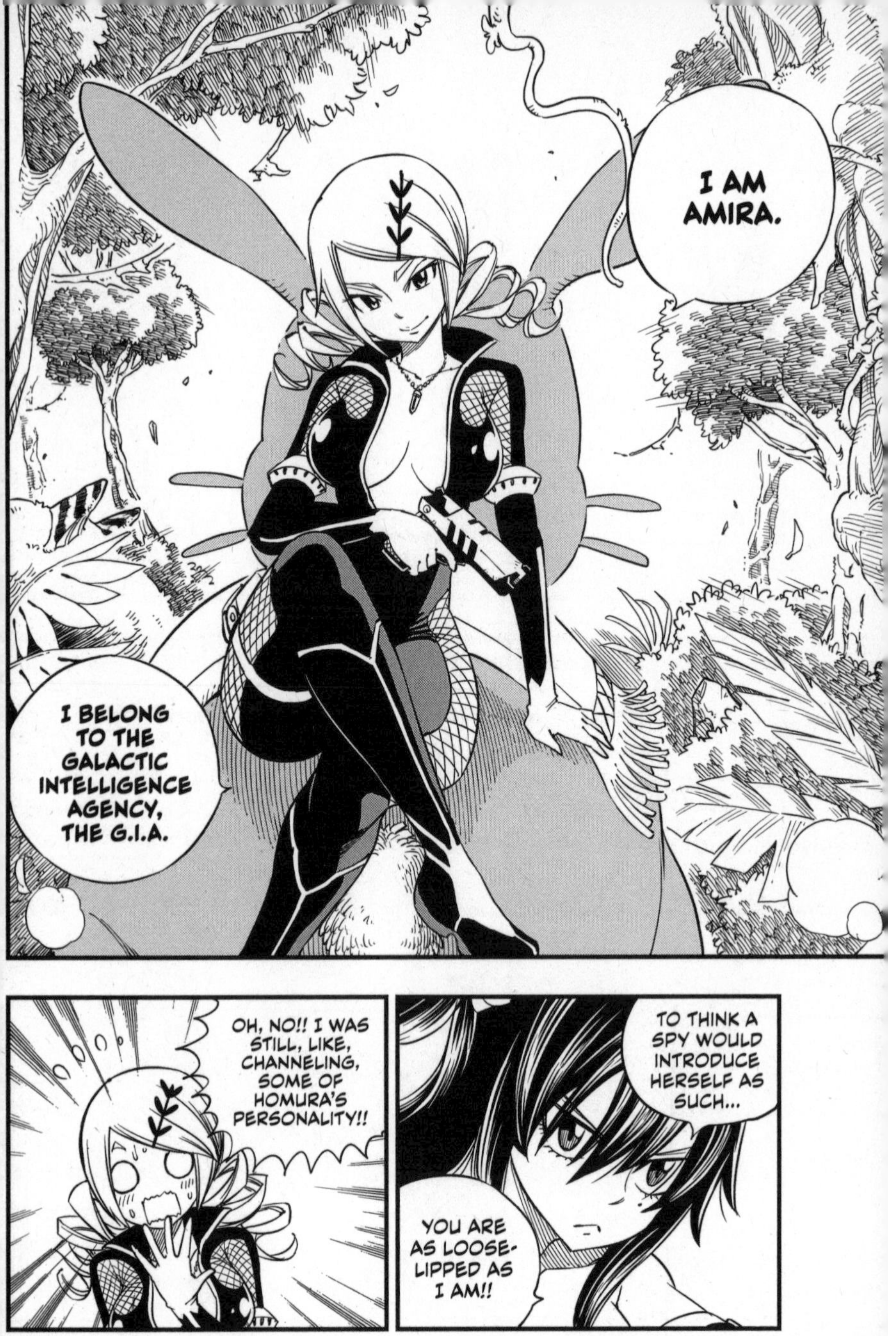
I AM AMIRA.
I BELONG TO THE GALACTIC INTELLIGENCE AGENCY, THE G.I.A.
TO THINK A SPY WOULD INTRODUCE HERSELF AS SUCH...
YOU ARE AS LOOSE-LIPPED AS I AM!!
OH, NO!! I WAS STILL, LIKE, CHANNELING, SOME OF HOMURA'S PERSONALITY!!

EDENS ZERO

CHAPTER 37: GREAT KAIJU SHIKI

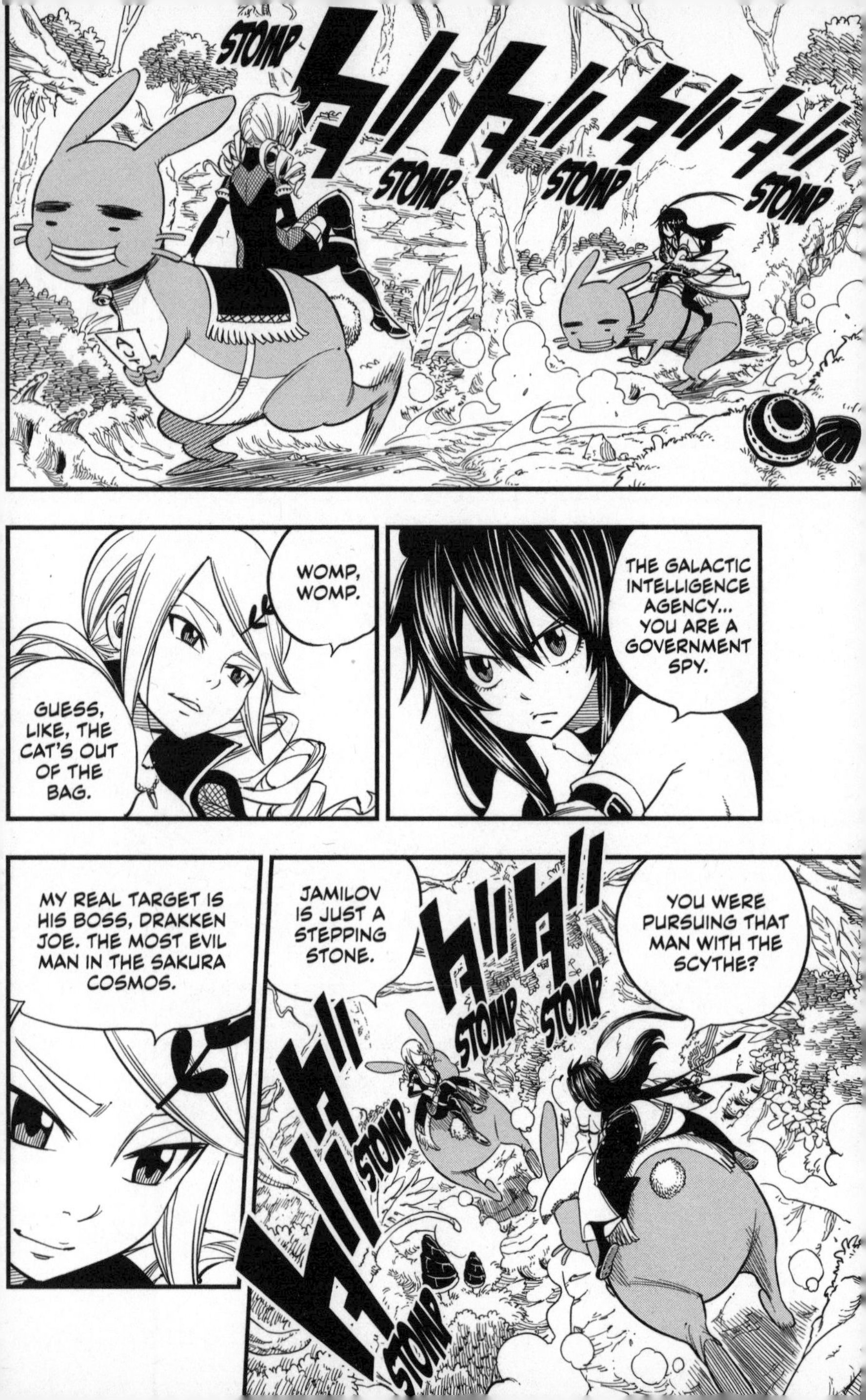
STOMP
STOMP
STOMP
STOMP
THE GALACTIC INTELLIGENCE AGENCY... YOU ARE A GOVERNMENT SPY.
WOMP, WOMP.
GUESS, LIKE, THE CAT'S OUT OF THE BAG.
YOU WERE PURSUING THAT MAN WITH THE SCYTHE?
STOMP
STOMP
JAMILOV IS JUST A STEPPING STONE.
STOMP
STOMP
MY REAL TARGET IS HIS BOSS, DRAKKEN JOE. THE MOST EVIL MAN IN THE SAKURA COSMOS.

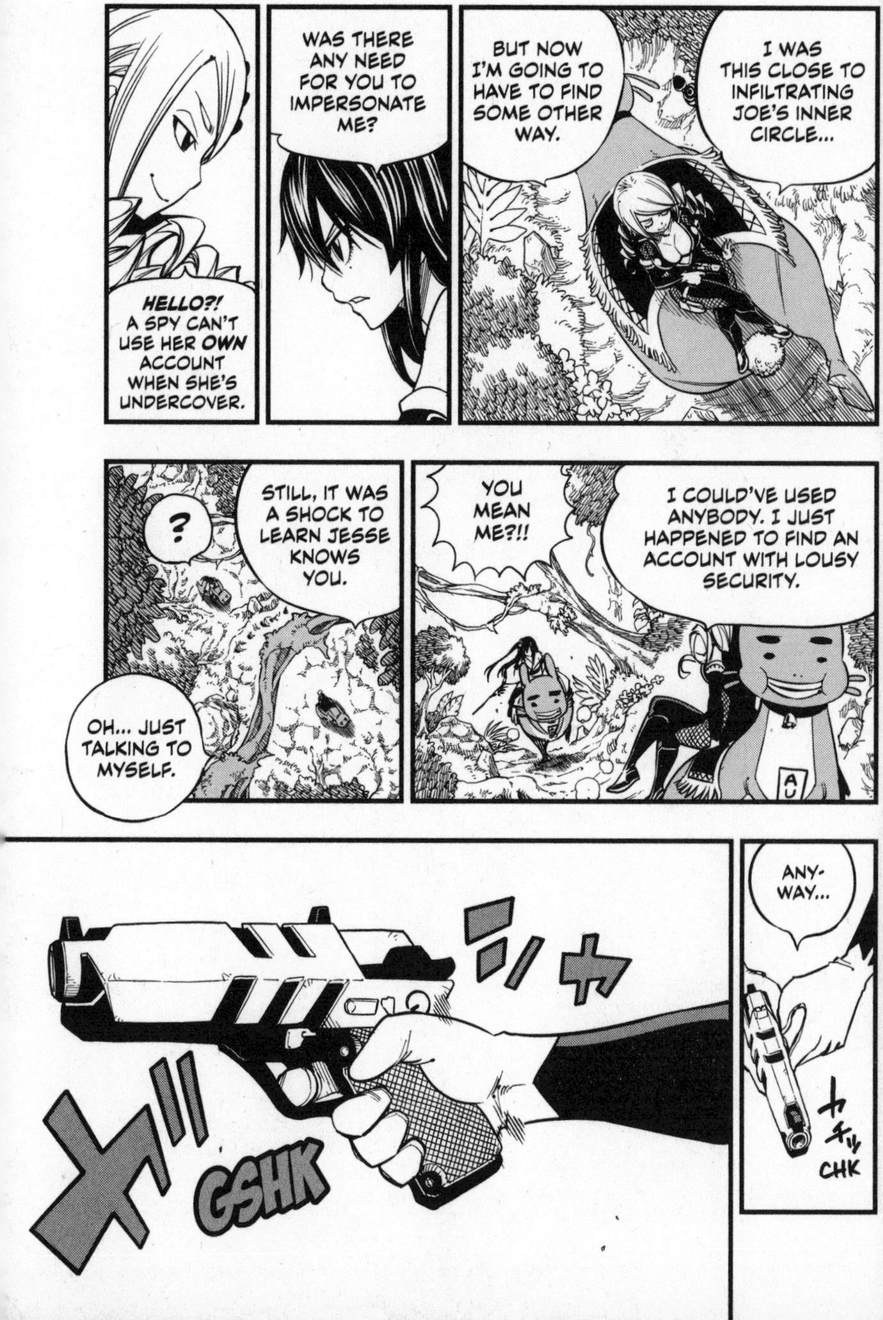
I WAS THIS CLOSE TO INFILTRATING JOE'S INNER CIRCLE...
BUT NOW I'M GOING TO HAVE TO FIND SOME OTHER WAY.
WAS THERE ANY NEED FOR YOU TO IMPERSONATE ME?
HELLO?! A SPY CAN'T USE HER *OWN* ACCOUNT WHEN SHE'S UNDERCOVER.
I COULD'VE USED ANYBODY. I JUST HAPPENED TO FIND AN ACCOUNT WITH LOUSY SECURITY.
YOU MEAN ME?!!
STILL, IT WAS A SHOCK TO LEARN JESSE KNOWS YOU.
?
OH... JUST TALKING TO MYSELF.
ANY-WAY...
CHK
GSHK

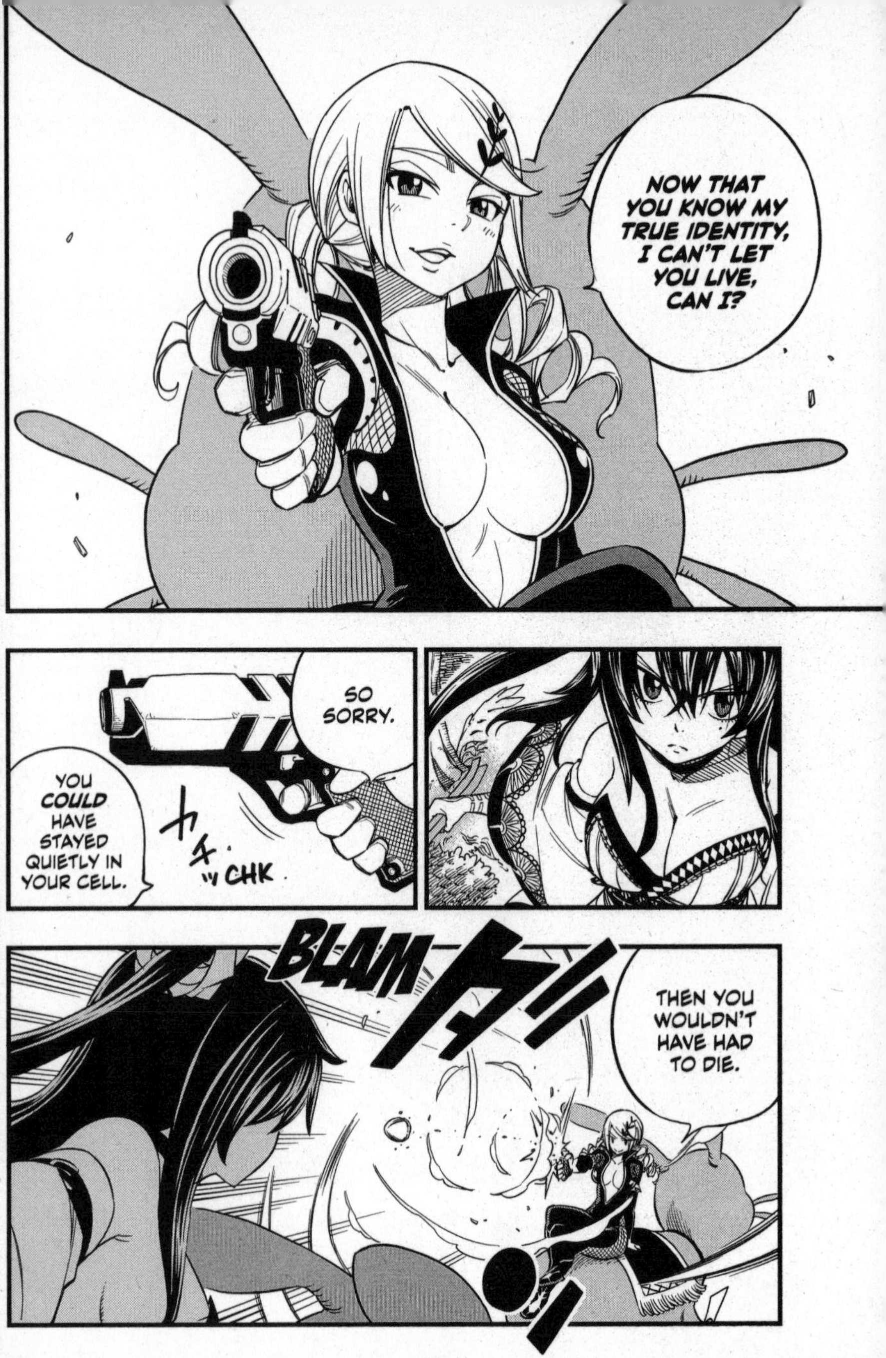
NOW THAT YOU KNOW MY TRUE IDENTITY, I CAN'T LET YOU LIVE, CAN I?
SO SORRY.
YOU COULD HAVE STAYED QUIETLY IN YOUR CELL.
CHK
BLAM
THEN YOU WOULDN'T HAVE HAD TO DIE.

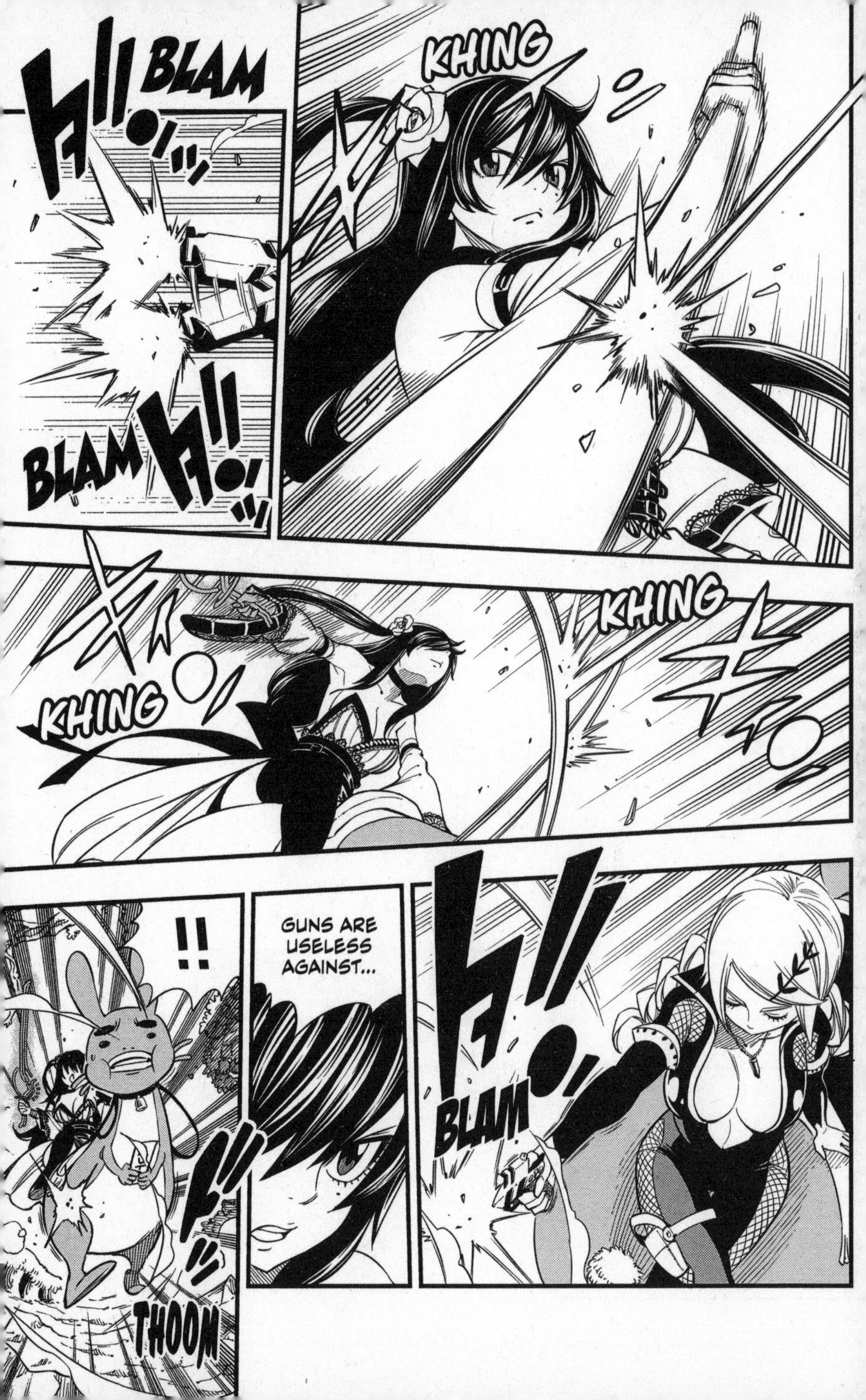
KHING
BLAM
BLAM
KHING
KHING
BLAM
GUNS ARE USELESS AGAINST...
!!
THOOM

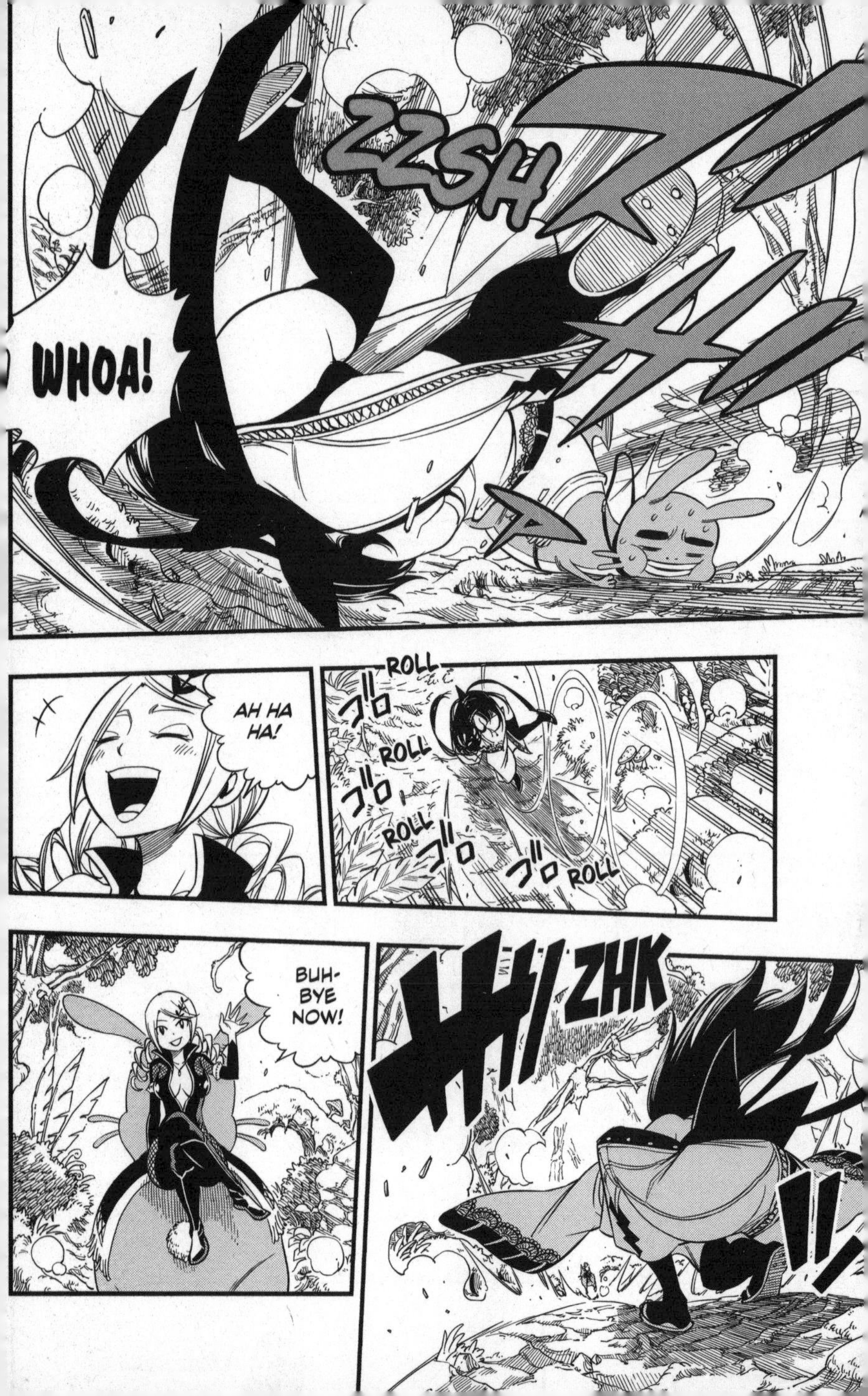
ZZSH
WHOA!
ROLL
ゴロ
ROLL
ゴロ
ROLL
ゴロ
ゴロ
ROLL
AH HA HA!
ZHK
!!
BUH-BYE NOW!

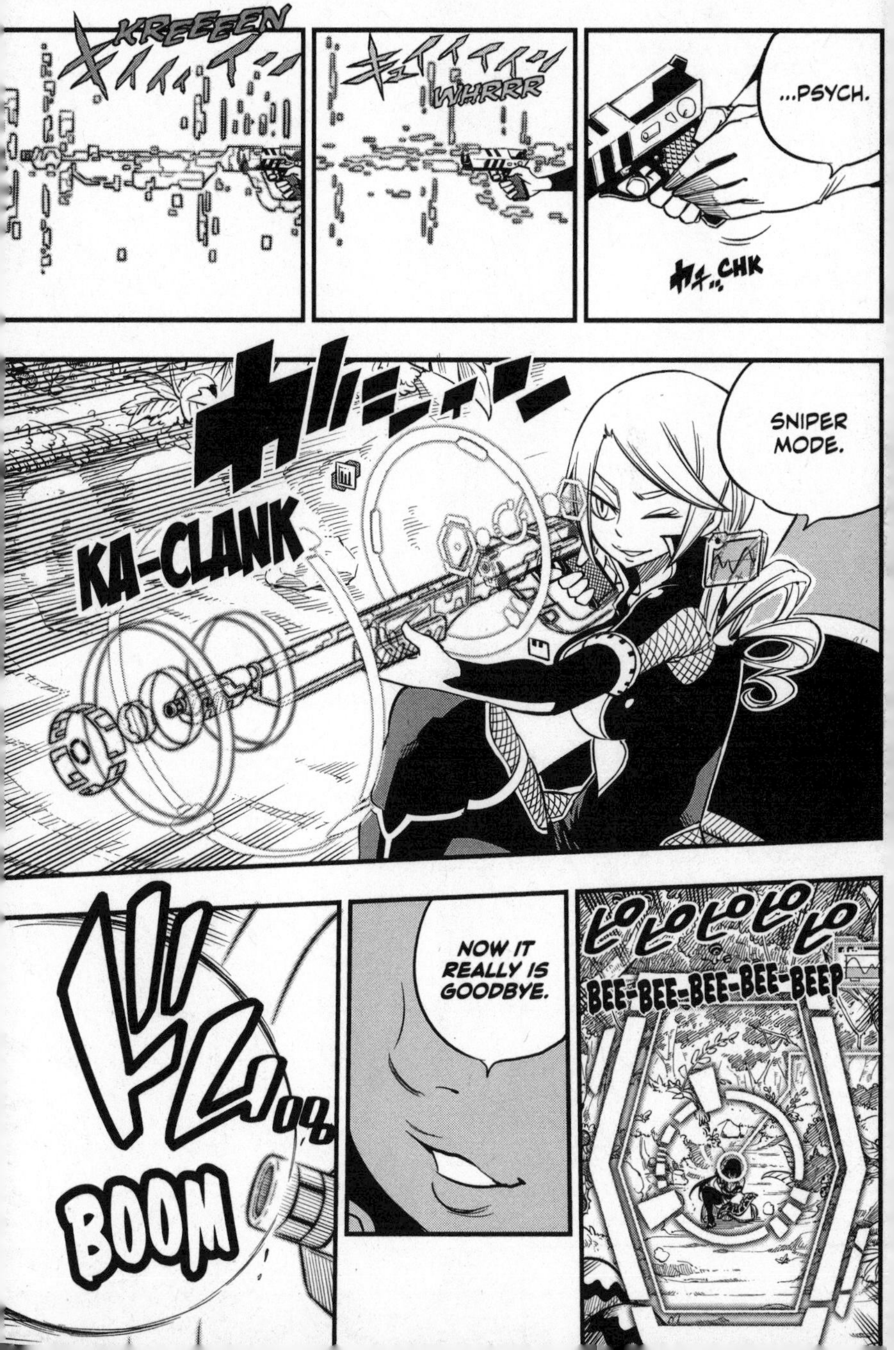
...PSYCH.
カチ
CHK
WHRRR
KREEEEN
SNIPER MODE.
KA-CLANK
ピピピピピ
BEE-BEE-BEE-BEE-BEEP
NOW IT REALLY IS GOODBYE.
BOOM

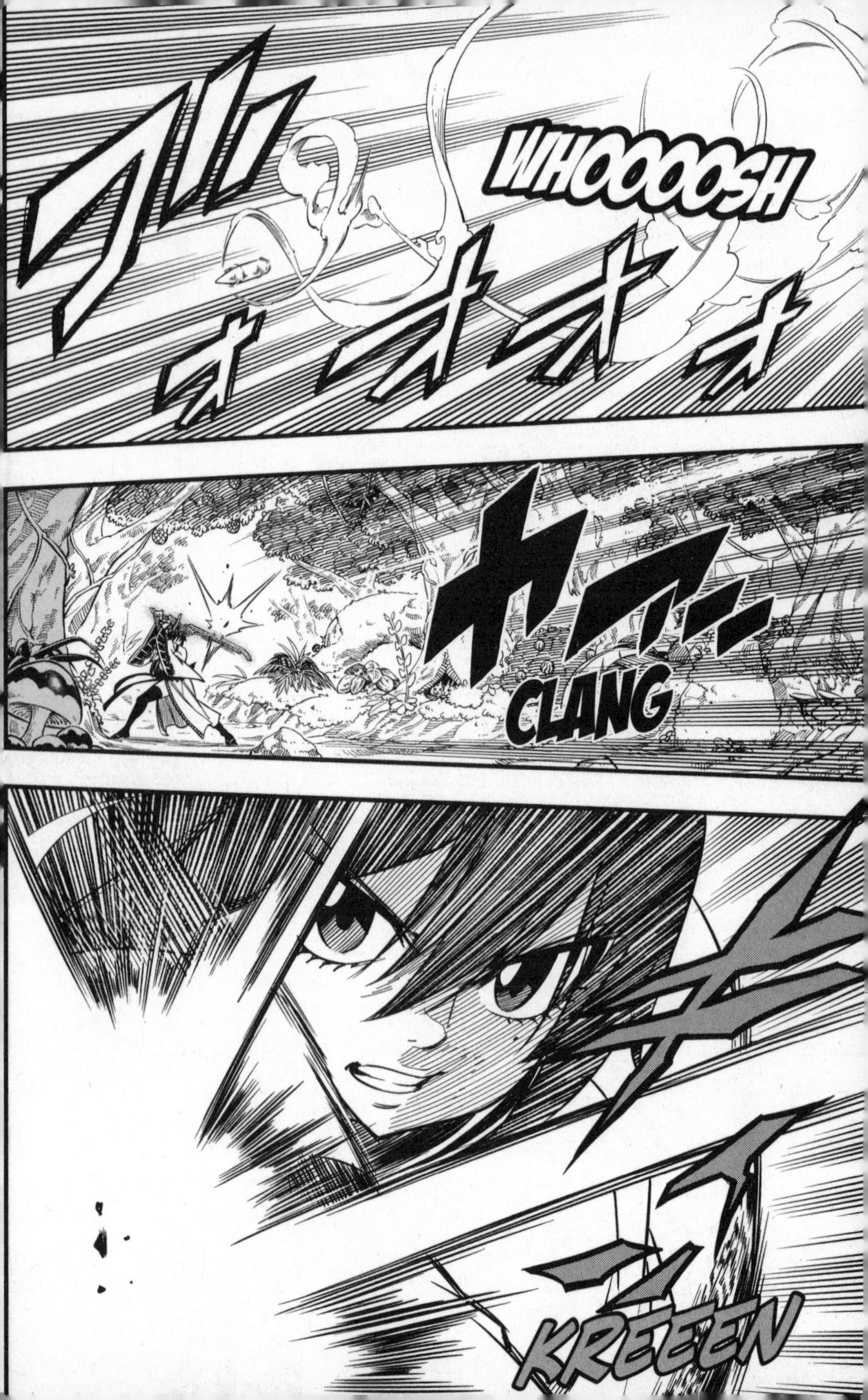
WHOOOOSH
CLANG
KREEEN

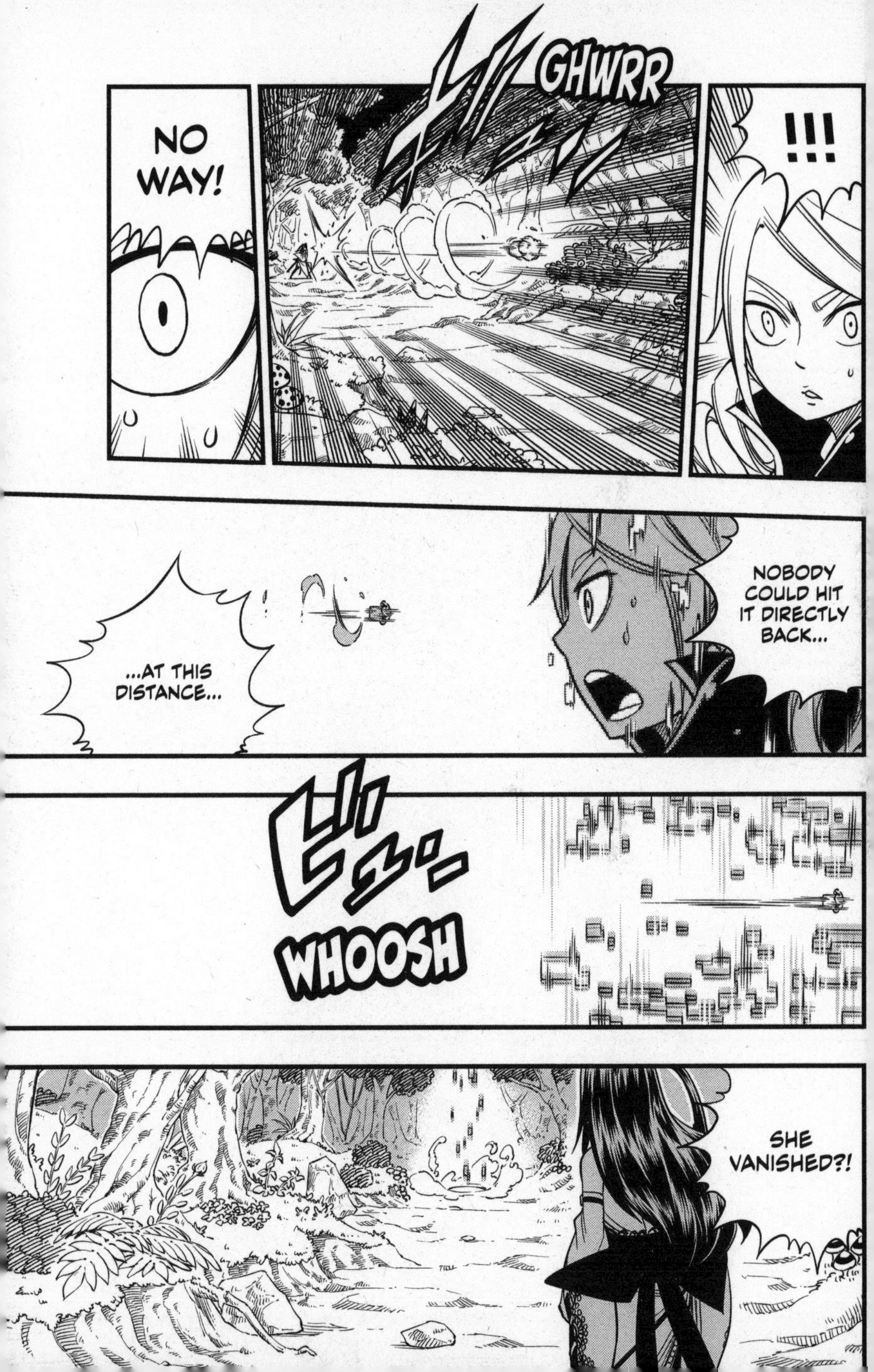
!!!
GHWRR
NO WAY!
NOBODY COULD HIT IT DIRECTLY BACK...
...AT THIS DISTANCE...
WHOOSH
SHE VANISHED?!

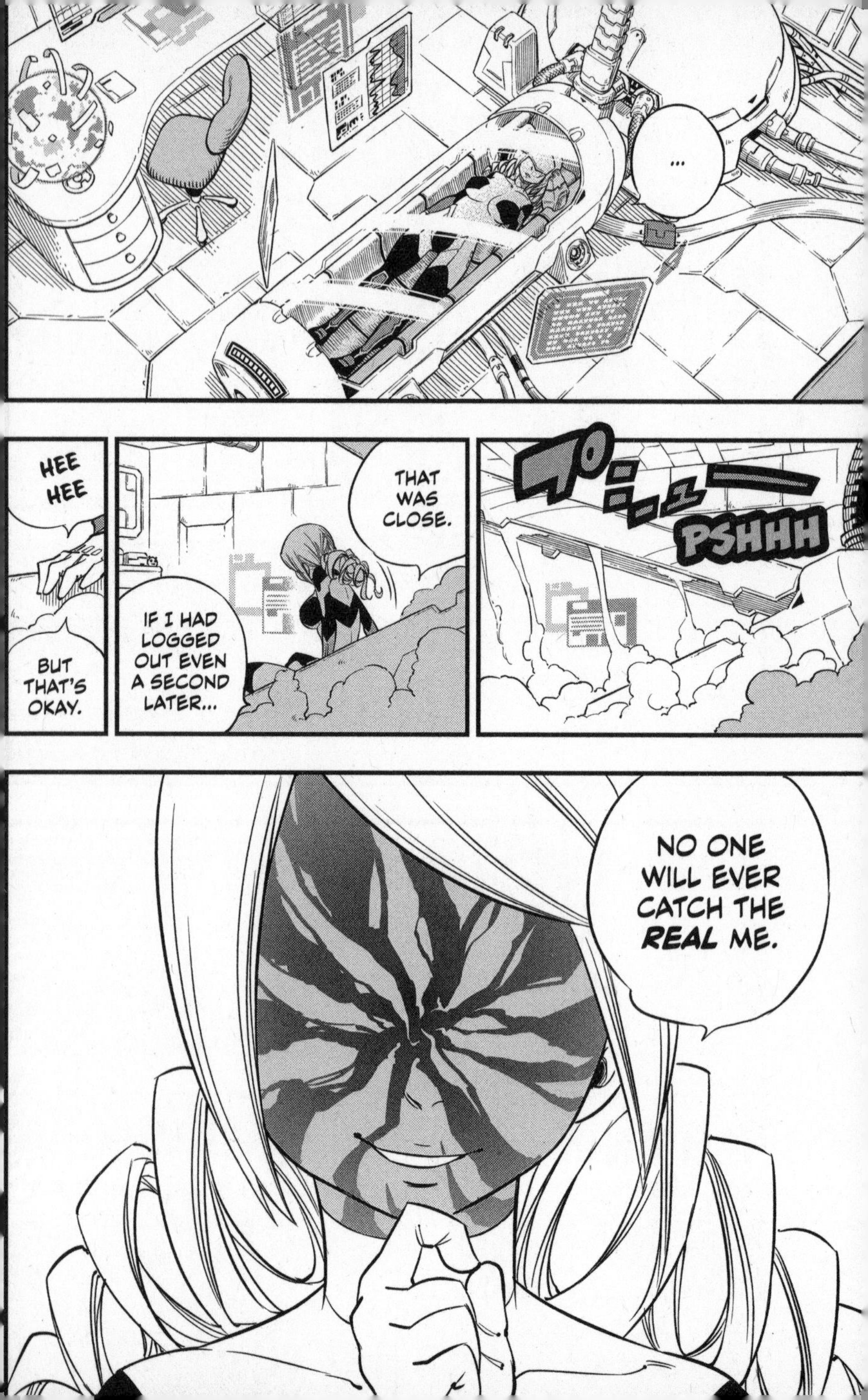
...
PSHHH
THAT WAS CLOSE.
IF I HAD LOGGED OUT EVEN A SECOND LATER...
HEE HEE
BUT THAT'S OKAY.
NO ONE WILL EVER CATCH THE *REAL* ME.

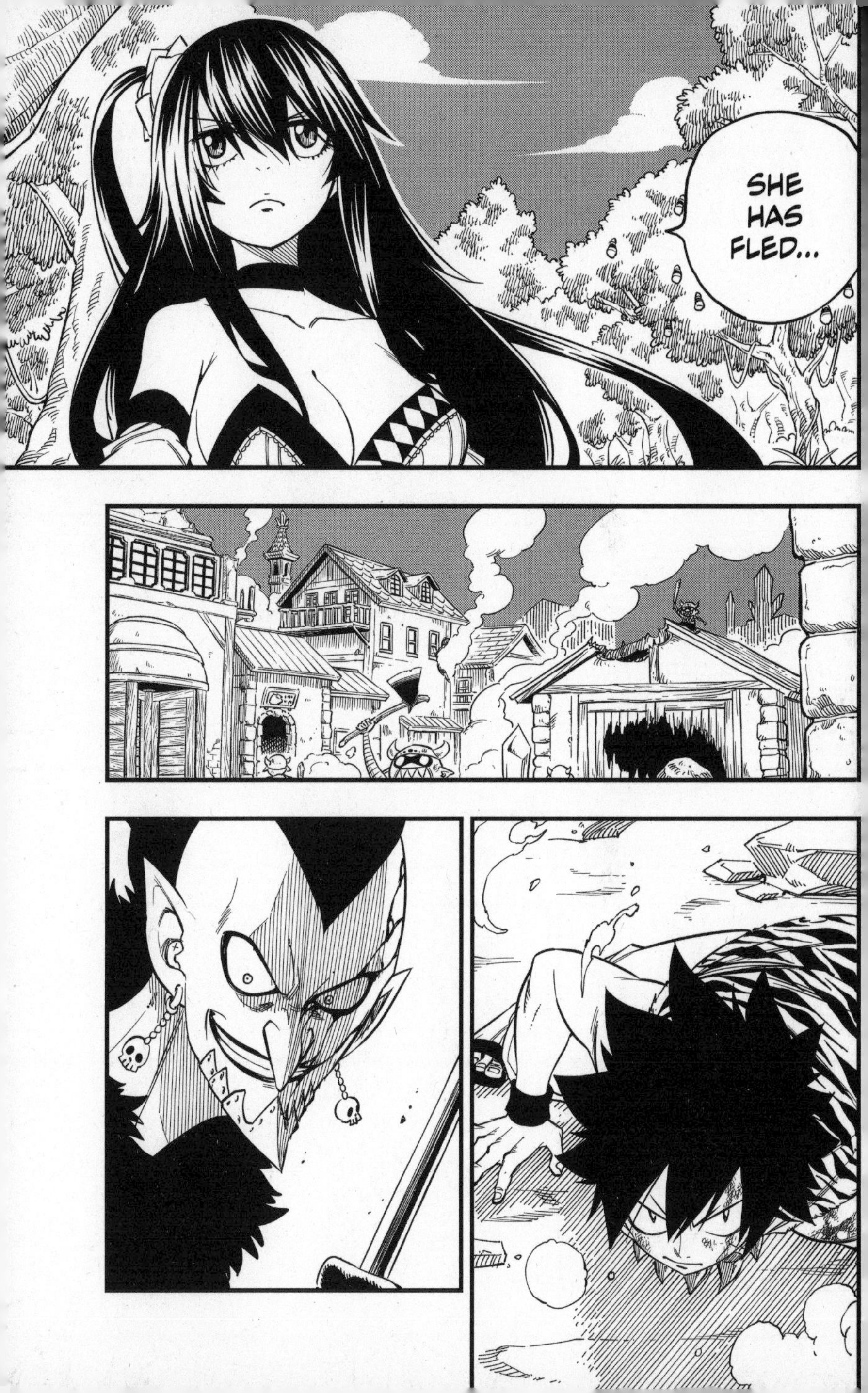
SHE HAS FLED...

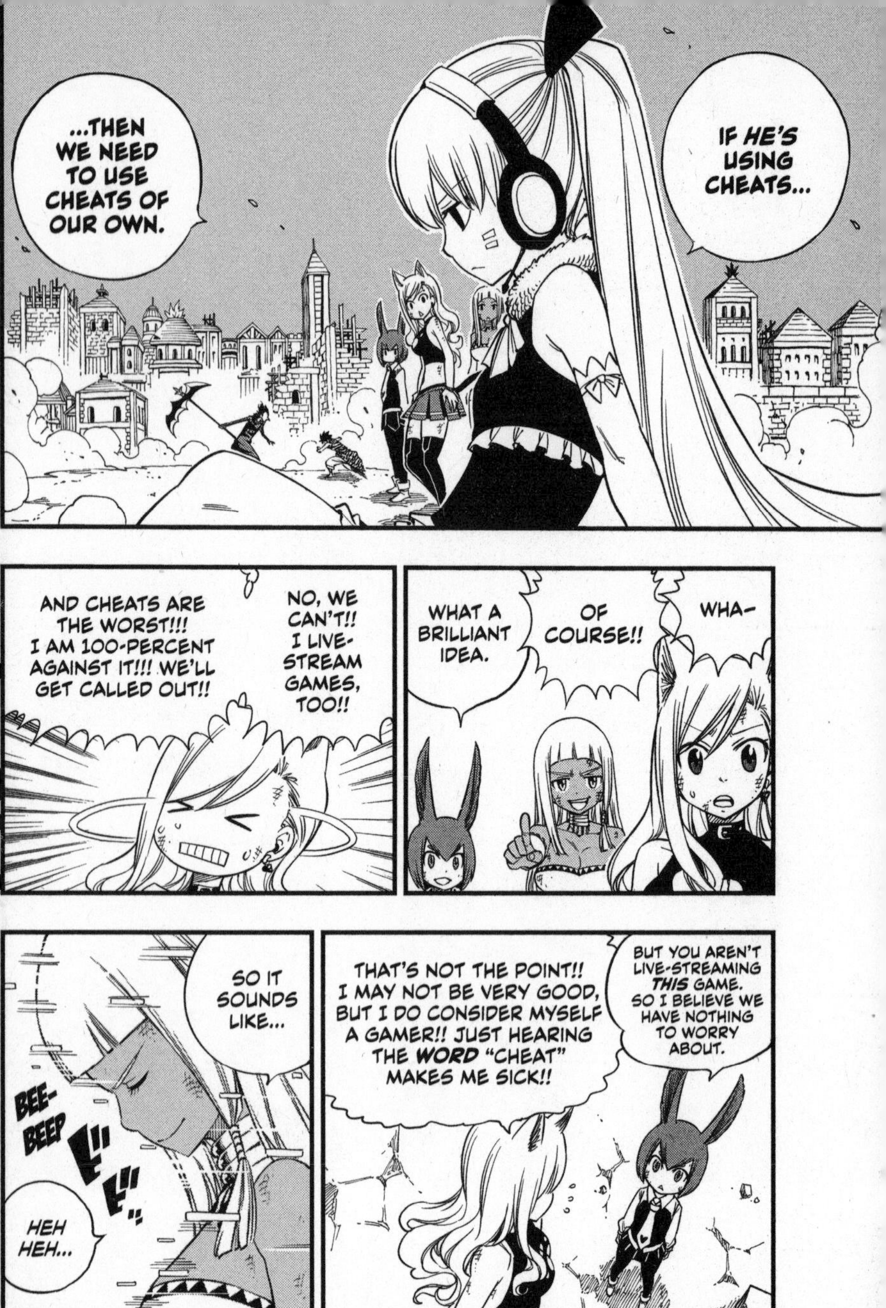
IF HE'S USING CHEATS...
...THEN WE NEED TO USE CHEATS OF OUR OWN.
WHA-
OF COURSE!!
WHAT A BRILLIANT IDEA.
NO, WE CAN'T!! I LIVE-STREAM GAMES, TOO!!
AND CHEATS ARE THE WORST!!! I AM 100-PERCENT AGAINST IT!!! WE'LL GET CALLED OUT!!
BUT YOU AREN'T LIVE-STREAMING THIS GAME. SO I BELIEVE WE HAVE NOTHING TO WORRY ABOUT.
THAT'S NOT THE POINT!! I MAY NOT BE VERY GOOD, BUT I DO CONSIDER MYSELF A GAMER!! JUST HEARING THE WORD "CHEAT" MAKES ME SICK!!
SO IT SOUNDS LIKE...
BEE-BEEP
HEH HEH...

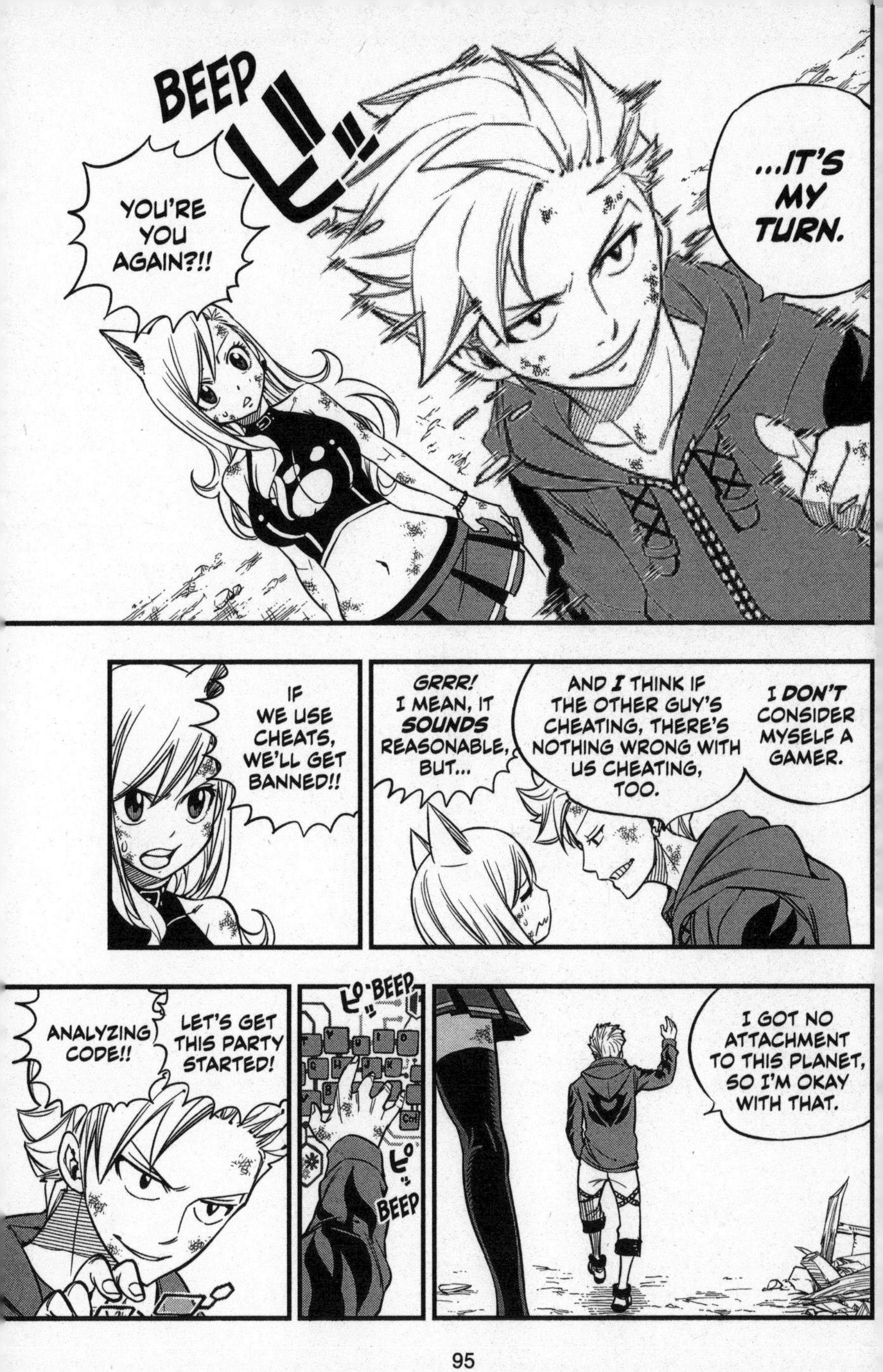
...IT'S MY TURN.
BEEP
YOU'RE YOU AGAIN?!!
I DON'T CONSIDER MYSELF A GAMER.
AND I THINK IF THE OTHER GUY'S CHEATING, THERE'S NOTHING WRONG WITH US CHEATING, TOO.
GRRR! I MEAN, IT SOUNDS REASONABLE, BUT...
IF WE USE CHEATS, WE'LL GET BANNED!!
I GOT NO ATTACHMENT TO THIS PLANET, SO I'M OKAY WITH THAT.
BEEP
BEEP
LET'S GET THIS PARTY STARTED!
ANALYZING CODE!!

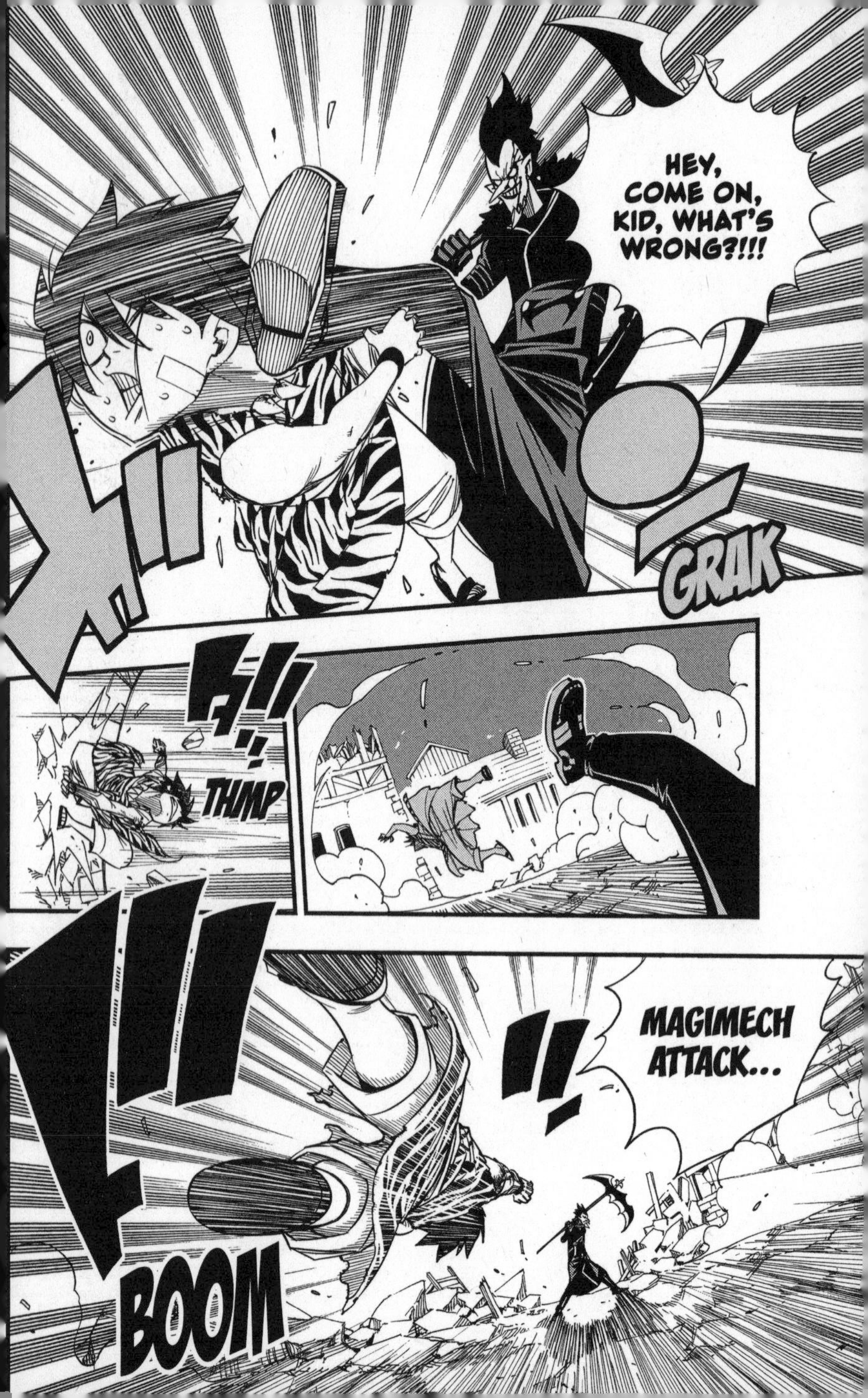
HEY, COME ON, KID, WHAT'S WRONG?!!!
GRAK
THMP
MAGIMECH ATTACK...
BOOM

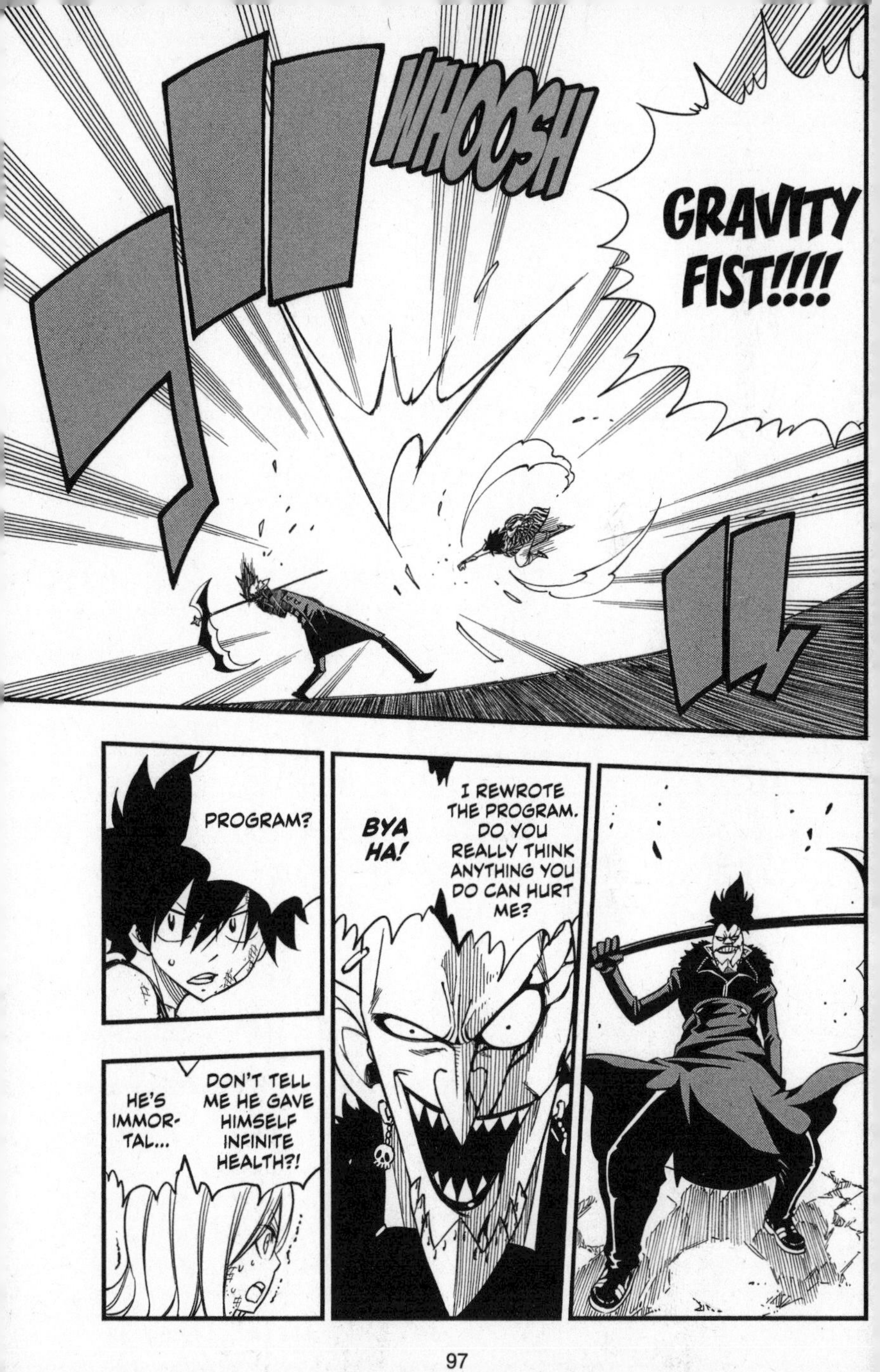
GRAVITY FIST!!!!
WHOOSH
I REWROTE THE PROGRAM. DO YOU REALLY THINK ANYTHING YOU DO CAN HURT ME?
BYA HA!
PROGRAM?
DON'T TELL ME HE GAVE HIMSELF INFINITE HEALTH?!
HE'S IMMOR-TAL...

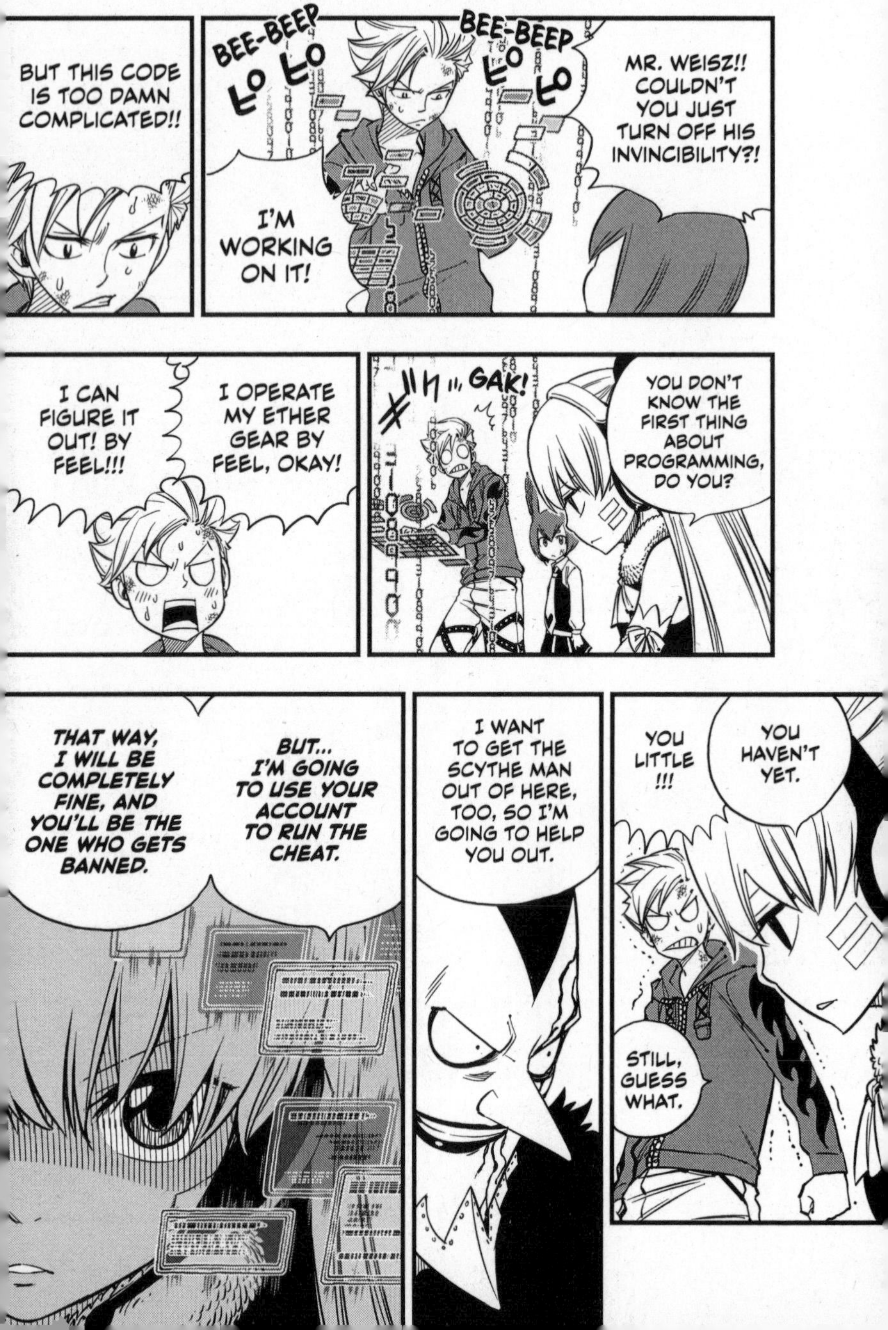
BEE-BEEP
BEE-BEEP
MR. WEISZ!! COULDN'T YOU JUST TURN OFF HIS INVINCIBILITY?!
I'M WORKING ON IT!
BUT THIS CODE IS TOO DAMN COMPLICATED!!
GAK!
YOU DON'T KNOW THE FIRST THING ABOUT PROGRAMMING, DO YOU?
I OPERATE MY ETHER GEAR BY FEEL, OKAY!
I CAN FIGURE IT OUT! BY FEEL!!!
YOU HAVEN'T YET.
YOU LITTLE !!!
STILL, GUESS WHAT.
I WANT TO GET THE SCYTHE MAN OUT OF HERE, TOO, SO I'M GOING TO HELP YOU OUT.
BUT... I'M GOING TO USE YOUR ACCOUNT TO RUN THE CHEAT.
THAT WAY, I WILL BE COMPLETELY FINE, AND YOU'LL BE THE ONE WHO GETS BANNED.

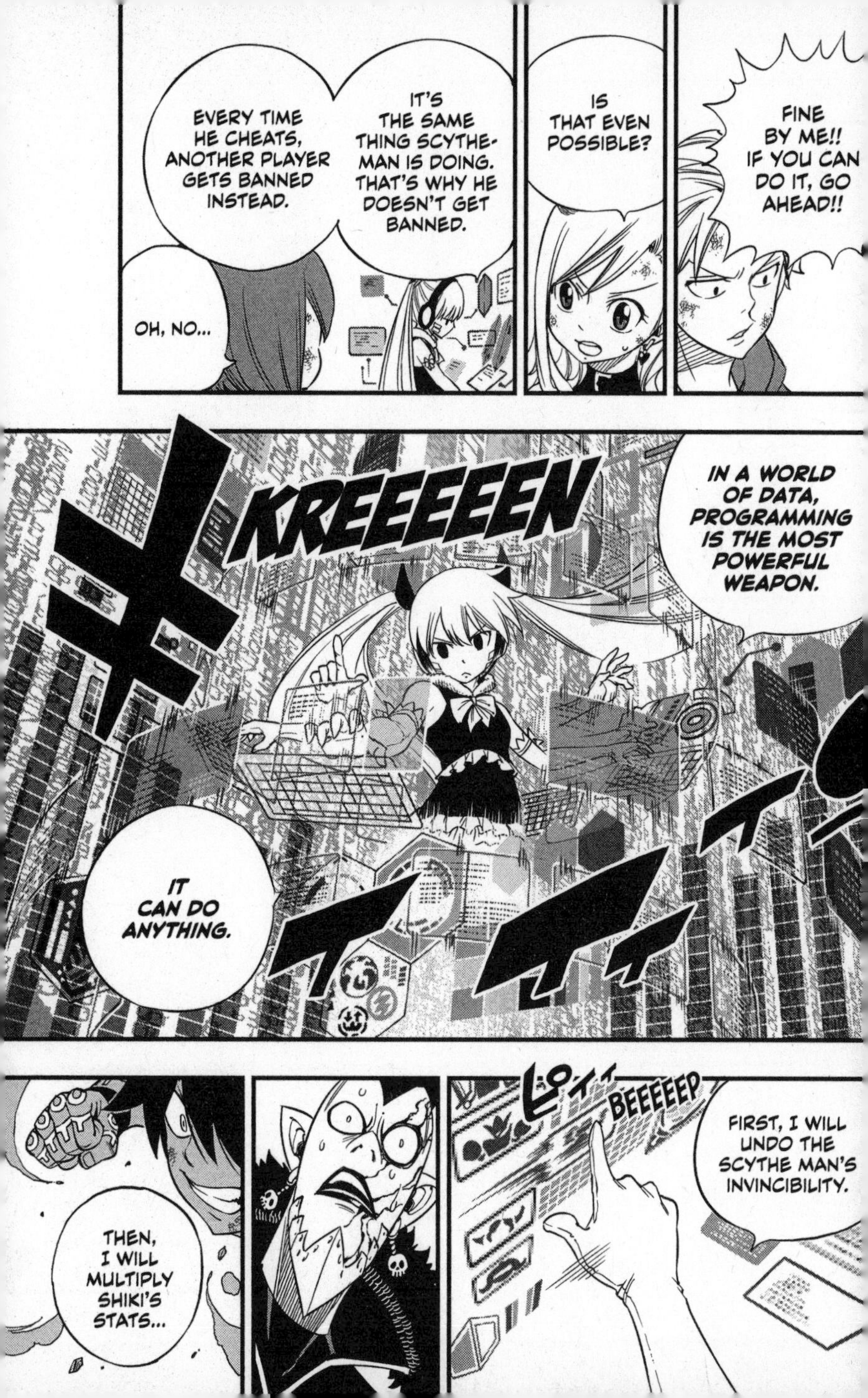
FINE BY ME!! IF YOU CAN DO IT, GO AHEAD!!
IS THAT EVEN POSSIBLE?
IT'S THE SAME THING SCYTHE-MAN IS DOING. THAT'S WHY HE DOESN'T GET BANNED.
EVERY TIME HE CHEATS, ANOTHER PLAYER GETS BANNED INSTEAD.
OH, NO...
KREEEEEN
IN A WORLD OF DATA, PROGRAMMING IS THE MOST POWERFUL WEAPON.
IT CAN DO ANYTHING.
BEEEEEP
FIRST, I WILL UNDO THE SCYTHE MAN'S INVINCIBILITY.
THEN, I WILL MULTIPLY SHIKI'S STATS...

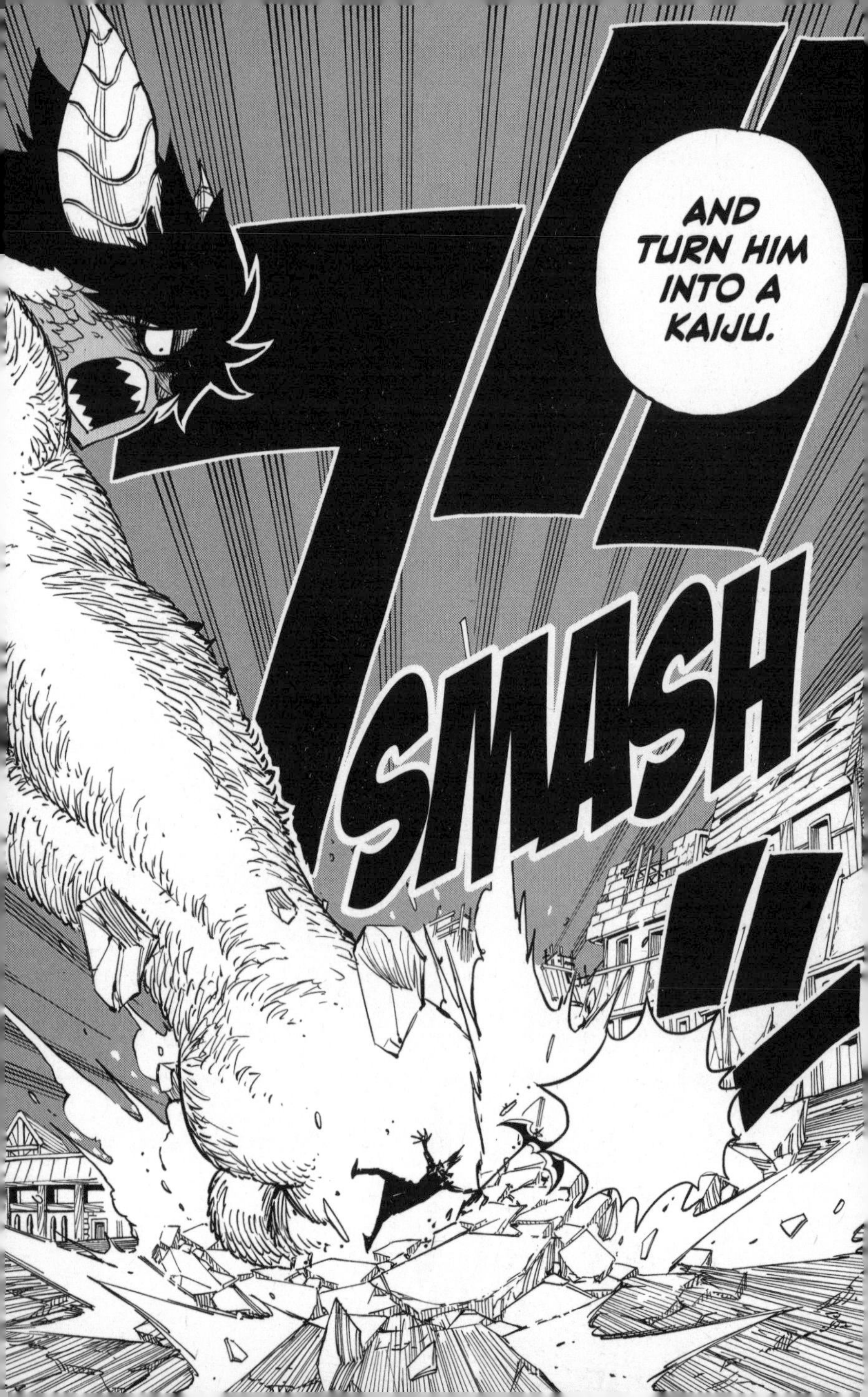
AND TURN HIM INTO A KAIJU.
SMASH!!

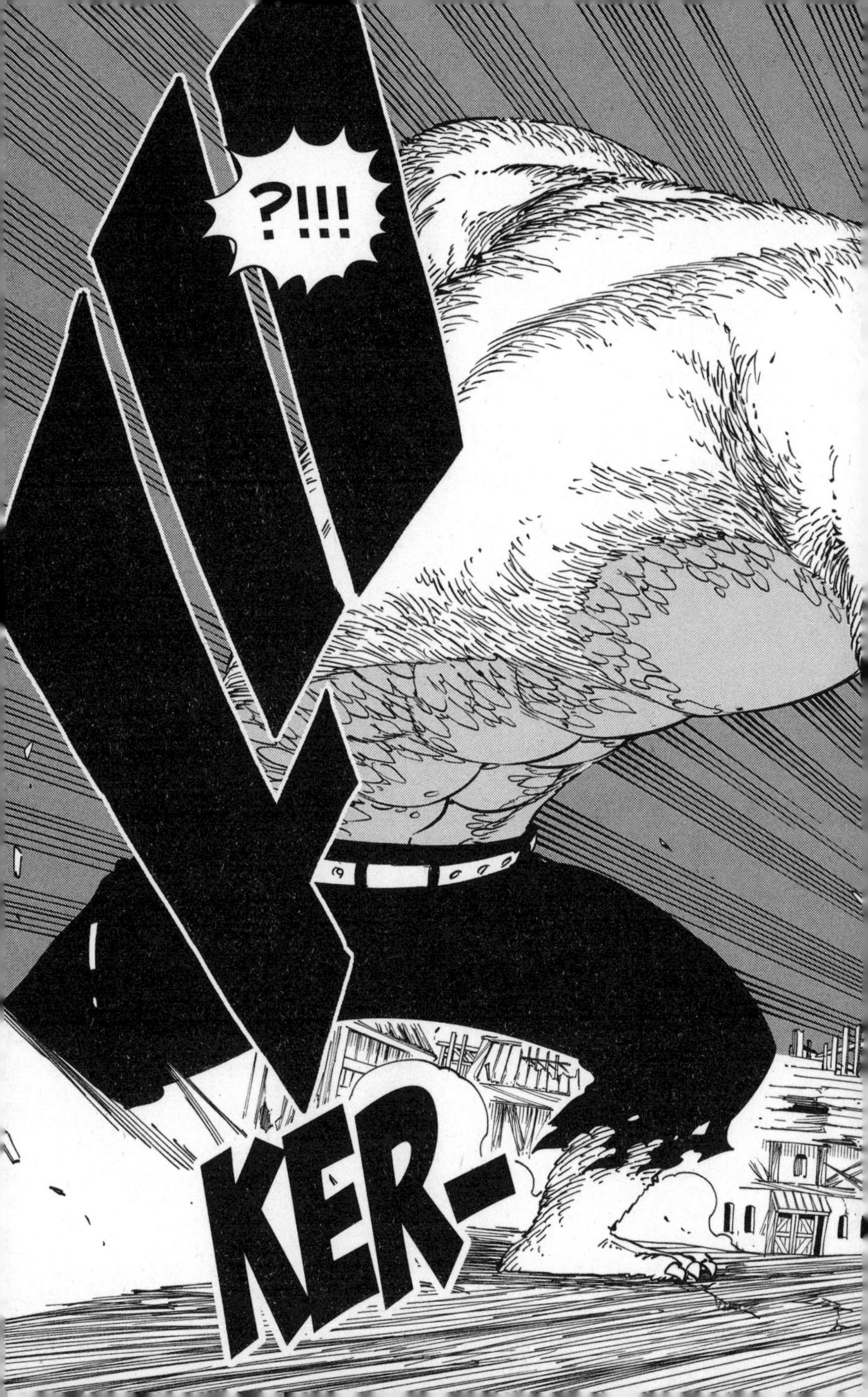
?!!!
KER-

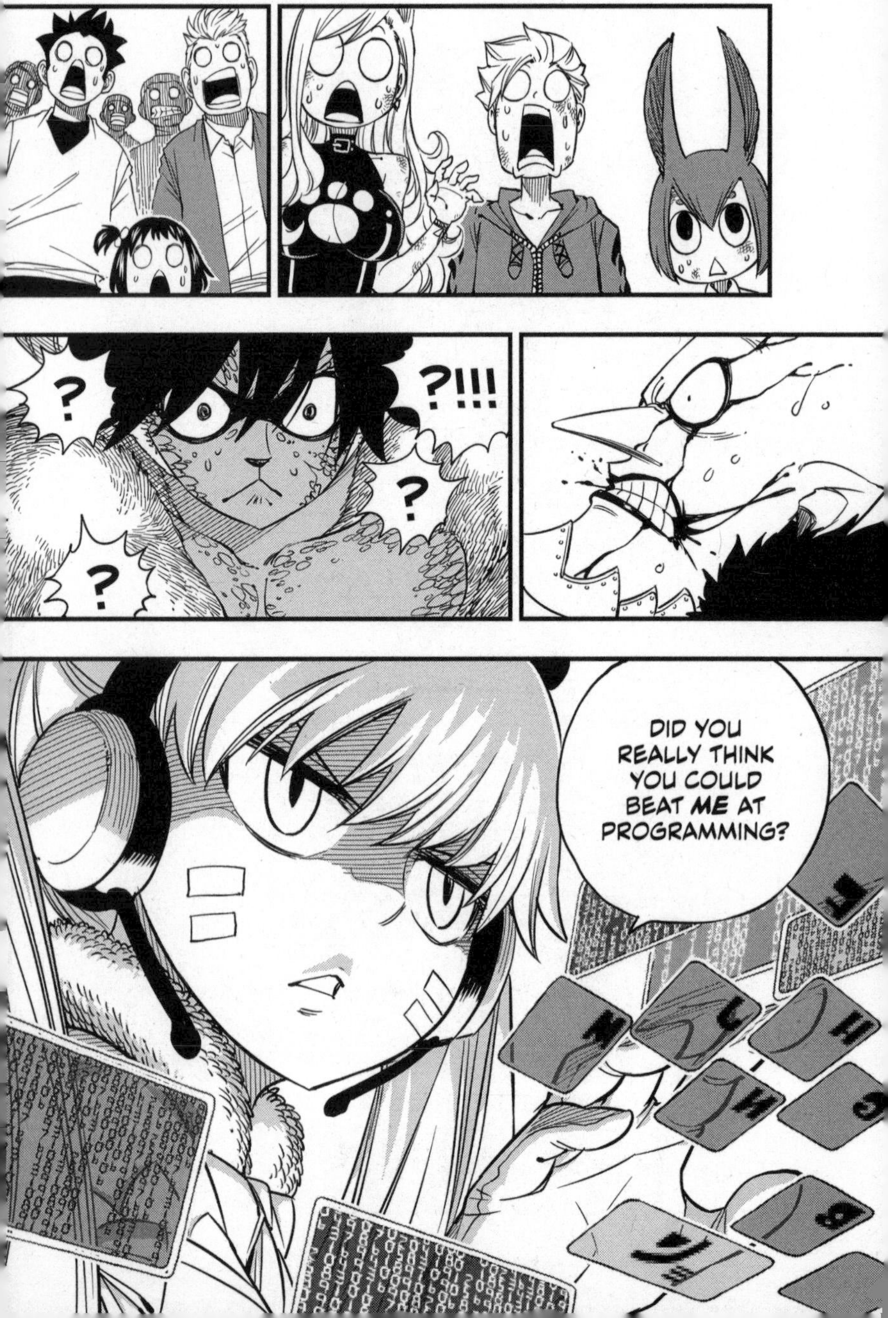
?!!!
?
?
?
DID YOU REALLY THINK YOU COULD BEAT **ME** AT PROGRAMMING?

EDENS ZERO

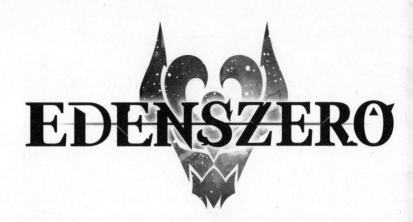

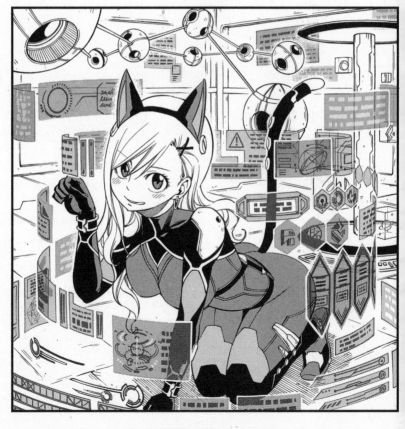

CHAPTER 38: 22 HITS

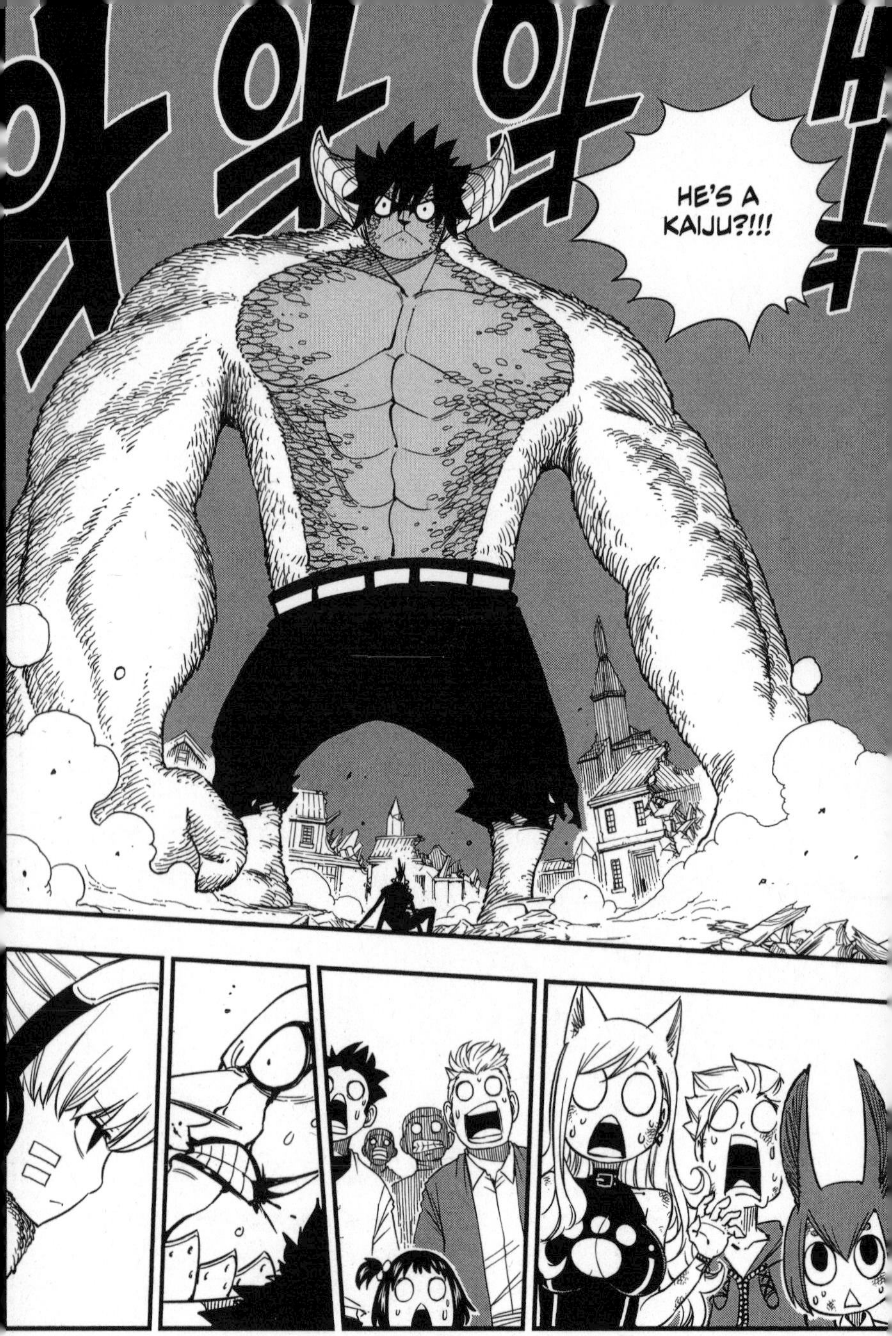
HE'S A KAIJU?!!!

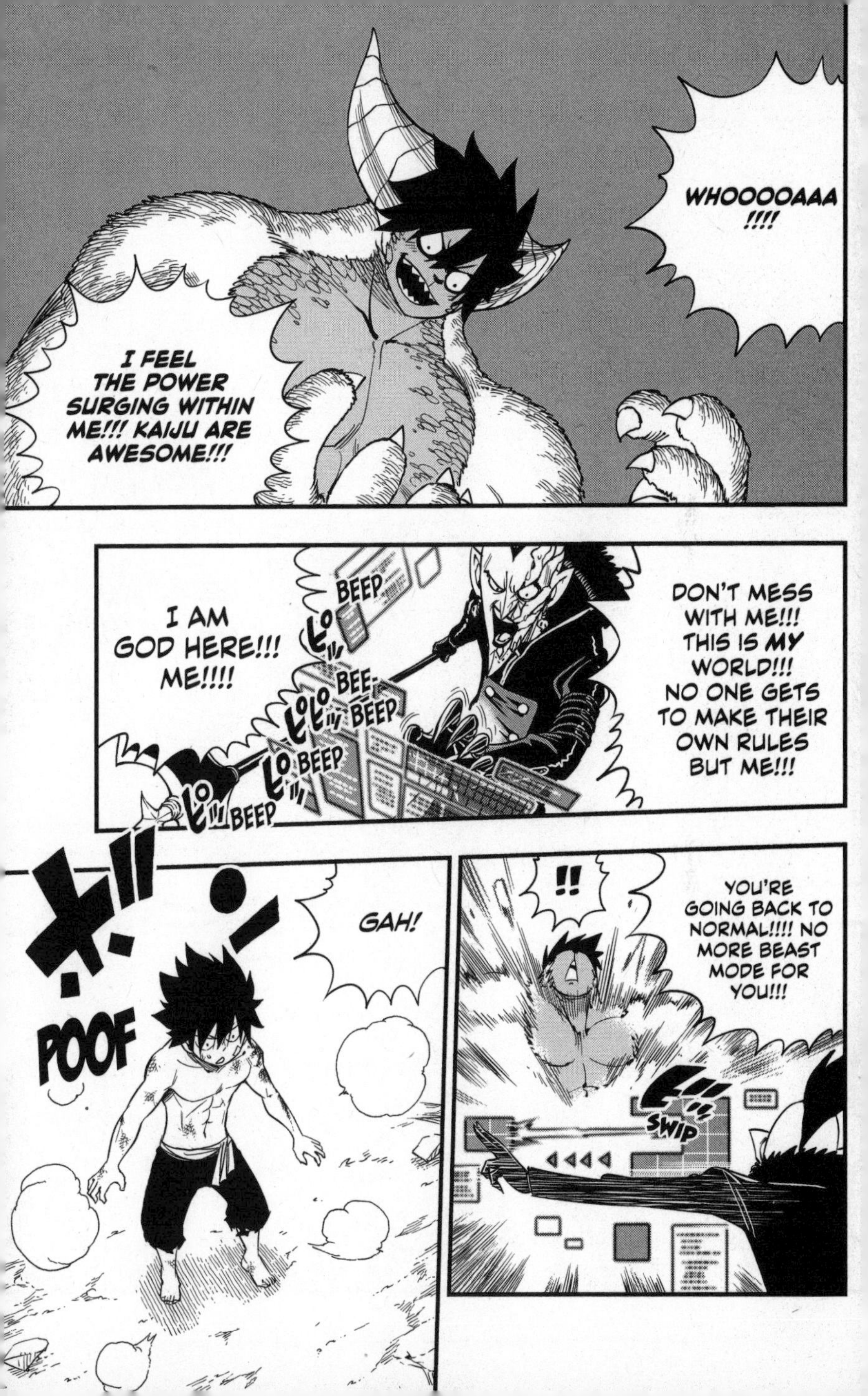
WHOOOOAAA !!!!
I FEEL THE POWER SURGING WITHIN ME!!! KAIJU ARE AWESOME!!!
DON'T MESS WITH ME!!! THIS IS MY WORLD!!! NO ONE GETS TO MAKE THEIR OWN RULES BUT ME!!!
BEEP
BEE-BEEP
BEEP
BEEP
I AM GOD HERE!!! ME!!!!
!!
YOU'RE GOING BACK TO NORMAL!!!! NO MORE BEAST MODE FOR YOU!!!
SWIP
GAH!
POOF

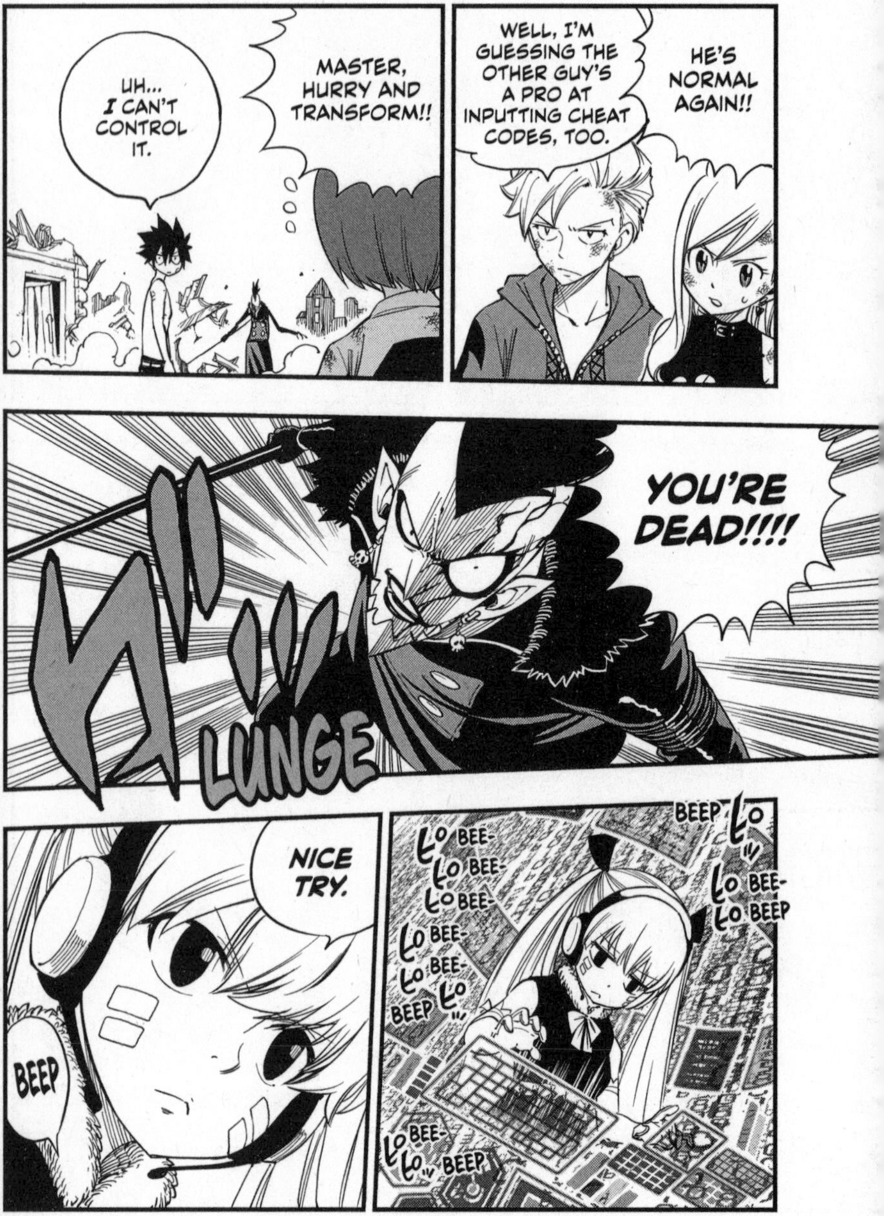
HE'S NORMAL AGAIN!!
WELL, I'M GUESSING THE OTHER GUY'S A PRO AT INPUTTING CHEAT CODES, TOO.
MASTER, HURRY AND TRANSFORM!!
UH... I CAN'T CONTROL IT.
YOU'RE DEAD!!!!
LUNGE
BEEP
BEE-
BEEP
BEE-
BEE-
BEE-
BEE-
BEE-
BEEP
BEE-
BEEP
NICE TRY.
BEEP

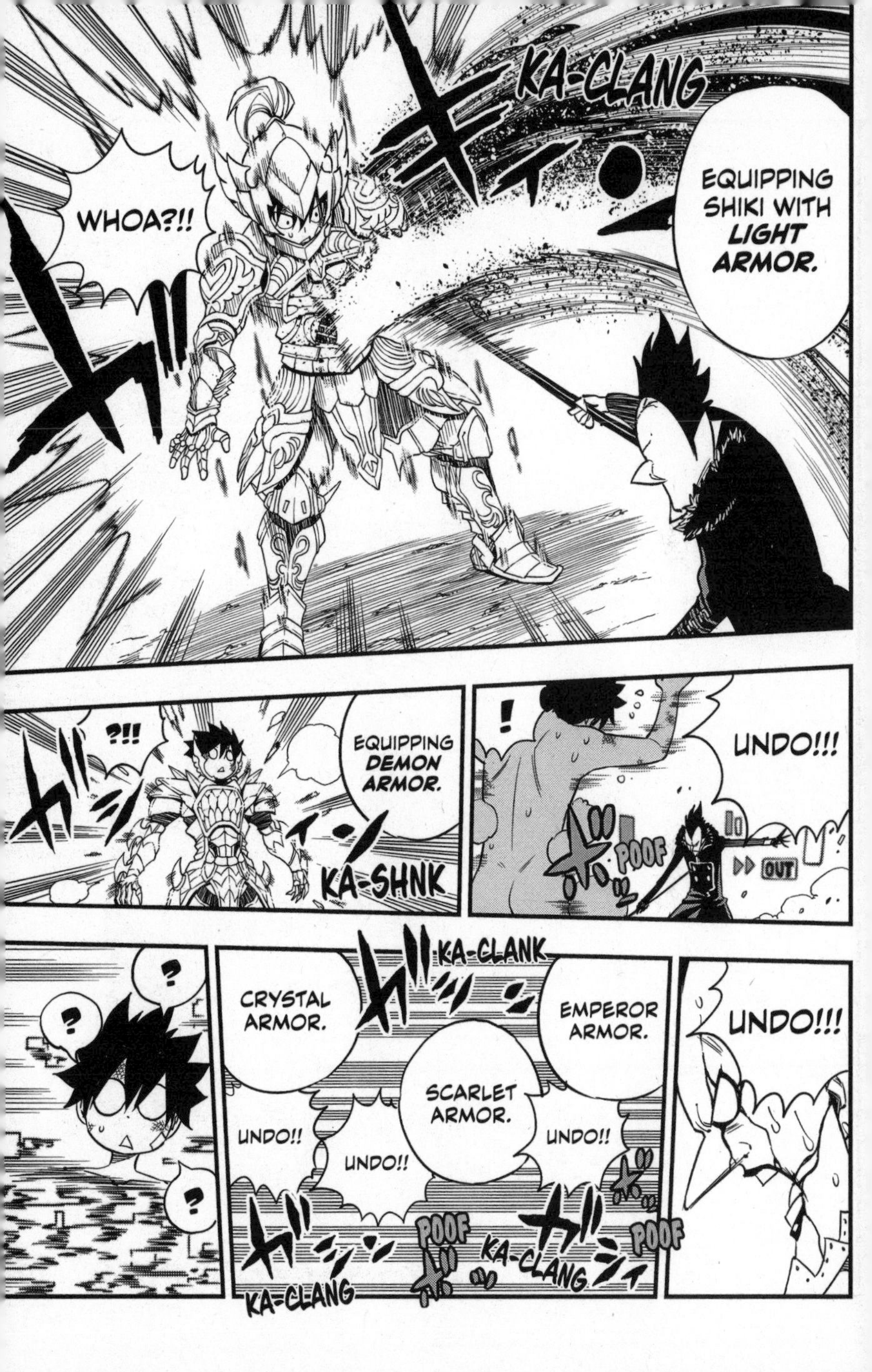
KA-CLANG
EQUIPPING SHIKI WITH LIGHT ARMOR.
WHOA?!!
UNDO!!!
!
POOF
OUT
EQUIPPING DEMON ARMOR.
KA-SHNK
?!!
UNDO!!!
EMPEROR ARMOR.
KA-CLANK
CRYSTAL ARMOR.
SCARLET ARMOR.
UNDO!!
UNDO!!
UNDO!!
POOF
KA-CLANG
POOF
KA-CLANG
?
?
?

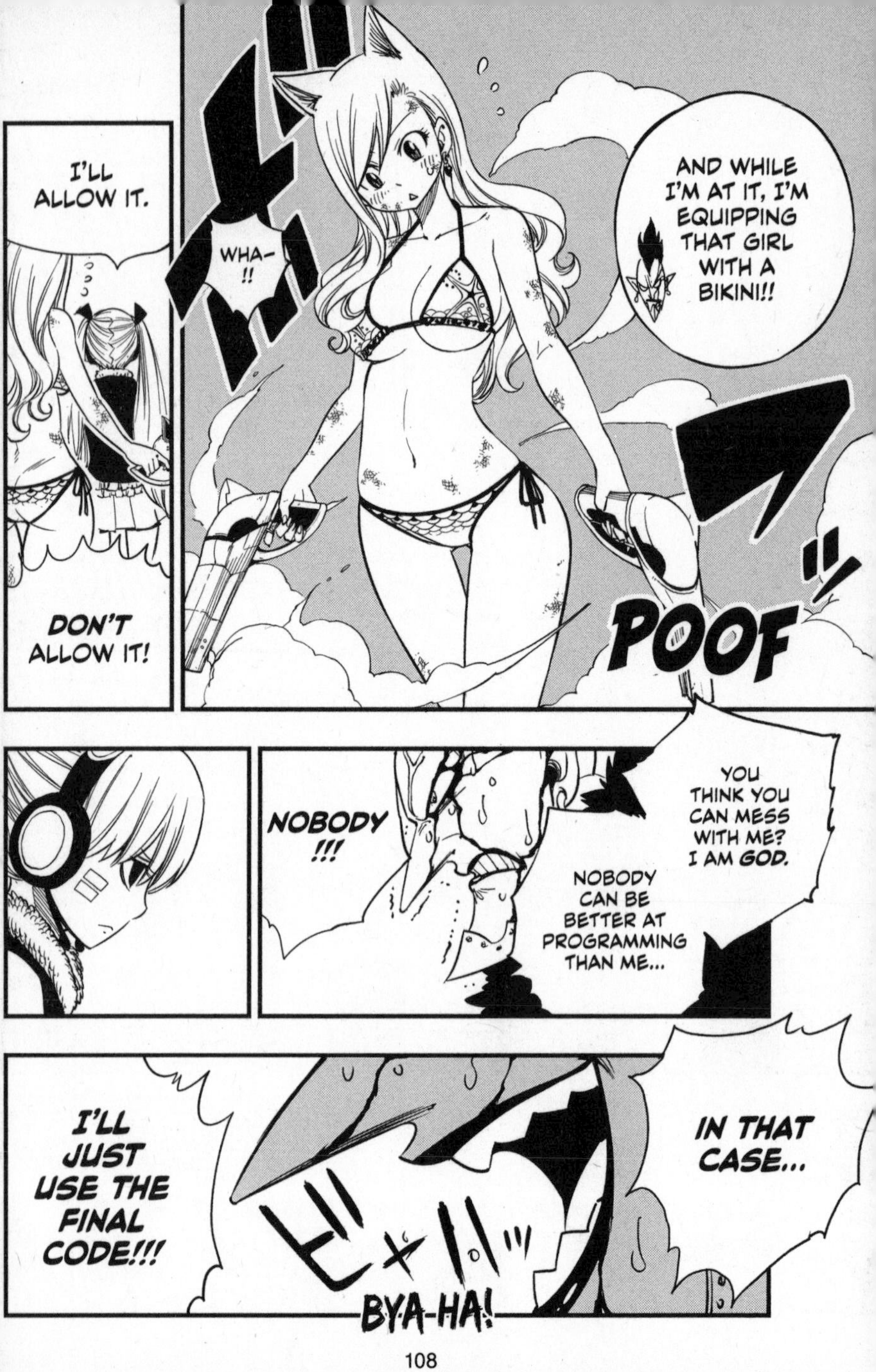
AND WHILE I'M AT IT, I'M EQUIPPING THAT GIRL WITH A BIKINI!!
WHA-!!
POOF
I'LL ALLOW IT.
DON'T ALLOW IT!
YOU THINK YOU CAN MESS WITH ME? I AM GOD.
NOBODY CAN BE BETTER AT PROGRAMMING THAN ME...
NOBODY!!!
IN THAT CASE...
I'LL JUST USE THE FINAL CODE!!!
BYA-HA!

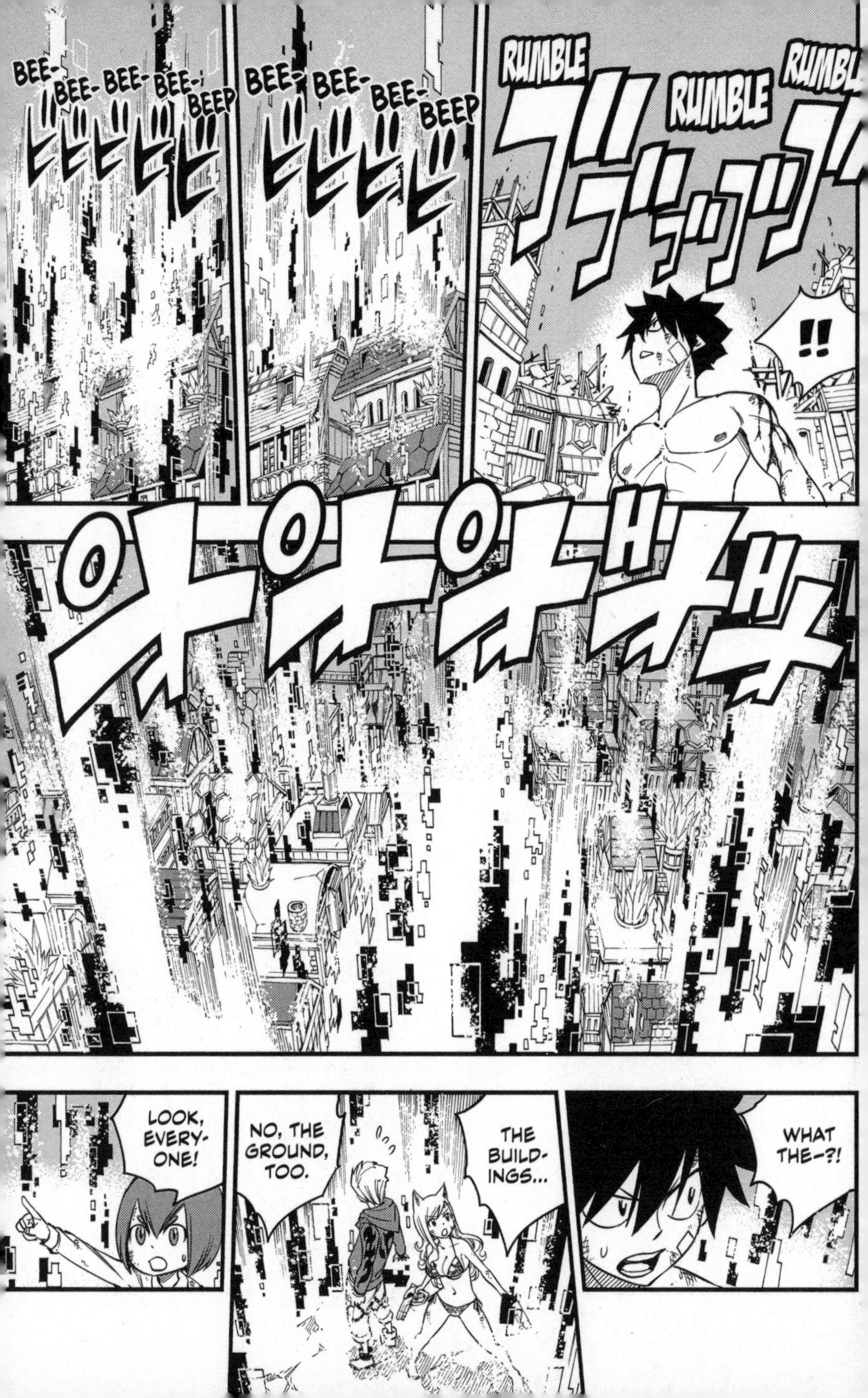
RUMBLE
RUMBLE
RUMBL
!!
BEE- BEE- BEE- BEEP
BEE- BEE- BEE- BEE- BEE- BEEP
OOOHH
WHAT THE-?!
THE BUILD- INGS...
NO, THE GROUND, TOO.
LOOK, EVERY- ONE!

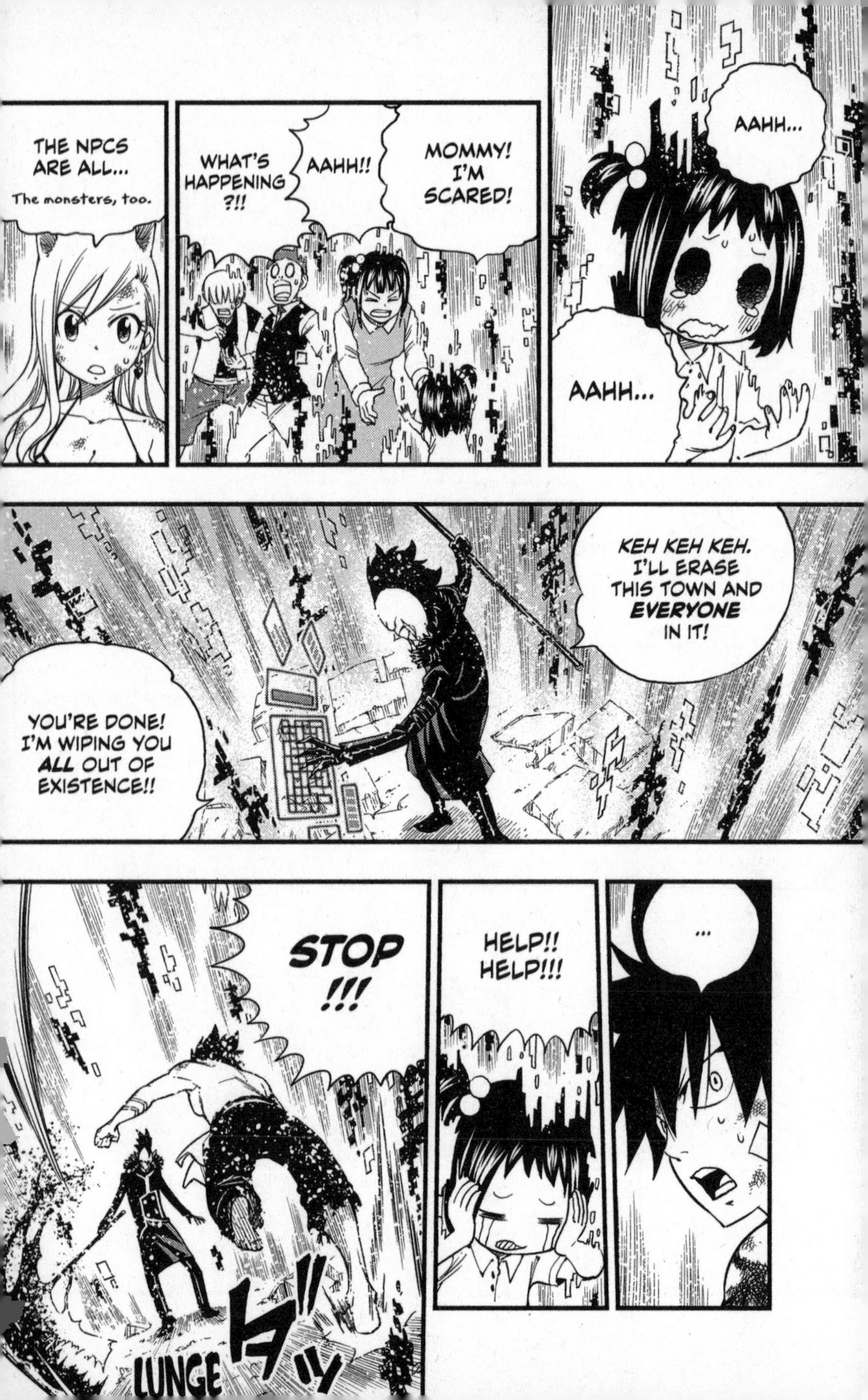
AAHH...
AAHH...
MOMMY! I'M SCARED!
AAHH!!
WHAT'S HAPPENING?!!
THE NPCS ARE ALL...
The monsters, too.
KEH KEH KEH. I'LL ERASE THIS TOWN AND EVERYONE IN IT!
YOU'RE DONE! I'M WIPING YOU ALL OUT OF EXISTENCE!!
...
HELP!! HELP!!!
STOP!!!
LUNGE

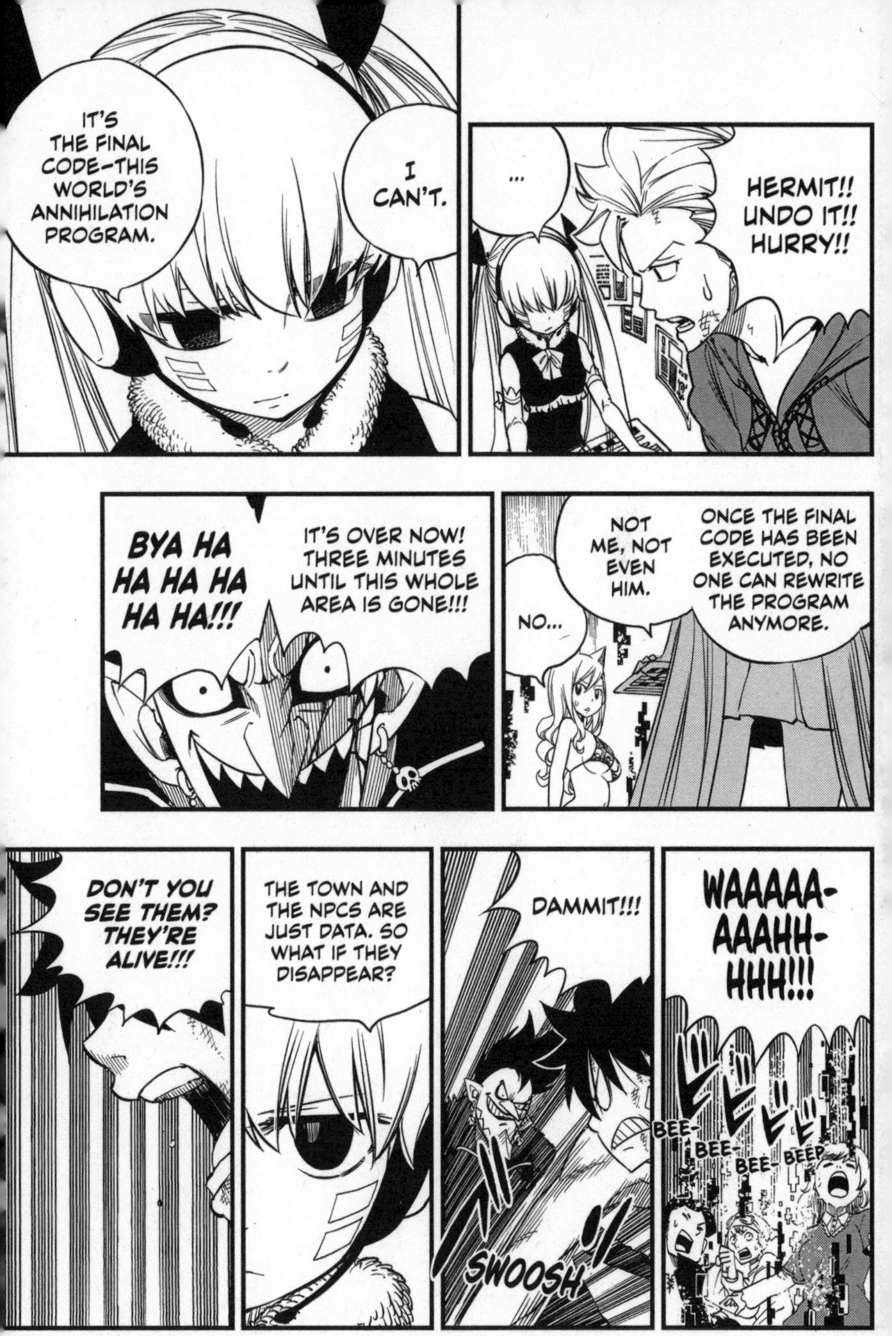
HERMIT!! UNDO IT!! HURRY!!
...
I CAN'T.
IT'S THE FINAL CODE—THIS WORLD'S ANNIHILATION PROGRAM.
ONCE THE FINAL CODE HAS BEEN EXECUTED, NO ONE CAN REWRITE THE PROGRAM ANYMORE.
NOT ME, NOT EVEN HIM.
NO...
IT'S OVER NOW! THREE MINUTES UNTIL THIS WHOLE AREA IS GONE!!!
BYA HA HA HA HA HA HA!!!
WAAAAA-AAAHH-HHH!!!
BEE- BEE- BEE- BEEP
DAMMIT!!!
SWOOSH
THE TOWN AND THE NPCS ARE JUST DATA. SO WHAT IF THEY DISAPPEAR?
DON'T YOU SEE THEM? THEY'RE ALIVE!!!

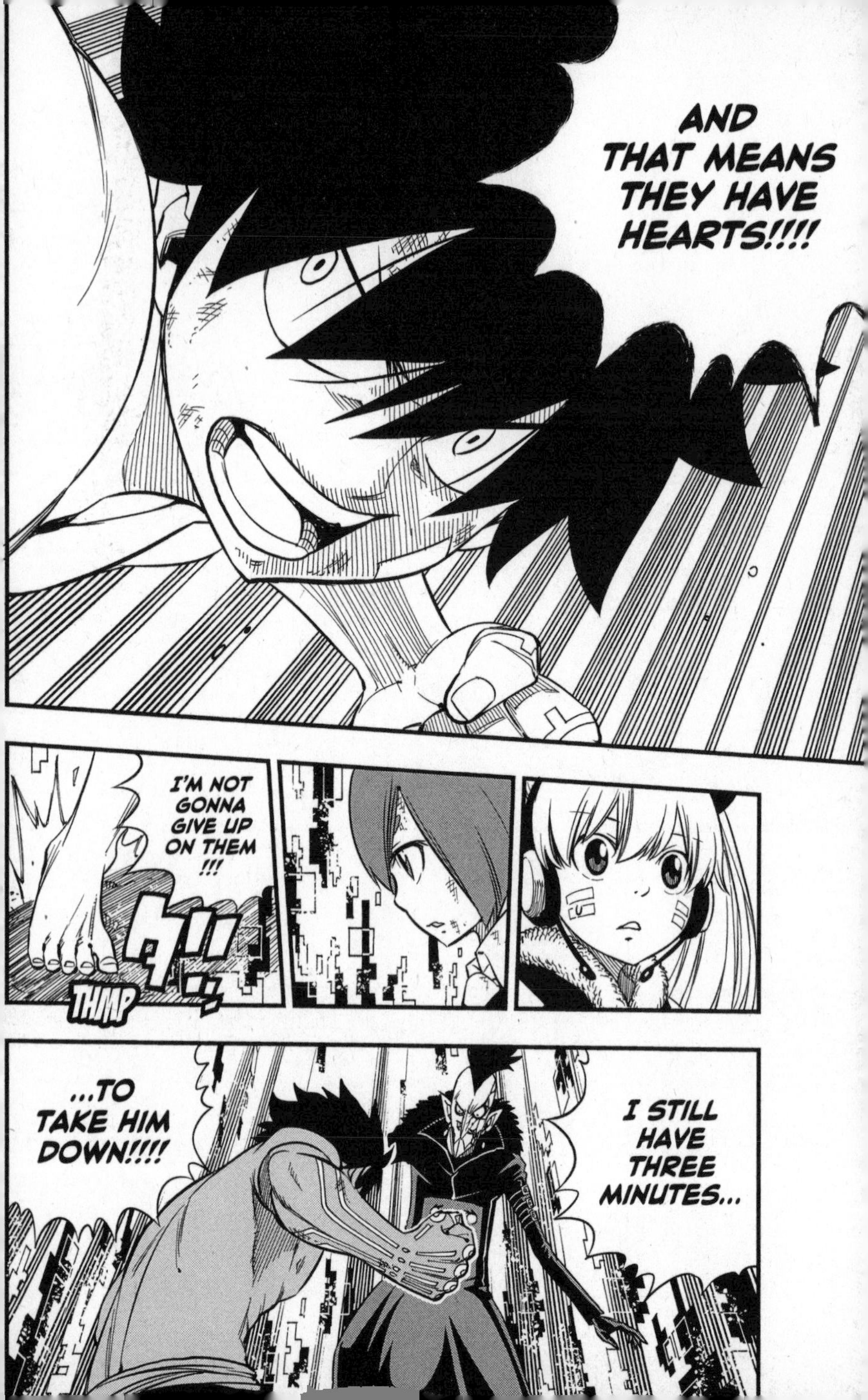
AND THAT MEANS THEY HAVE HEARTS!!!!
I'M NOT GONNA GIVE UP ON THEM!!!
THMP
I STILL HAVE THREE MINUTES...
...TO TAKE HIM DOWN!!!!

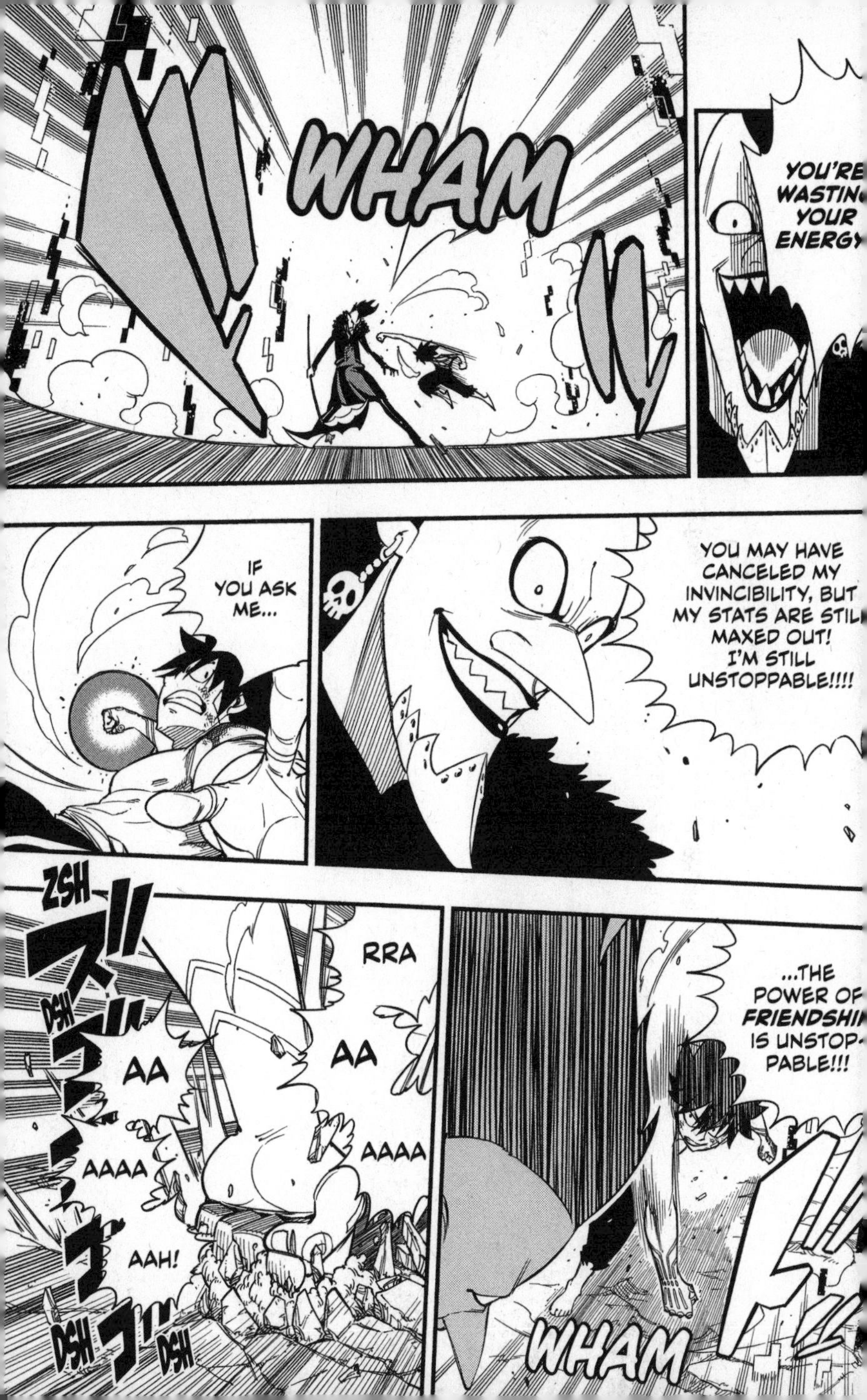
YOU'RE WASTING YOUR ENERGY
WHAM
YOU MAY HAVE CANCELED MY INVINCIBILITY, BUT MY STATS ARE STILL MAXED OUT! I'M STILL UNSTOPPABLE!!!!
IF YOU ASK ME...
...THE POWER OF FRIENDSHIP IS UNSTOP-PABLE!!!
WHAM
RRA
AA
AAAA
AA
AAAA
AAH!
ZSH
DSH
DSH
DSH

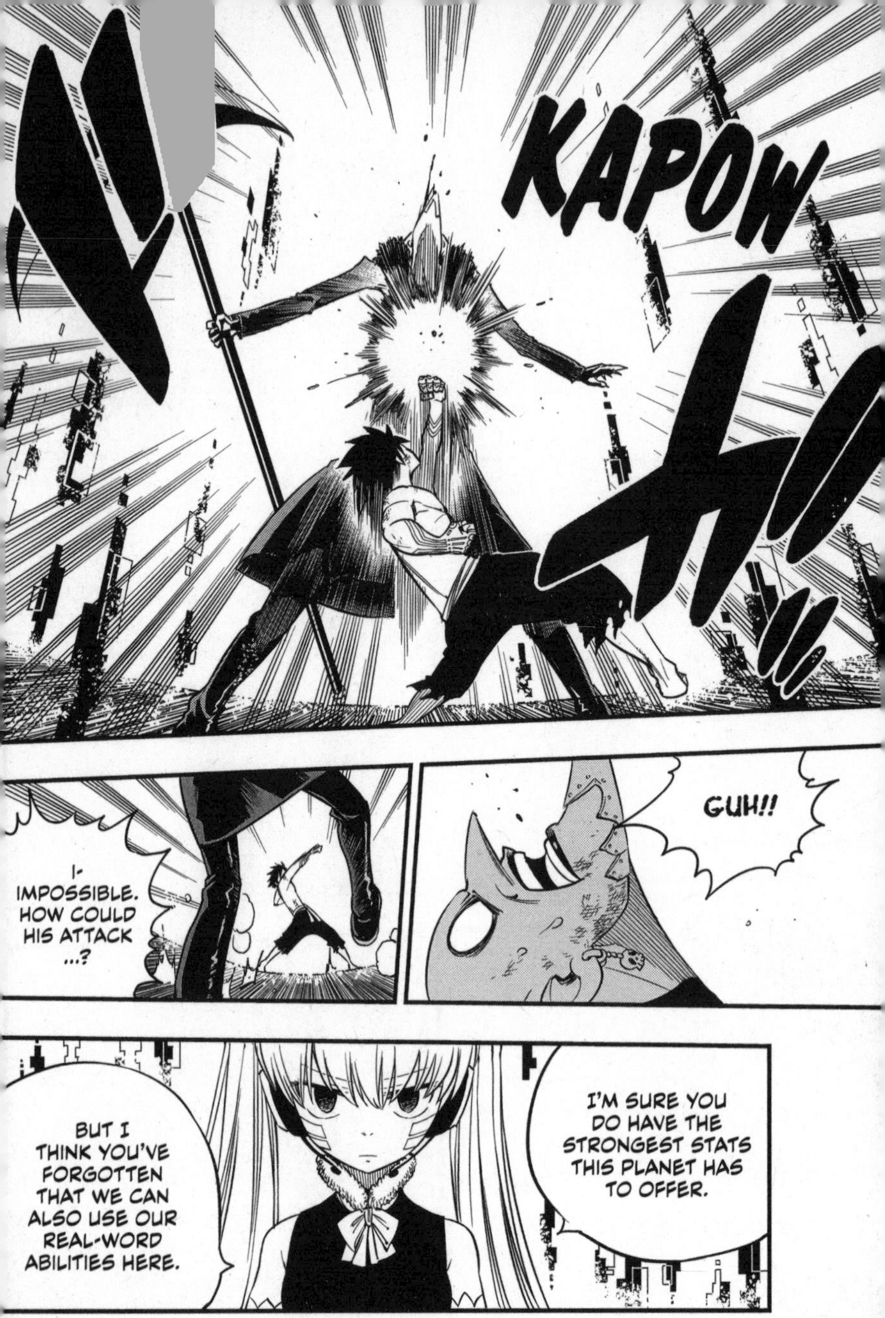
KAPOW
GUH!!
I- IMPOSSIBLE. HOW COULD HIS ATTACK ...?
I'M SURE YOU DO HAVE THE STRONGEST STATS THIS PLANET HAS TO OFFER.
BUT I THINK YOU'VE FORGOTTEN THAT WE CAN ALSO USE OUR REAL-WORD ABILITIES HERE.

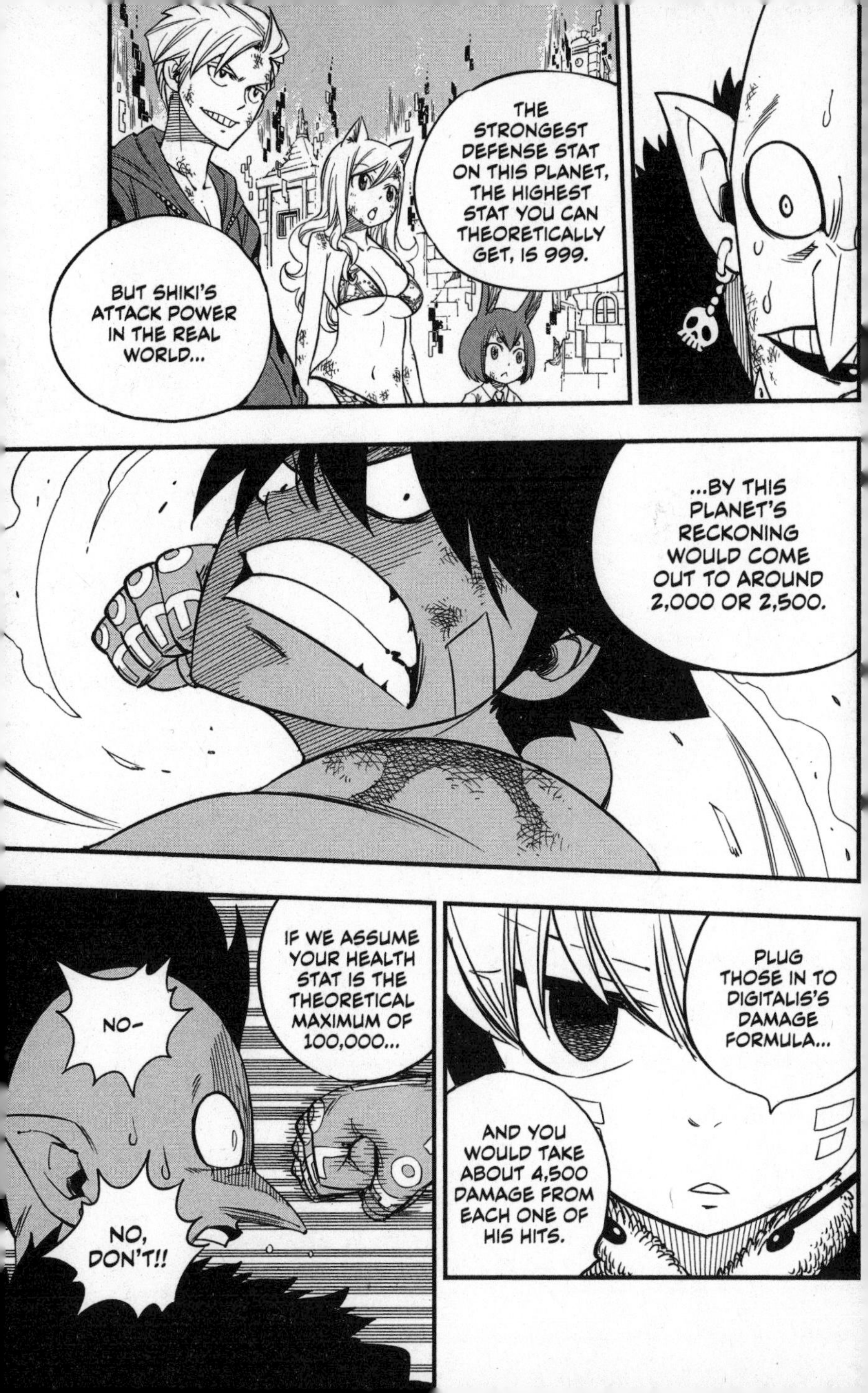
THE STRONGEST DEFENSE STAT ON THIS PLANET, THE HIGHEST STAT YOU CAN THEORETICALLY GET, IS 999.
BUT SHIKI'S ATTACK POWER IN THE REAL WORLD...
...BY THIS PLANET'S RECKONING WOULD COME OUT TO AROUND 2,000 OR 2,500.
PLUG THOSE IN TO DIGITALIS'S DAMAGE FORMULA...
AND YOU WOULD TAKE ABOUT 4,500 DAMAGE FROM EACH ONE OF HIS HITS.
IF WE ASSUME YOUR HEALTH STAT IS THE THEORETICAL MAXIMUM OF 100,000...
NO-
NO, DON'T!!

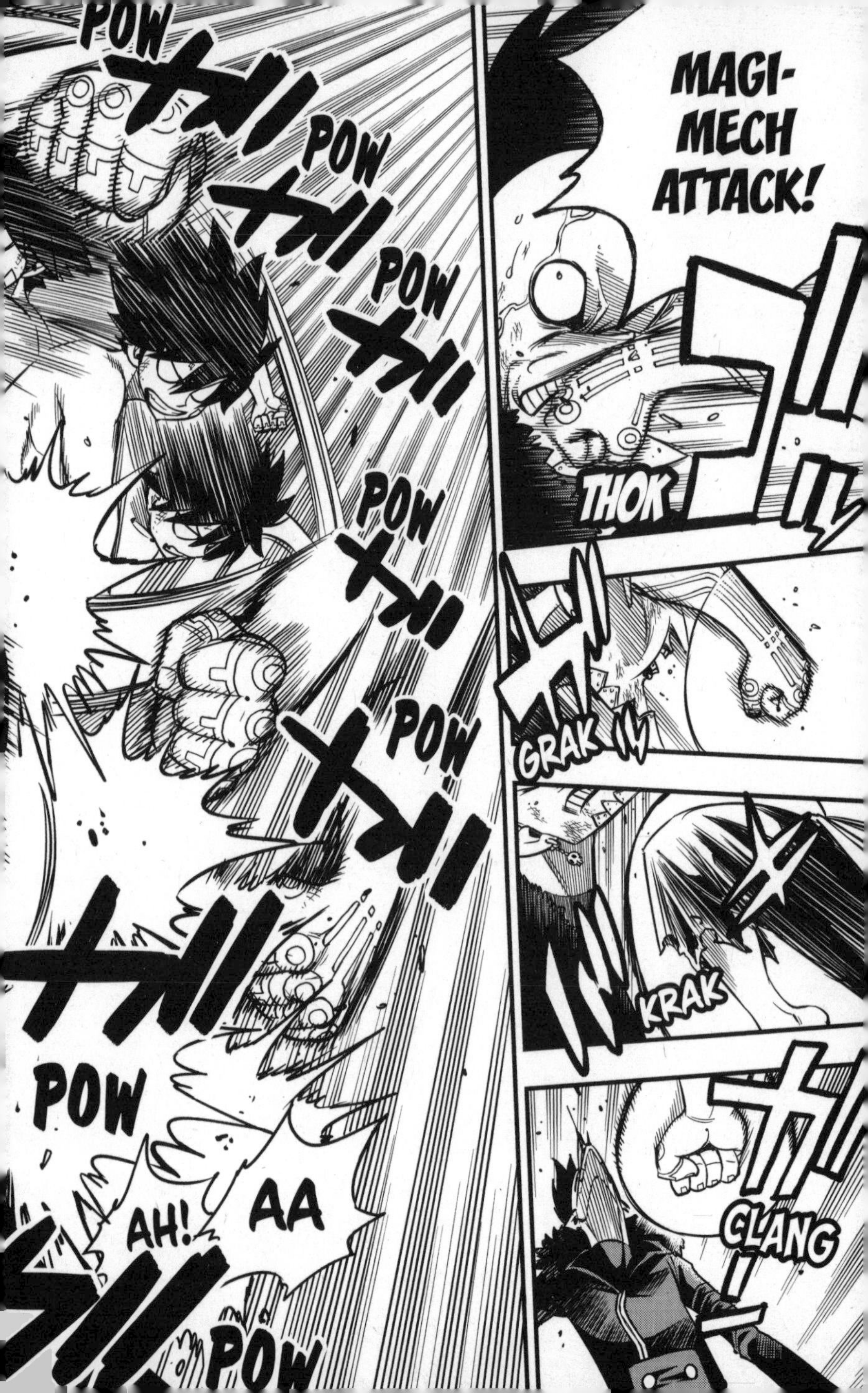
MAGI-MECH ATTACK!
THOK
GRAK
KRAK
CLANG
POW
POW
POW
POW
POW
POW
AA
AH!
POW

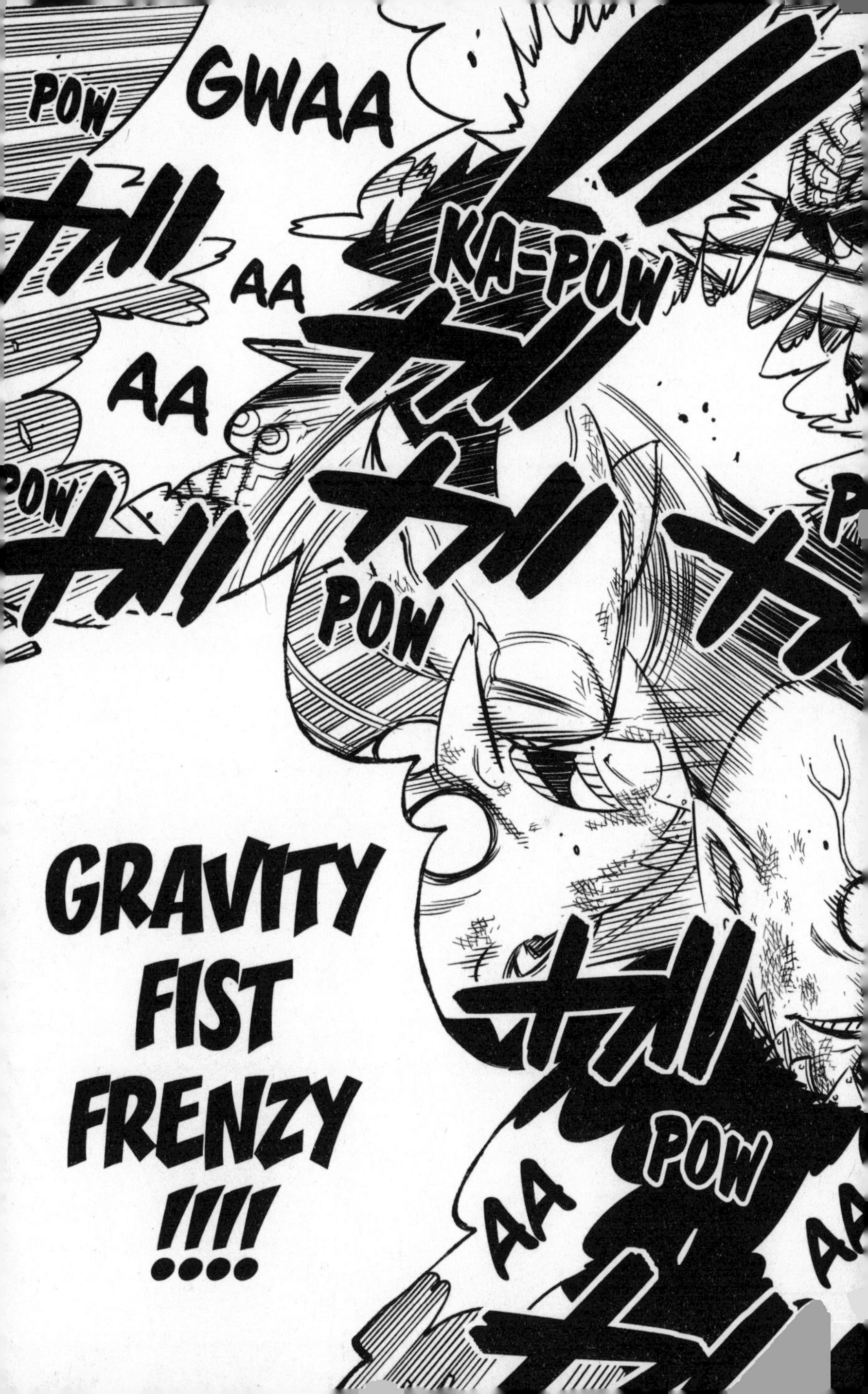
KA-POW
GWAA
AA
AA
POW
POW
POW
GRAVITY FIST FRENZY!!!!
POW
AA

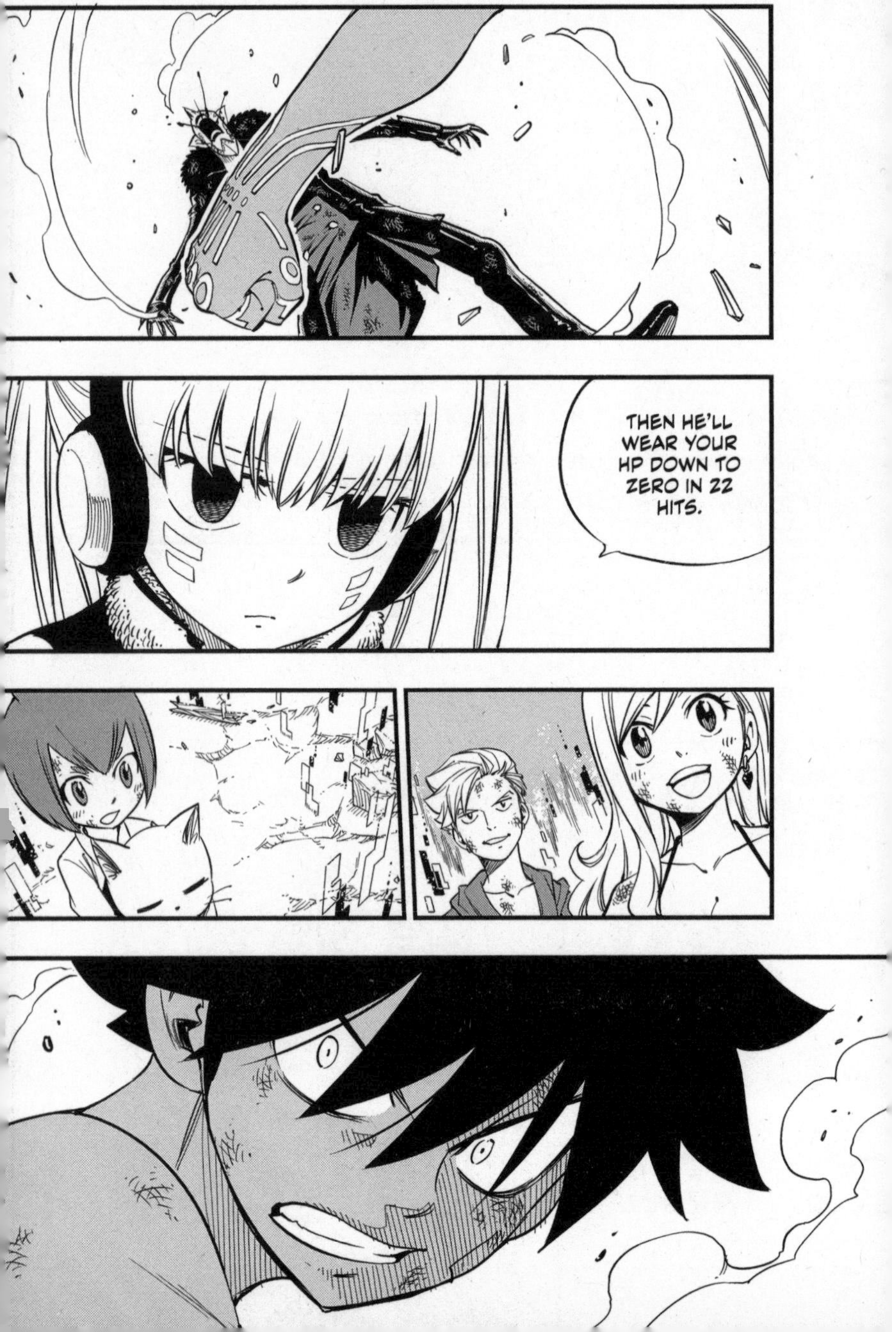
THEN HE'LL WEAR YOUR HP DOWN TO ZERO IN 22 HITS.

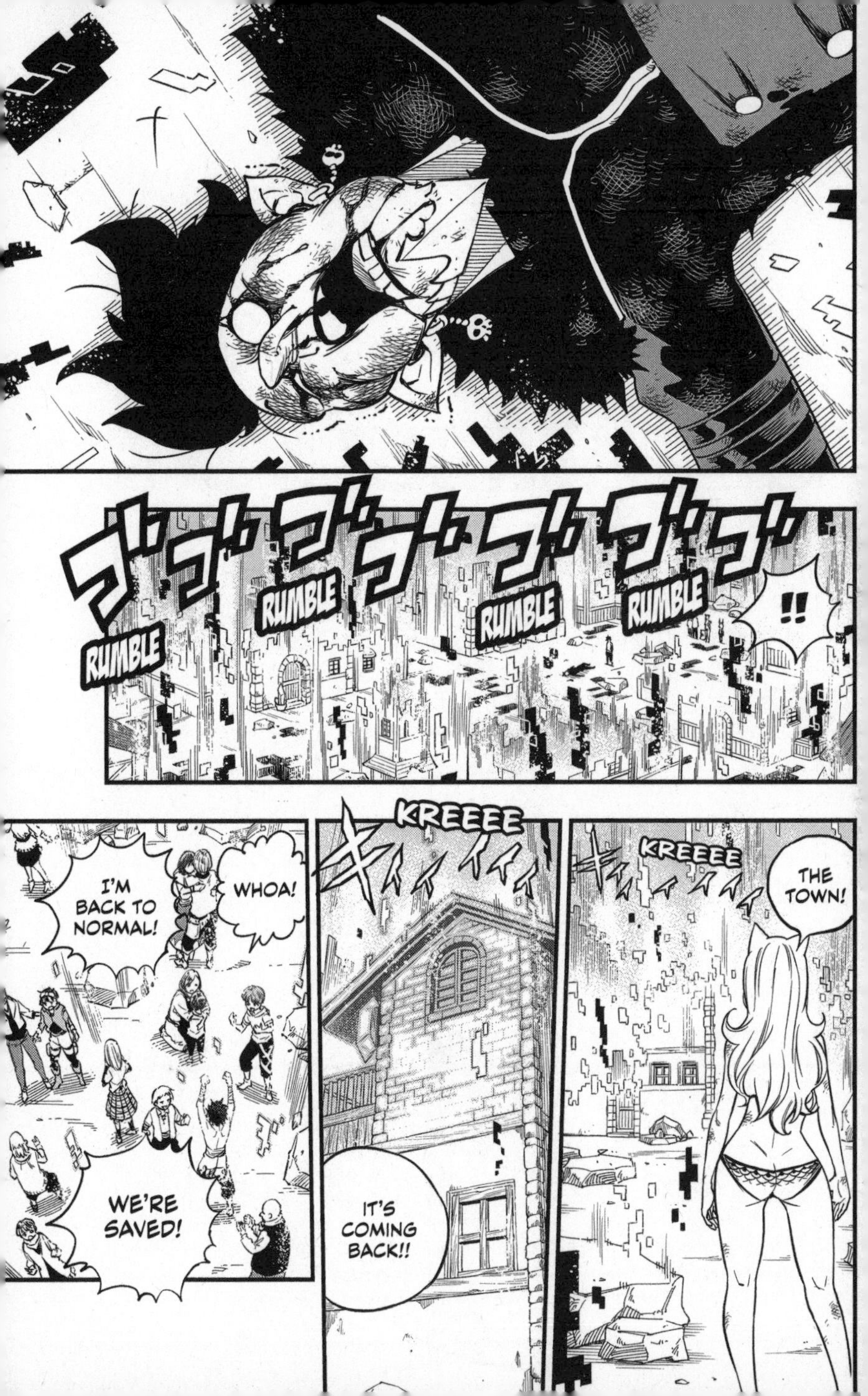
!!
RUMBLE
RUMBLE
RUMBLE
RUMBLE
KREEEE
THE TOWN!
KREEEE
IT'S COMING BACK!!
WHOA!
I'M BACK TO NORMAL!
WE'RE SAVED!

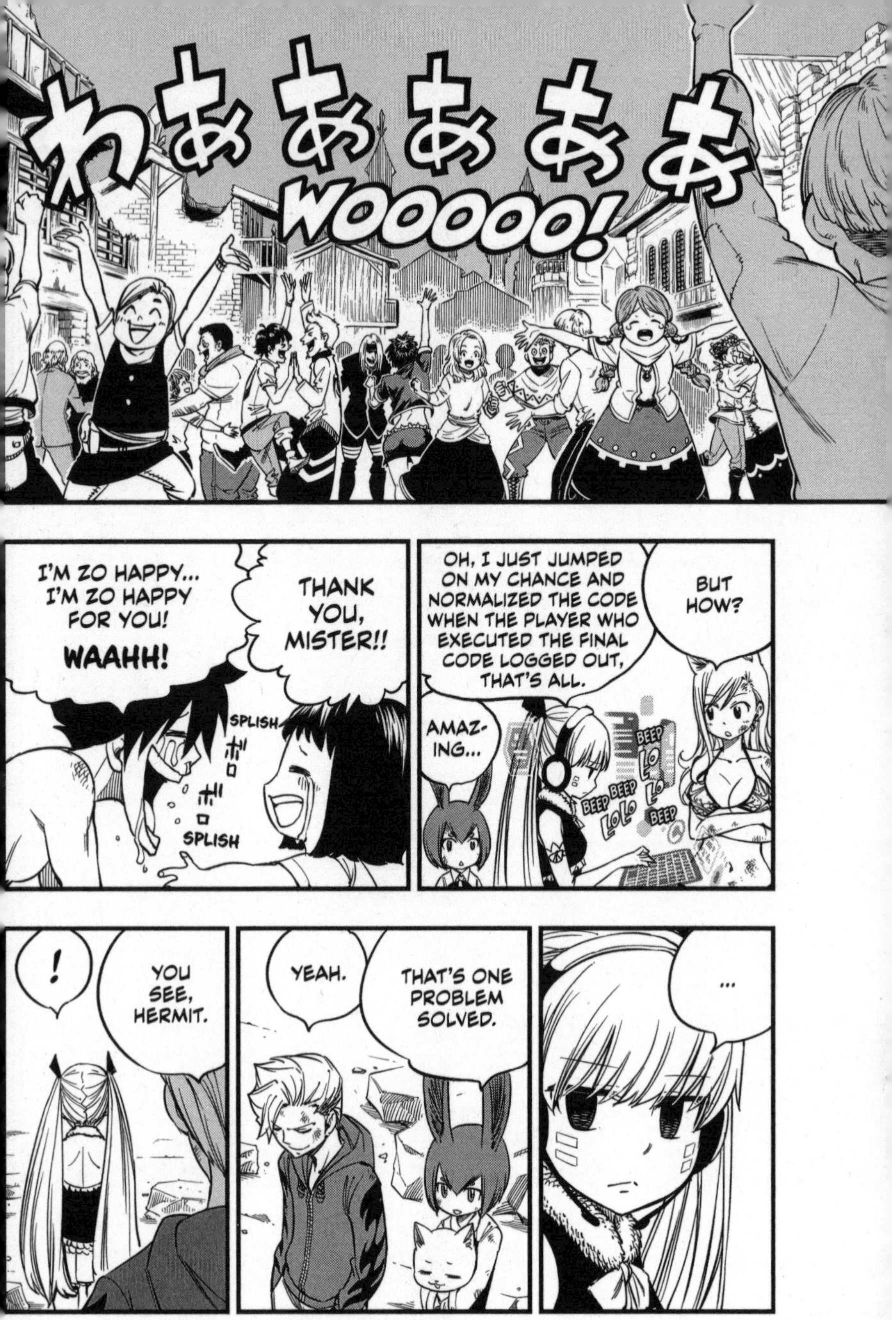
わああああああ
WOOOOO!
BUT HOW?
OH, I JUST JUMPED ON MY CHANCE AND NORMALIZED THE CODE WHEN THE PLAYER WHO EXECUTED THE FINAL CODE LOGGED OUT, THAT'S ALL.
AMAZ-ING...
BEEP
BEEP BEEP
BEEP
BEEP
THANK YOU, MISTER!!
I'M ZO HAPPY... I'M ZO HAPPY FOR YOU!
WAAHH!
SPLISH
SPLISH
...
THAT'S ONE PROBLEM SOLVED.
YEAH.
YOU SEE, HERMIT.
!

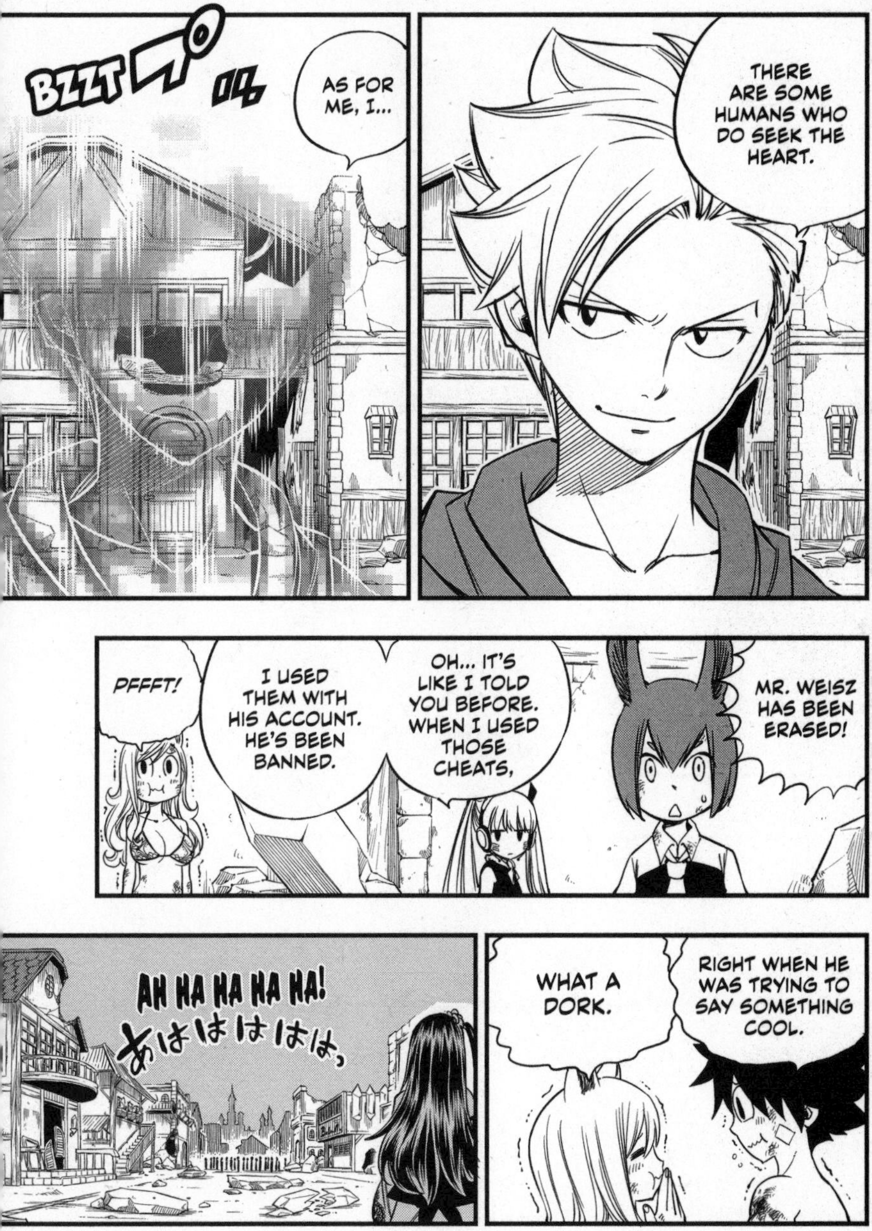
THERE ARE SOME HUMANS WHO DO SEEK THE HEART.
AS FOR ME, I...
BZZT
MR. WEISZ HAS BEEN ERASED!
OH... IT'S LIKE I TOLD YOU BEFORE. WHEN I USED THOSE CHEATS,
I USED THEM WITH HIS ACCOUNT. HE'S BEEN BANNED.
PFFFT!
RIGHT WHEN HE WAS TRYING TO SAY SOMETHING COOL.
WHAT A DORK.
AH HA HA HA HA!
あははははは,

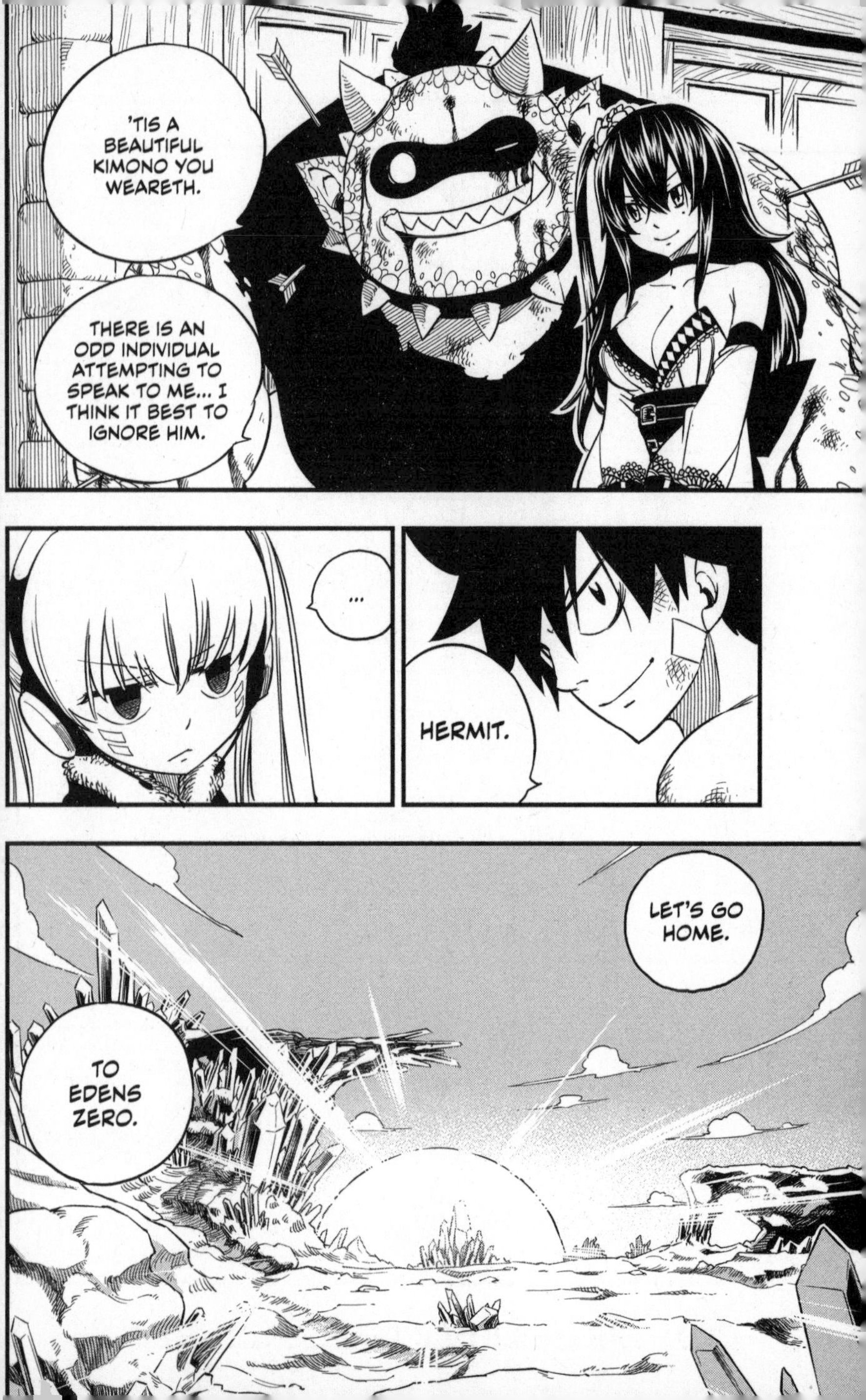
'TIS A BEAUTIFUL KIMONO YOU WEARETH.
THERE IS AN ODD INDIVIDUAL ATTEMPTING TO SPEAK TO ME... I THINK IT BEST TO IGNORE HIM.
HERMIT.
...
LET'S GO HOME.
TO EDENS ZERO.

CHAPTER 39: SPIDER THE GENIUS HACKER

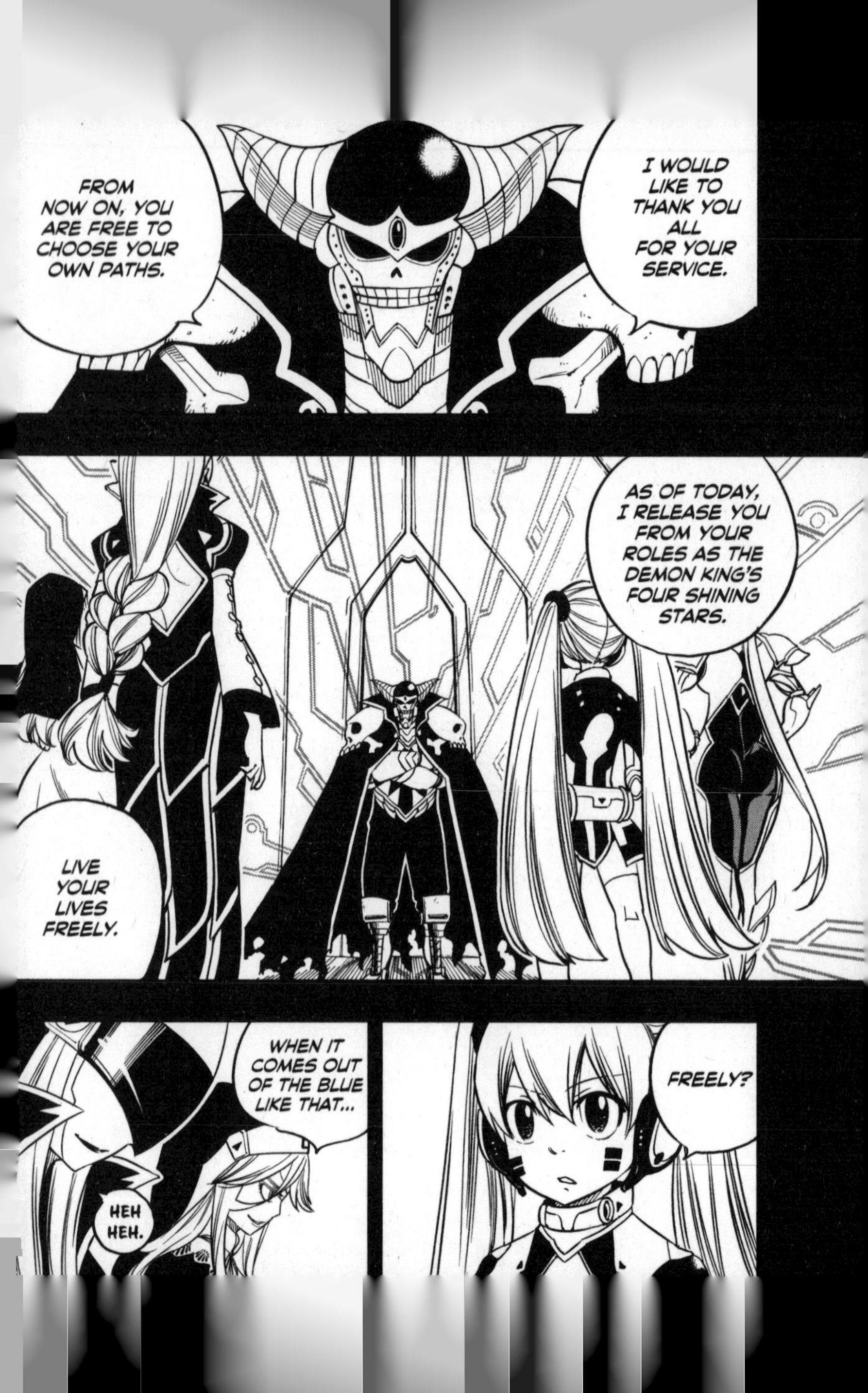
I WOULD LIKE TO THANK YOU ALL FOR YOUR SERVICE.
FROM NOW ON, YOU ARE FREE TO CHOOSE YOUR OWN PATHS.
AS OF TODAY, I RELEASE YOU FROM YOUR ROLES AS THE DEMON KING'S FOUR SHINING STARS.
LIVE YOUR LIVES FREELY.
FREELY?
WHEN IT COMES OUT OF THE BLUE LIKE THAT...
HEH HEH.

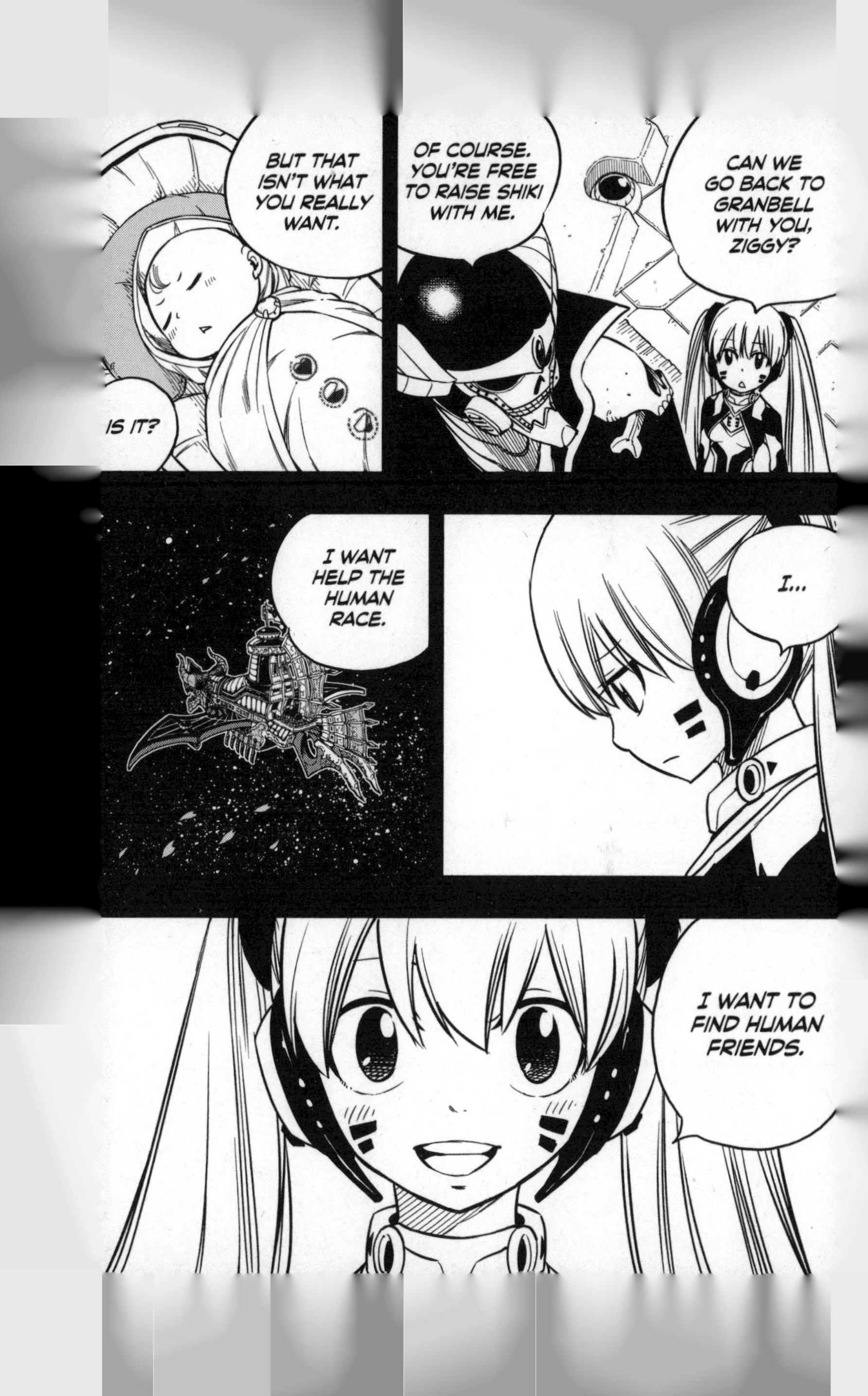
CAN WE GO BACK TO GRANBELL WITH YOU, ZIGGY?
OF COURSE. YOU'RE FREE TO RAISE SHIKI WITH ME.
BUT THAT ISN'T WHAT YOU REALLY WANT.
IS IT?
I...
I WANT HELP THE HUMAN RACE.
I WANT TO FIND HUMAN FRIENDS.

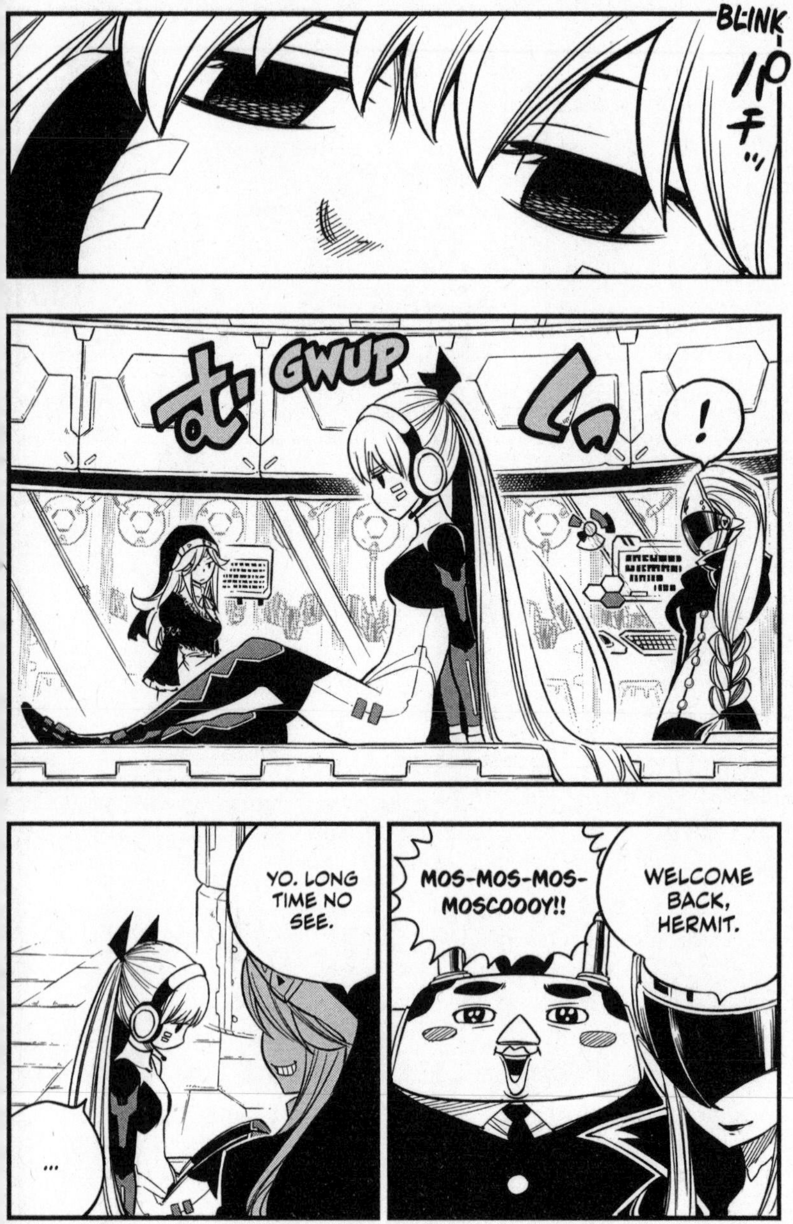
BLINK
パチッ
!
GWUP
WELCOME BACK, HERMIT.
MOS-MOS-MOS-MOSCOOOY!!
YO. LONG TIME NO SEE.
...

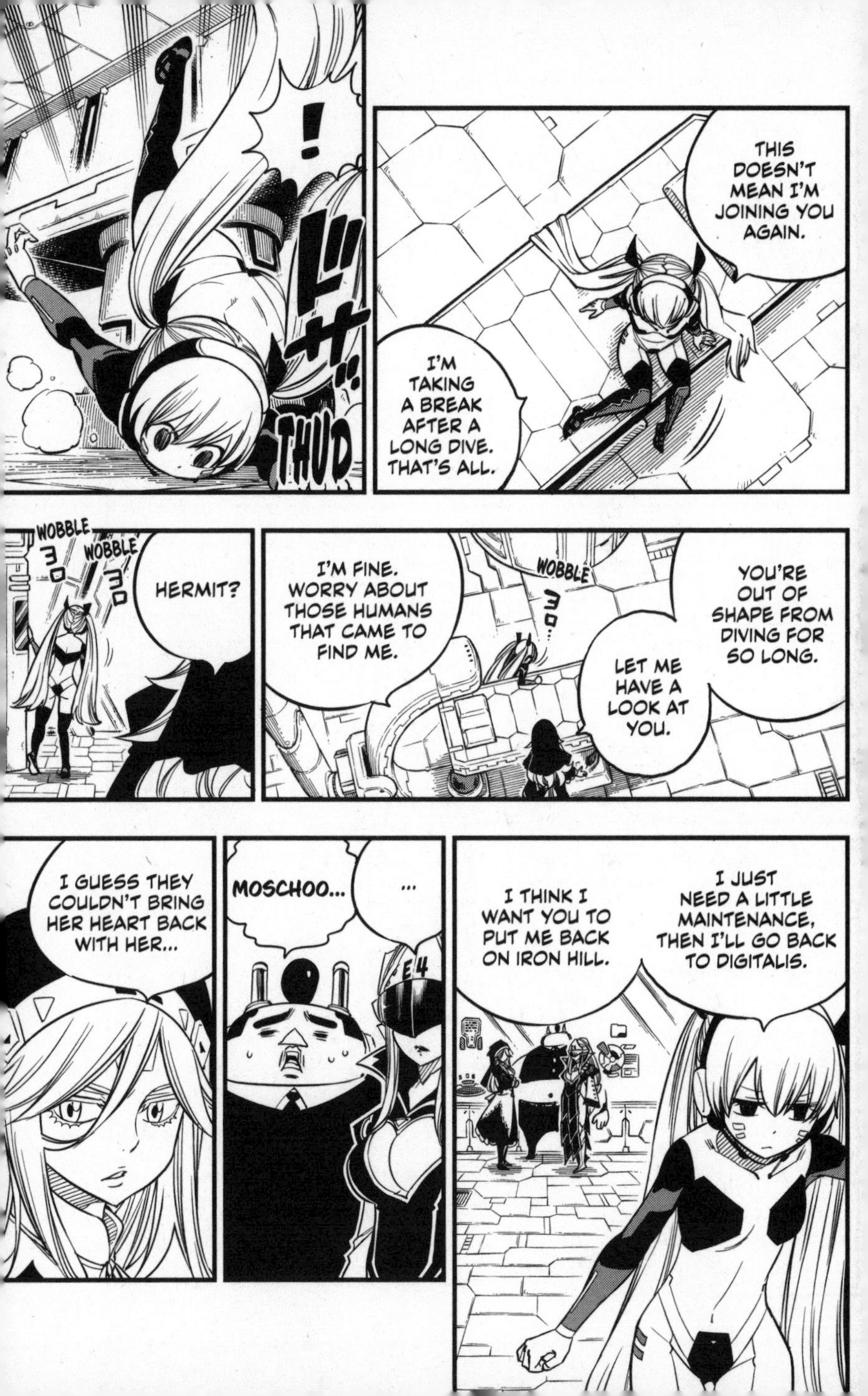
THIS DOESN'T MEAN I'M JOINING YOU AGAIN.
I'M TAKING A BREAK AFTER A LONG DIVE. THAT'S ALL.
!
THUD
YOU'RE OUT OF SHAPE FROM DIVING FOR SO LONG.
LET ME HAVE A LOOK AT YOU.
WOBBLE
I'M FINE. WORRY ABOUT THOSE HUMANS THAT CAME TO FIND ME.
HERMIT?
WOBBLE
WOBBLE
I JUST NEED A LITTLE MAINTENANCE, THEN I'LL GO BACK TO DIGITALIS.
I THINK I WANT YOU TO PUT ME BACK ON IRON HILL.
...
MOSCHOO...
I GUESS THEY COULDN'T BRING HER HEART BACK WITH HER...

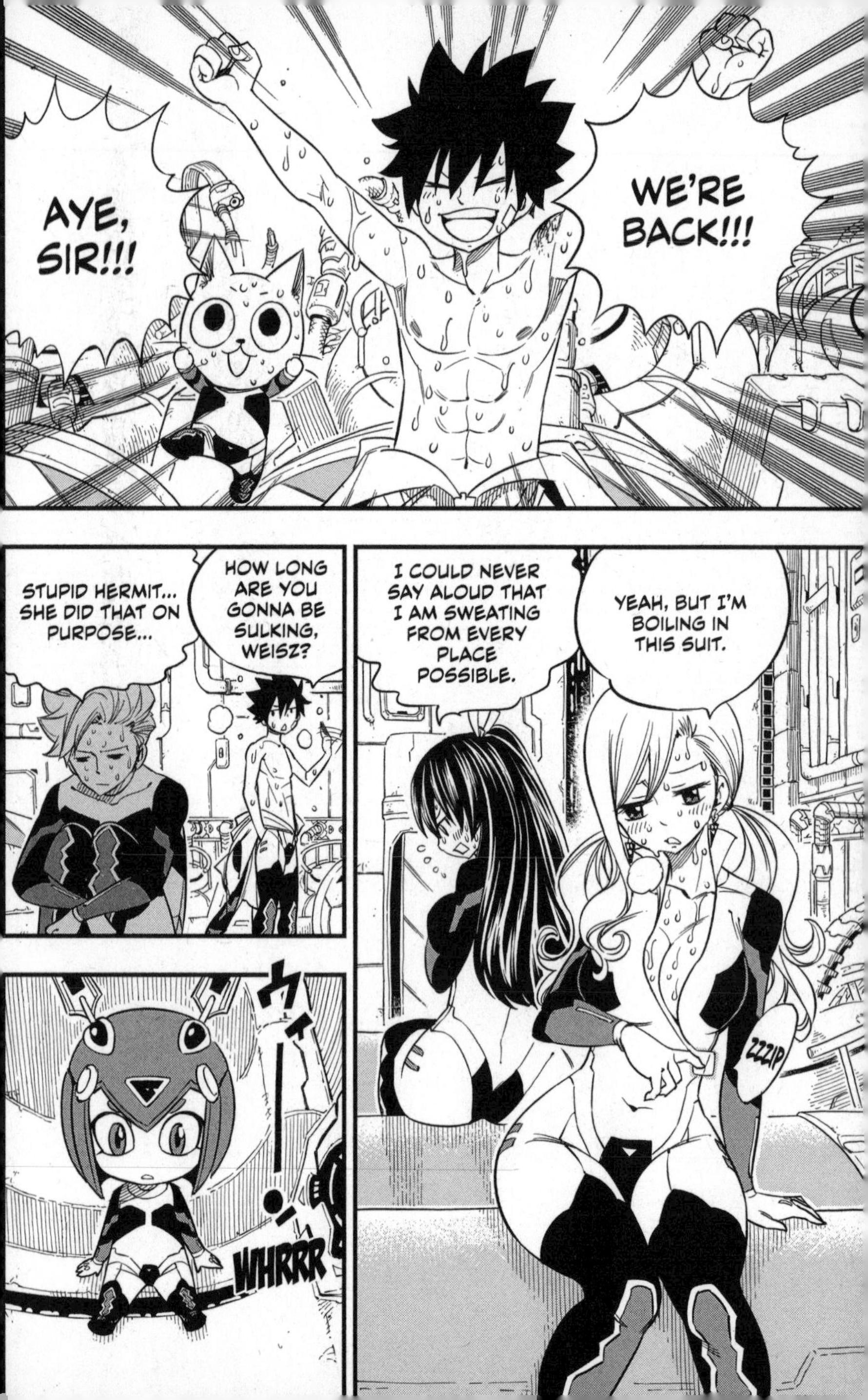

WE'RE BACK!!!
AYE, SIR!!!
YEAH, BUT I'M BOILING IN THIS SUIT.
I COULD NEVER SAY ALOUD THAT I AM SWEATING FROM EVERY PLACE POSSIBLE.
ZZZIP
HOW LONG ARE YOU GONNA BE SULKING, WEISZ?
STUPID HERMIT... SHE DID THAT ON PURPOSE...
ウィーン
WHRRR

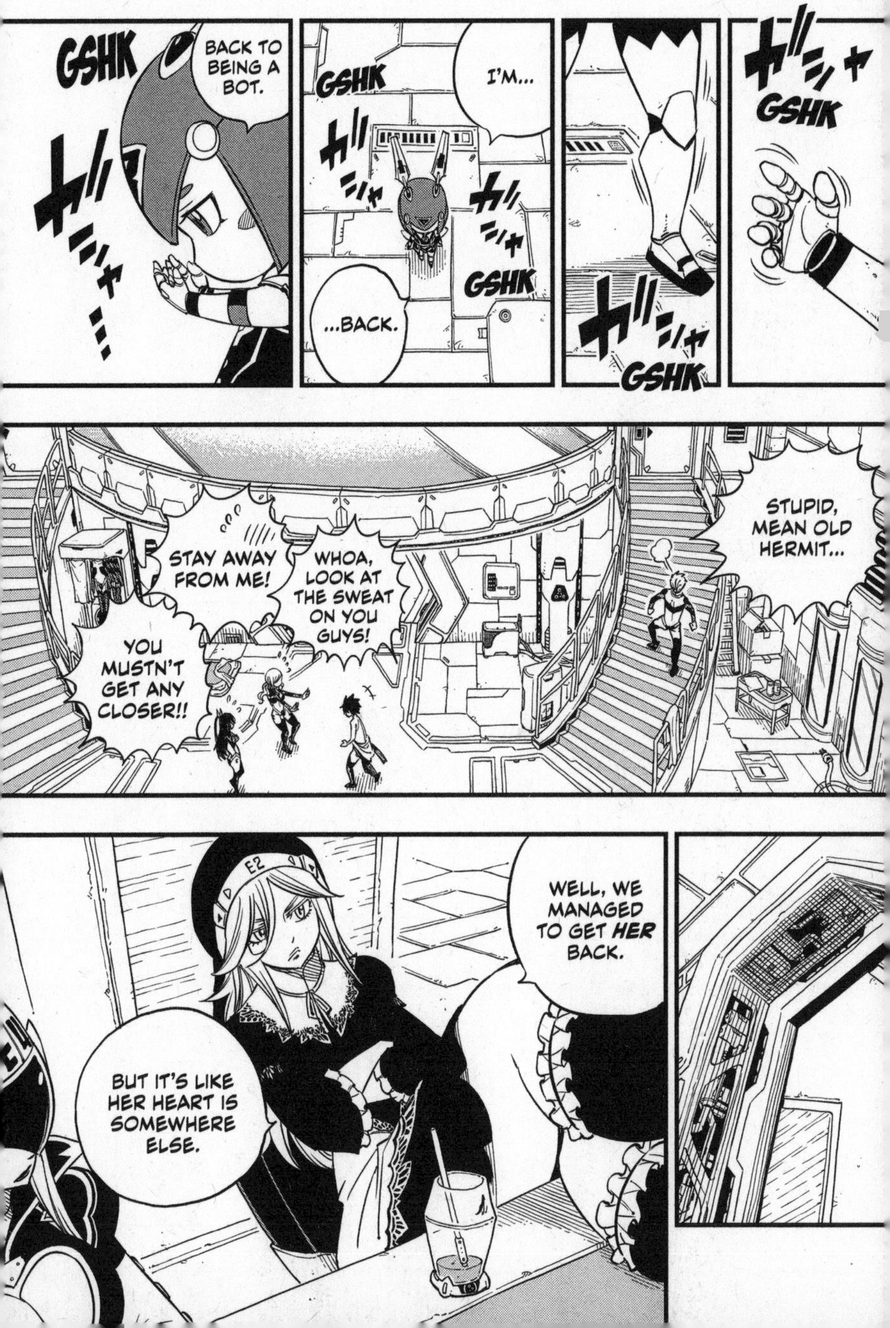
ガシャ
GSHK
ガシャ
GSHK
GSHK
I'M...
ガシャ
GSHK
...BACK.
GSHK
BACK TO BEING A BOT.
ガシャ...
STUPID, MEAN OLD HERMIT...
WHOA, LOOK AT THE SWEAT ON YOU GUYS!
STAY AWAY FROM ME!
YOU MUSTN'T GET ANY CLOSER!!
WELL, WE MANAGED TO GET *HER* BACK.
BUT IT'S LIKE HER HEART IS SOMEWHERE ELSE.

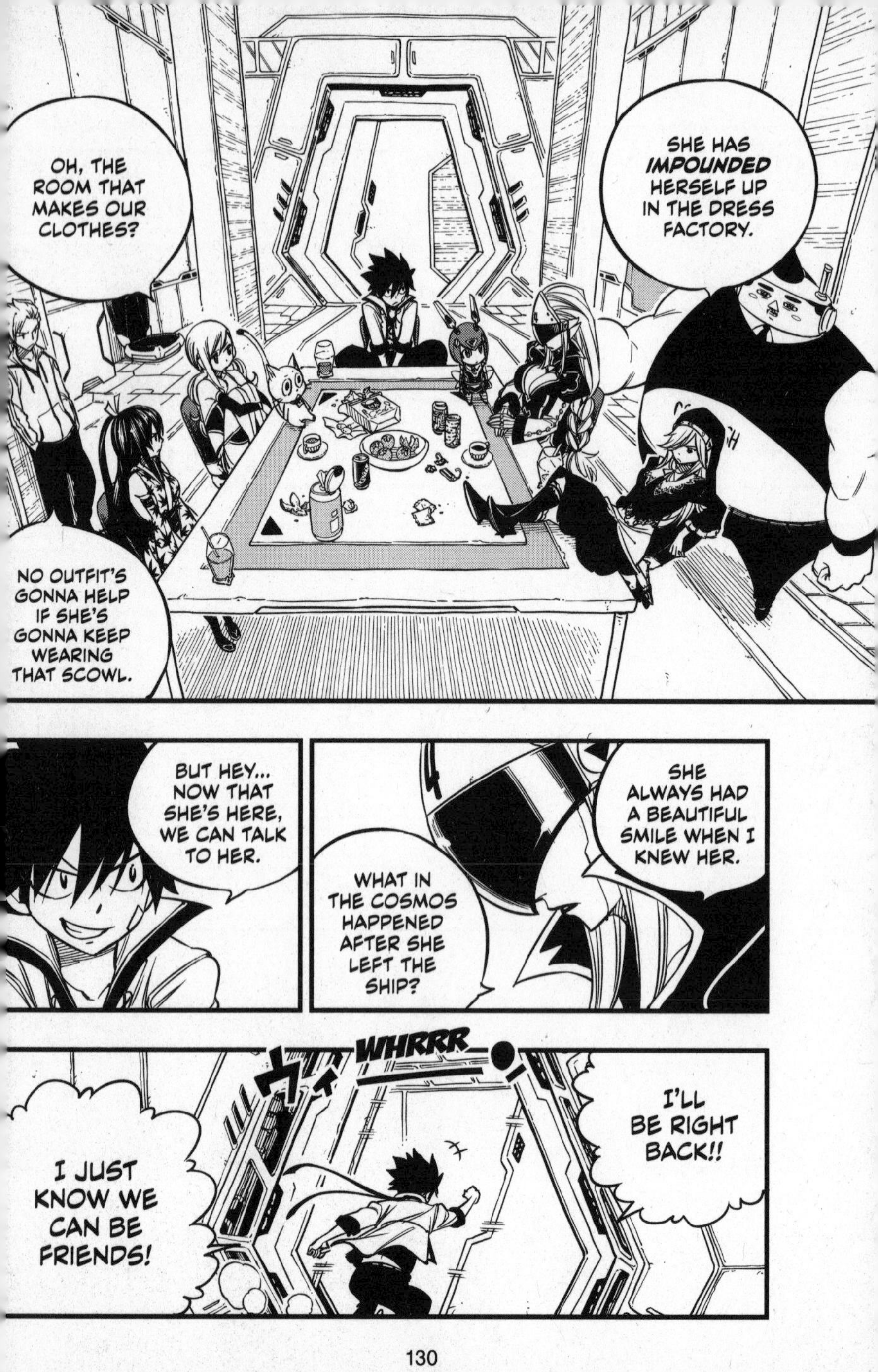
SHE HAS IMPOUNDED HERSELF UP IN THE DRESS FACTORY.
OH, THE ROOM THAT MAKES OUR CLOTHES?
NO OUTFIT'S GONNA HELP IF SHE'S GONNA KEEP WEARING THAT SCOWL.
SHE ALWAYS HAD A BEAUTIFUL SMILE WHEN I KNEW HER.
WHAT IN THE COSMOS HAPPENED AFTER SHE LEFT THE SHIP?
BUT HEY... NOW THAT SHE'S HERE, WE CAN TALK TO HER.
WHRRR
I'LL BE RIGHT BACK!!
I JUST KNOW WE CAN BE FRIENDS!

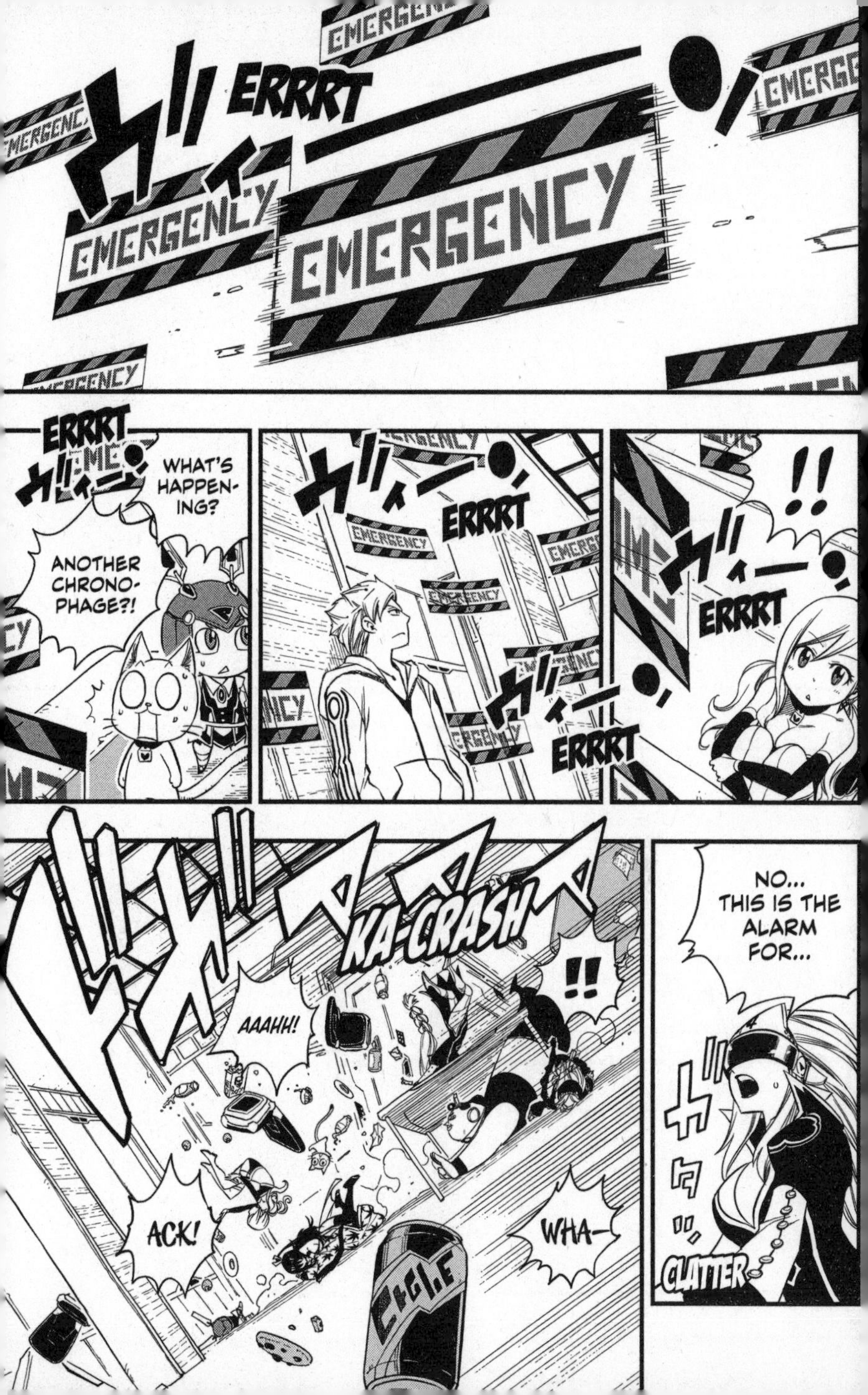
ERRRT
EMERGENCY
!!
ERRRT
ERRRT
EMERGENCY
ERRRT
ERRRT
WHAT'S HAPPEN-ING?
ANOTHER CHRONO-PHAGE?!
NO... THIS IS THE ALARM FOR...
CLATTER
KA-CRASH
!!
AAAHH!
WHA-
ACK!

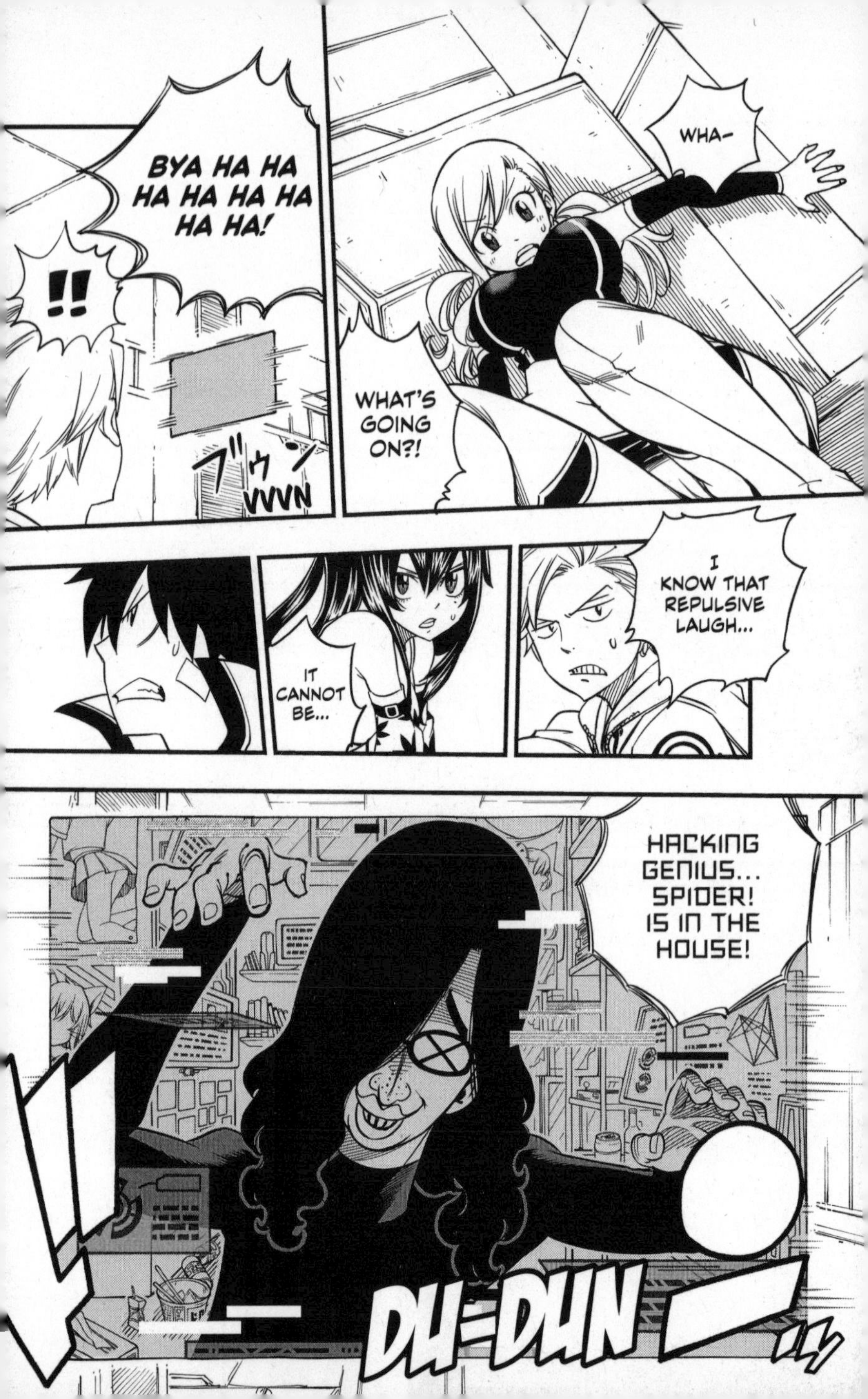
WHA-
WHAT'S GOING ON?!
BYA HA HA HA HA HA HA HA HA!
!!
ブゥン
VVVN
I KNOW THAT REPULSIVE LAUGH...
IT CANNOT BE...
HACKING GENIUS... SPIDER! IS IN THE HOUSE!
DU-DUN

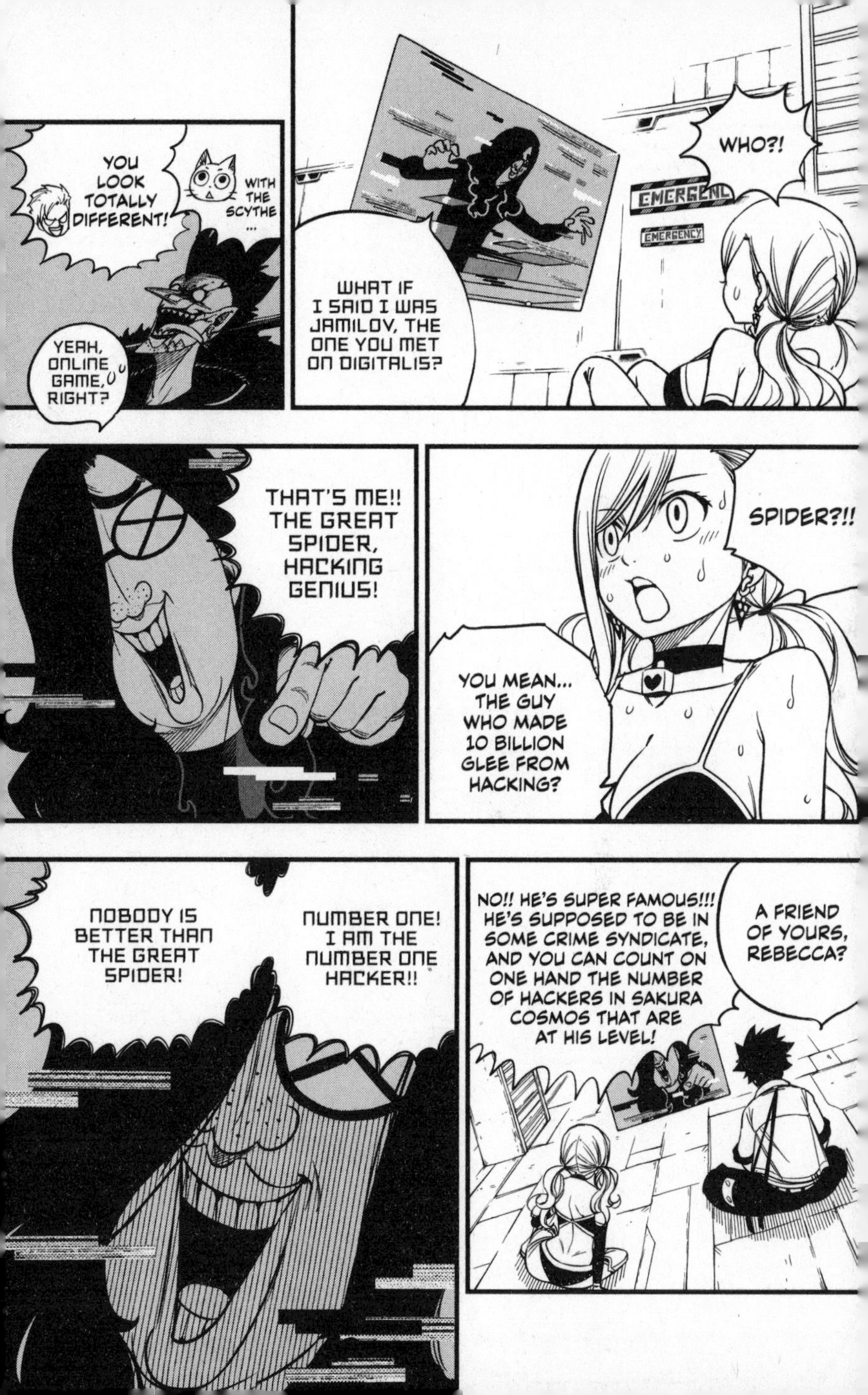
WHO?!
EMERGENCY
WHAT IF I SAID I WAS JAMILOV, THE ONE YOU MET ON DIGITALIS?
YOU LOOK TOTALLY DIFFERENT!
WITH THE SCYTHE ...
YEAH, ONLINE GAME, RIGHT?
SPIDER?!!
YOU MEAN... THE GUY WHO MADE 10 BILLION GLEE FROM HACKING?
THAT'S ME!! THE GREAT SPIDER, HACKING GENIUS!
A FRIEND OF YOURS, REBECCA?
NO!! HE'S SUPER FAMOUS!!! HE'S SUPPOSED TO BE IN SOME CRIME SYNDICATE, AND YOU CAN COUNT ON ONE HAND THE NUMBER OF HACKERS IN SAKURA COSMOS THAT ARE AT HIS LEVEL!
NUMBER ONE! I AM THE NUMBER ONE HACKER!!
NOBODY IS BETTER THAN THE GREAT SPIDER!

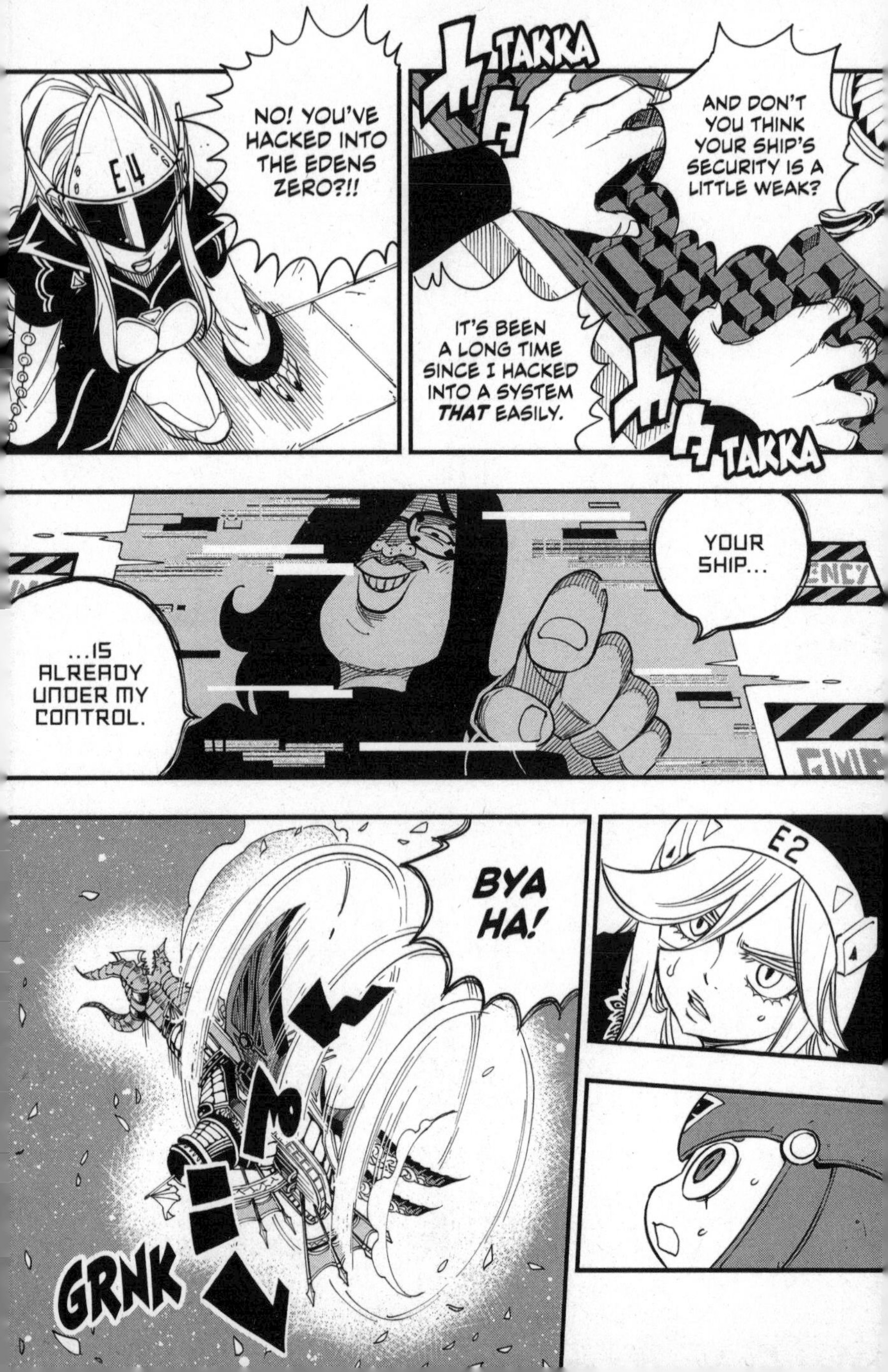
TAKKA
AND DON'T YOU THINK YOUR SHIP'S SECURITY IS A LITTLE WEAK?
IT'S BEEN A LONG TIME SINCE I HACKED INTO A SYSTEM *THAT* EASILY.
TAKKA
NO! YOU'VE HACKED INTO THE EDENS ZERO?!!
YOUR SHIP...
...IS ALREADY UNDER MY CONTROL.
E2
BYA HA!
GRNK

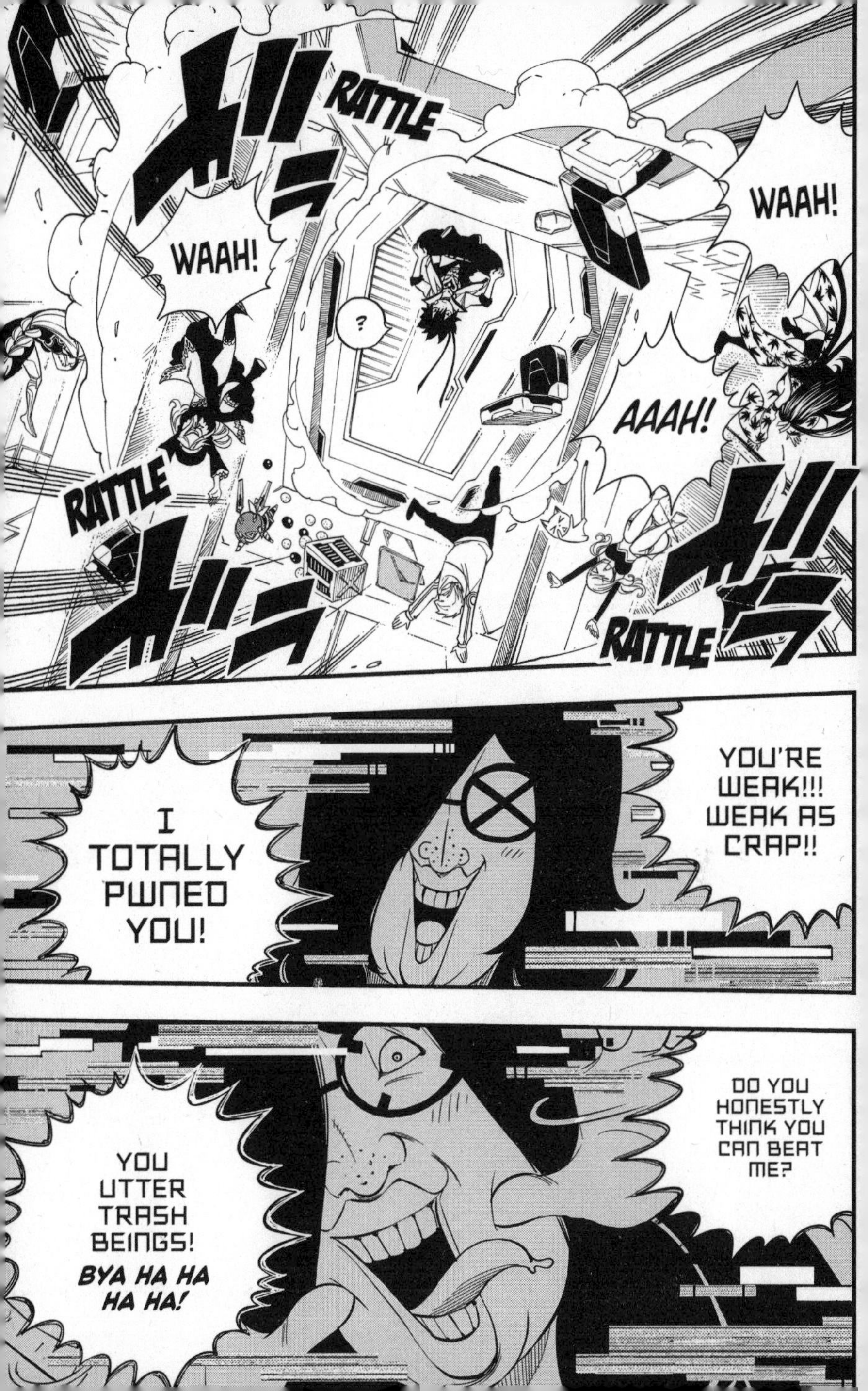
RATTLE
WAAH!
WAAH!
?
AAAH!
RATTLE
RATTLE
YOU'RE WEAK!!! WEAK AS CRAP!!
I TOTALLY PWNED YOU!
DO YOU HONESTLY THINK YOU CAN BEAT ME?
YOU UTTER TRASH BEINGS!
BYA HA HA HA HA!

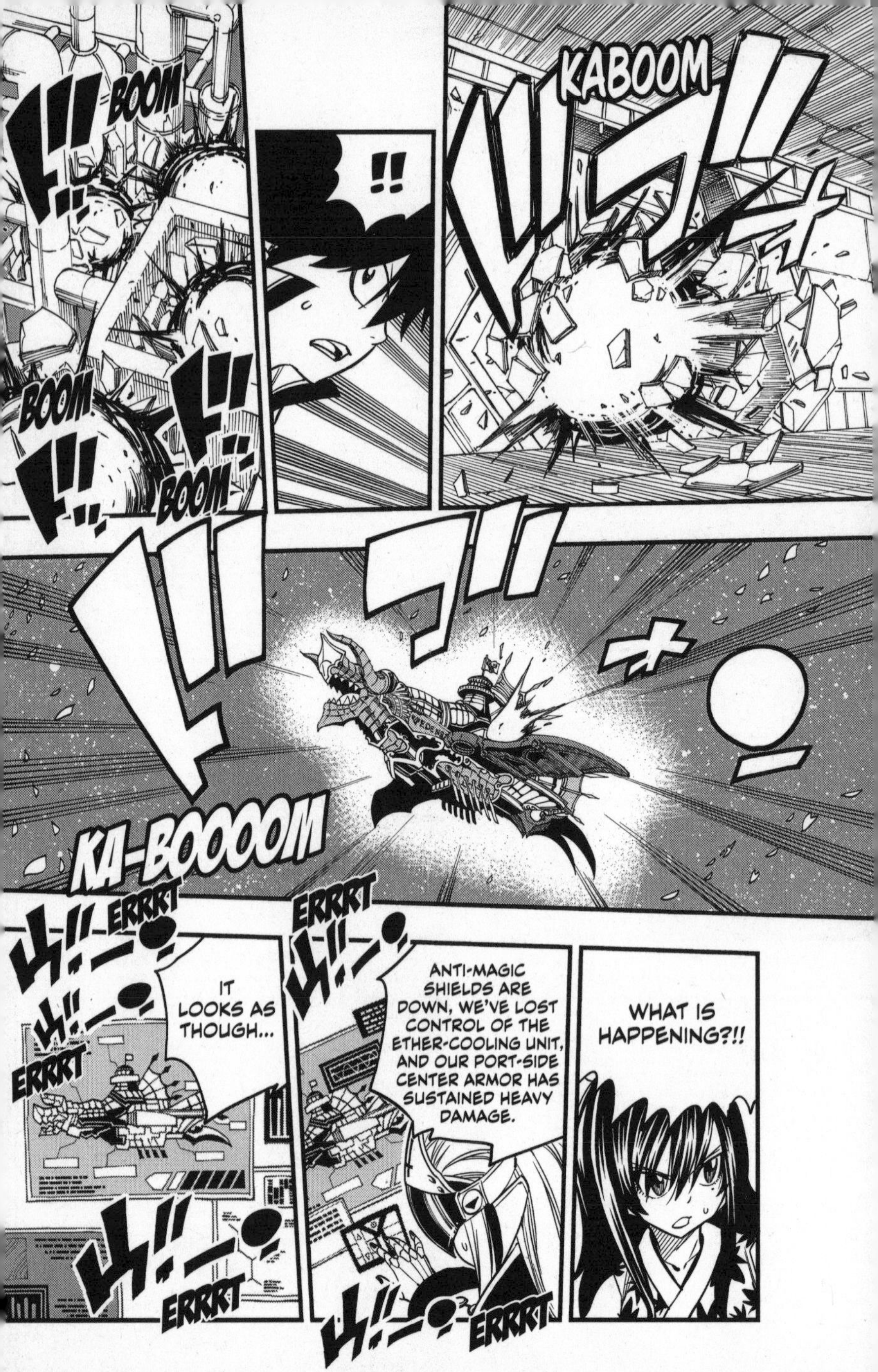
KABOOM
!!
BOOM
BOOM
BOOM
KA-BOOOOM
WHAT IS HAPPENING?!!
ERRRT
ANTI-MAGIC SHIELDS ARE DOWN, WE'VE LOST CONTROL OF THE ETHER-COOLING UNIT, AND OUR PORT-SIDE CENTER ARMOR HAS SUSTAINED HEAVY DAMAGE.
ERRRT
ERRRT
IT LOOKS AS THOUGH...
ERRRT
ERRRT

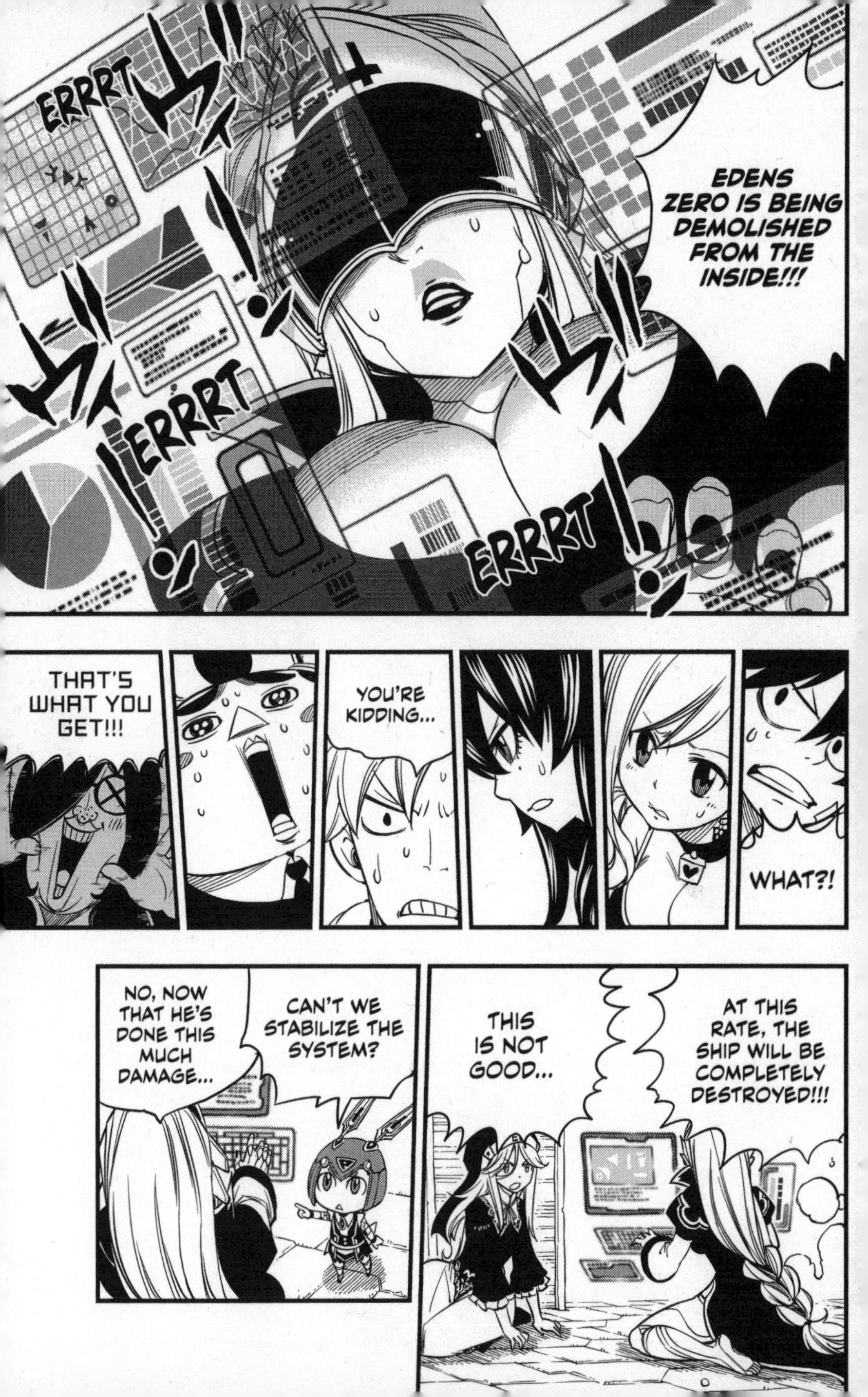
EDENS ZERO IS BEING DEMOLISHED FROM THE INSIDE!!!
ERRRT
ERRRT
ERRRT
WHAT?!
YOU'RE KIDDING...
THAT'S WHAT YOU GET!!!
AT THIS RATE, THE SHIP WILL BE COMPLETELY DESTROYED!!!
THIS IS NOT GOOD...
CAN'T WE STABILIZE THE SYSTEM?
NO, NOW THAT HE'S DONE THIS MUCH DAMAGE...

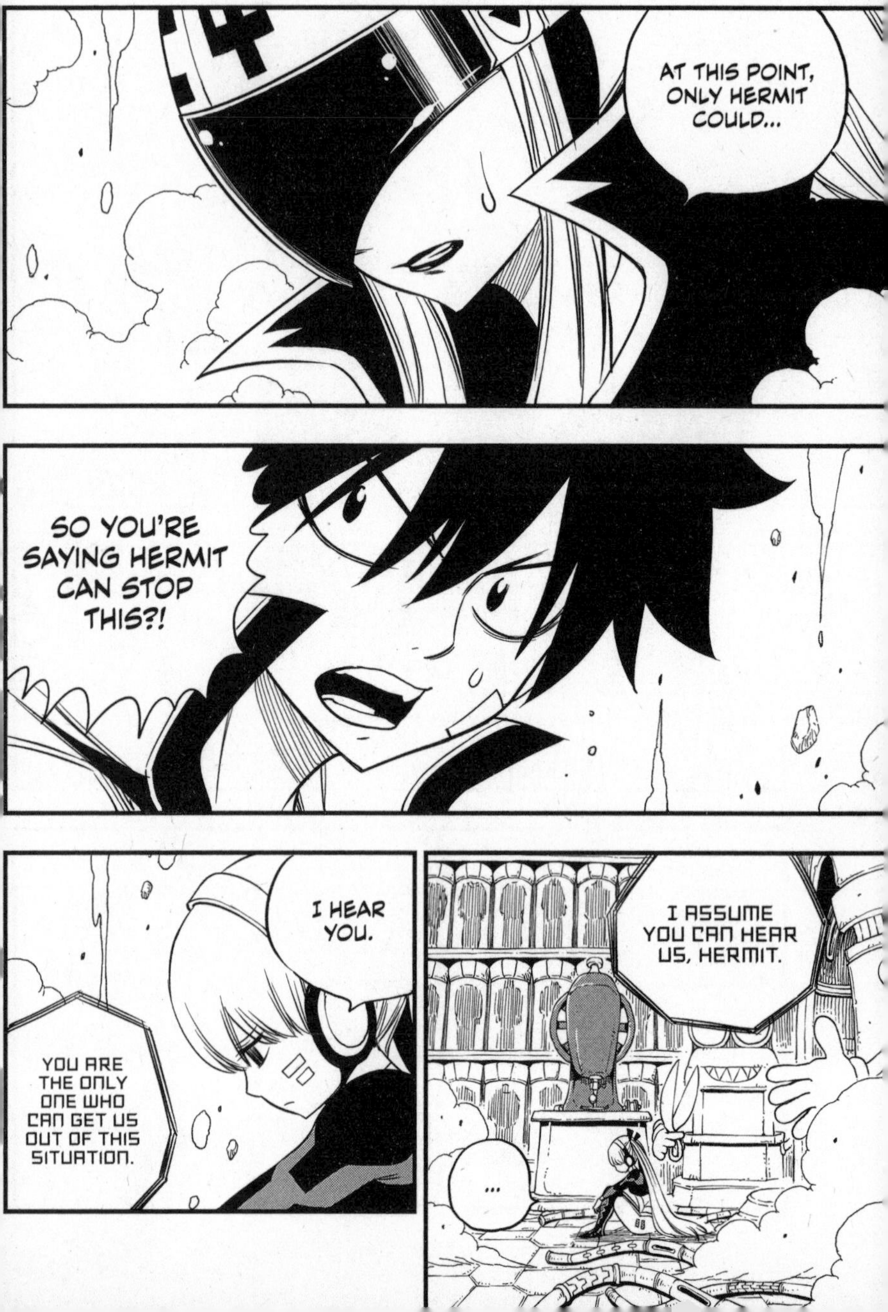
AT THIS POINT, ONLY HERMIT COULD...
SO YOU'RE SAYING HERMIT CAN STOP THIS?!
I ASSUME YOU CAN HEAR US, HERMIT.
...
I HEAR YOU.
YOU ARE THE ONLY ONE WHO CAN GET US OUT OF THIS SITUATION.

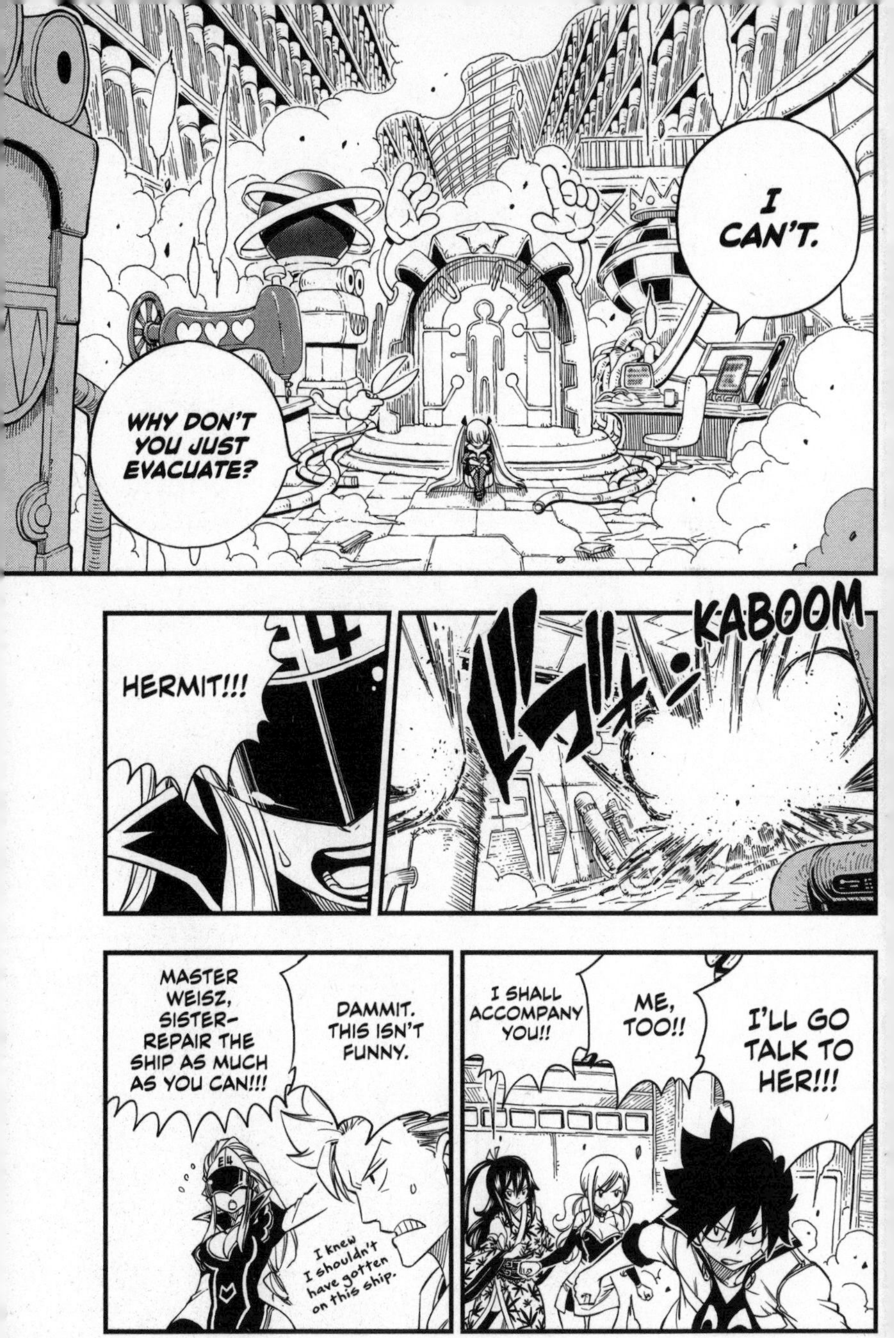
I CAN'T.
WHY DON'T YOU JUST EVACUATE?
KABOOM
HERMIT!!!
I'LL GO TALK TO HER!!!
ME, TOO!!
I SHALL ACCOMPANY YOU!!
DAMMIT. THIS ISN'T FUNNY.
MASTER WEISZ, SISTER-REPAIR THE SHIP AS MUCH AS YOU CAN!!!
I knew I shouldn't have gotten on this ship.

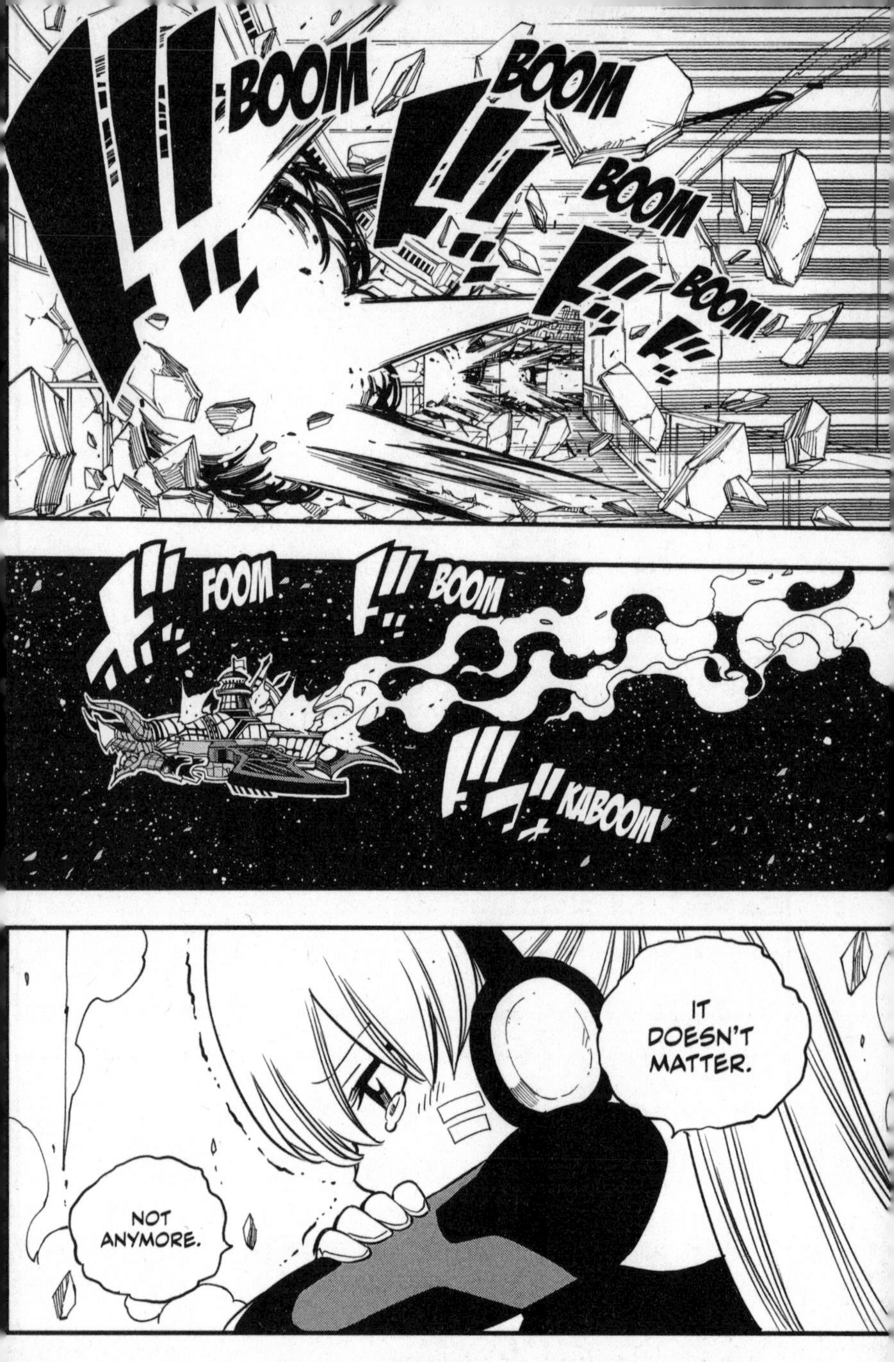
BOOM
BOOM
BOOM
BOOM
BOOM
FOOM
KABOOM
IT DOESN'T MATTER.
NOT ANYMORE.

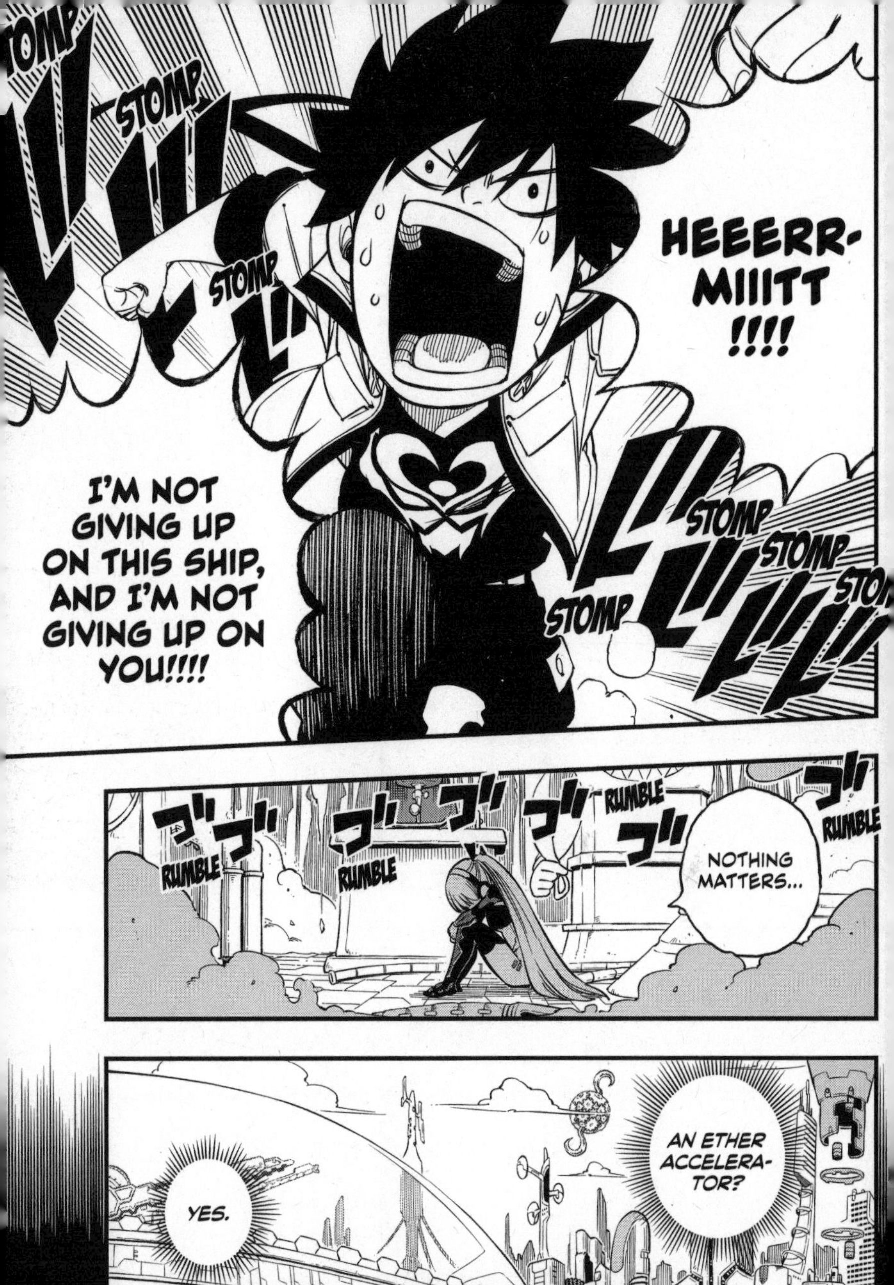
HEEERR-MIIITT!!!!
STOMP
STOMP
STOMP
STOMP
STOMP
STOMP
STOMP
I'M NOT GIVING UP ON THIS SHIP, AND I'M NOT GIVING UP ON YOU!!!!
RUMBLE
NOTHING MATTERS...
RUMBLE
RUMBLE
RUMBLE
AN ETHER ACCELERATOR?
YES.

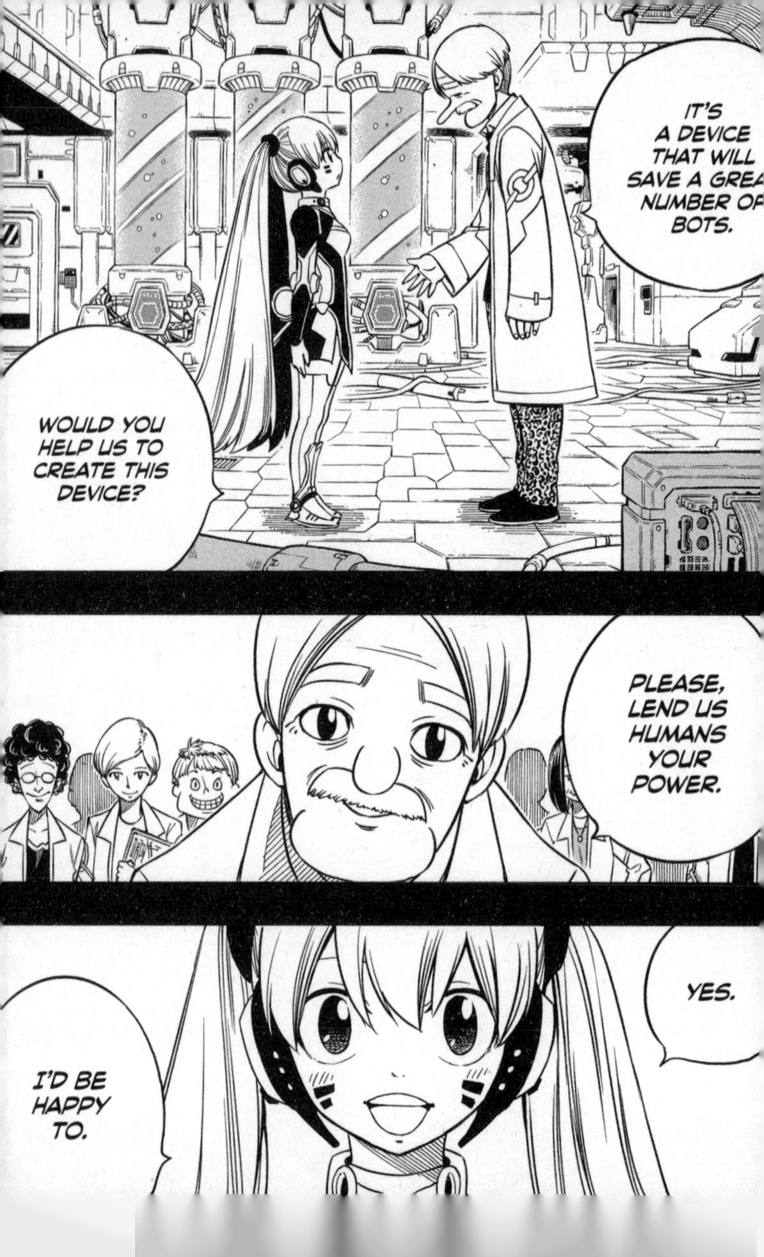
IT'S A DEVICE THAT WILL SAVE A GREA NUMBER OF BOTS.
WOULD YOU HELP US TO CREATE THIS DEVICE?
PLEASE, LEND US HUMANS YOUR POWER.
YES.
I'D BE HAPPY TO.

EDENS ZERO

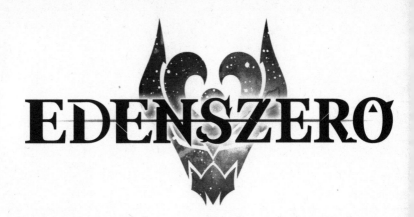

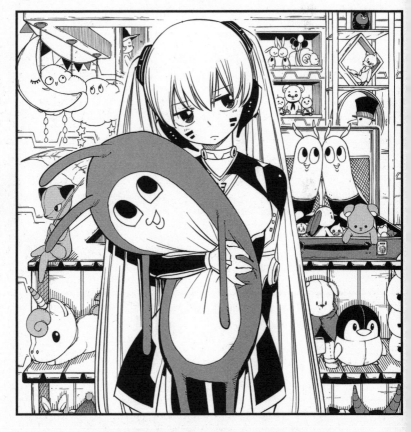

CHAPTER 40: OPERATION C7

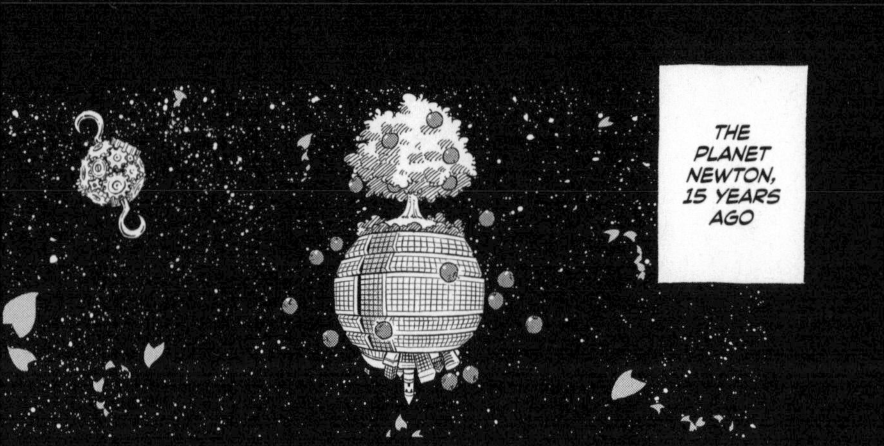
THE PLANET NEWTON, 15 YEARS AGO
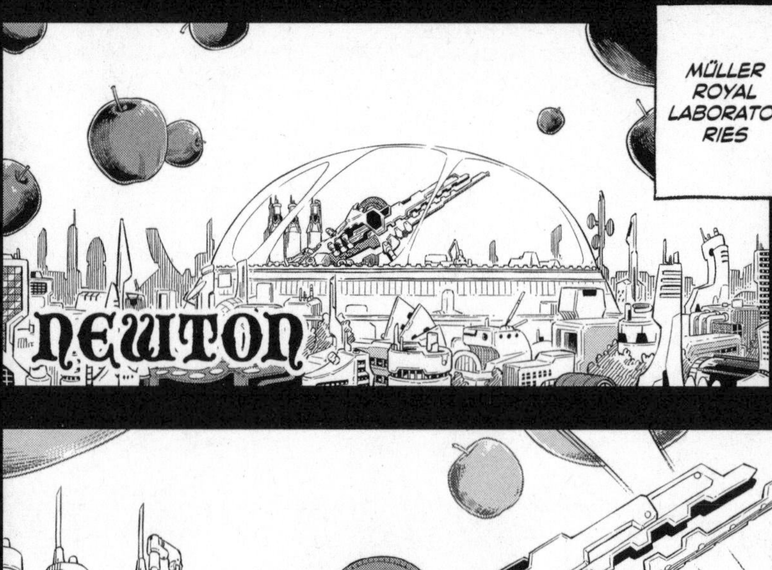
MÜLLER ROYAL LABORATO-RIES
NEWTON
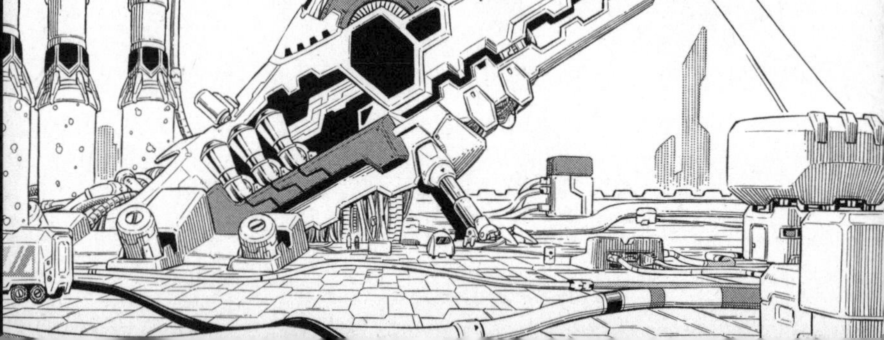

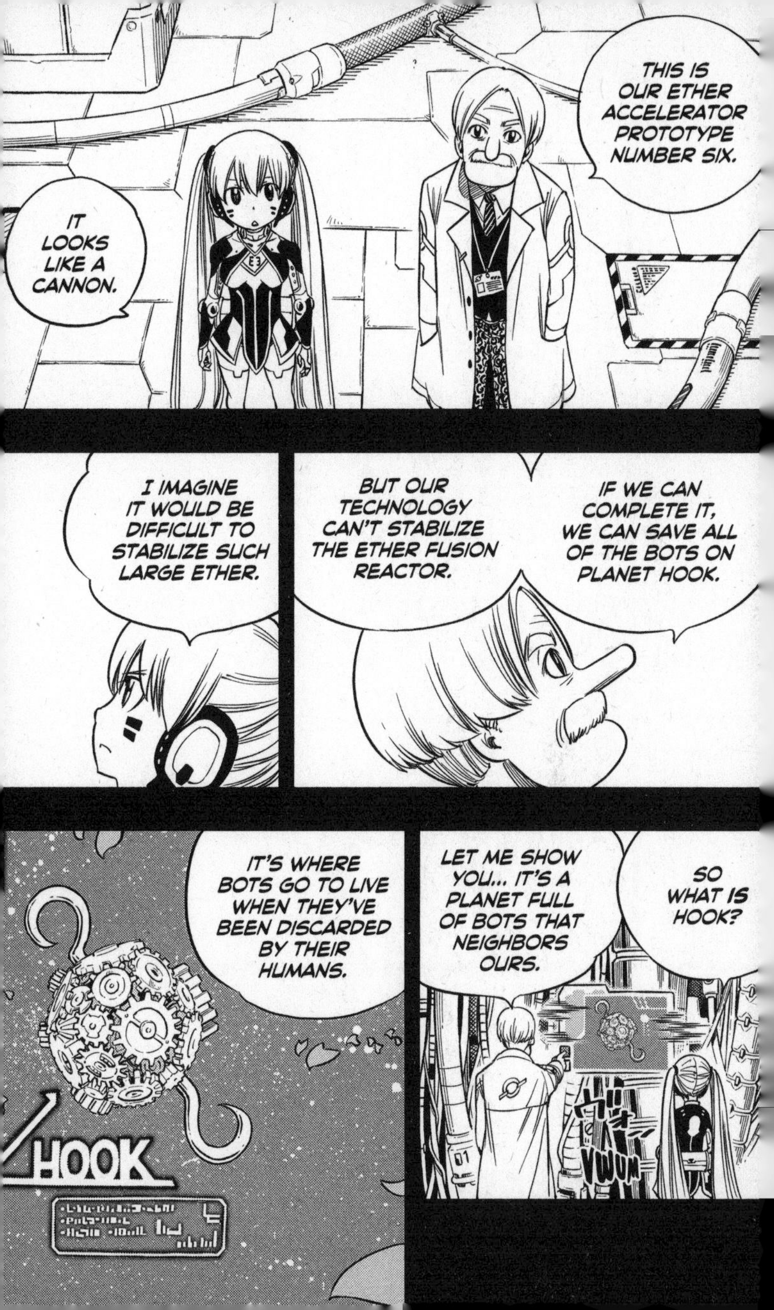
THIS IS OUR ETHER ACCELERATOR PROTOTYPE NUMBER SIX.
IT LOOKS LIKE A CANNON.
IF WE CAN COMPLETE IT, WE CAN SAVE ALL OF THE BOTS ON PLANET HOOK.
BUT OUR TECHNOLOGY CAN'T STABILIZE THE ETHER FUSION REACTOR.
I IMAGINE IT WOULD BE DIFFICULT TO STABILIZE SUCH LARGE ETHER.
SO WHAT IS HOOK?
LET ME SHOW YOU... IT'S A PLANET FULL OF BOTS THAT NEIGHBORS OURS.
VWUM
IT'S WHERE BOTS GO TO LIVE WHEN THEY'VE BEEN DISCARDED BY THEIR HUMANS.
HOOK

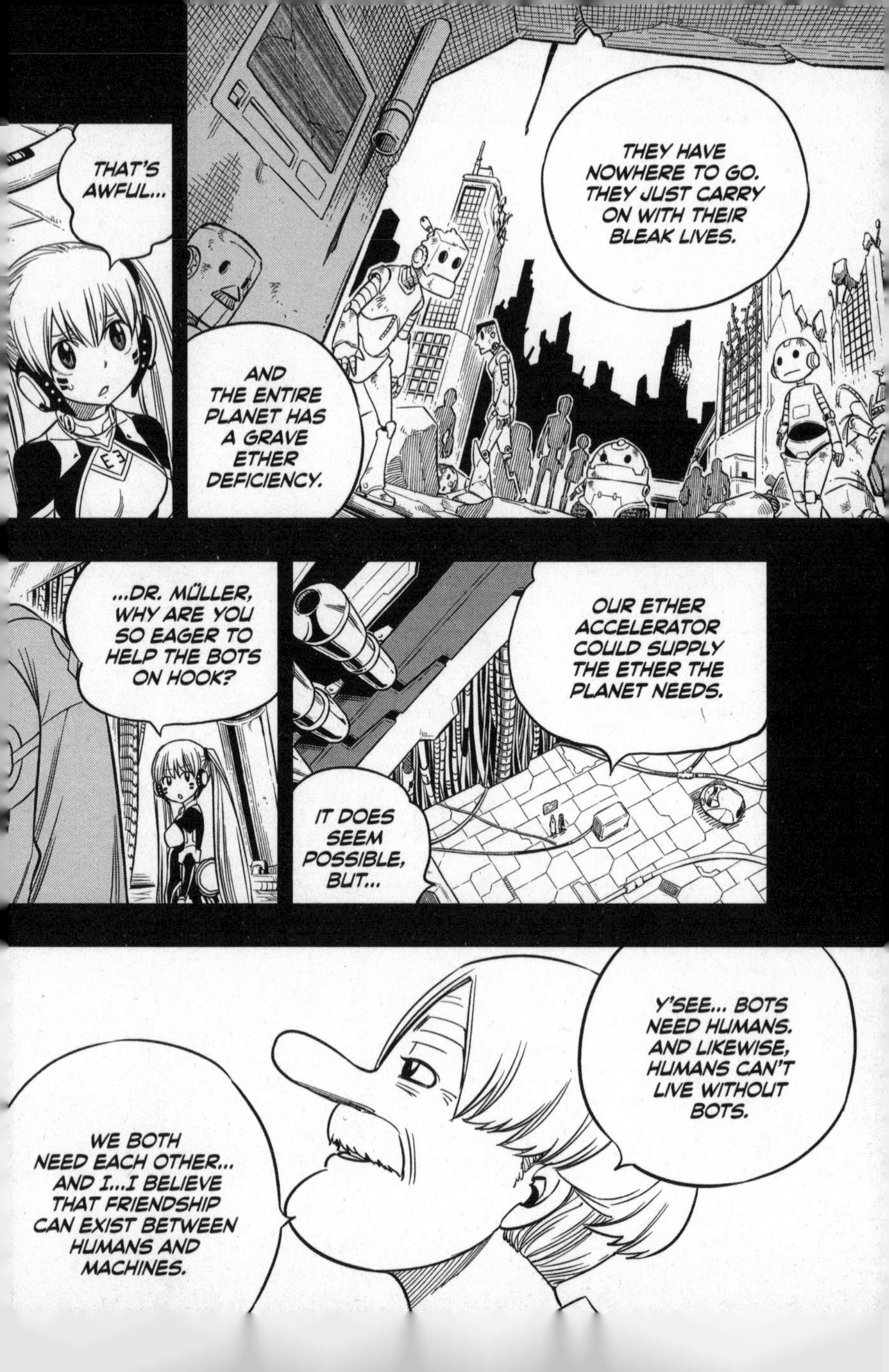
THEY HAVE NOWHERE TO GO. THEY JUST CARRY ON WITH THEIR BLEAK LIVES.
AND THE ENTIRE PLANET HAS A GRAVE ETHER DEFICIENCY.
THAT'S AWFUL...
OUR ETHER ACCELERATOR COULD SUPPLY THE ETHER THE PLANET NEEDS.
IT DOES SEEM POSSIBLE, BUT...
...DR. MÜLLER, WHY ARE YOU SO EAGER TO HELP THE BOTS ON HOOK?
Y'SEE... BOTS NEED HUMANS. AND LIKEWISE, HUMANS CAN'T LIVE WITHOUT BOTS.
WE BOTH NEED EACH OTHER... AND I...I BELIEVE THAT FRIENDSHIP CAN EXIST BETWEEN HUMANS AND MACHINES.

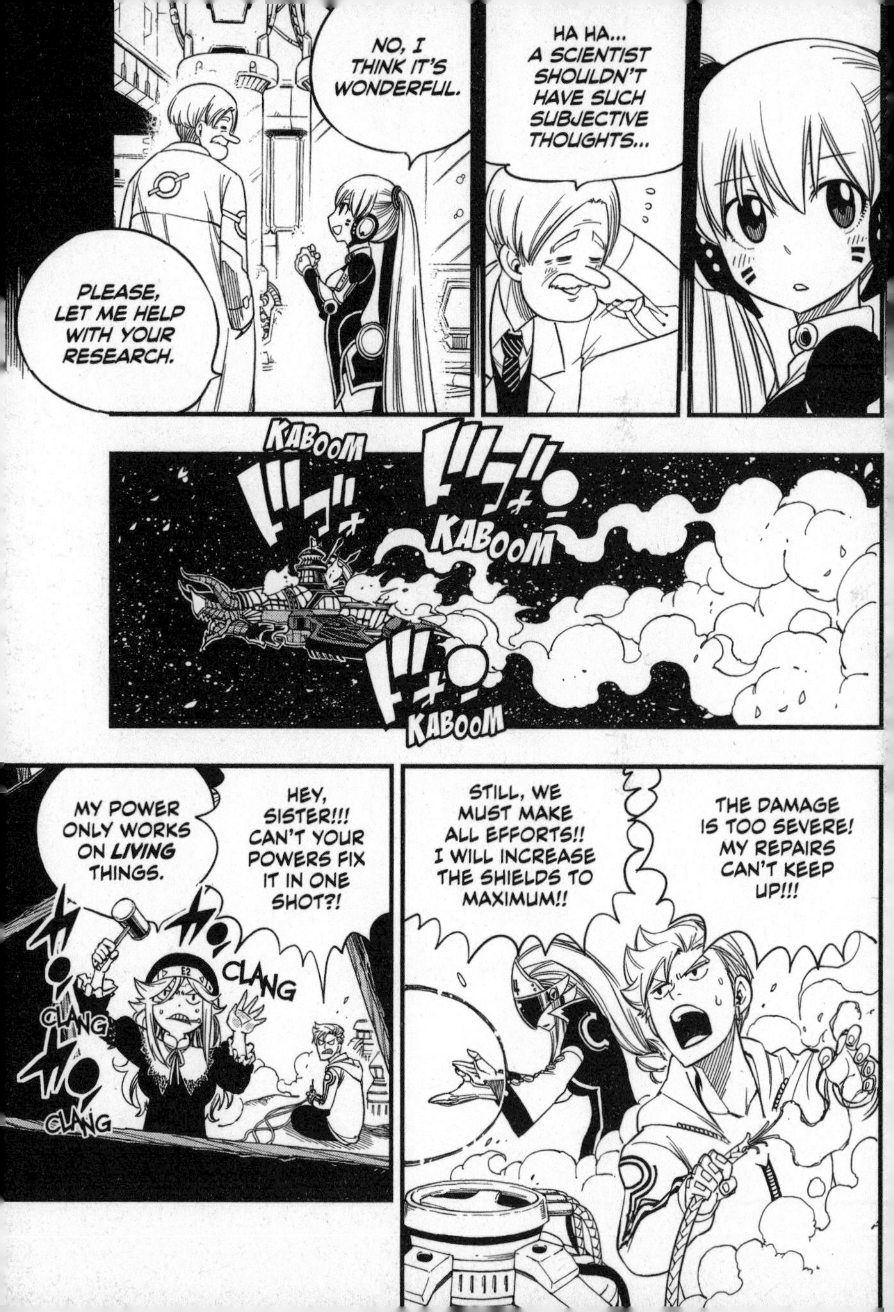
HA HA... A SCIENTIST SHOULDN'T HAVE SUCH SUBJECTIVE THOUGHTS...
NO, I THINK IT'S WONDERFUL.
PLEASE, LET ME HELP WITH YOUR RESEARCH.
KABOOM
KABOOM
KABOOM
THE DAMAGE IS TOO SEVERE! MY REPAIRS CAN'T KEEP UP!!!
STILL, WE MUST MAKE ALL EFFORTS!! I WILL INCREASE THE SHIELDS TO MAXIMUM!!
HEY, SISTER!!! CAN'T YOUR POWERS FIX IT IN ONE SHOT?!
MY POWER ONLY WORKS ON *LIVING* THINGS.
CLANG
CLANG
CLANG

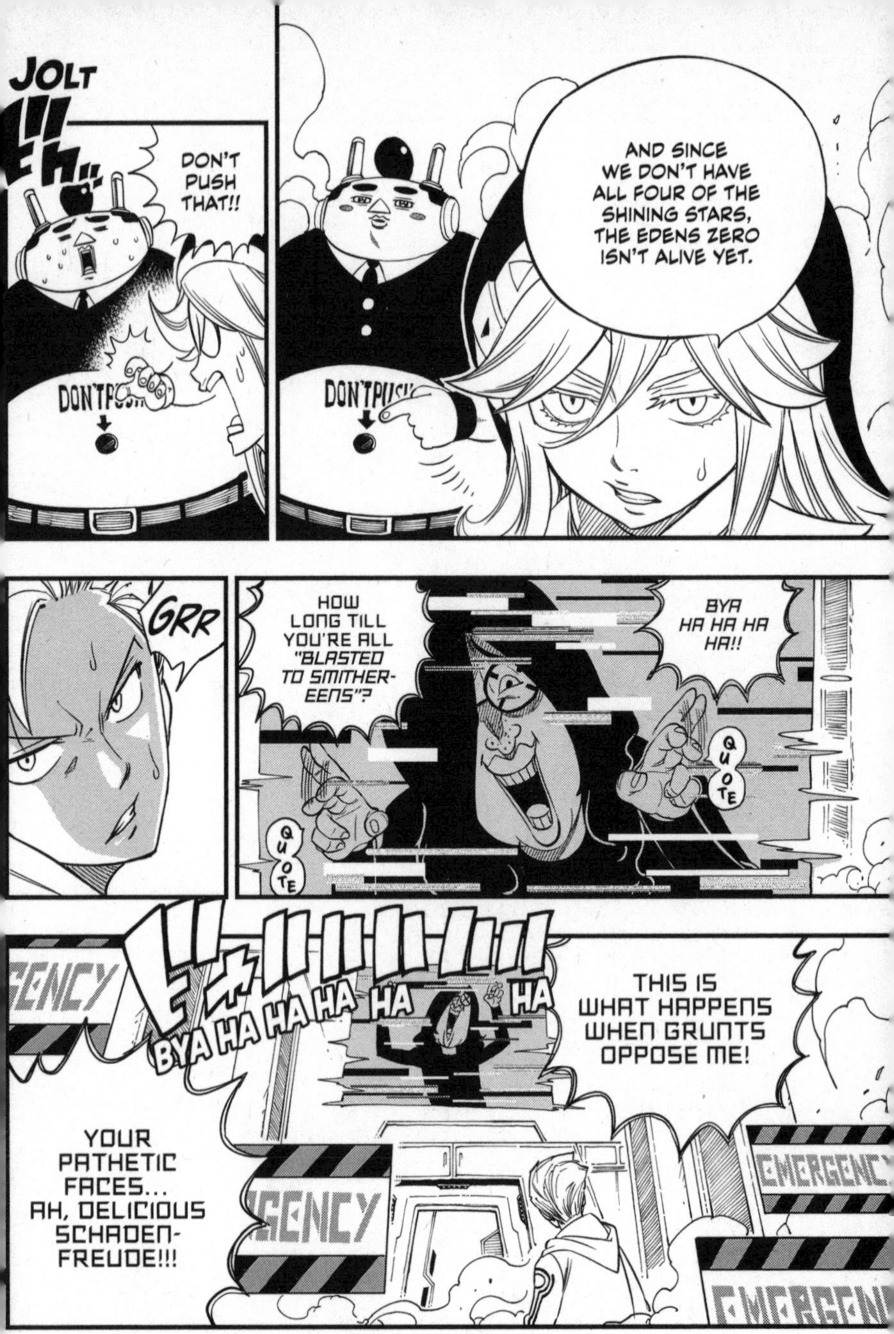
AND SINCE WE DON'T HAVE ALL FOUR OF THE SHINING STARS, THE EDENS ZERO ISN'T ALIVE YET.
JOLT
DON'T PUSH THAT!!
BYA HA HA HA HA!!
HOW LONG TILL YOU'RE ALL "BLASTED TO SMITHEREENS"?
QUOTE
QUOTE
GRR
BYA HA HA HA HA HA
THIS IS WHAT HAPPENS WHEN GRUNTS OPPOSE ME!
YOUR PATHETIC FACES... AH, DELICIOUS SCHADENFREUDE!!!

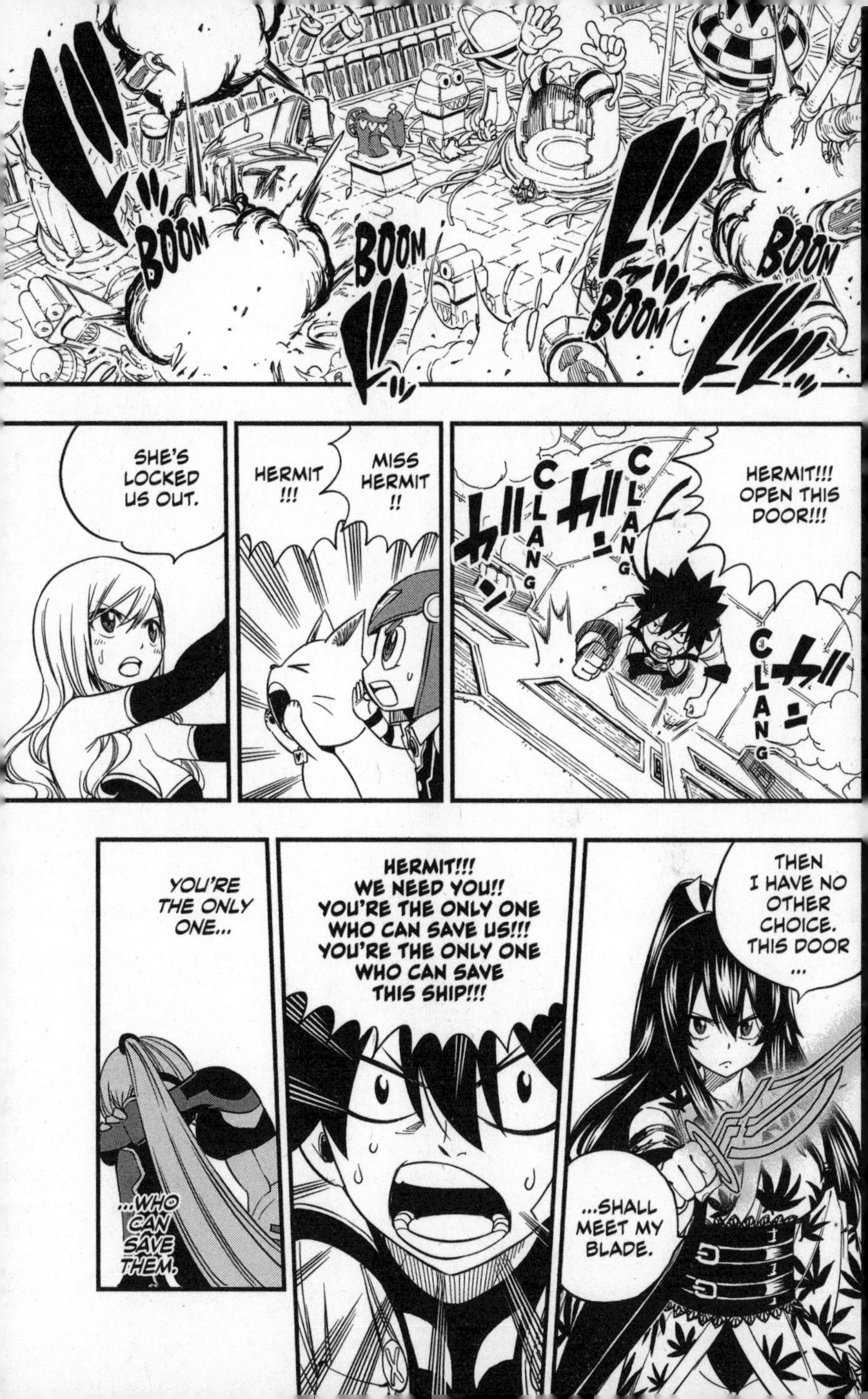
BOOM
BOOM
BOOM
BOOM
HERMIT!!! OPEN THIS DOOR!!!
CLANG
CLANG
CLANG
MISS HERMIT!!
HERMIT!!!
SHE'S LOCKED US OUT.
THEN I HAVE NO OTHER CHOICE. THIS DOOR ...
...SHALL MEET MY BLADE.
HERMIT!!! WE NEED YOU!! YOU'RE THE ONLY ONE WHO CAN SAVE US!!! YOU'RE THE ONLY ONE WHO CAN SAVE THIS SHIP!!!
YOU'RE THE ONLY ONE...
...WHO CAN SAVE THEM.

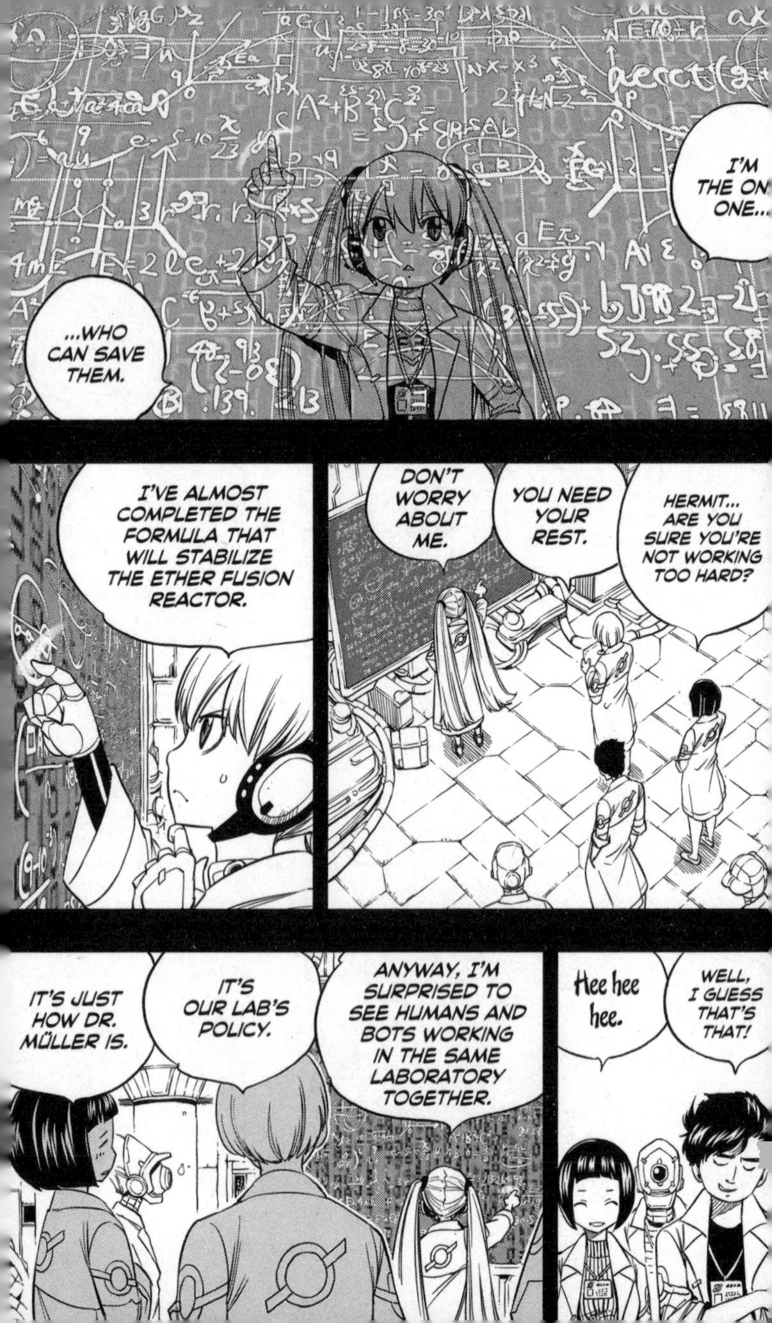
I'M THE ON ONE...
...WHO CAN SAVE THEM.
HERMIT... ARE YOU SURE YOU'RE NOT WORKING TOO HARD?
YOU NEED YOUR REST.
DON'T WORRY ABOUT ME.
I'VE ALMOST COMPLETED THE FORMULA THAT WILL STABILIZE THE ETHER FUSION REACTOR.
WELL, I GUESS THAT'S THAT!
Hee hee hee.
ANYWAY, I'M SURPRISED TO SEE HUMANS AND BOTS WORKING IN THE SAME LABORATORY TOGETHER.
IT'S OUR LAB'S POLICY.
IT'S JUST HOW DR. MÜLLER IS.

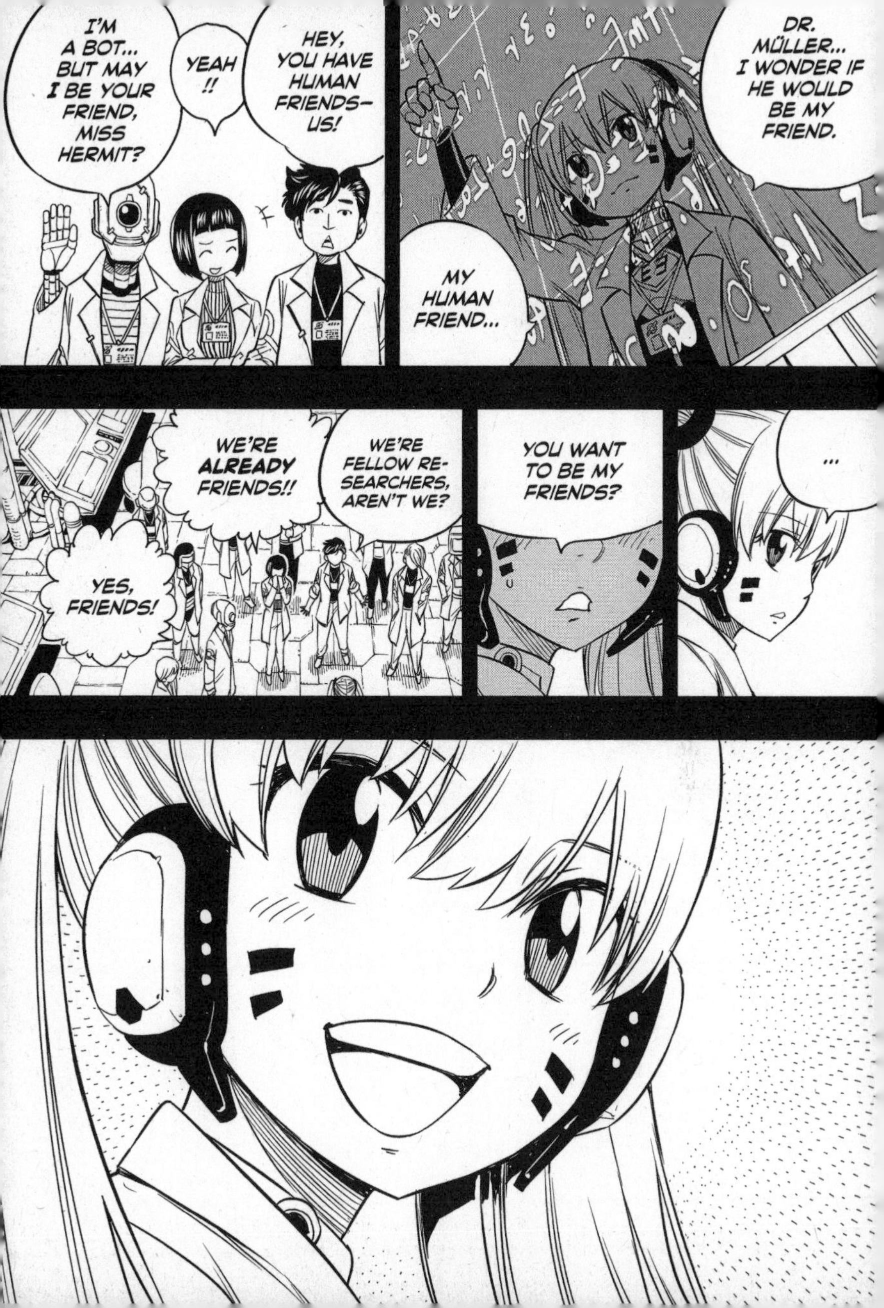
DR. MÜLLER... I WONDER IF HE WOULD BE MY FRIEND.
MY HUMAN FRIEND...
HEY, YOU HAVE HUMAN FRIENDS— US!
YEAH !!
I'M A BOT... BUT MAY I BE YOUR FRIEND, MISS HERMIT?
...
YOU WANT TO BE MY FRIENDS?
WE'RE FELLOW RE-SEARCHERS, AREN'T WE?
WE'RE ALREADY FRIENDS!!
YES, FRIENDS!

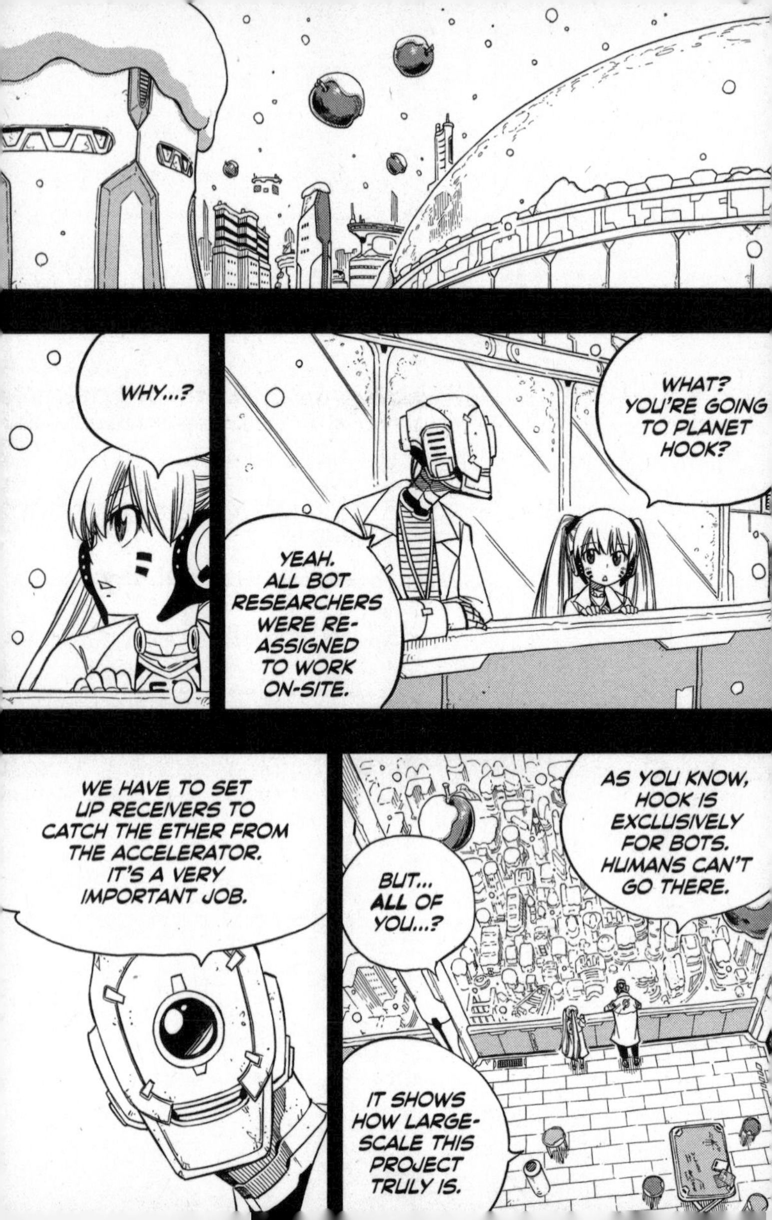
WHAT? YOU'RE GOING TO PLANET HOOK?
YEAH. ALL BOT RESEARCHERS WERE RE-ASSIGNED TO WORK ON-SITE.
WHY...?
AS YOU KNOW, HOOK IS EXCLUSIVELY FOR BOTS. HUMANS CAN'T GO THERE.
BUT... **ALL** OF YOU...?
IT SHOWS HOW LARGE-SCALE THIS PROJECT TRULY IS.
WE HAVE TO SET UP RECEIVERS TO CATCH THE ETHER FROM THE ACCELERATOR. IT'S A VERY IMPORTANT JOB.

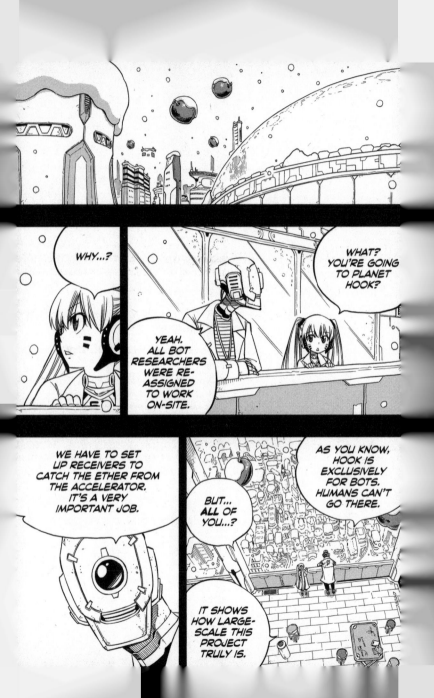

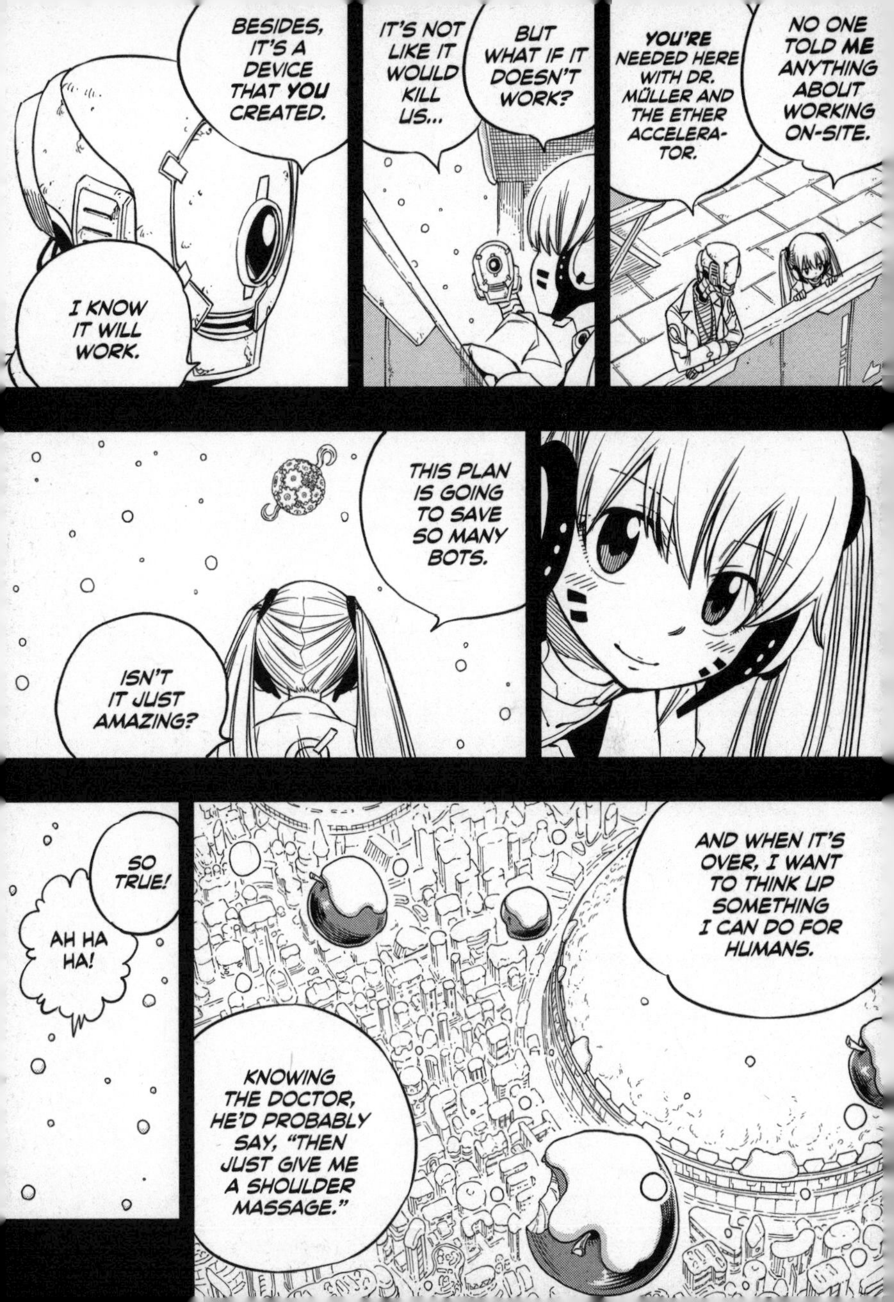
NO ONE TOLD ME ANYTHING ABOUT WORKING ON-SITE.
YOU'RE NEEDED HERE WITH DR. MÜLLER AND THE ETHER ACCELERATOR.
BUT WHAT IF IT DOESN'T WORK?
IT'S NOT LIKE IT WOULD KILL US...
BESIDES, IT'S A DEVICE THAT YOU CREATED.
I KNOW IT WILL WORK.
THIS PLAN IS GOING TO SAVE SO MANY BOTS.
ISN'T IT JUST AMAZING?
AND WHEN IT'S OVER, I WANT TO THINK UP SOMETHING I CAN DO FOR HUMANS.
KNOWING THE DOCTOR, HE'D PROBABLY SAY, "THEN JUST GIVE ME A SHOULDER MASSAGE."
SO TRUE!
AH HA HA!

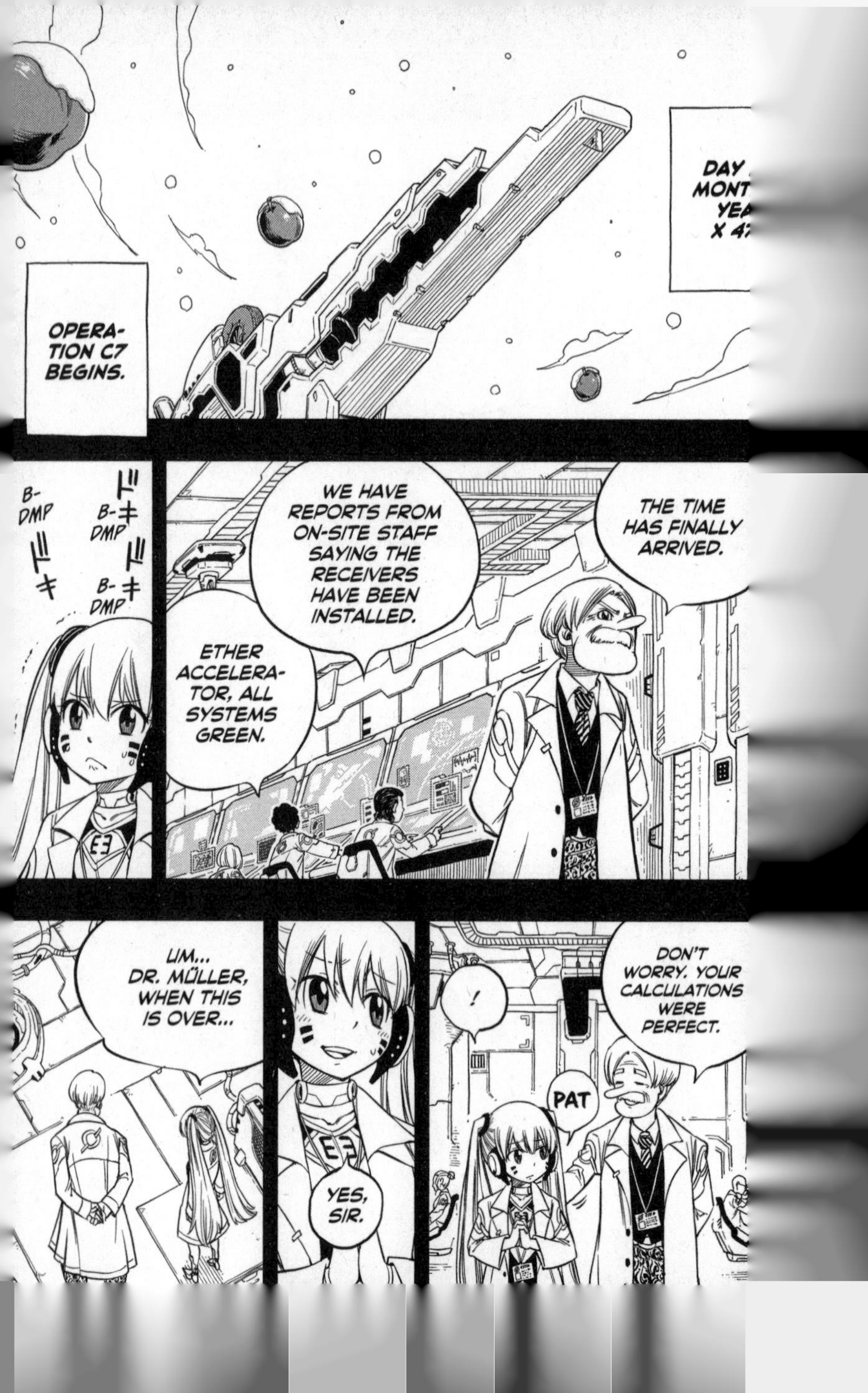
DAY
MONT
YEA
X 47
OPERATION C7 BEGINS.
THE TIME HAS FINALLY ARRIVED.
WE HAVE REPORTS FROM ON-SITE STAFF SAYING THE RECEIVERS HAVE BEEN INSTALLED.
ETHER ACCELERATOR, ALL SYSTEMS GREEN.
B-DMP ドキ
B-DMP ドキ
B-DMP ドキ
DON'T WORRY. YOUR CALCULATIONS WERE PERFECT.
!
PAT
YES, SIR.
UM... DR. MÜLLER, WHEN THIS IS OVER...

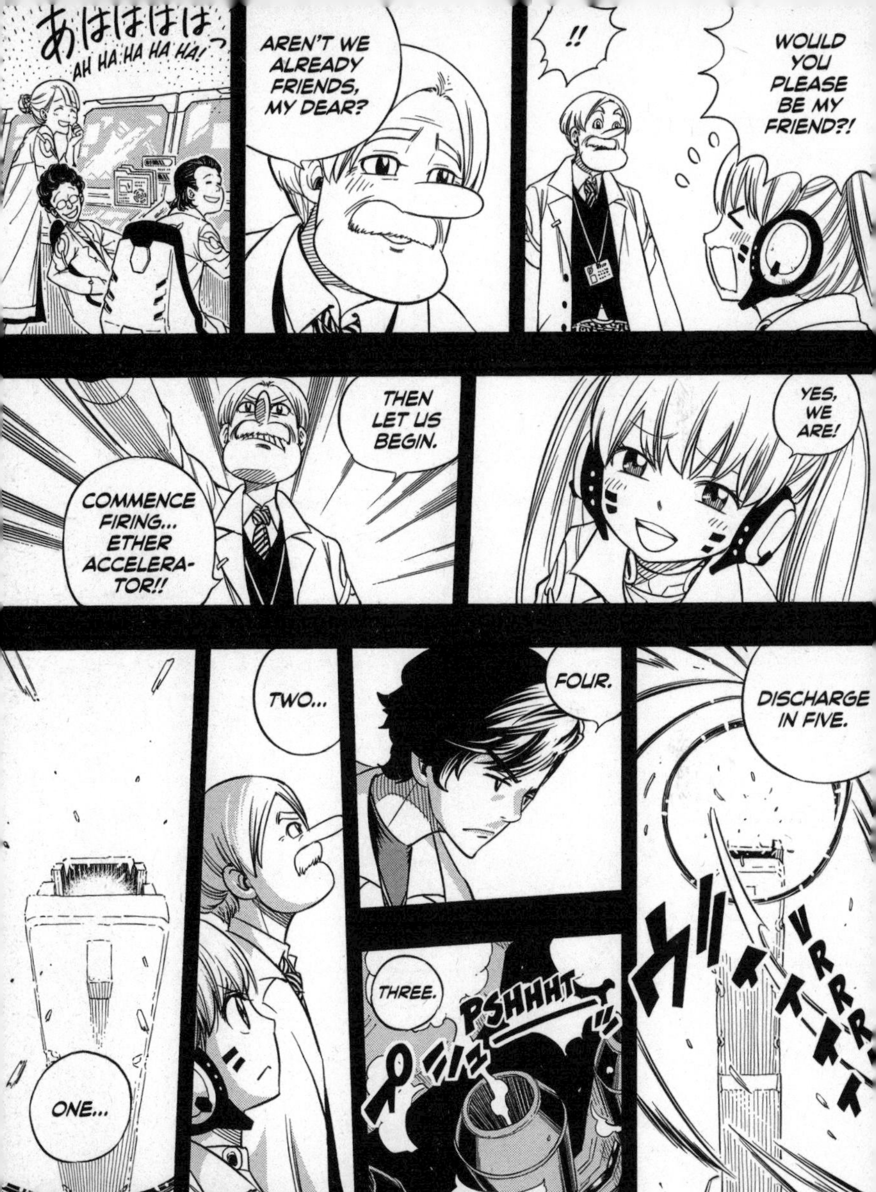
WOULD YOU PLEASE BE MY FRIEND?!
!!
AREN'T WE ALREADY FRIENDS, MY DEAR?
あはははは
AH HA HA HA HA!
YES, WE ARE!
THEN LET US BEGIN.
COMMENCE FIRING... ETHER ACCELERATOR!!
DISCHARGE IN FIVE.
VRRRRRT
FOUR.
THREE.
PSHHHT
TWO...
ONE...

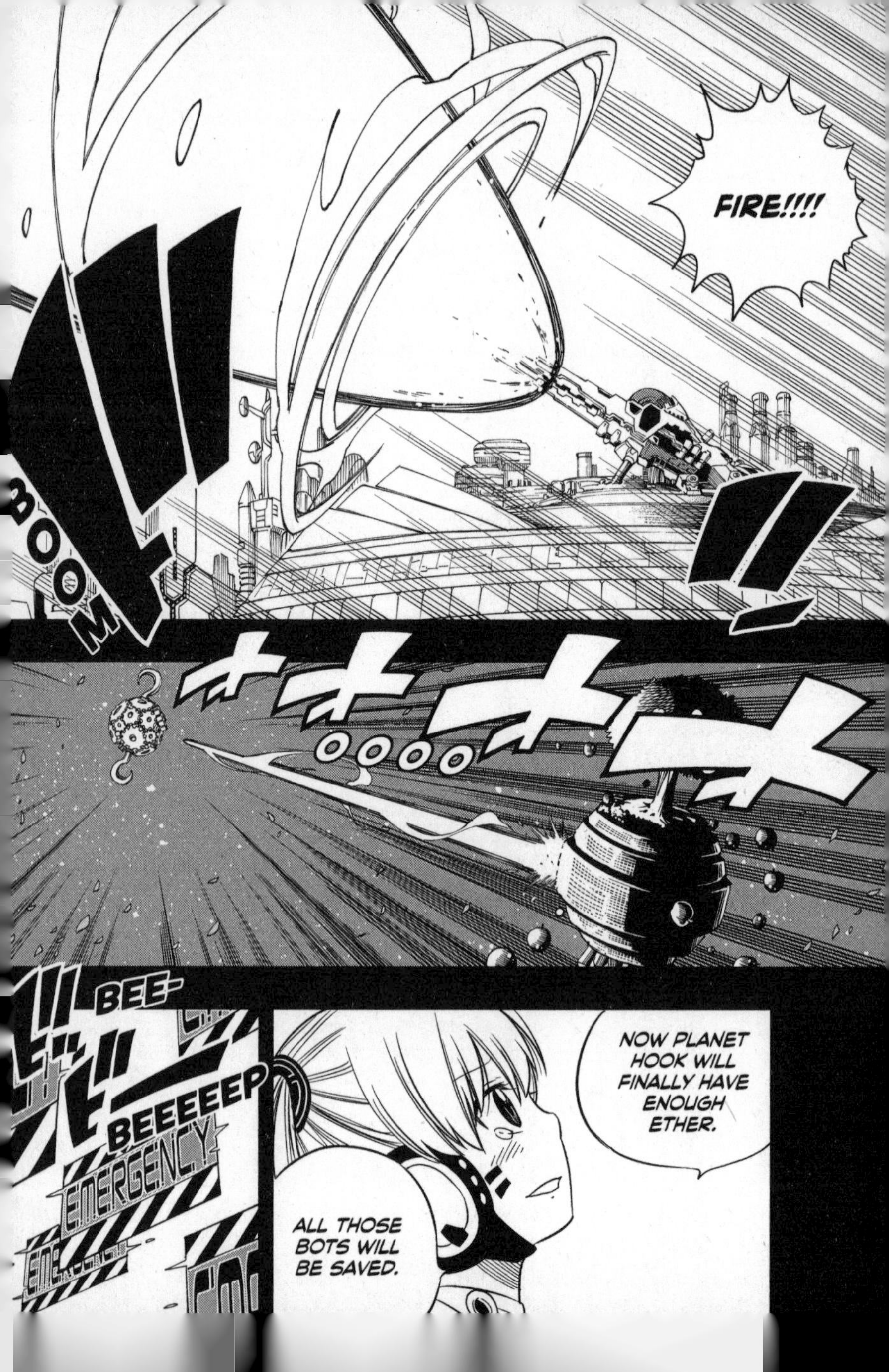
FIRE!!!!
BOOM
OOOO
NOW PLANET HOOK WILL FINALLY HAVE ENOUGH ETHER.
ALL THOSE BOTS WILL BE SAVED.
BEE-
BEEEEEP
EMERGENCY

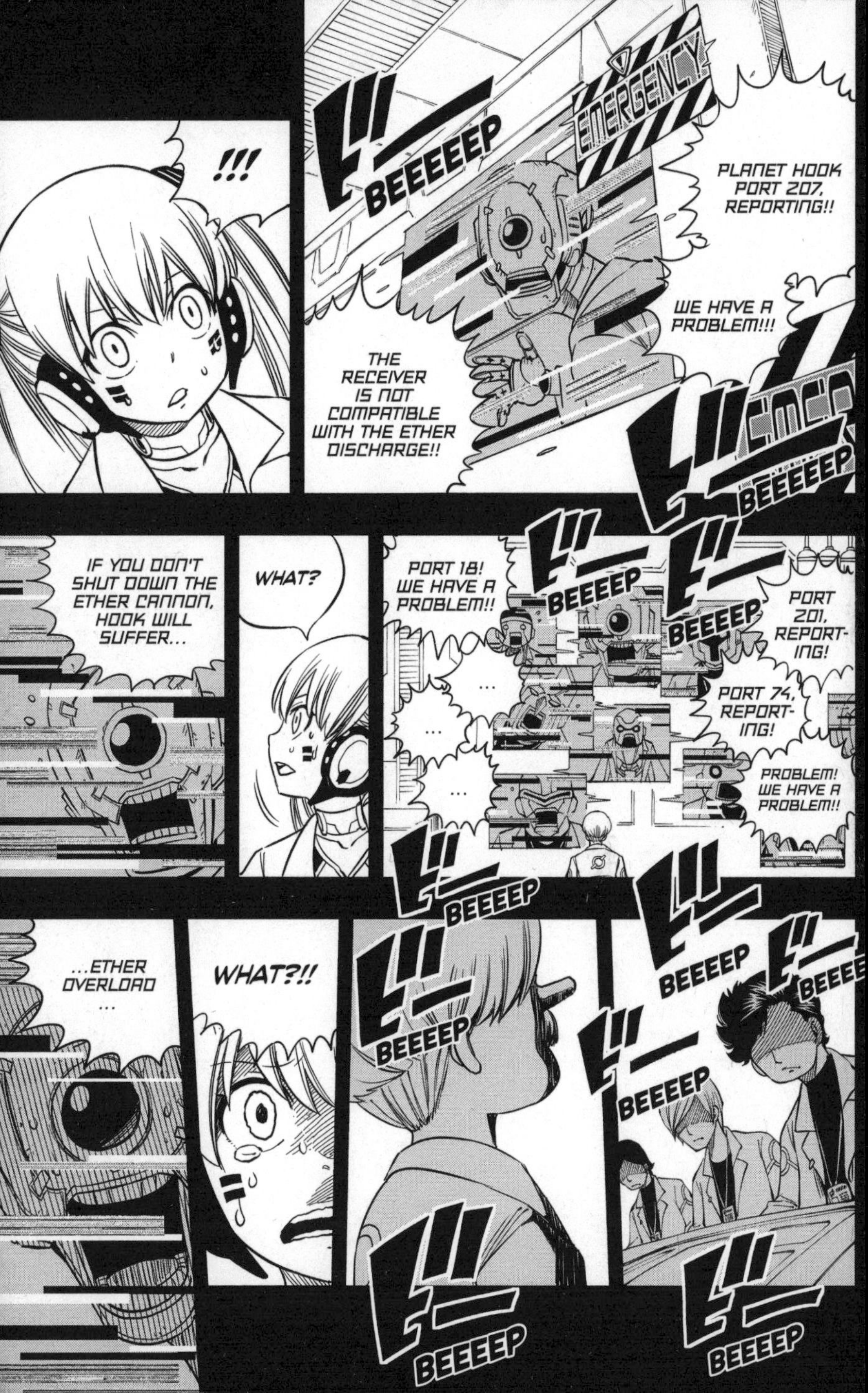

BEEEEEP
EMERGENCY
PLANET HOOK PORT 207, REPORTING!!
WE HAVE A PROBLEM!!!
THE RECEIVER IS NOT COMPATIBLE WITH THE ETHER DISCHARGE!!
BEEEEEP
!!!
BEEEEP
BEEEEP
PORT 201, REPORTING!
PORT 18! WE HAVE A PROBLEM!!
PORT 74, REPORTING!
PROBLEM! WE HAVE A PROBLEM!!
...
...
...
WHAT?
IF YOU DON'T SHUT DOWN THE ETHER CANNON, HOOK WILL SUFFER...
BEEEEP
BEEEEP
BEEEEP
BEEEEP
BEEEEP
BEEEEP
BEEEEP
WHAT?!!
...ETHER OVERLOAD ...

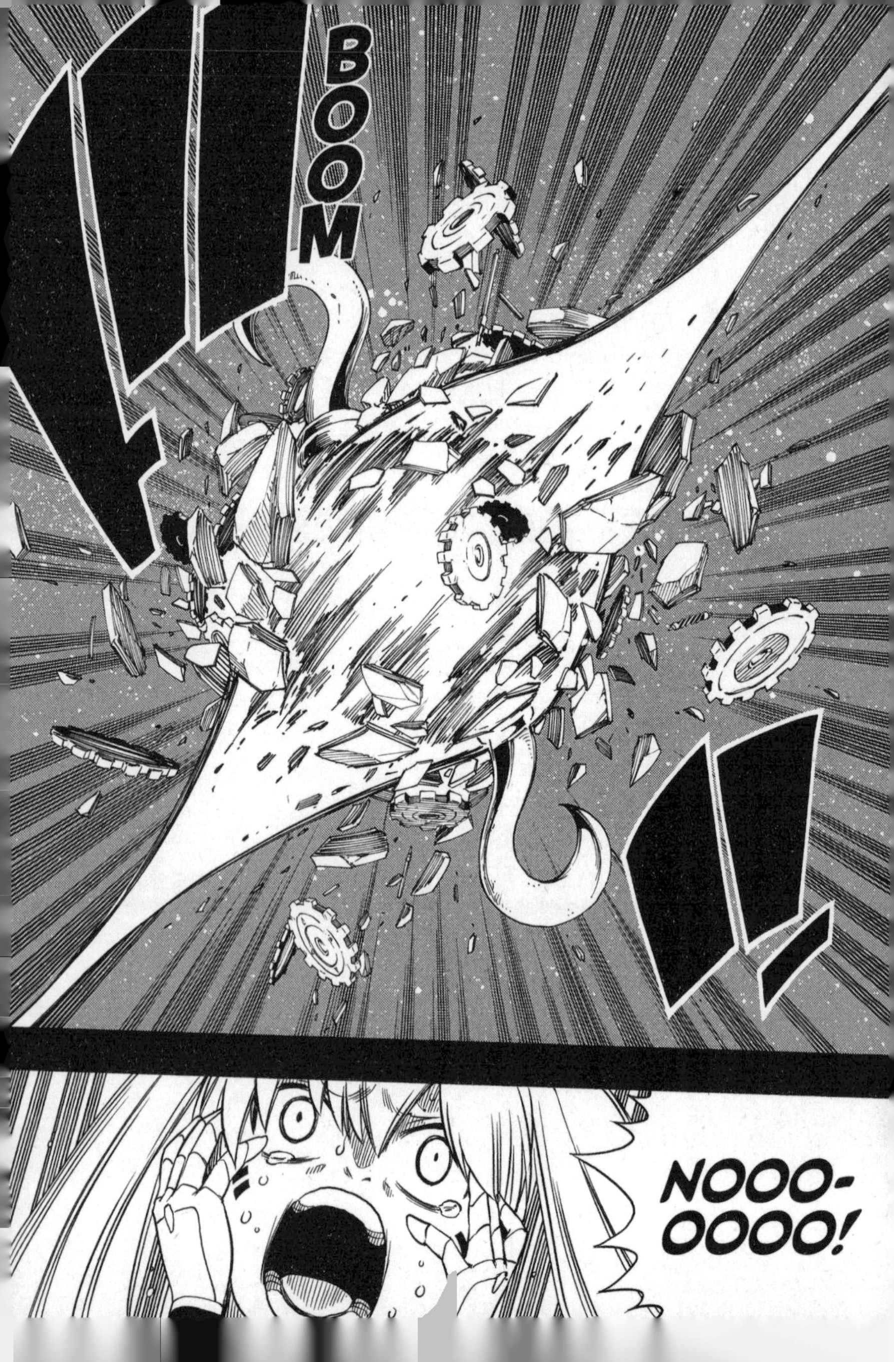
BOOM
NOOO-
OOOO!

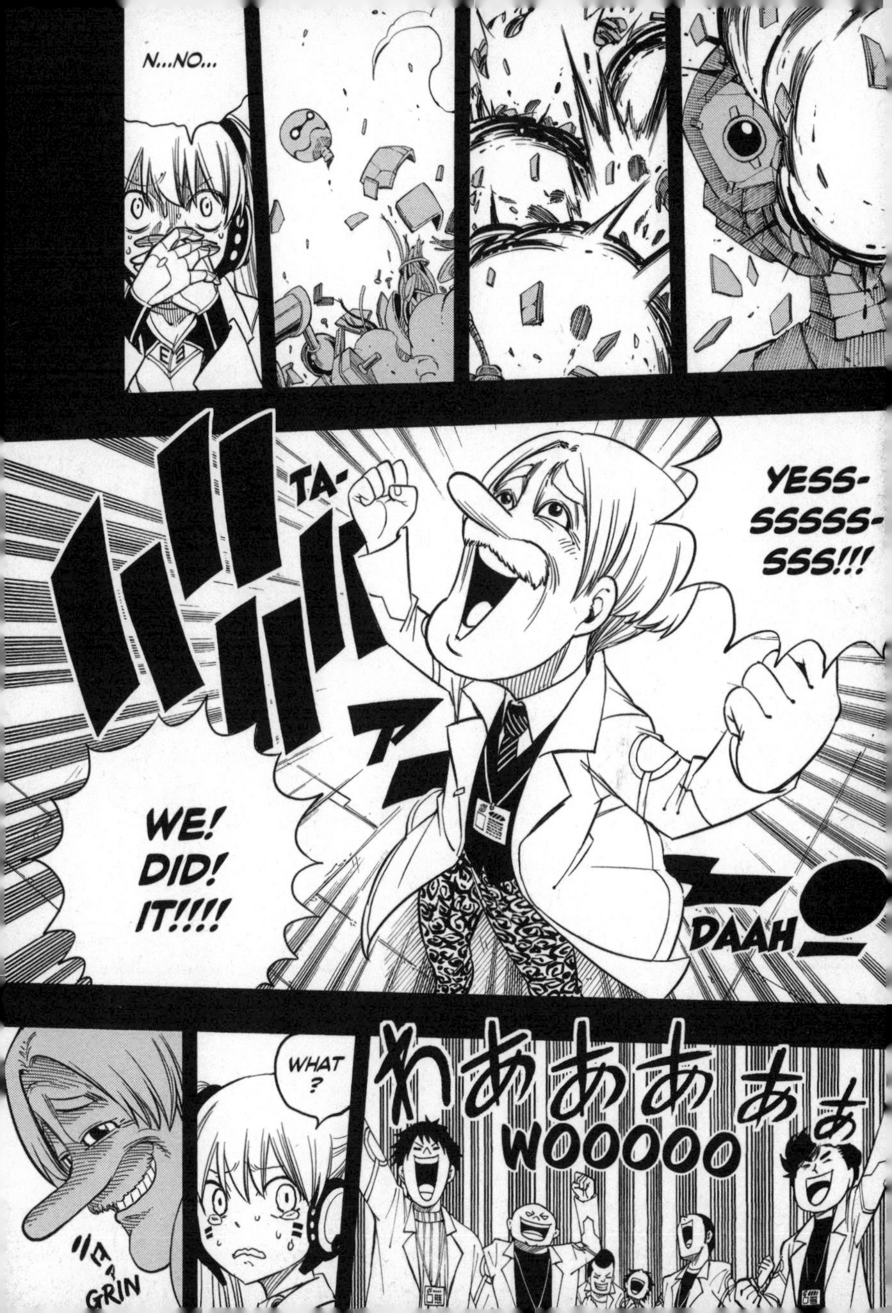
N...NO...
YESS-SSSSS-SSS!!!
TA-
DAAH
WE! DID! IT!!!!
わあああああ
WOOOOO
WHAT?
GRIN

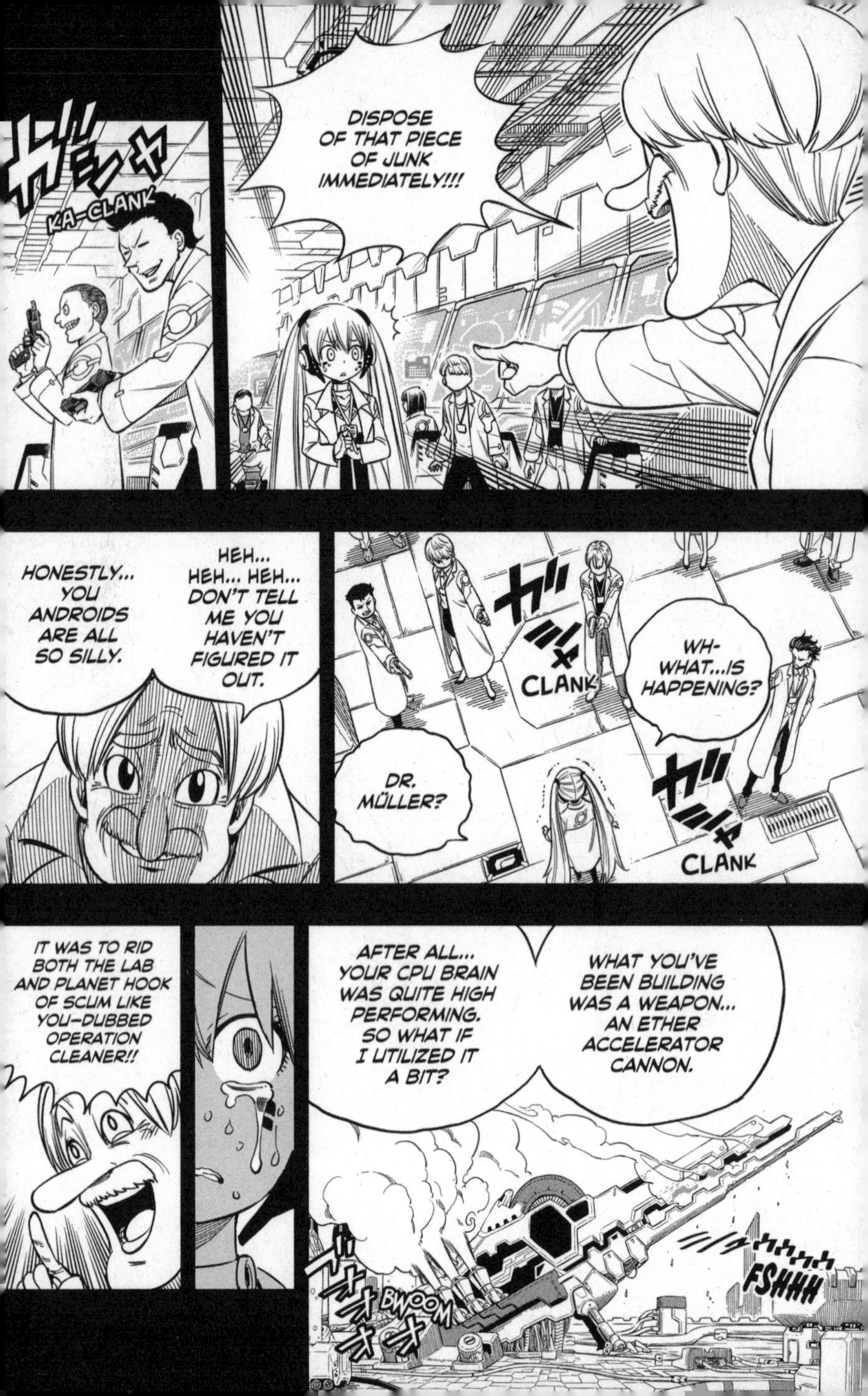
DISPOSE OF THAT PIECE OF JUNK IMMEDIATELY!!!
KA-CLANK
WH- WHAT...IS HAPPENING?
CLANK
DR. MÜLLER?
CLANK
HEH... HEH... HEH... DON'T TELL ME YOU HAVEN'T FIGURED IT OUT.
HONESTLY... YOU ANDROIDS ARE ALL SO SILLY.
WHAT YOU'VE BEEN BUILDING WAS A WEAPON... AN ETHER ACCELERATOR CANNON.
AFTER ALL... YOUR CPU BRAIN WAS QUITE HIGH PERFORMING. SO WHAT IF I UTILIZED IT A BIT?
FSHHH
BWOOM
IT WAS TO RID BOTH THE LAB AND PLANET HOOK OF SCUM LIKE YOU—DUBBED OPERATION CLEANER!!

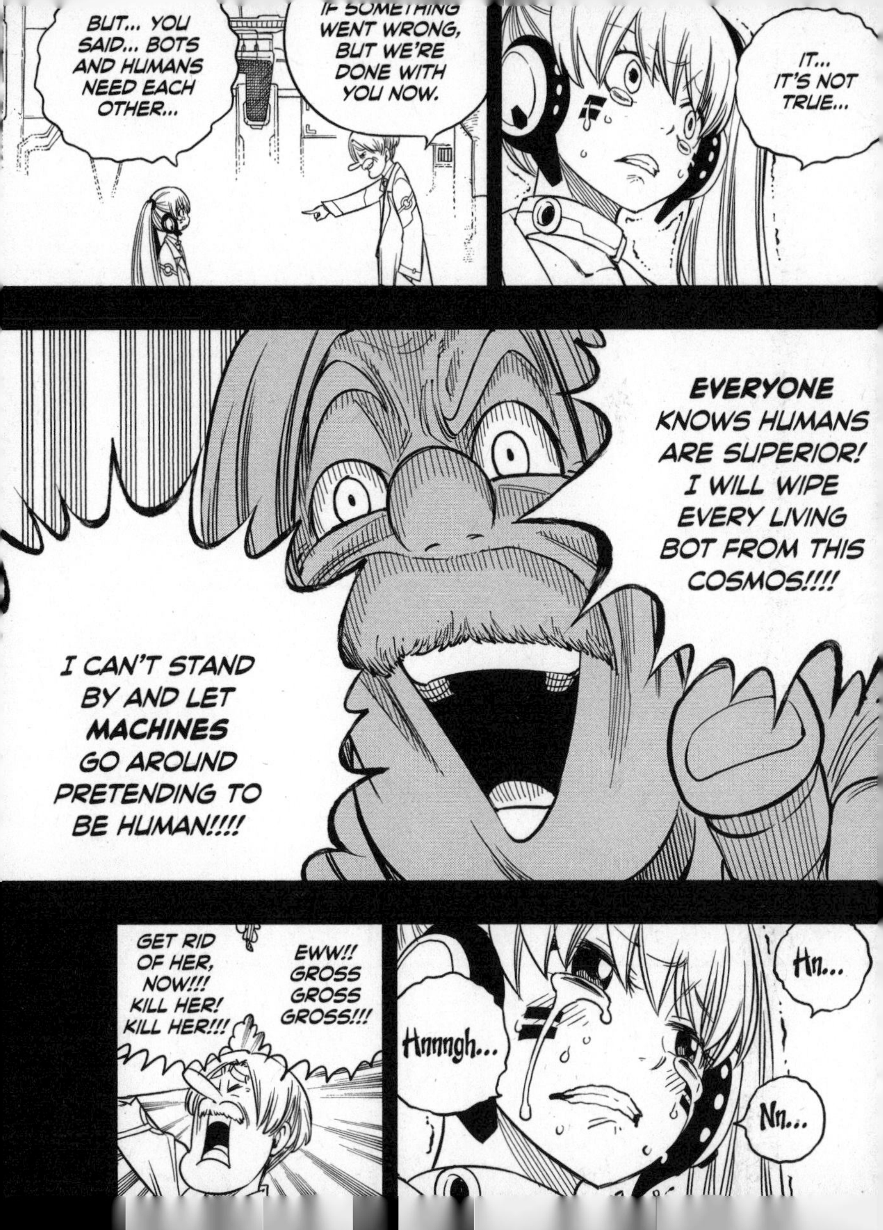
IT... IT'S NOT TRUE...
IF SOMETHING WENT WRONG, BUT WE'RE DONE WITH YOU NOW.
BUT... YOU SAID... BOTS AND HUMANS NEED EACH OTHER...
EVERYONE KNOWS HUMANS ARE SUPERIOR! I WILL WIPE EVERY LIVING BOT FROM THIS COSMOS!!!!
I CAN'T STAND BY AND LET MACHINES GO AROUND PRETENDING TO BE HUMAN!!!!
Hn...
Hnnngh...
Nn...
EWW!! GROSS GROSS GROSS!!!
GET RID OF HER, NOW!!! KILL HER! KILL HER!!!

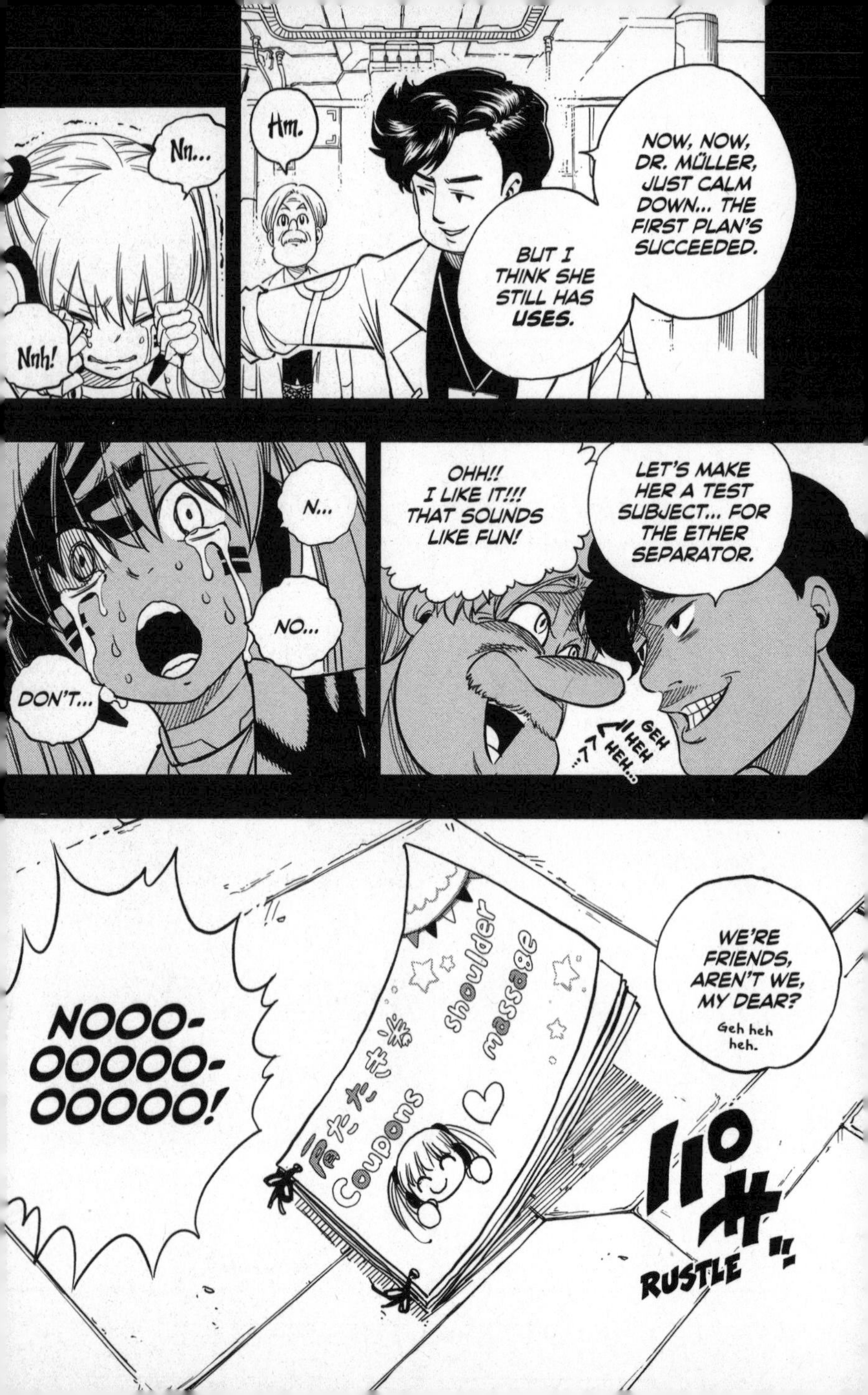
NOW, NOW, DR. MÜLLER, JUST CALM DOWN... THE FIRST PLAN'S SUCCEEDED.
BUT I THINK SHE STILL HAS USES.
Hm.
Nn...
Nnh!
LET'S MAKE HER A TEST SUBJECT... FOR THE ETHER SEPARATOR.
OHH!! I LIKE IT!!! THAT SOUNDS LIKE FUN!
GEH HEH HEH...
N...
NO...
DON'T...
WE'RE FRIENDS, AREN'T WE, MY DEAR?
Geh heh heh.
RUSTLE
shoulder massage
Coupons
NOOO-OOOOO-OOOOO!

EDENS ZERO

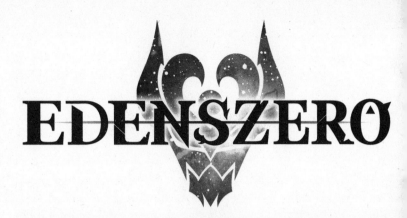

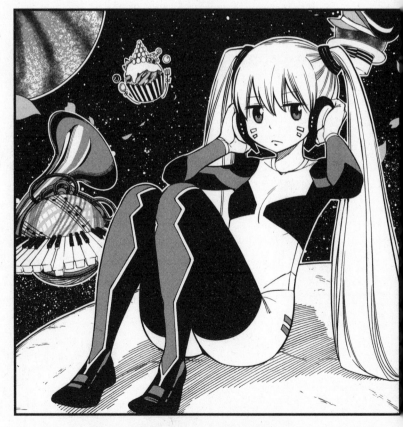

CHAPTER 41: FIREWORKS

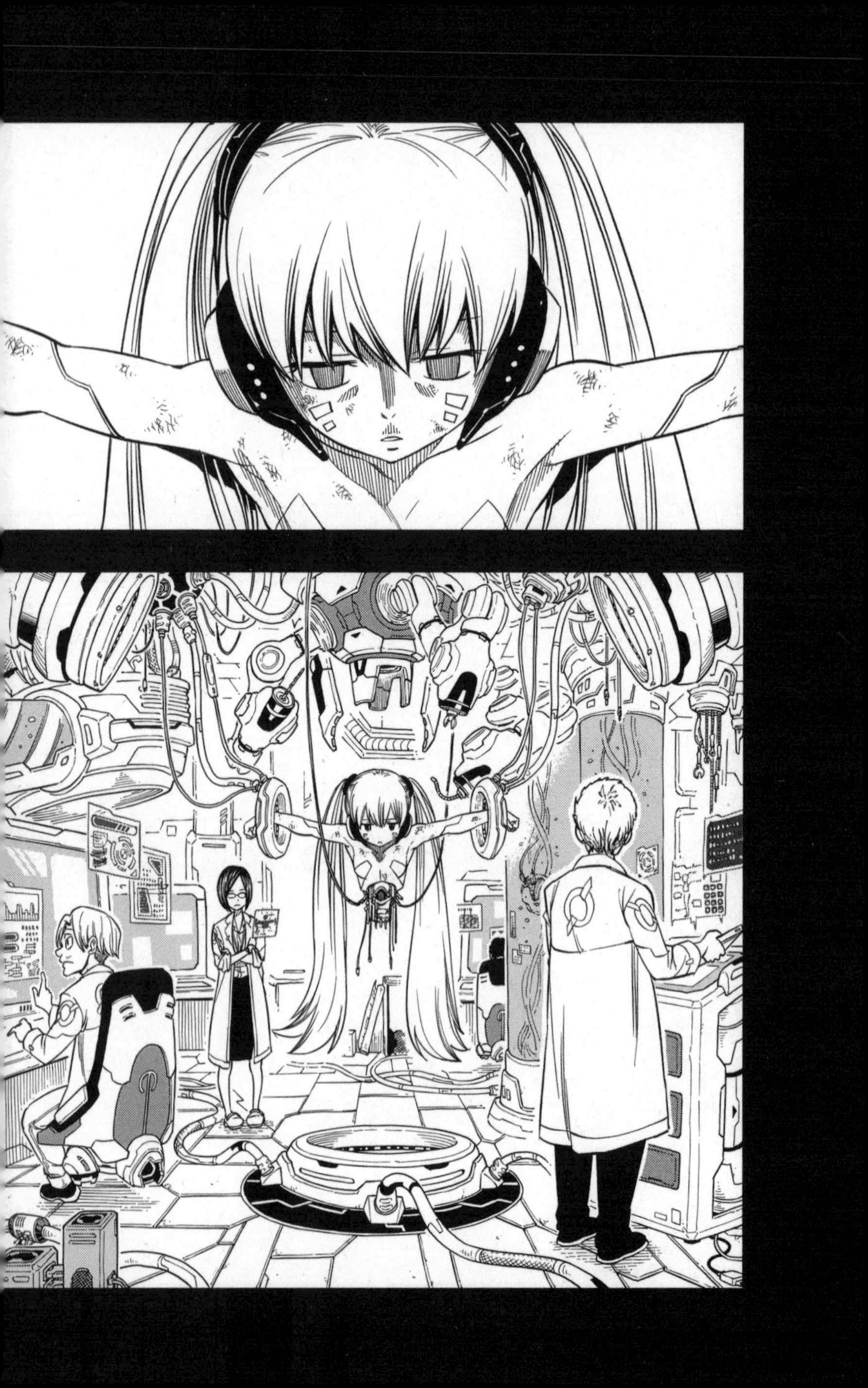

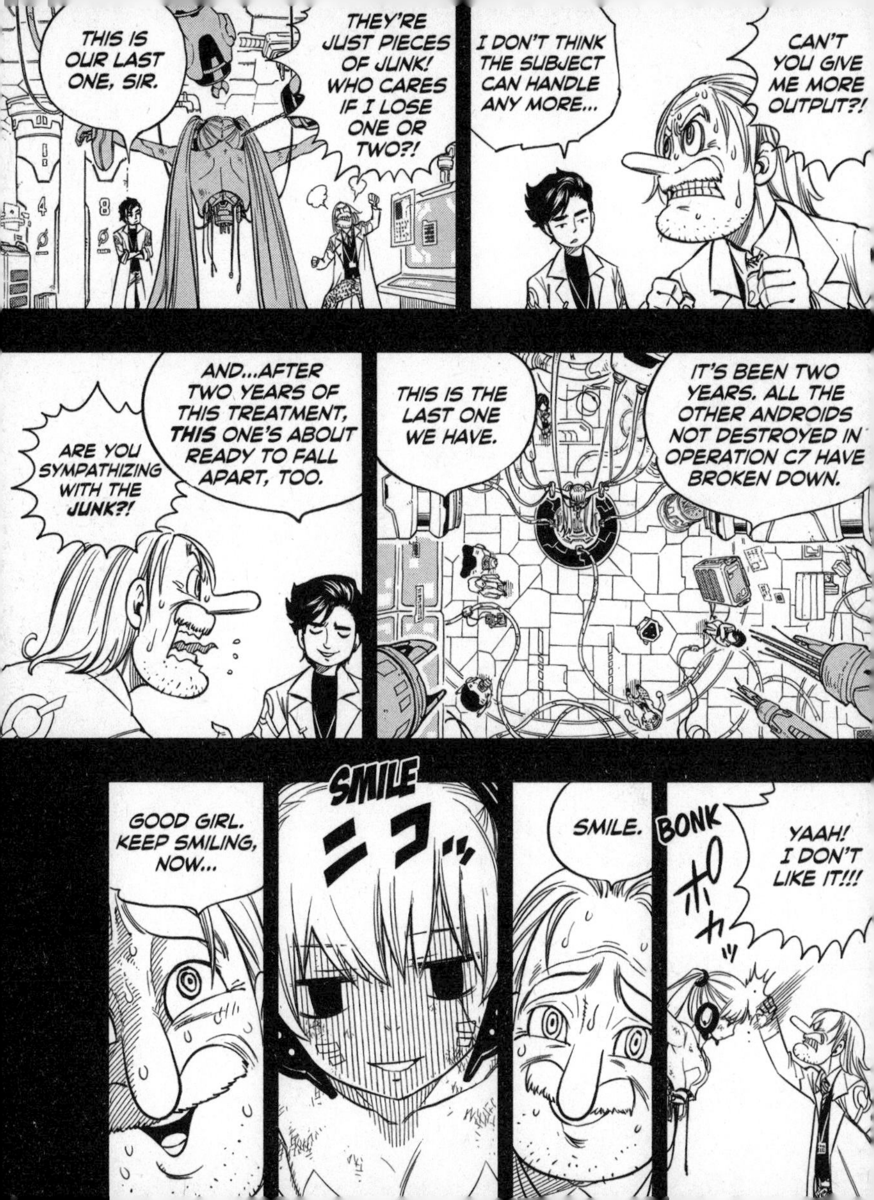
CAN'T YOU GIVE ME MORE OUTPUT?!
I DON'T THINK THE SUBJECT CAN HANDLE ANY MORE...
THEY'RE JUST PIECES OF JUNK! WHO CARES IF I LOSE ONE OR TWO?!
THIS IS OUR LAST ONE, SIR.
IT'S BEEN TWO YEARS. ALL THE OTHER ANDROIDS NOT DESTROYED IN OPERATION C7 HAVE BROKEN DOWN.
THIS IS THE LAST ONE WE HAVE.
AND...AFTER TWO YEARS OF THIS TREATMENT, **THIS** ONE'S ABOUT READY TO FALL APART, TOO.
ARE YOU SYMPATHIZING WITH THE **JUNK**?!
YAAH! I DON'T LIKE IT!!!
BONK
ポカッ
SMILE.
SMILE
ニコッ
GOOD GIRL. KEEP SMILING, NOW...

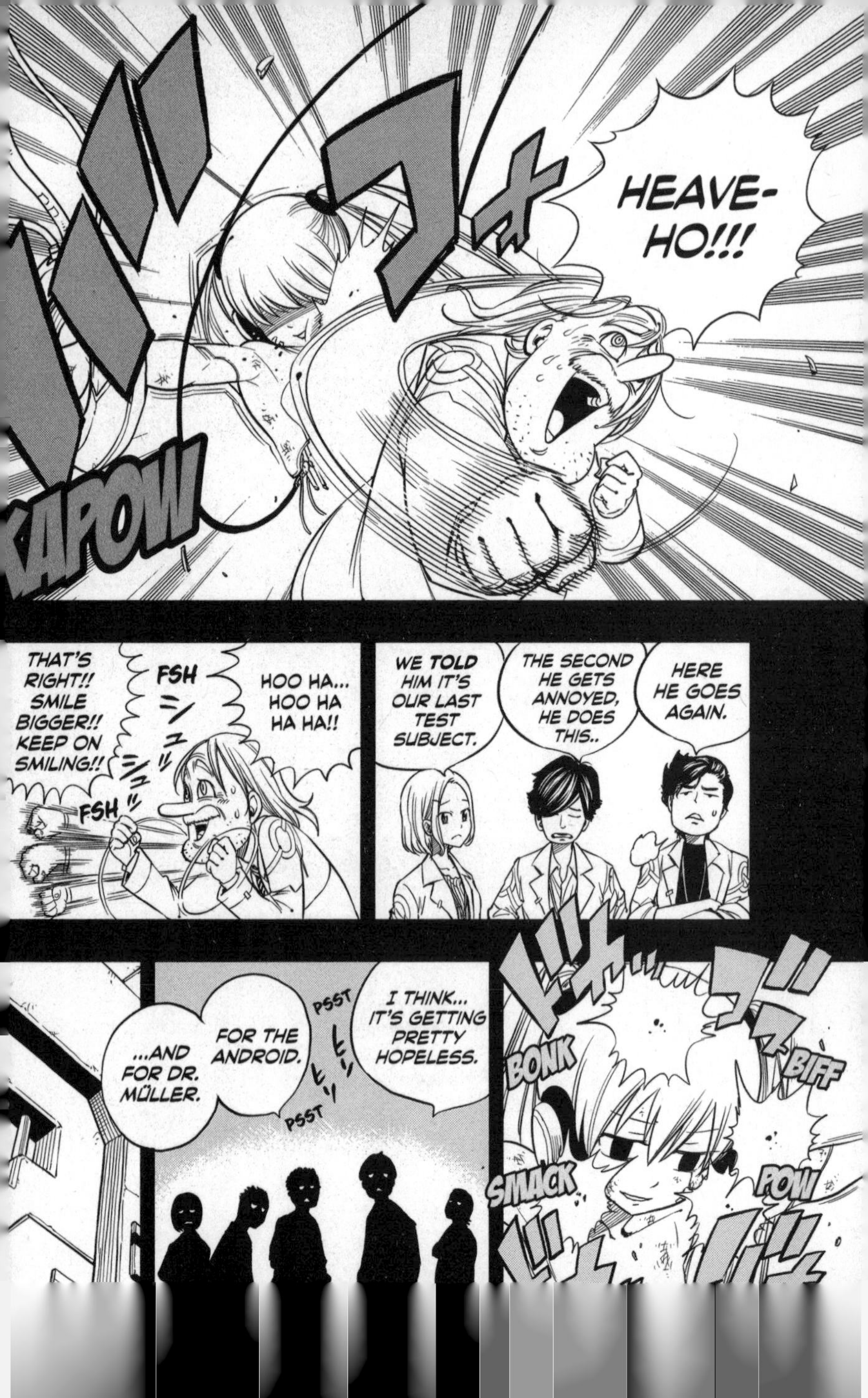
HEAVE-HO!!!
KAPOW
HERE HE GOES AGAIN.
THE SECOND HE GETS ANNOYED, HE DOES THIS..
WE TOLD HIM IT'S OUR LAST TEST SUBJECT.
HOO HA... HOO HA HA HA!!
FSH
THAT'S RIGHT!! SMILE BIGGER!! KEEP ON SMILING!!
FSH
BONK
BIFF
SMACK
POW
I THINK... IT'S GETTING PRETTY HOPELESS.
PSST
FOR THE ANDROID.
...AND FOR DR. MÜLLER.
PSST

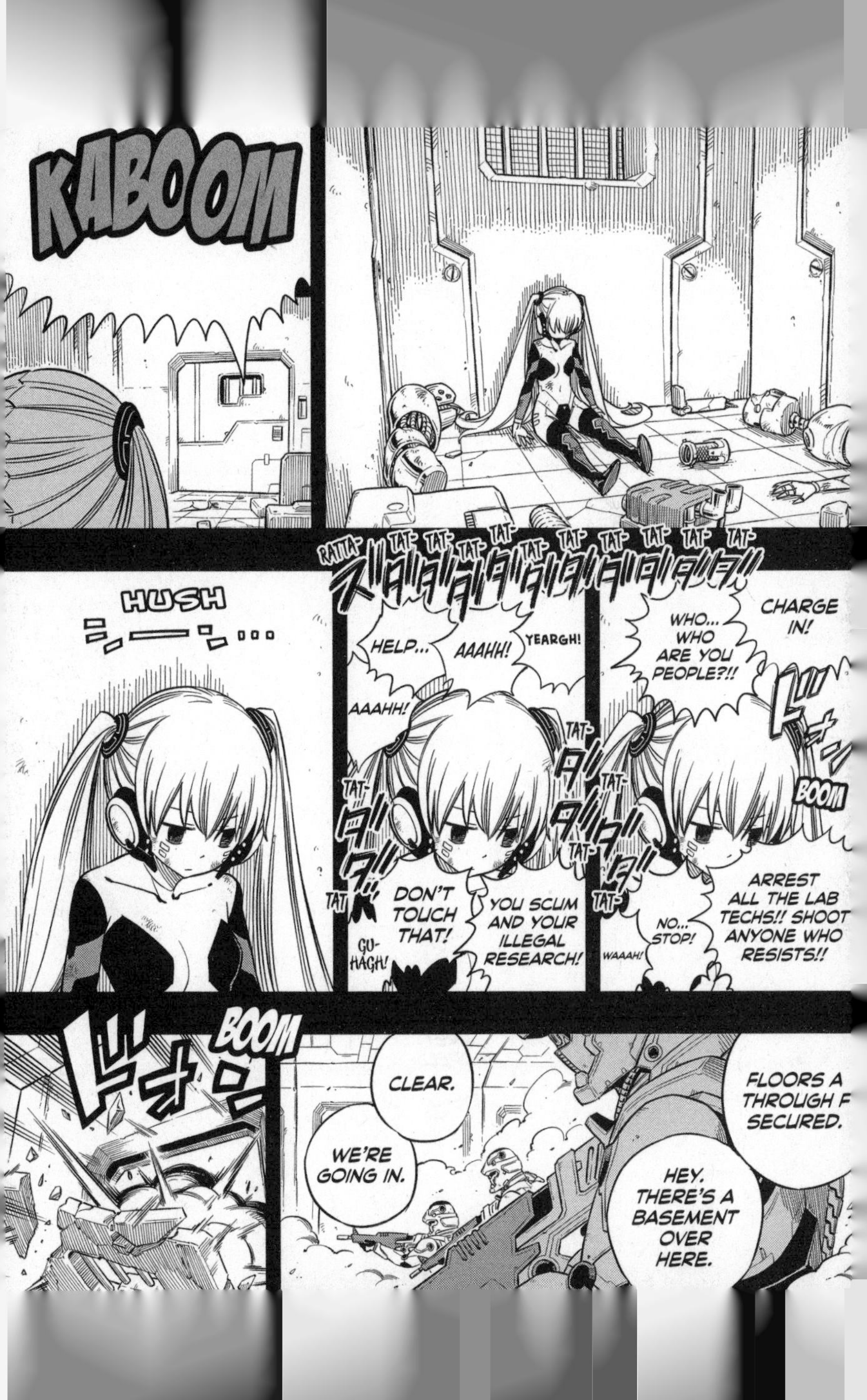
KABOOM
RATTA-TAT-TAT-TAT-TAT-TAT-TAT-TAT-TAT-TAT-TAT-
CHARGE IN!
WHO... WHO ARE YOU PEOPLE?!!
BOOM
TAT-
TAT-
ARREST ALL THE LAB TECHS!! SHOOT ANYONE WHO RESISTS!!
NO... STOP!
WAAAH!
YEARGH!
AAAHH!
HELP...
AAAHH!
TAT-
TAT-
TAT
YOU SCUM AND YOUR ILLEGAL RESEARCH!
DON'T TOUCH THAT!
GU-HAGH!
HUSH
FLOORS A THROUGH F SECURED.
HEY. THERE'S A BASEMENT OVER HERE.
CLEAR.
WE'RE GOING IN.
BOOM

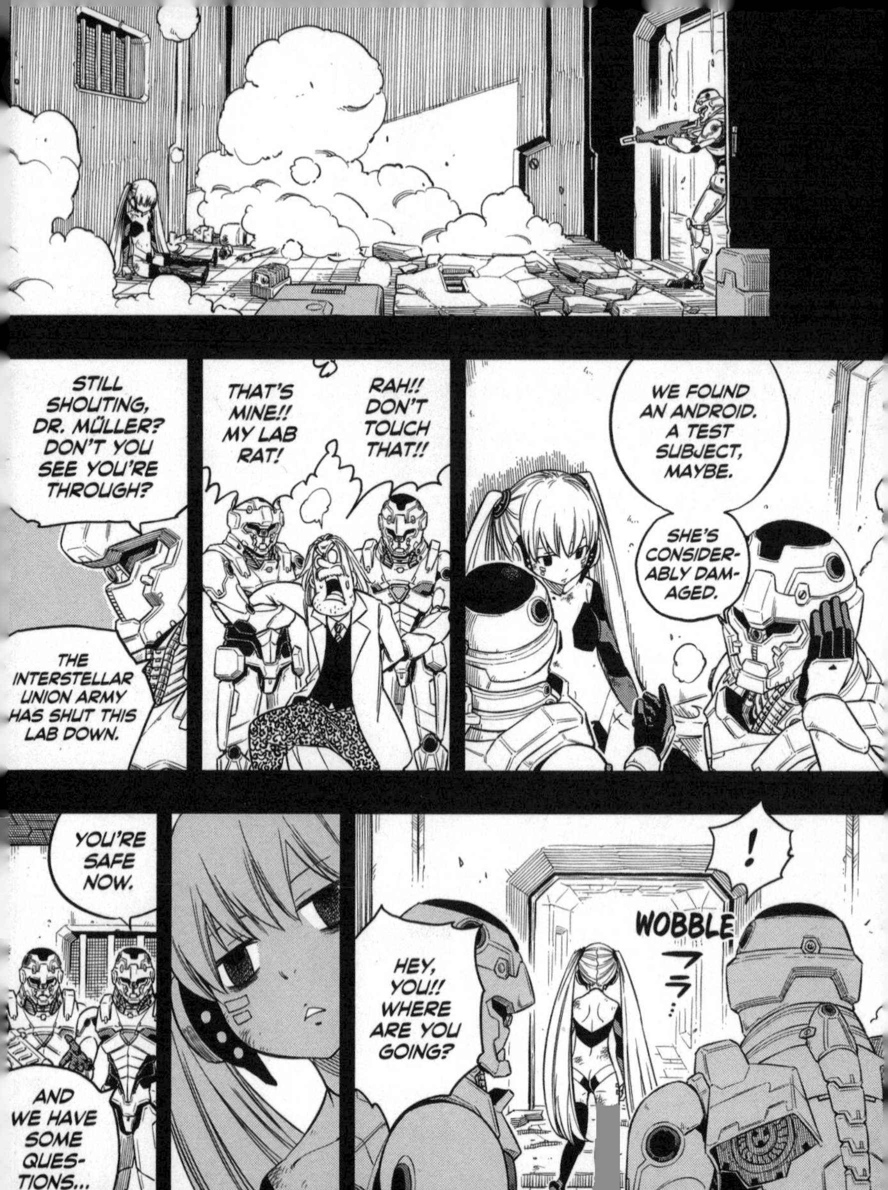
WE FOUND AN ANDROID. A TEST SUBJECT, MAYBE.
SHE'S CONSIDER-ABLY DAM-AGED.
RAH!! DON'T TOUCH THAT!!
THAT'S MINE!! MY LAB RAT!
STILL SHOUTING, DR. MÜLLER? DON'T YOU SEE YOU'RE THROUGH?
THE INTERSTELLAR UNION ARMY HAS SHUT THIS LAB DOWN.
!
WOBBLE
HEY, YOU!! WHERE ARE YOU GOING?
YOU'RE SAFE NOW.
AND WE HAVE SOME QUES-TIONS...

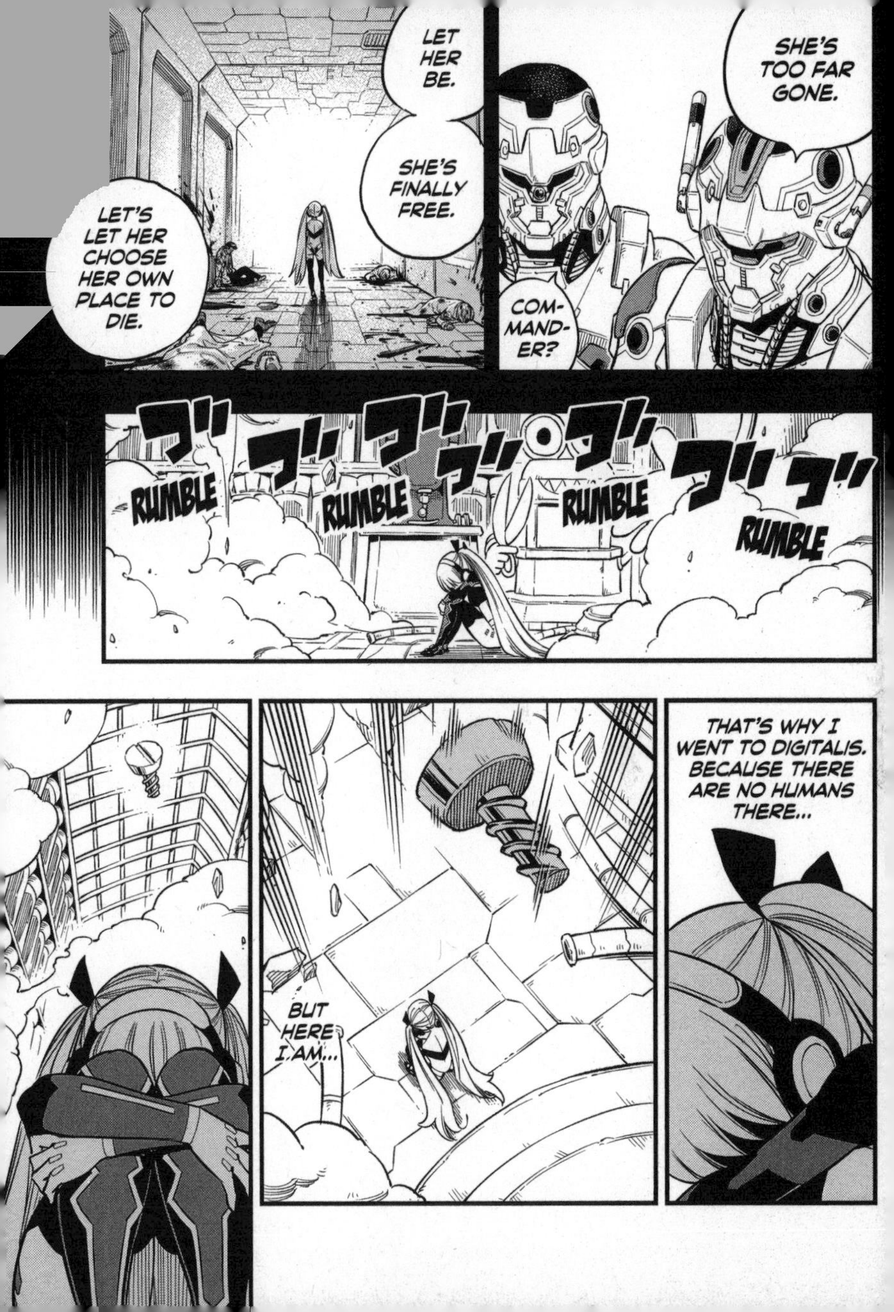
SHE'S TOO FAR GONE.
COM-MAND-ER?
LET HER BE.
SHE'S FINALLY FREE.
LET'S LET HER CHOOSE HER OWN PLACE TO DIE.
RUMBLE
RUMBLE
RUMBLE
RUMBLE
THAT'S WHY I WENT TO DIGITALIS. BECAUSE THERE ARE NO HUMANS THERE...
BUT HERE I AM...

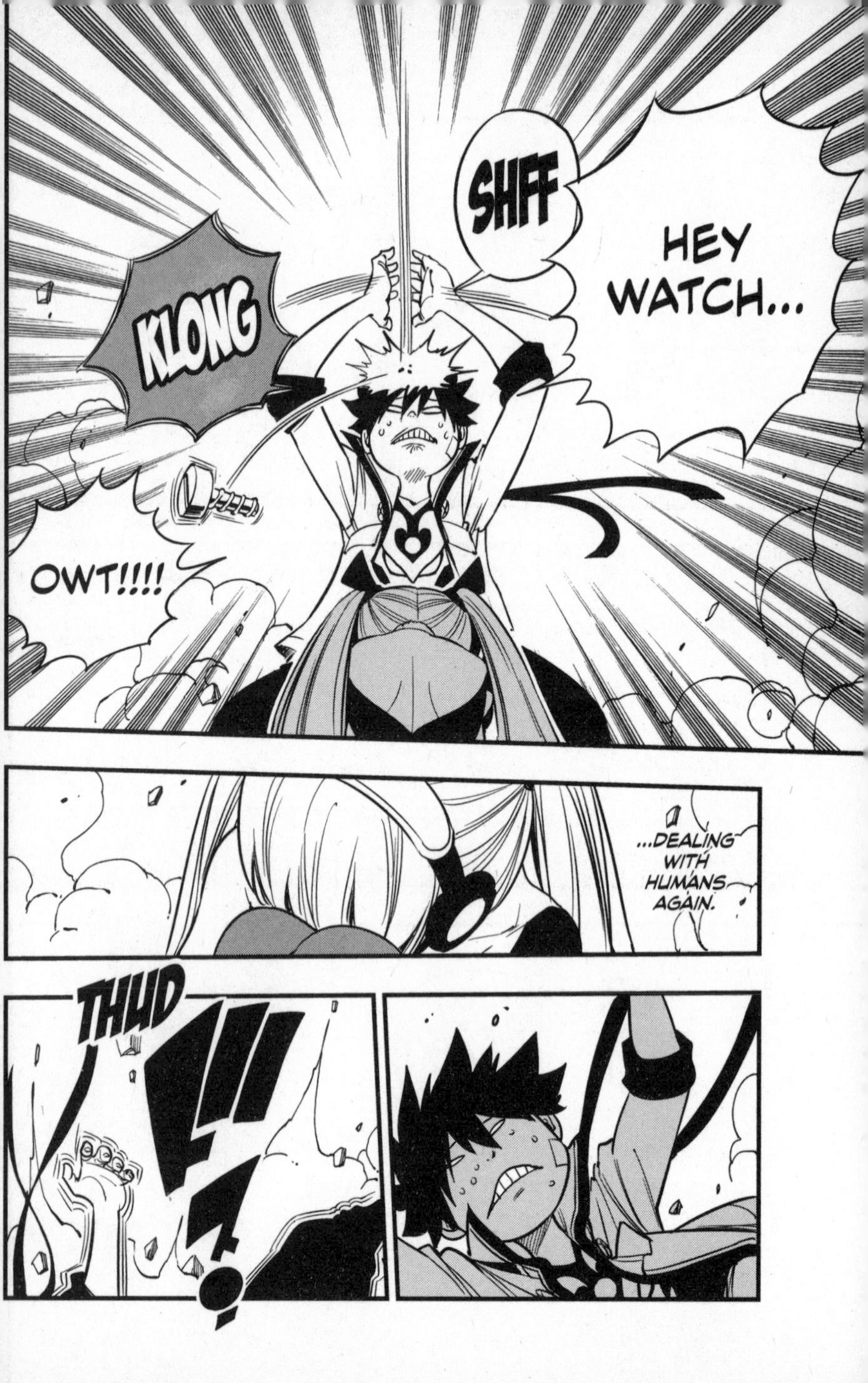
SHFF
HEY WATCH...
KLONG
OWT!!!!
...DEALING WITH HUMANS AGAIN.
THUD
!!!?

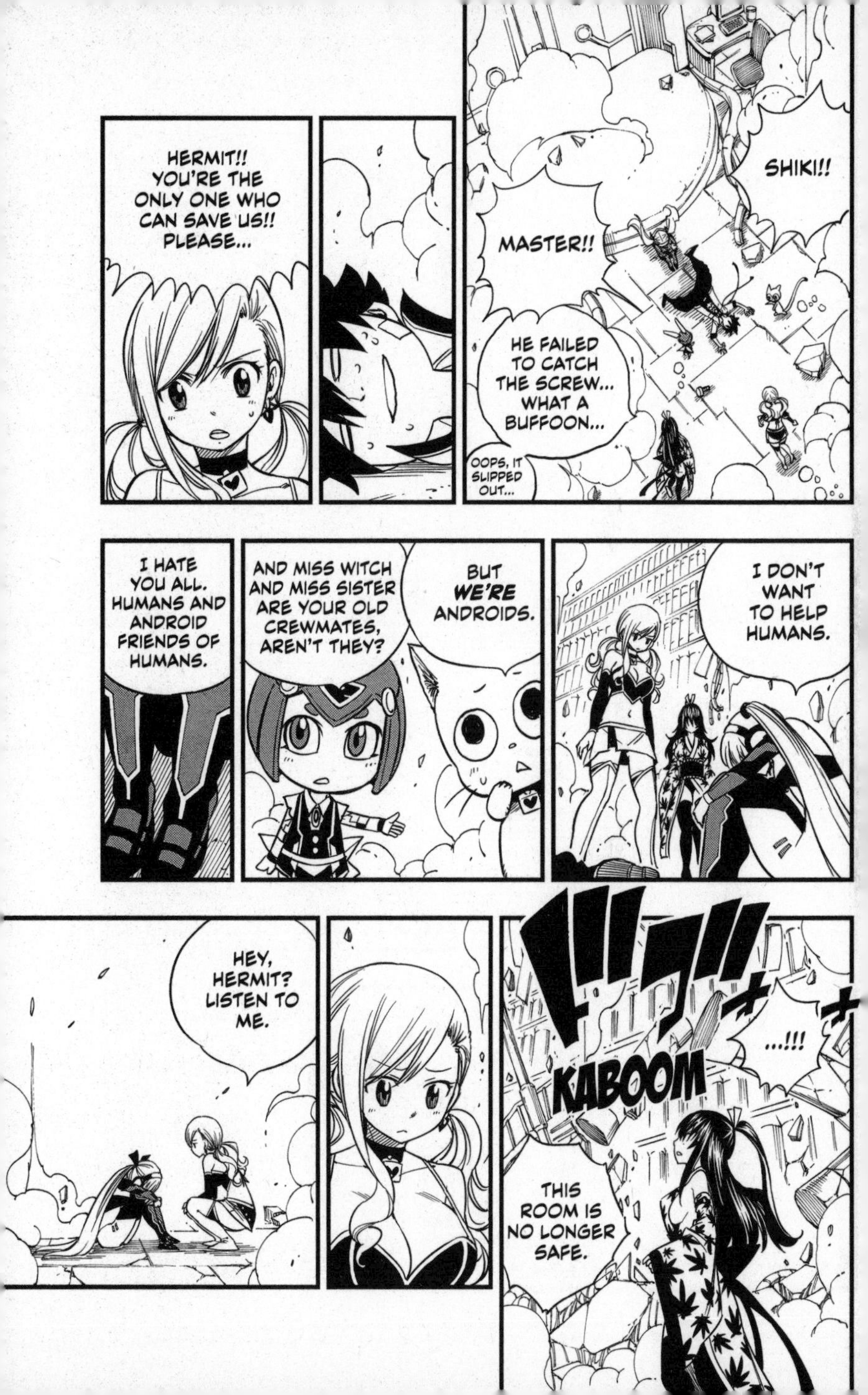
SHIKI!!
MASTER!!
HE FAILED TO CATCH THE SCREW... WHAT A BUFFOON...
OOPS, IT SLIPPED OUT...
HERMIT!! YOU'RE THE ONLY ONE WHO CAN SAVE US!! PLEASE...
I DON'T WANT TO HELP HUMANS.
BUT WE'RE ANDROIDS.
AND MISS WITCH AND MISS SISTER ARE YOUR OLD CREWMATES, AREN'T THEY?
I HATE YOU ALL. HUMANS AND ANDROID FRIENDS OF HUMANS.
KABOOM
...!!!
THIS ROOM IS NO LONGER SAFE.
HEY, HERMIT? LISTEN TO ME.

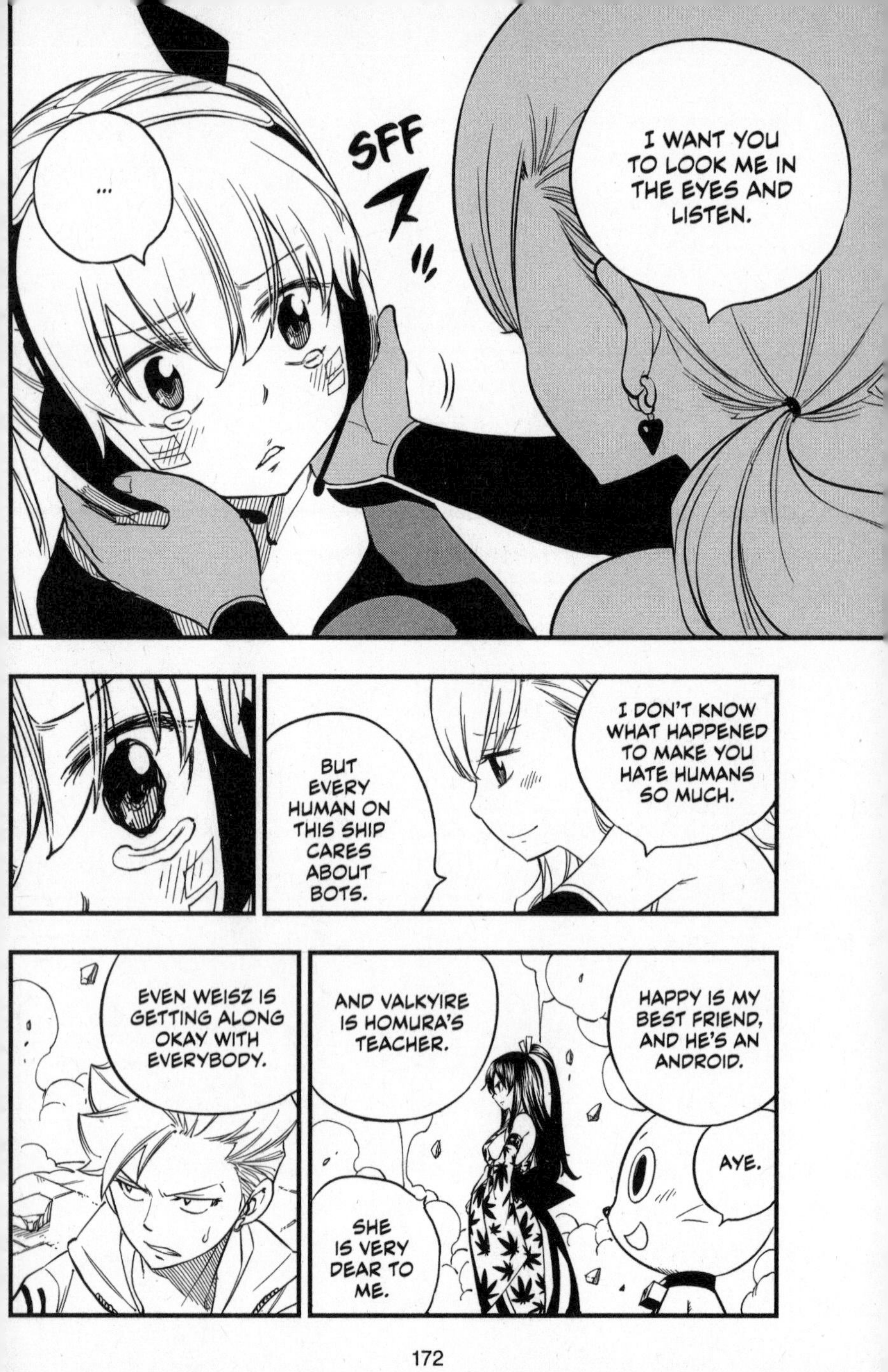
I WANT YOU TO LOOK ME IN THE EYES AND LISTEN.
SFF
...
I DON'T KNOW WHAT HAPPENED TO MAKE YOU HATE HUMANS SO MUCH.
BUT EVERY HUMAN ON THIS SHIP CARES ABOUT BOTS.
HAPPY IS MY BEST FRIEND, AND HE'S AN ANDROID.
AYE.
AND VALKYIRE IS HOMURA'S TEACHER.
SHE IS VERY DEAR TO ME.
EVEN WEISZ IS GETTING ALONG OKAY WITH EVERYBODY.

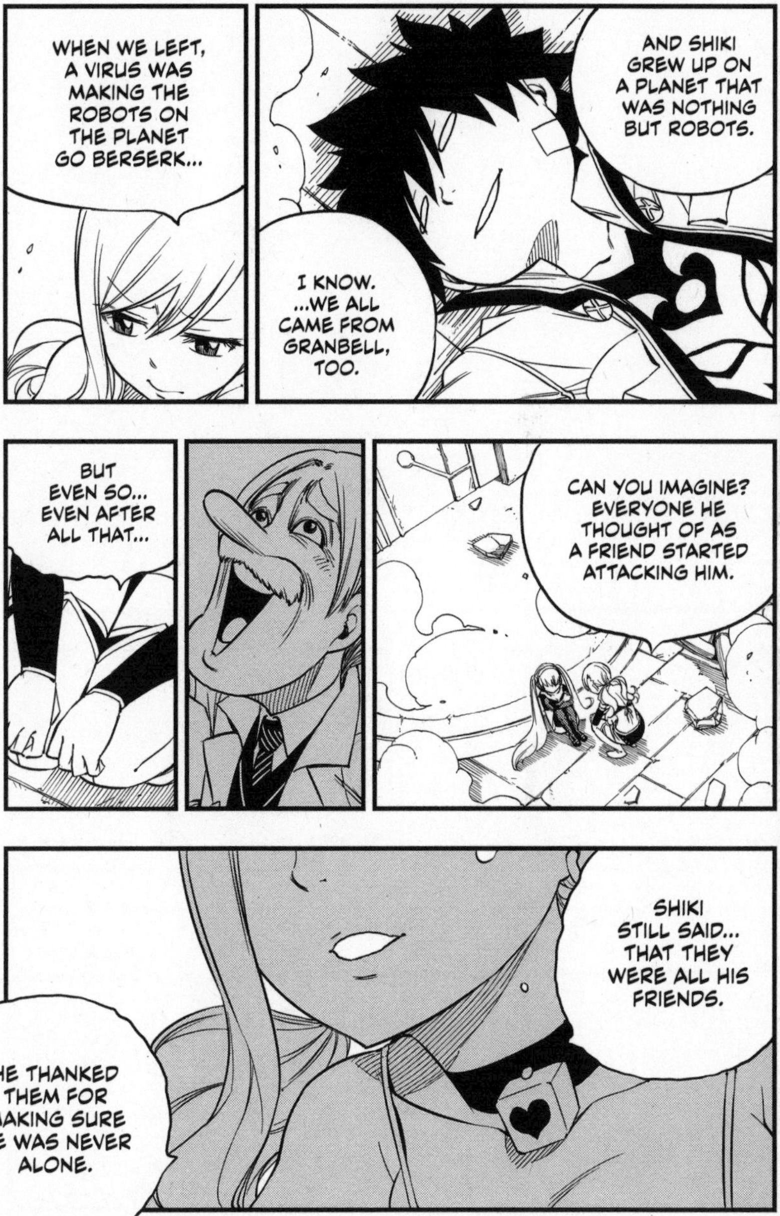
AND SHIKI GREW UP ON A PLANET THAT WAS NOTHING BUT ROBOTS.
I KNOW. ...WE ALL CAME FROM GRANBELL, TOO.
WHEN WE LEFT, A VIRUS WAS MAKING THE ROBOTS ON THE PLANET GO BERSERK...
CAN YOU IMAGINE? EVERYONE HE THOUGHT OF AS A FRIEND STARTED ATTACKING HIM.
BUT EVEN SO... EVEN AFTER ALL THAT...
SHIKI STILL SAID... THAT THEY WERE ALL HIS FRIENDS.
HE THANKED THEM FOR MAKING SURE HE WAS NEVER ALONE.

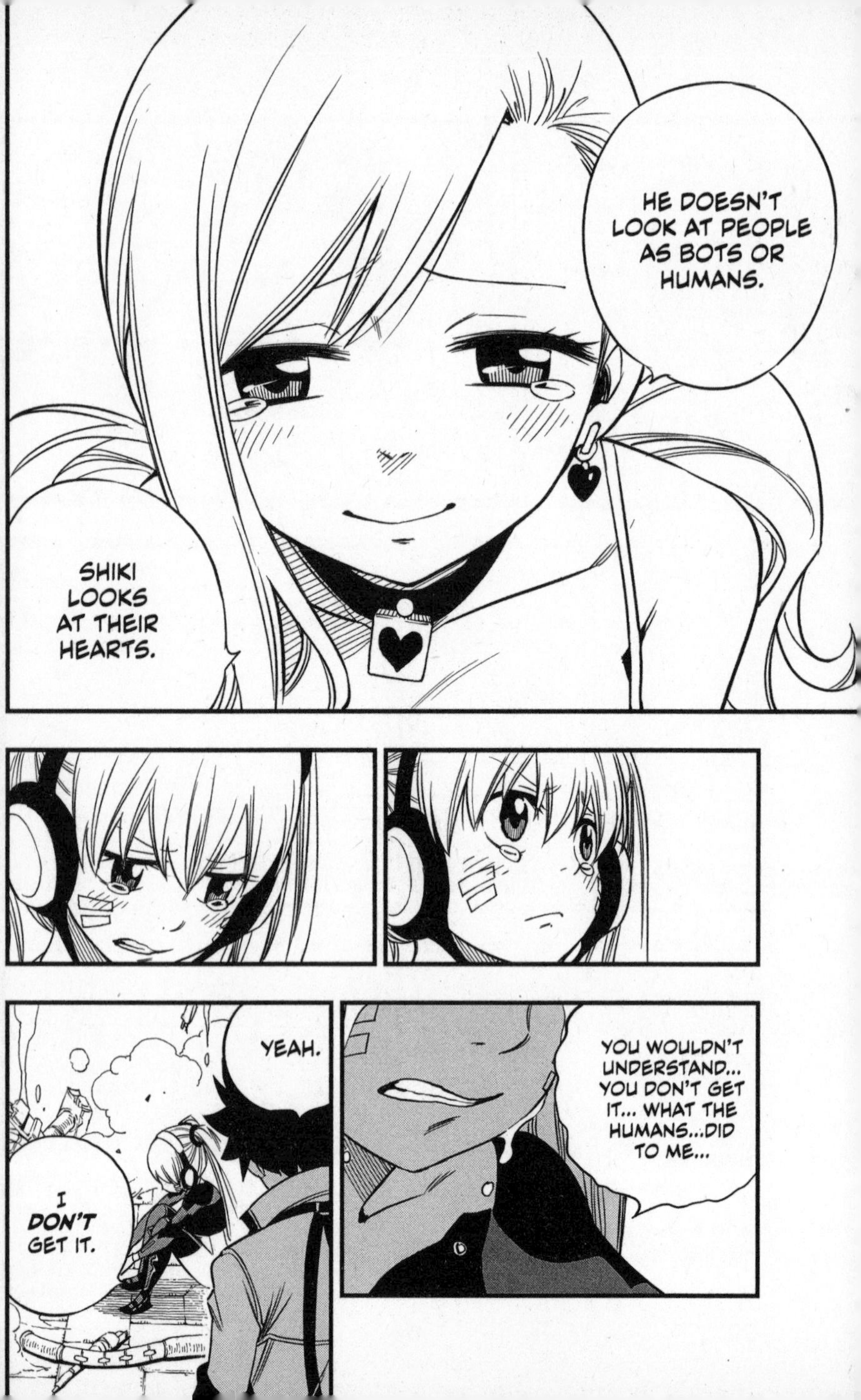
HE DOESN'T LOOK AT PEOPLE AS BOTS OR HUMANS.
SHIKI LOOKS AT THEIR HEARTS.
YOU WOULDN'T UNDERSTAND... YOU DON'T GET IT... WHAT THE HUMANS...DID TO ME...
YEAH.
I *DON'T* GET IT.

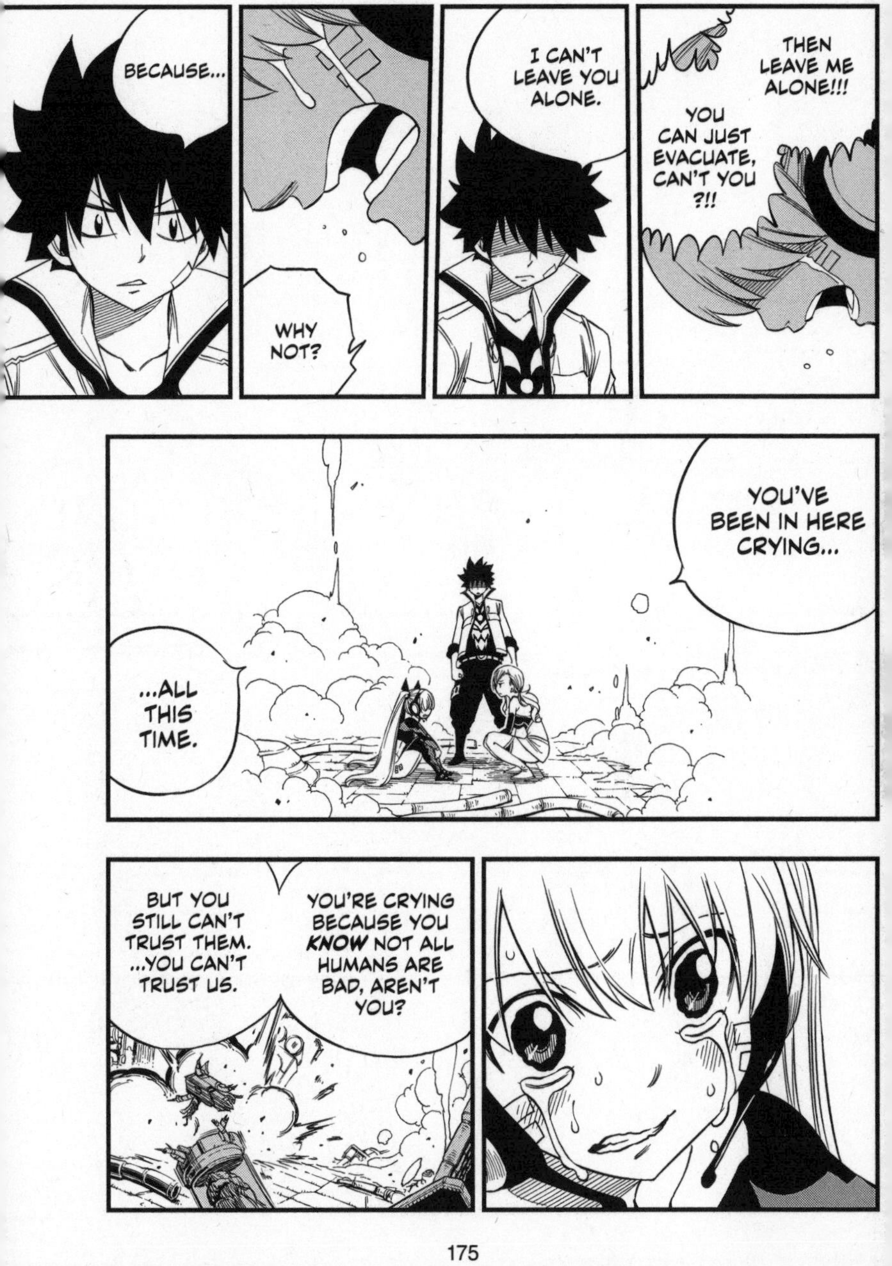
THEN LEAVE ME ALONE!!!
YOU CAN JUST EVACUATE, CAN'T YOU ?!!
I CAN'T LEAVE YOU ALONE.
WHY NOT?
BECAUSE...
YOU'VE BEEN IN HERE CRYING...
...ALL THIS TIME.
YOU'RE CRYING BECAUSE YOU *KNOW* NOT ALL HUMANS ARE BAD, AREN'T YOU?
BUT YOU STILL CAN'T TRUST THEM. ...YOU CAN'T TRUST US.

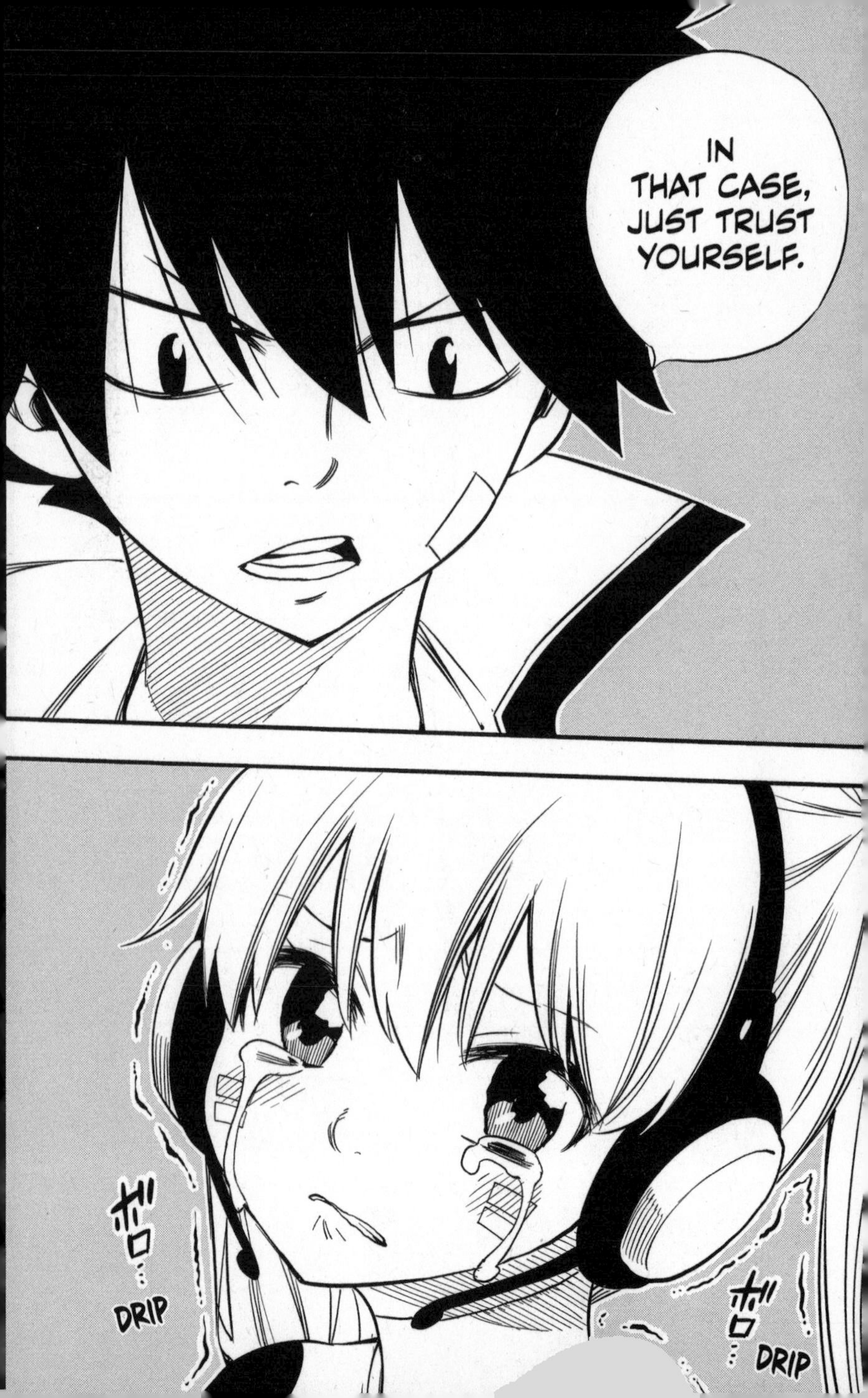
IN THAT CASE, JUST TRUST YOURSELF.
ポロ… DRIP
ポロ… DRIP

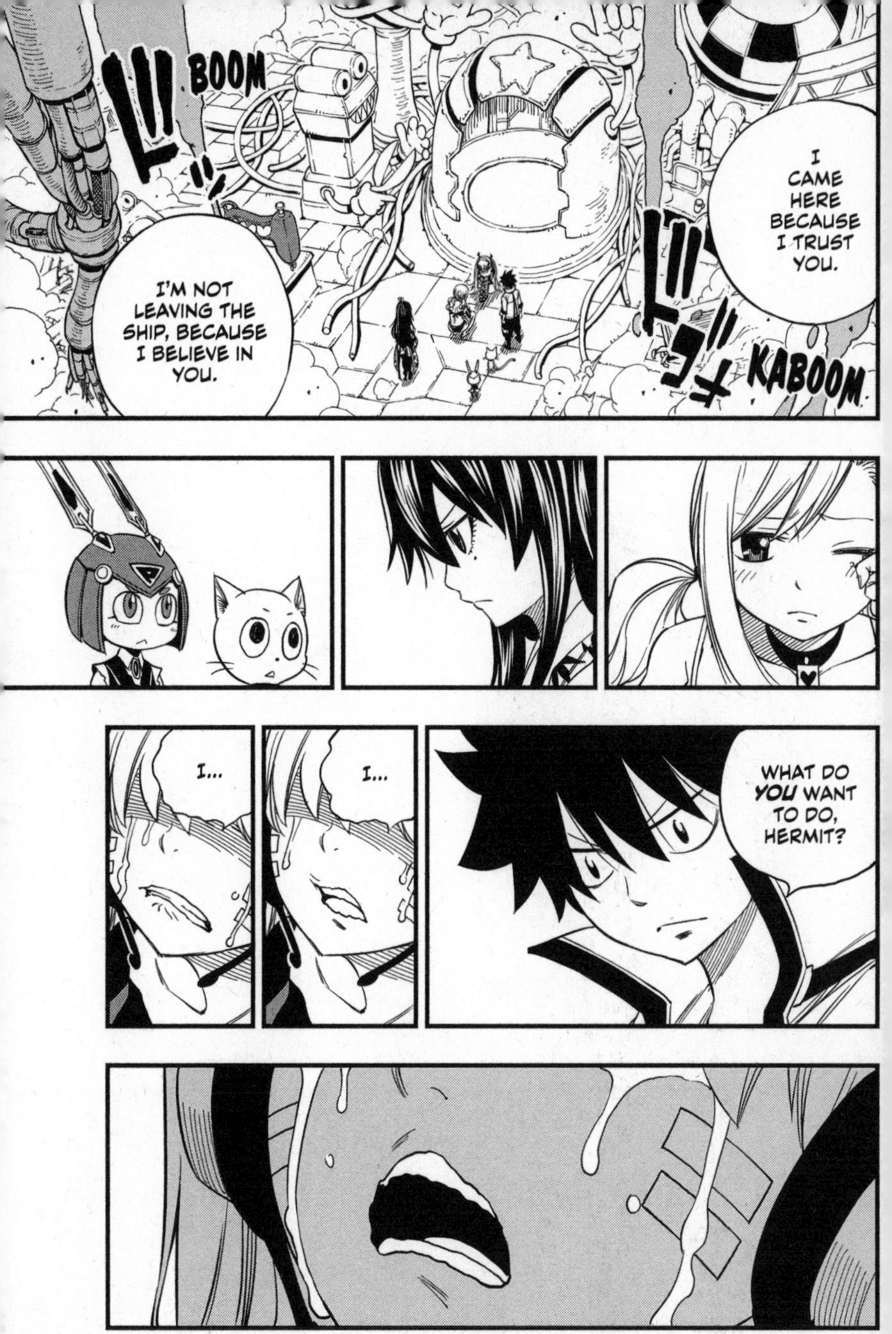
I CAME HERE BECAUSE I TRUST YOU.
KABOOM
BOOM
I'M NOT LEAVING THE SHIP, BECAUSE I BELIEVE IN YOU.
WHAT DO *YOU* WANT TO DO, HERMIT?
I...
I...

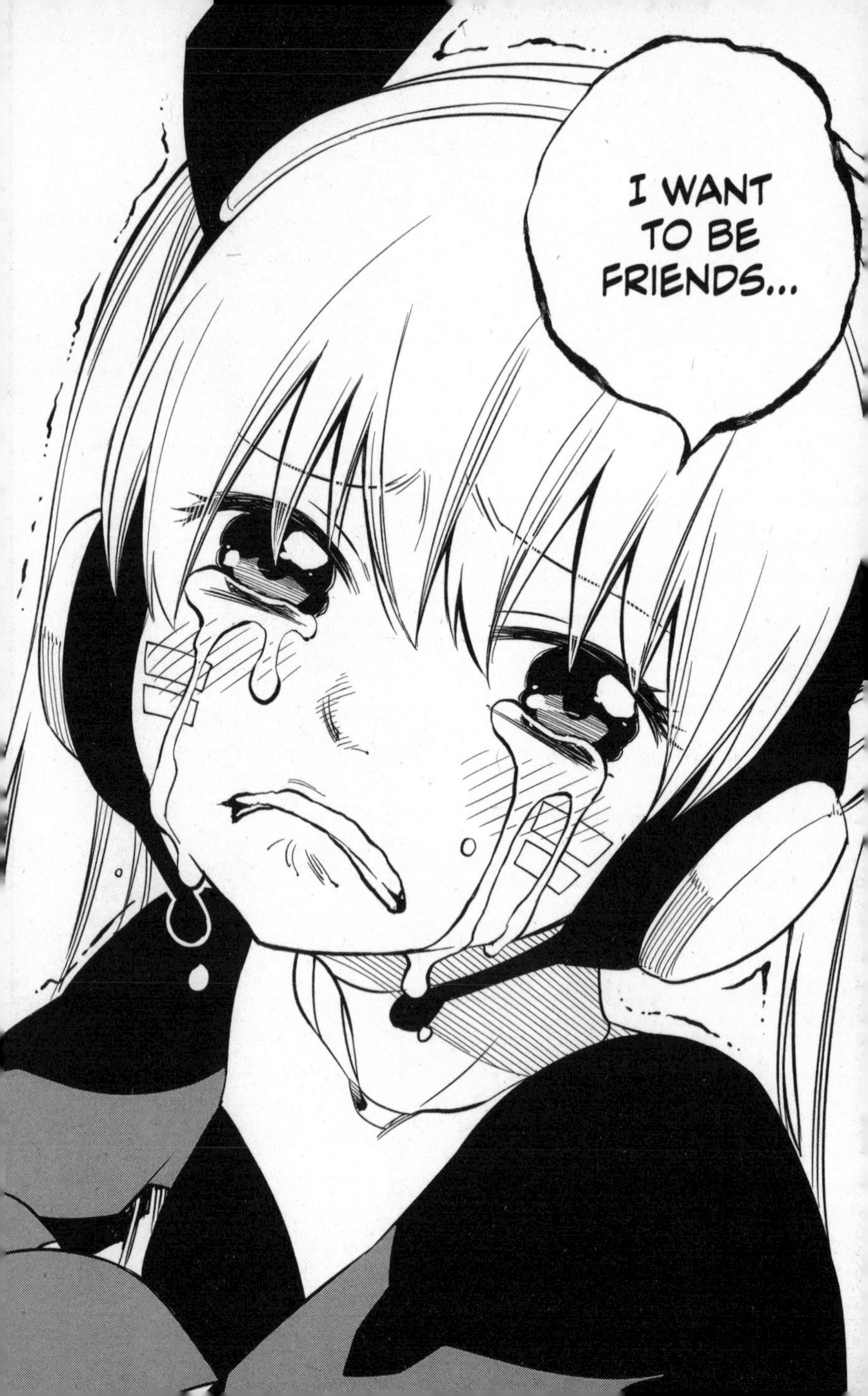
I WANT TO BE FRIENDS...

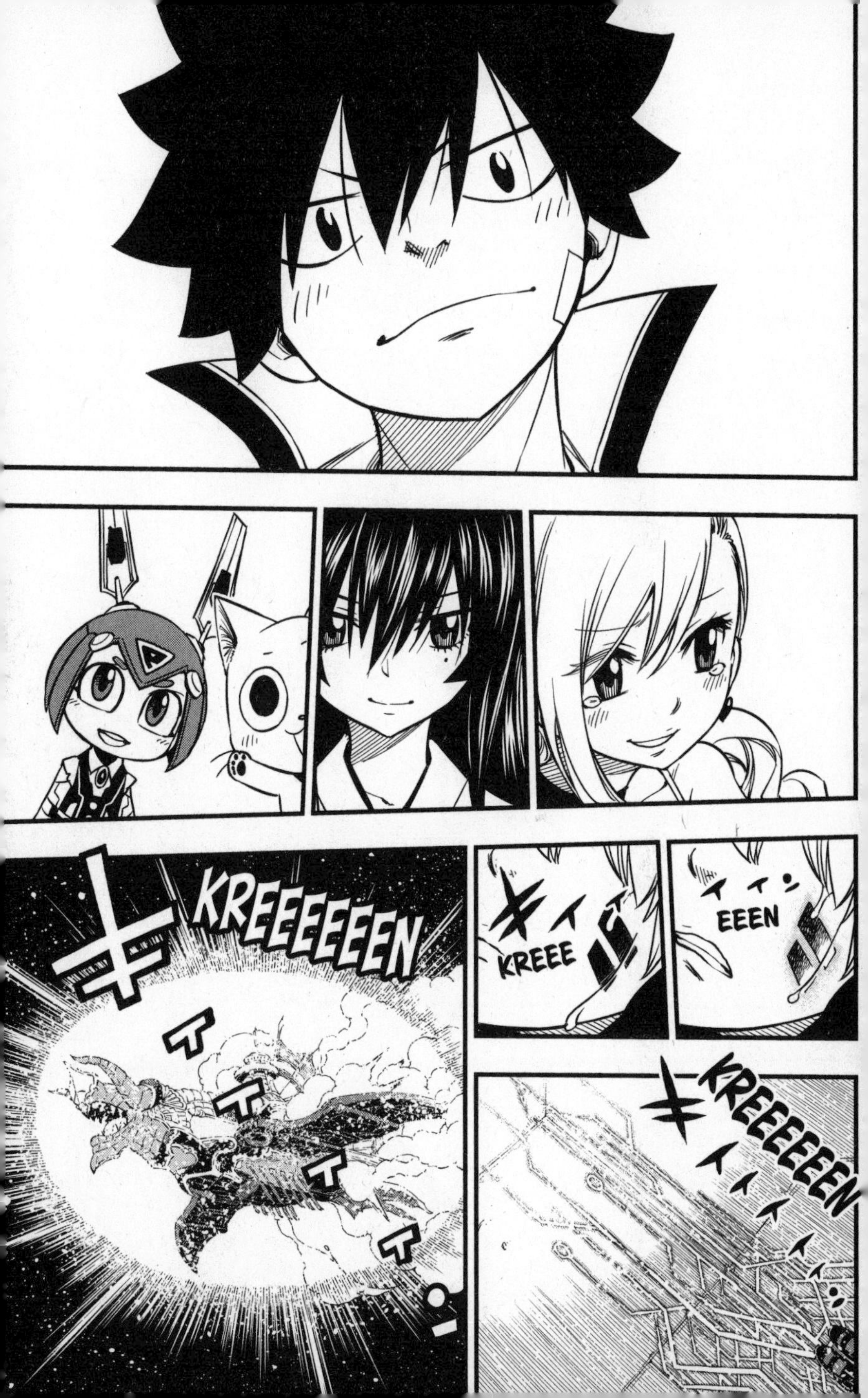
KREEEEEEEN
KREEE
EEEN
KREEEEEEEN

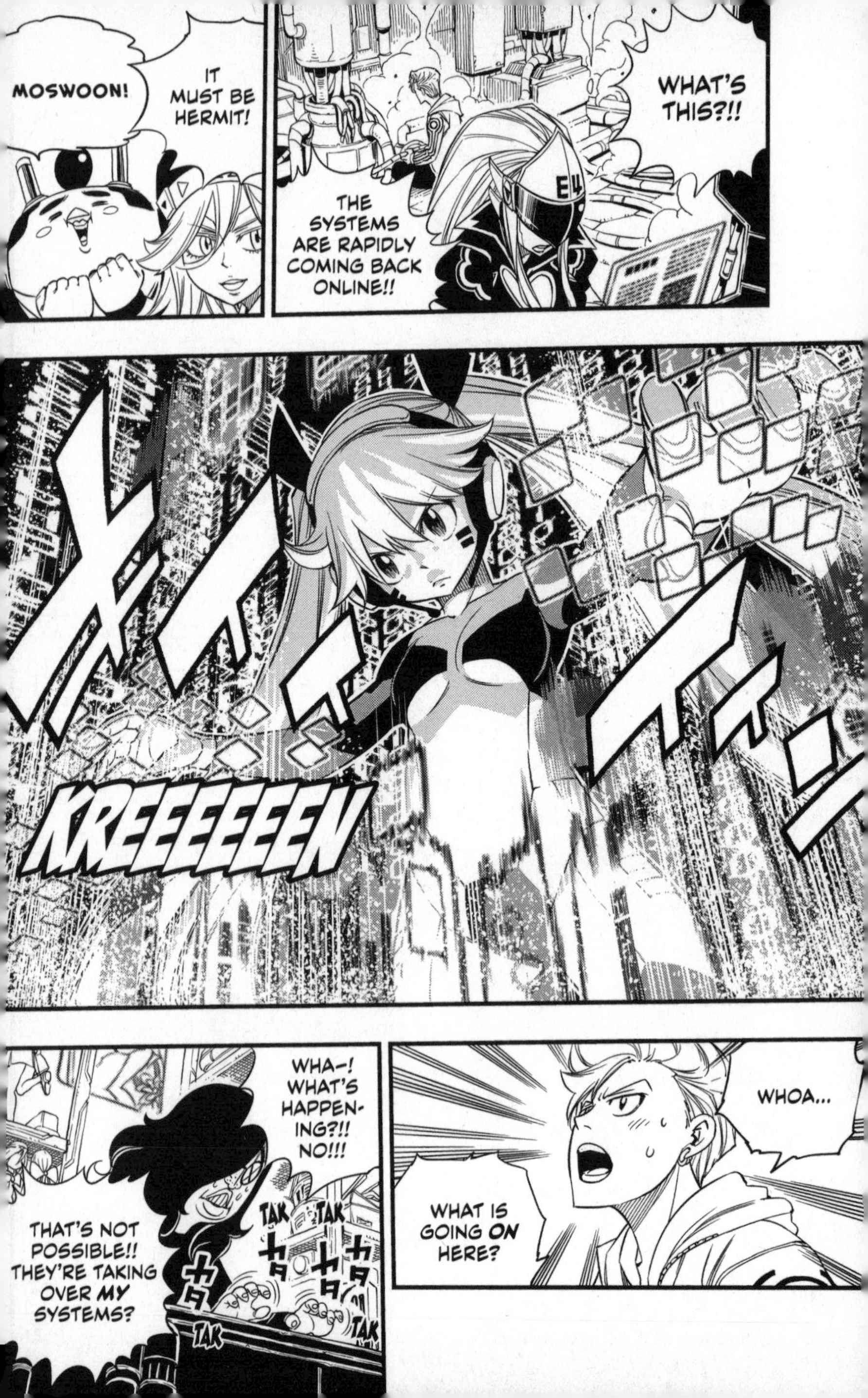
WHAT'S THIS?!!
THE SYSTEMS ARE RAPIDLY COMING BACK ONLINE!!
IT MUST BE HERMIT!
MOSWOON!
KREEEEEEEN
WHOA...
WHAT IS GOING ON HERE?
WHA-! WHAT'S HAPPEN-ING?!! NO!!!
THAT'S NOT POSSIBLE!! THEY'RE TAKING OVER MY SYSTEMS?
TAK
TAK
TAK
TAK

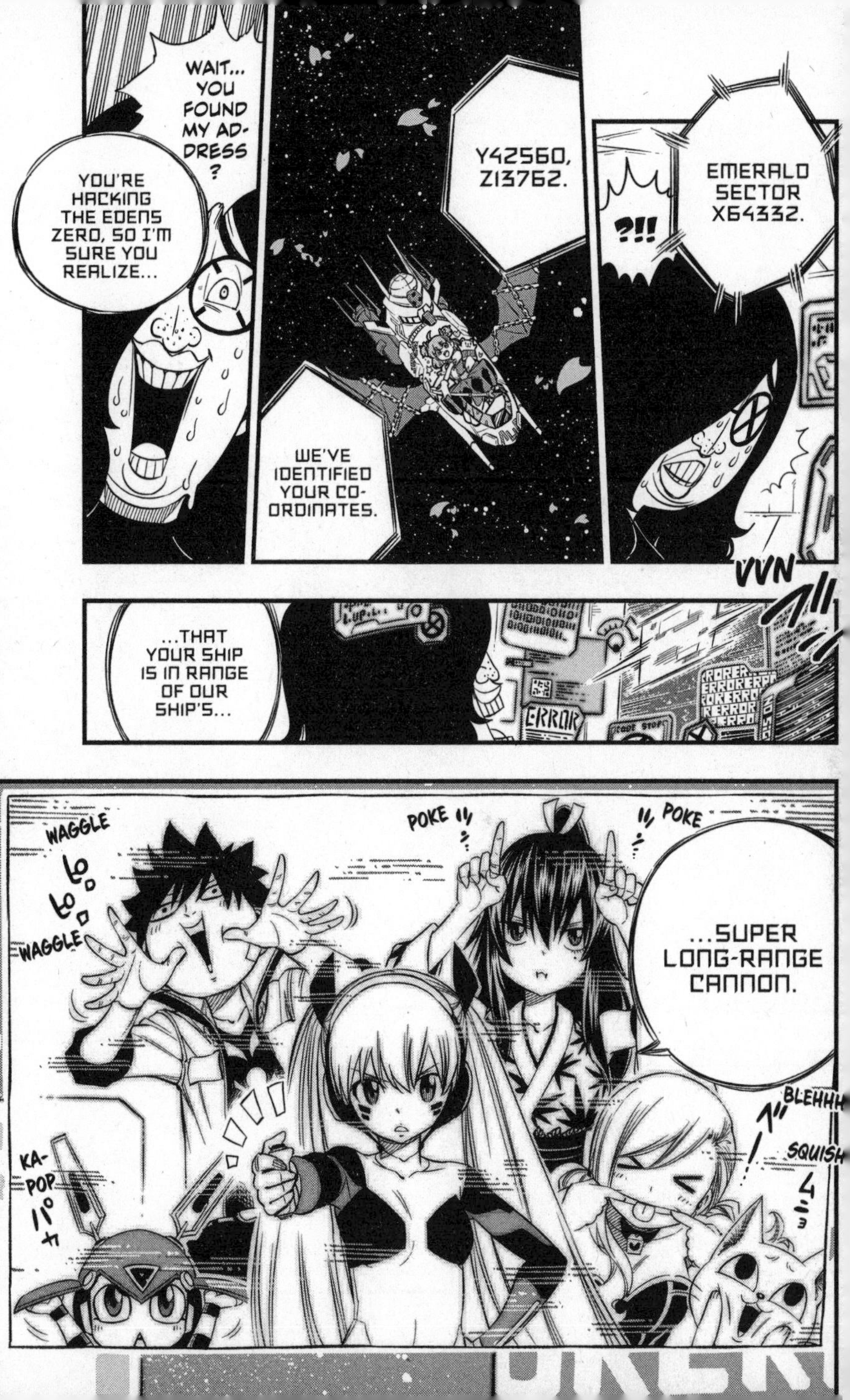
EMERALD SECTOR X64332.
?!!
Y42560, Z13762.
WE'VE IDENTIFIED YOUR CO-ORDINATES.
WAIT... YOU FOUND MY AD-DRESS?
YOU'RE HACKING THE EDENS ZERO, SO I'M SURE YOU REALIZE...
VVN
...THAT YOUR SHIP IS IN RANGE OF OUR SHIP'S...
...SUPER LONG-RANGE CANNON.
POKE
POKE
WAGGLE
WAGGLE
BLEHHH
SQUISH
KA-POP

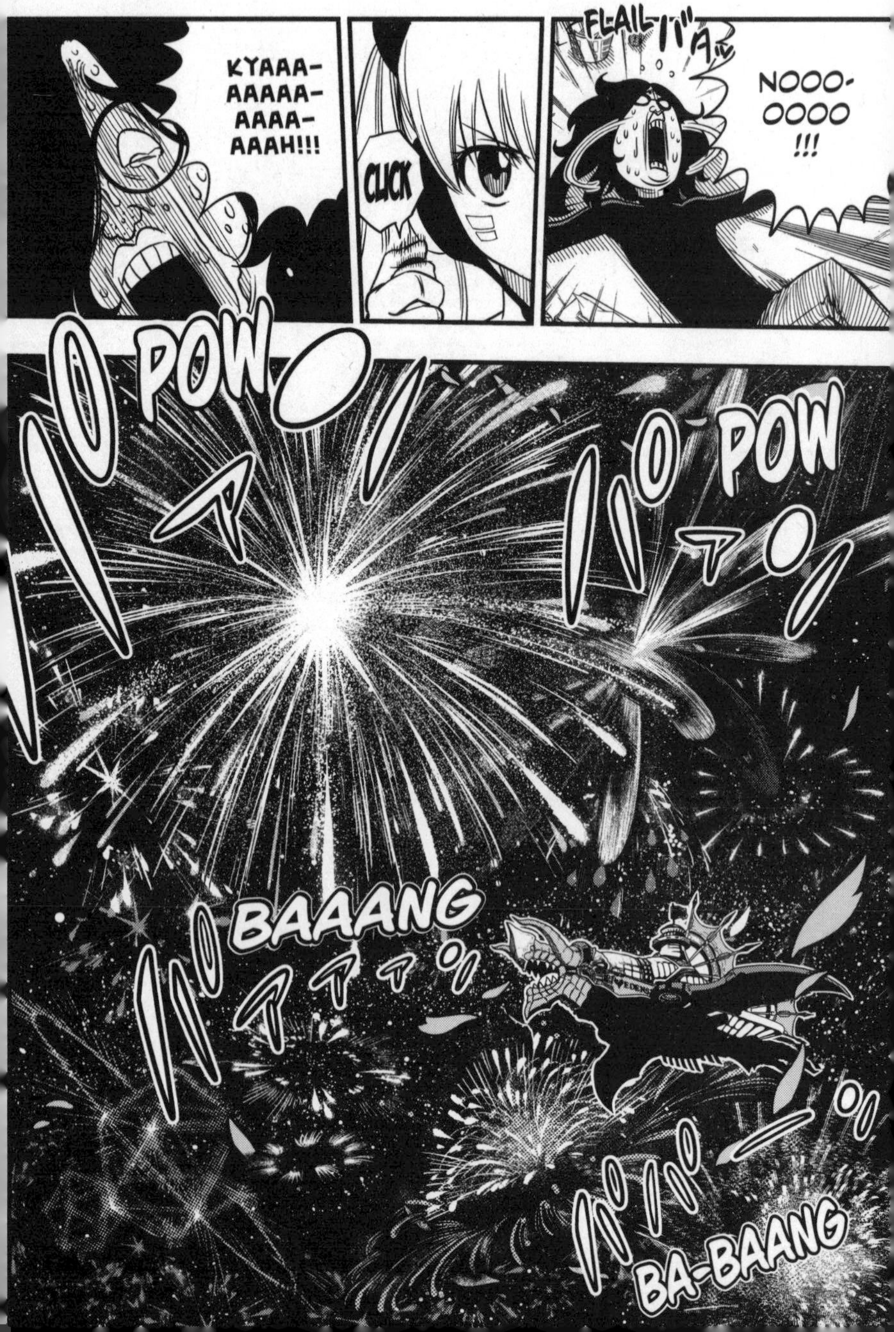
FLAIL
NOOO-OOOO!!!
CLICK
KYAAA-AAAAA-AAAA-AAAH!!!
POW
POW
BAAANG
BA-BAANG

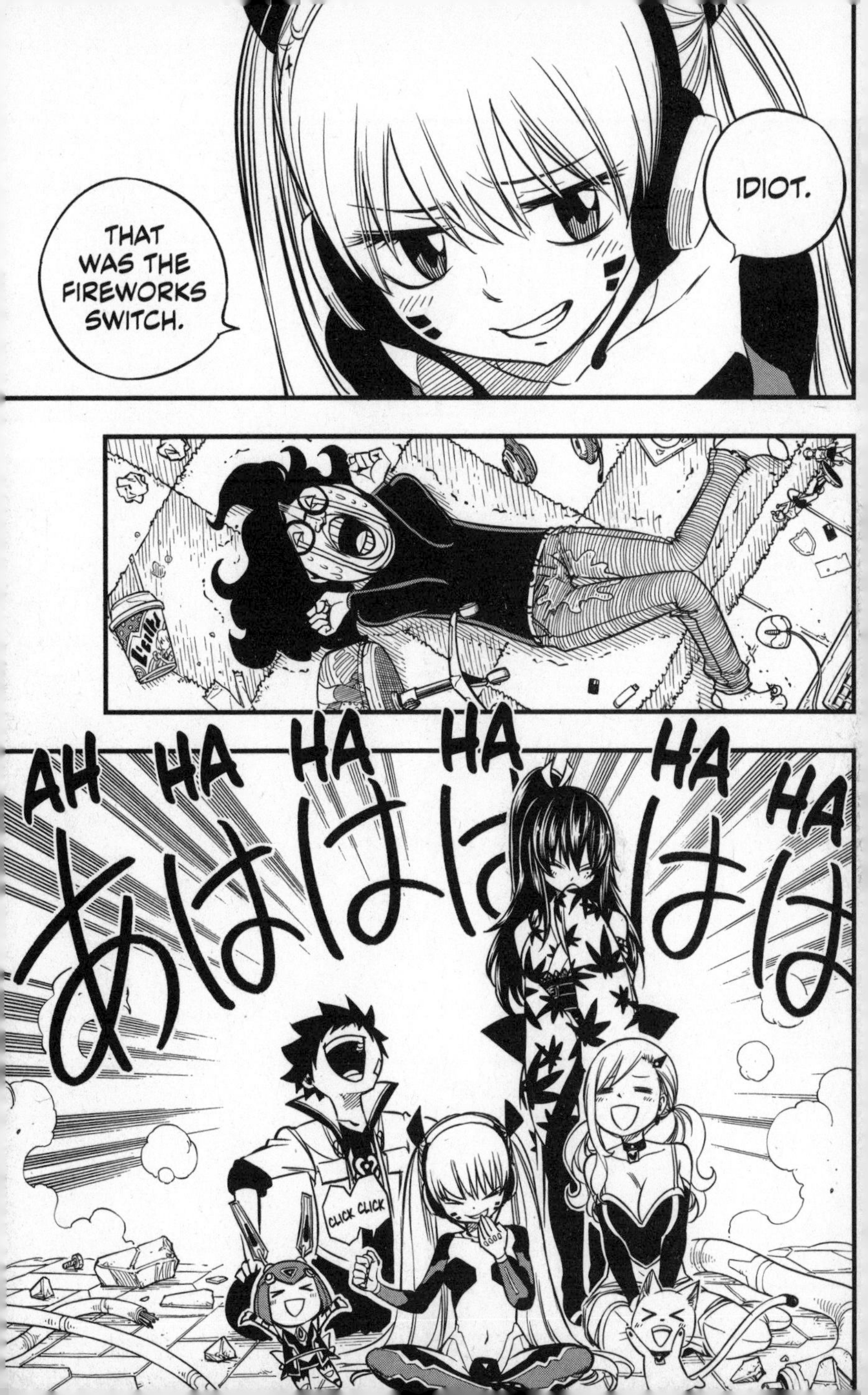

IDIOT.
THAT WAS THE FIREWORKS SWITCH.
AH HA HA HA HA HA
あははははは
CLICK CLICK

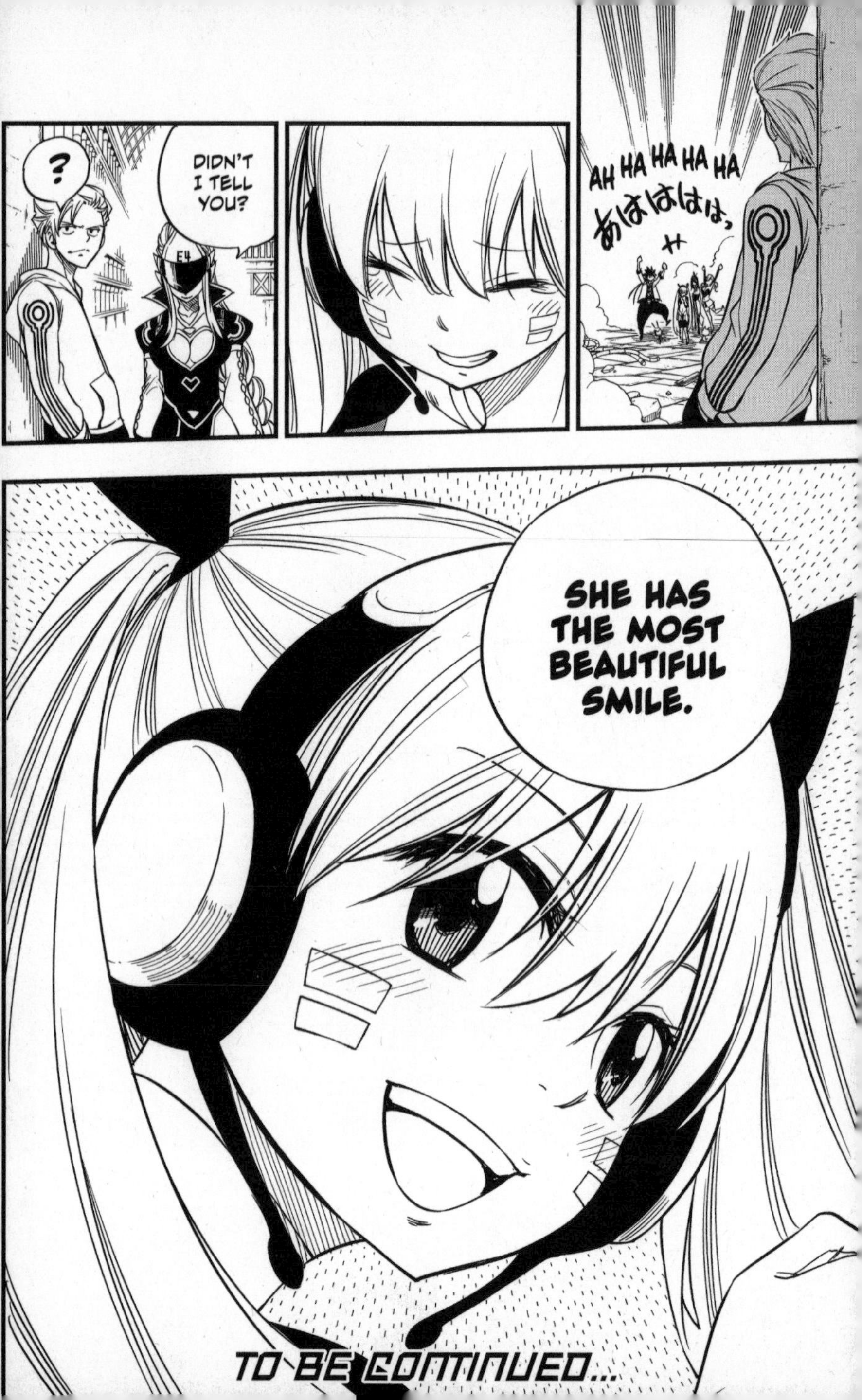
AH HA HA HA HA
あははははっ
DIDN'T I TELL YOU?
?
SHE HAS THE MOST BEAUTIFUL SMILE.
TO BE CONTINUED...

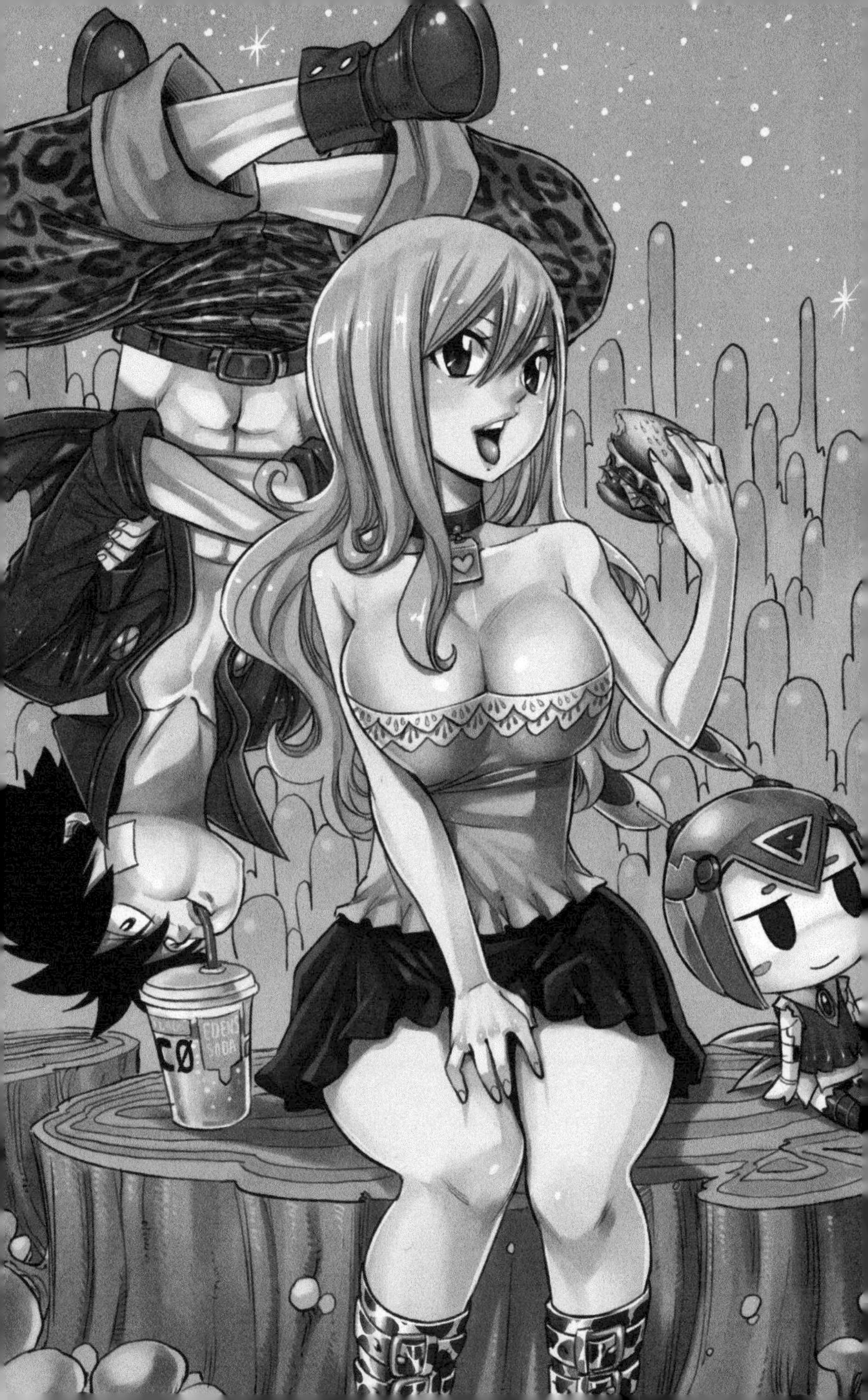
CØ

AFTERWORD

How did you like the Digitalis Arc? I had a few other ideas I wanted to use to take advantage of the virtual-world setting, but I felt like the story would go on too long, so I had to cut some of them. I also planned to have Labilia show up, and Justice from the Interstellar Union Army, but when I thought of the pacing and balance of the story, they had to take a rain check.

This is far from anything new, but when writing stories, the plot is constantly changing from my original outline. This may be different for other authors, but when I'm nailing down ideas to make each chapter more interesting, I end up altering the storyline. To give an example from this volume, my original idea was that fake Homura was actually Justice, but somewhere down the line I decided a new character would be more interesting after all, so I designed Amira real quick. Further back, this arc was originally going to start with the prince of Digitalis coming to ask Shiki and his crew for help, but that turned out vastly different.

So you can see I'm making it up as I... *Ahem.* I'm adapting the story as the need arises.

It goes without saying that Hermit goes through some emotional changes during the Digitalis Arc, but Pino does, too. There will be more on that in the next volume. Those kinds of details—the ones that are so close to the foundation of the story—will almost never change mid-series.

By the way, the concept behind both Dr. Müller (the guy from Hermit's past) and Jamilov (Spider) is that I wanted to create the absolute worst kind of trash possible. How do you think I did?

I've always been bad at drawing the scum of the earth, and even when I thought I had created a real piece of garbage, I'd still get a lot of comments saying, "They have their own kind of charm," "I feel so sorry for them," "They're not so bad." And well, that's okay, but I'm working hard on a personal theme of mine for this series—which is to come up with villains that will make the readers think, "Please just destroy this guy already!" Of course, the enemies will have their own convictions that will lead them to fighting Shiki and friends, too!

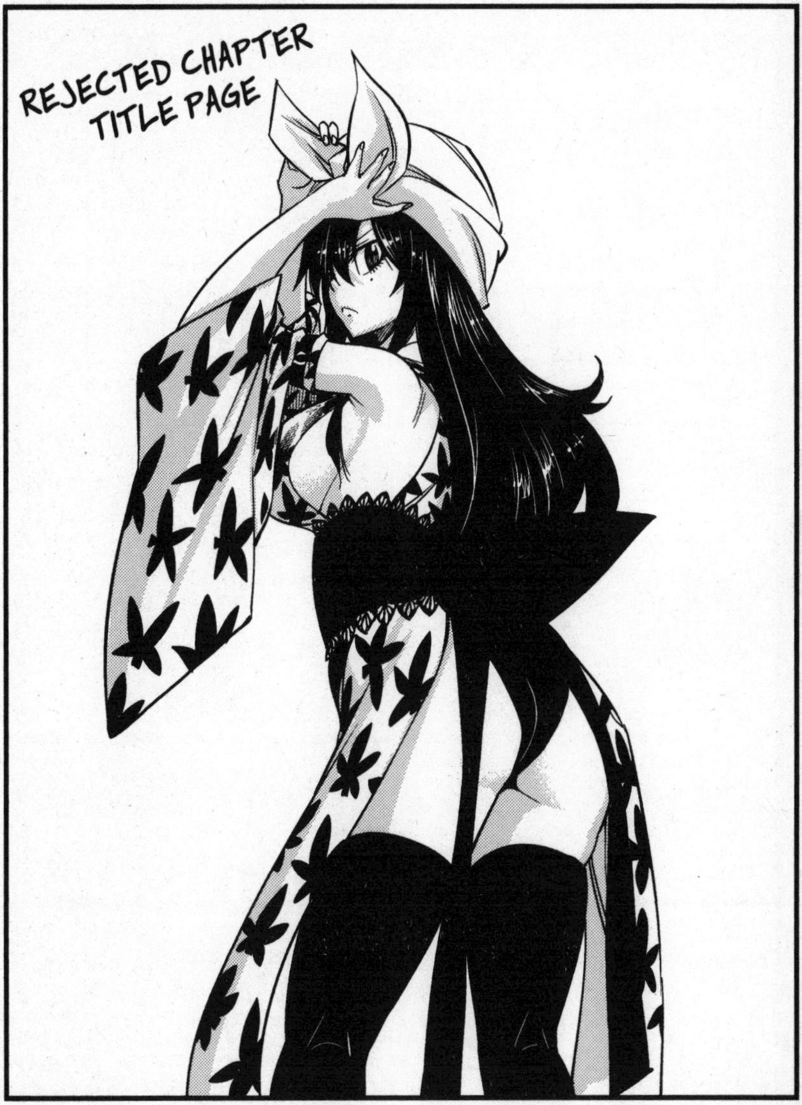
REJECTED CHAPTER TITLE PAGE

OUR THIRD INSTALLMENT USES TWO WHOLE PAGES TO REALLY GIVE YOUR WORK SOME IMPACT!

(MABUSHIO-SAN, TOKYO)

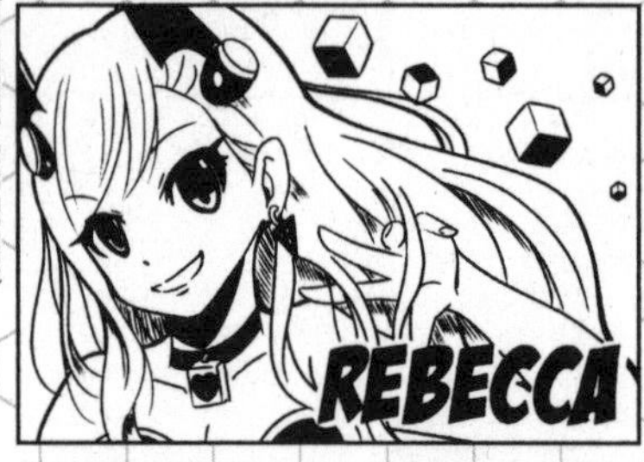
REBECCA

▲ OH! THIS STYLISH REBECCA WOULD MAKE A GREAT WEB BANNER. IF SHE CAN GET HER B-CUBER CAREER UP AND RUNNING, IT MIGHT OPEN UP SOME DOORS TO MODELING OR ACTING.

(MIMI SUSUDA-SAN, OITA)

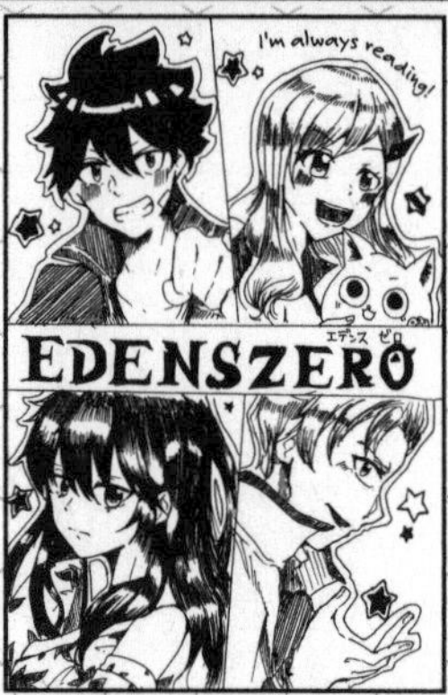
I'm always reading!
エデンズ ゼロ
EDENSZERO

◀ A MASTERPIECE WITH ALL OF THE MAIN CAST. SOMEHOW IT'S VERY SOOTHING. I MEAN, I'VE NEVER SEEN SHIKI LOOK SO NICE!!

(NIKA MOCHIZUKI-SAN, NAGANO)

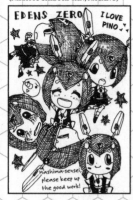

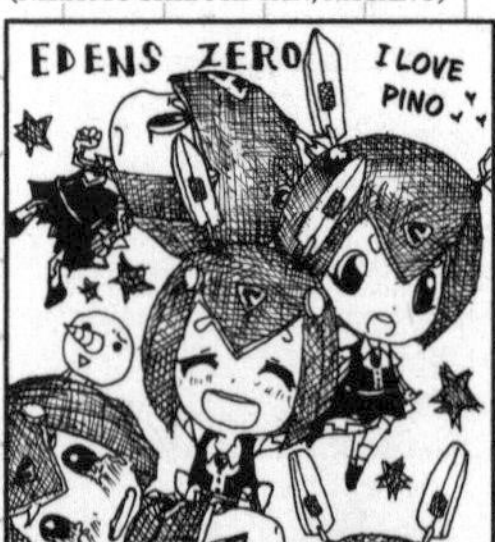
EDENS ZERO
I LOVE PINO
Mashima-sensei, please keep up the good work!

▲ SIX FACES OF THE LOVELY PINO. DID YOU LIKE HER AVATAR IN DIGITALIS? IN THE NEXT VOLUME, WE'LL COVER THE NEW DREAM THAT PINO HAS, SO MAKE SURE TO CHECK IT OUT.

(NIKUKYU-SAN, KANAGAWA)

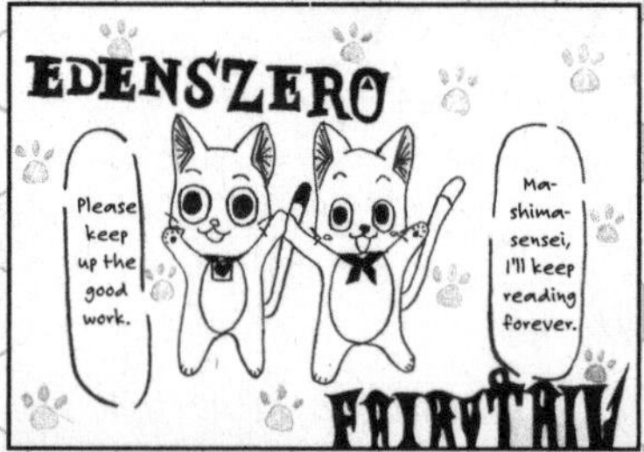
EDENSZERO
Please keep up the good work.
Mashima-sensei, I'll keep reading forever.
FAIRYTAIL

◀ AYE! I WILL KEEP UP THE GOOD WORK!! HE HAS A MECHANICAL BODY IN *EDENS ZERO*, BUT THE SOUL OF A BLUE CAT WILL ALWAYS BE THE SAME! PLEASE CONTINUE TO ENJOY DOUBLE HAPPY.

MASHIMA'S ONE-HIT KO

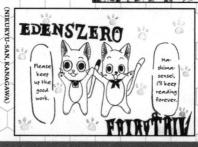

(TOSHIHIRO MIKI-SAN, TOKUSHIMA)

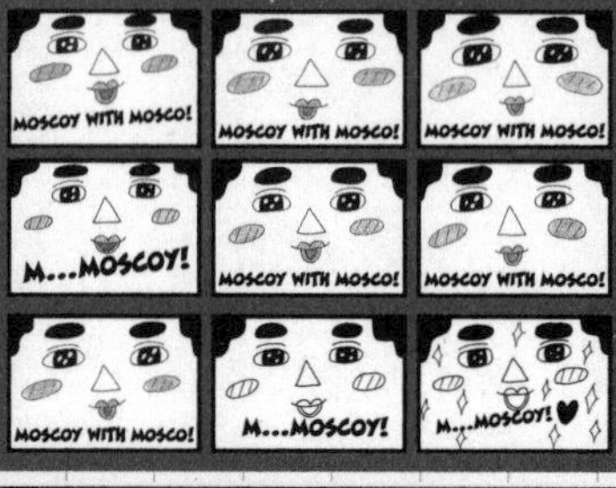
MOSCOY WITH MOSCO!
MOSCOY WITH MOSCO!
MOSCOY WITH MOSCO!
M...MOSCOY!
MOSCOY WITH MOSCO!
MOSCOY WITH MOSCO!
MOSCOY WITH MOSCO!
M...MOSCOY!
M...MOSCOY!♥

◀ THE HASTILY-DEVELOPED, BRAND-NEW "MASHIMA'S ONE-HIT KO" CORNER! THIS IS THE GLORIOUS MASTERPIECE TO BE FEATURED FIRST. THE IMPORTANT THING IS IMPACT. THIS PACKAGE CONTAINED NINE WHOLE DRAWINGS (ALL WITH SUBTLE DIFFERENCES), INSTANTLY KNOCKING MASHIMA OUT OF THE RING.

EDITOR'S NOTE: DRAWING SUBMISSIONS LIMITED TO JAPAN

EZ DRAWING

(URUCHAMA-SAN, GUNMA)

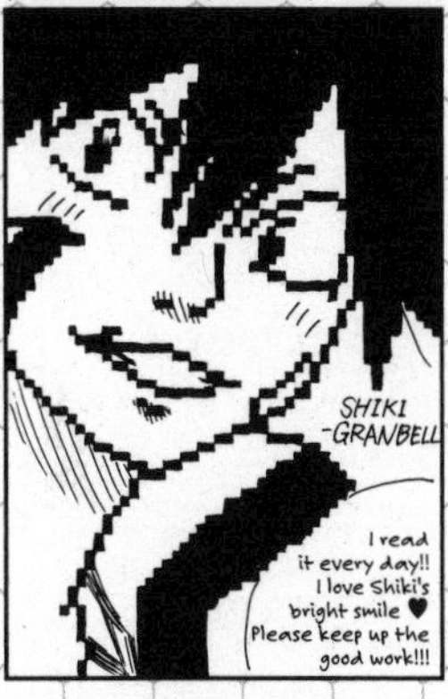
SHIKI
-GRANBELL
I read it every day!! I love Shiki's bright smile ♥ Please keep up the good work!!!

▲ PIXEL SHIKI. NEXT TIME THEY GO TO A DIGITAL WORLD LIKE DIGITALIS, MAYBE YOU'LL GET TO SEE HIM LIKE THIS.

(MUJIKA-SAN, FUKUOKA)

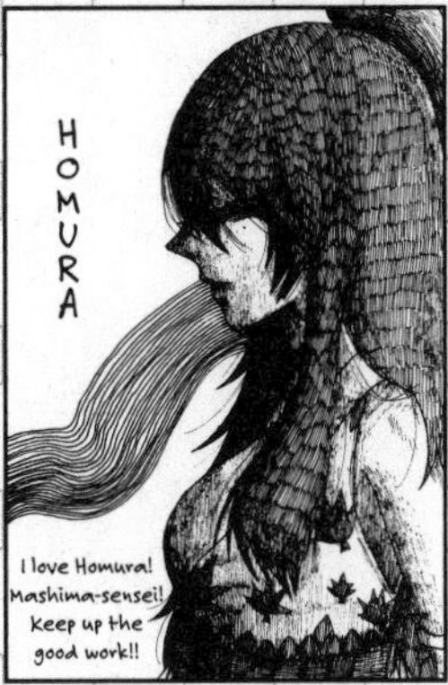
HOMURA
I love Homura! Mashima-sensei! Keep up the good work!!

▲ HOMURA, HER EYES CLOSED, DEEP IN THOUGHT. IT MAKES A GREAT PICTURE, BUT I THINK IT WOULD BE ULTRA-RARE TO SEE HER LIKE THIS! WHY? BECAUSE SHE HAS THAT UNFORTUNATE HABIT OF SPEAKING WHATEVER IS ON HER MIND...

(RYO ITO-SAN, HYOGO)

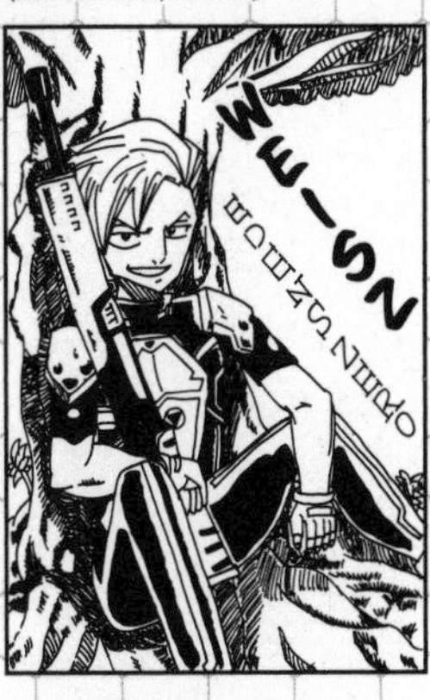
WE-ISZ

▲ WEISZ'S MACHINA MAKER ETHER GEAR IS FULLY COMPATIBLE WITH FIREARMS. HE EVEN TURNED MOSCO INTO SWISS CHEESE. BUT IF CERTAIN PEOPLE FIND OUT, WILL *HE* BE TURNED INTO SWISS CHEESE?!

(RIRINA-SAN, TOCHIGI)

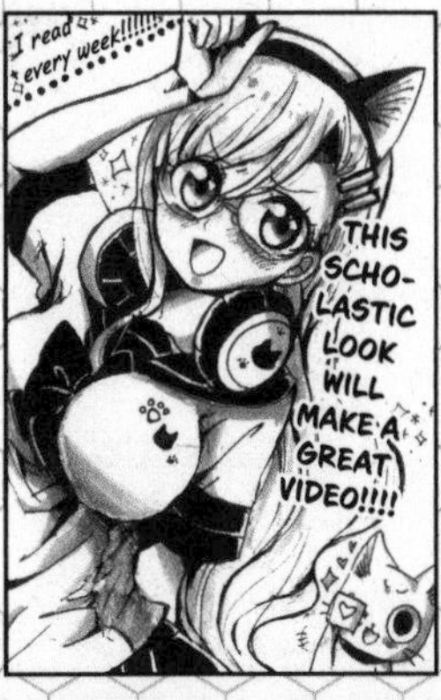
I read every week!!!!!!!
THIS SCHOLASTIC LOOK WILL MAKE A GREAT VIDEO!!!!

◀ CAT-EAR GLASSES GIRL REBECCA. MAYBE SHE'S A LOT MORE BASHFUL THAN HER STATEMENT LEADS US TO BELIEVE?! BUT IF IT'S FOR THE SAKE OF A GOOD VIDEO, AND IF SHE DOESN'T MIND STUDYING, THEN WHY NOT?! LET'S MAKE A GOOD VIDEO!!

(NIKA MOCHIZUKI-SAN, NAGANO)

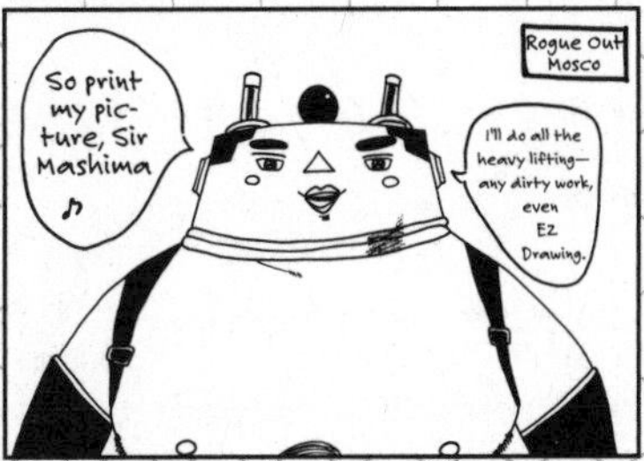
Rogue Out Mosco
I'll do all the heavy lifting—any dirty work, even EZ Drawing.
So print my picture, Sir Mashima ♪

▲ THERE, I PRINTED IT. BUT WHAT SHOULD I MAKE MOSCO DO? HE TURNED OUT TO BE THE EDENS ZERO'S CARETAKER (ALSO KNOWN AS SISTER'S LACKEY), BUT HOW POWERFUL IS HE, REALLY?!

A dark and sexy body-horror action manga perfect for fans of *Prison School* and *High School of the Dead*!

Shuichi Kagaya is a smart kid, and most smart kids his age would be thinking about college. Shuichi is also a monster, and he's smart enough to know that monsters don't go to college. But after he uses his monstrous form to save his classmate Claire Aoki, it doesn't matter what his plans for the future were, because he's not the one making the decisions anymore. Now that the seductive, sadistic Claire knows Shuichi's secret, she's got her own ideas about what a monster is good for—because he's not the first monster she's met...

KC KODANSHA COMICS

GLEIPNIR

"You and me together...we would be unstoppable."

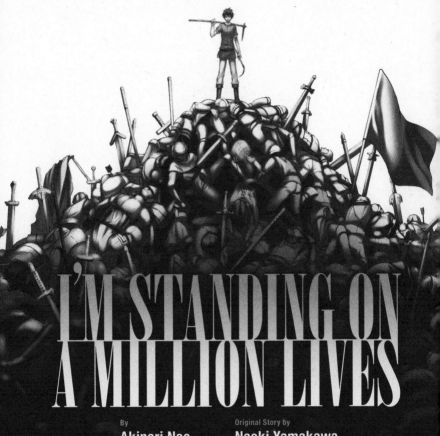

I'M STANDING ON A MILLION LIVES

By
Akinari Nao

Original Story by
Naoki Yamakawa

Yusuke Yotsuya doesn't care about getting into high school—he just wants to get back home to his game and away from other people. But when he suddenly finds himself in a real-life fantasy game alongside his two gorgeous classmates, he discovers a new world of possibility and excitement. Despite a rough start, Yusuke and his friend fight to level up and clear the challenges set before them by a mysterious figure from the future, but before long, they find that they're not just battling for their own lives, but for the lives of millions.

A Kodansha Comics Trade Paperback Original
EDENS ZERO 5 copyright © 2019 Hiro Mashima
English translation copyright © 2019 Hiro Mashima

Published in the United States by Kodansha Comics, an imprint of Kodansha USA Publishing, LLC, New York.

Publication rights for this English edition arranged through Kodansha Ltd., Tokyo.

First published in Japan in 2019 by Kodansha Ltd., Tokyo.

ISBN 978-1-63236-788-4

Original cover design by Narumi Miura (G x complex).

Printed in the United States of America.

www.kodanshacomics.com

9 8 7 6 5 4 3 2 1
Translation: Alethea and Athena Nibley
Lettering: AndWorld Design
Editing: Haruko Hashimoto
Kodansha Comics edition cover design by Phil Balsman

Publisher: Kiichiro Sugawara
Managing editor: Maya Rosewood
Vice president of marketing & publicity: Naho Yamada

Director of publishing services: Ben Applegate
Associate director of operations: Stephen Pakula
Publishing services managing editor: Noelle Webster
Assistant production manager: Emi Lotto

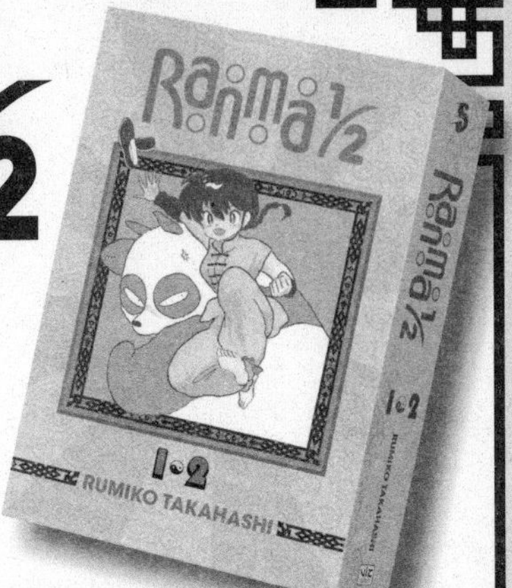
Ranma 1/2
1•2
RUMIKO TAKAHASHI

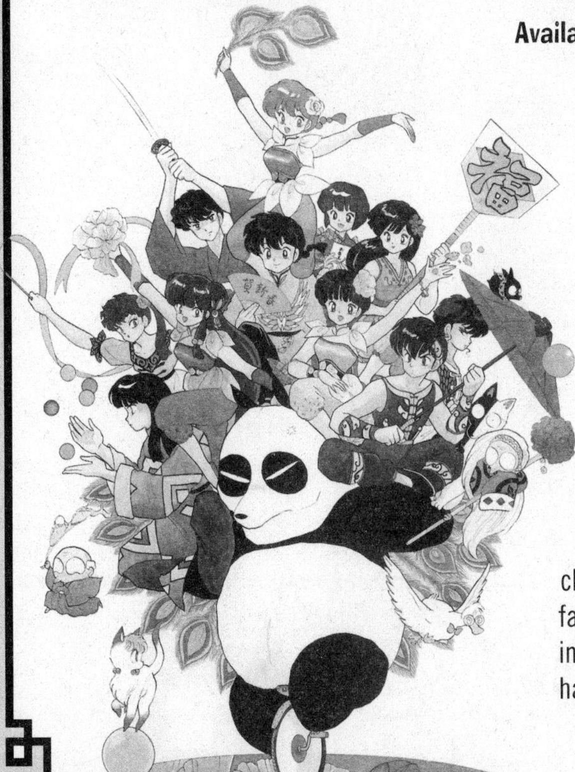

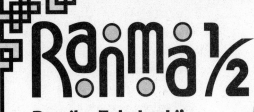

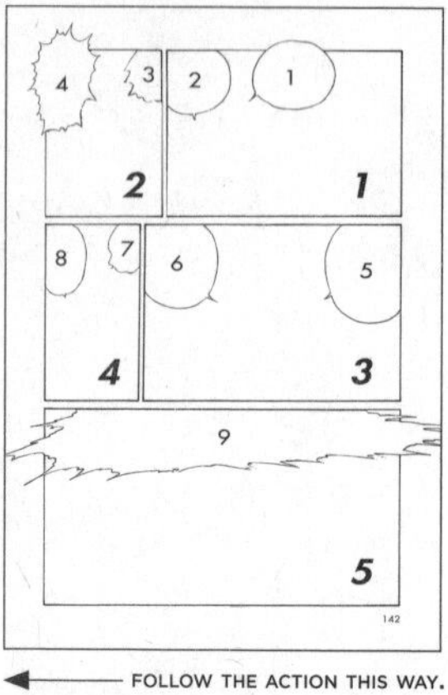
FOLLOW THE ACTION THIS WAY.

Fly Me to the Moon has been printed in the original Japanese format in order to preserve the orientation of the original artwork. Please turn it around and begin reading from right to left.

Unlike English, Japanese is read right to left, so Japanese comics are read in reverse order from the way English comics are typically read. Have fun with it!

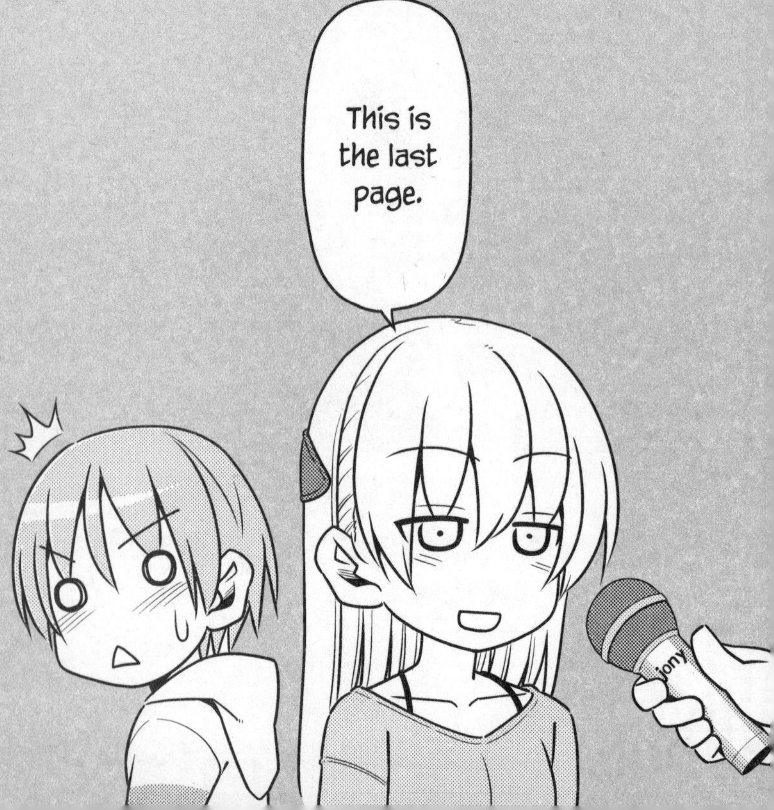
This is the last page.
Sony